*Japan
Before
Tokugawa*

*This book is based on a conference
sponsored by the
Joint Committee on Japanese Studies of
the Social Science Research Council and
the American Council of Learned Societies
and by the Japan Society
for the Promotion of Science*

Japan Before Tokugawa

Political Consolidation and Economic Growth, 1500 to 1650

EDITED BY JOHN WHITNEY HALL,
NAGAHARA KEIJI, AND
KOZO YAMAMURA

PRINCETON UNIVERSITY PRESS
PRINCETON, NEW JERSEY

Contributors and Collaborators

PETER J. ARNESEN
ASAO NAOHIRO
MARTIN COLLCUTT
GEORGE ELISON
FUJIKI HISASHI
JOHN WHITNEY HALL
SUSAN B. HANLEY
WILLIAM B. HAUSER
MARIUS B. JANSEN
KATSUMATA SHIZUO

MATSUOKA HISATO
JAMES L. MCCLAIN
NAGAHARA KEIJI
SASAKI GIN'YA
SASAKI JUNNOSUKE
RONALD P. TOBY
WAKITA HARUKO
WAKITA OSAMU
KOZO YAMAMURA

Editorial Assistants

PETER J. ARNESEN
JAMES L. MCCLAIN
ADRIANNE V. SUDDARD

Contents

List of Illustrations   ix

List of Maps   xi

Acknowledgments   xiii

Introduction   7
JOHN WHITNEY HALL, NAGAHARA KEIJI, AND KOZO YAMAMURA

1 The Sengoku Daimyo and the Kandaka System   27
NAGAHARA KEIJI WITH KOZO YAMAMURA

2 The Sengoku Daimyo of Western Japan: The Case of the
Ōuchi   64
MATSUOKA HISATO WITH PETER J. ARNESEN

3 The Development of Sengoku Law   101
KATSUMATA SHIZUO WITH MARTIN COLLCUTT

4 Sengoku Daimyo Rule and Commerce   125
SASAKI GIN'YA WITH WILLIAM B. HAUSER

5 The Political Posture of Oda Nobunaga   149
FUJIKI HISASHI WITH GEORGE ELISON

6 Hideyoshi's Domestic Policies   194
JOHN WHITNEY HALL

7 The Commercial and Urban Policies of Oda Nobunaga
and Toyotomi Hideyoshi   224
WAKITA OSAMU WITH JAMES L. MCCLAIN

8 Shogun and Tennō   248
ASAO NAOHIRO WITH MARIUS B. JANSEN

9 The Changing Rationale of Daimyo Control in the
Emergence of the Bakuhan State   271
SASAKI JUNNOSUKE WITH RONALD P. TOBY

10 Dimensions of Development: Cities in Fifteenth- and
Sixteenth-Century Japan   295
WAKITA HARUKO WITH SUSAN B. HANLEY

Contents

11 *Returns on Unification: Economic Growth in Japan,*
 1550-1650   327
 Kozo Yamamura

 Glossary   373
 Notes on Contributors   383
 Index   387

List of Illustrations

(following page 148)

1. Portrait of Oda Nobunaga dating from shortly after his death.
2. Oda Nobunaga's "Tenka Fubu" seal affixed to an order to two of his retainers.
3. The battle of Nagashino, 1575, showing Nobunaga's early use of firearms.
4. Sketch map of the base plan of Azuchi castle showing moats, walls, and the main keep.
5. Hikone castle retains today many features of Oda-Toyotomi era castle architecture.
6. Portrait of Toyotomi Hideyoshi in court robes.
7. Osaka castle before its destruction, sketched by a Dutch resident in Japan.
8. Example of a *kenchi-chō* dated 1594. In this instance assessment is still stated in kandaka terms.
9. Officials surveying rice fields.
10. The storming of Osaka castle in 1615.
11. Nijō castle, Tokugawa headquarters in Kyoto, begun in 1603 by Ieyasu.
12. Horses laden with bales of rice.
13. Women transplanting rice to the rhythm of children beating drum and gong.
14. Improved irrigation techniques were among the technological features that increased agricultural production during the sixteenth century.

List of Maps

1. The Provinces of Medieval Japan 2
2. The Ōuchi Domain (ca. 1550) 3
3. Major Sengoku Daimyo (ca. 1572) 4
4. Cities and Major Transportation Routes (ca. 1600) 5

Acknowledgments

THIS VOLUME results from a binational conference held in the summer of 1977 called at the time the "Conference on Sengoku Japan." As will be evident to the reader, the actual content of the conference was somewhat broader than the term Sengoku would imply. The meeting was one of a series of academic conferences organized and supported by the Joint Committee on Japanese Studies of the American Council of Learned Societies and the Social Science Research Council in the United States. In this instance support for the Japanese side of the conference was provided by the Japan Society for the Promotion of Science (Nihon Gakujutsu Shinkōkai) of Tokyo.

The Conference on Sengoku Japan took place on Maui, Hawaii, from August 28 to September 2, 1977. It was attended, in addition to those listed as contributors or collaborators on the title page of this volume, by Mrs. Nagahara Kazuko, who served as rapporteur for the Japanese participants, and by Gary S. Shea (Washington University) and Michael Burton (Princeton University), who served as rapporteurs on the American side. Ronald Aqua represented the SSRC at the meeting and took charge of local arrangements.

The conference adopted the common format for scholarly meetings, which called for papers to be written on designated themes for circulation in advance of the meeting so that they could be thoroughly discussed and criticized during the conference. Following the Maui meeting, authors were asked to revise their papers in response to suggestions made during the conference discussion. These revised papers, together with Mrs. Nagahara's notes on the conference discussion, became the basis for the Japanese version of the conference proceedings.

Acknowledgments

As is so often the case, the Japanese version, published by Yoshikawa Kōbunkan, has appeared ahead of the English version. There were several reasons for this other than the greater efficiency of the publishing process in Japan. The main cause of delay in the English version was the problem of translation and editing. Following receipt of revised manuscripts from Japanese authors with the assistance of Professor Nagahara, the American translator-adaptors reworked each essay for general editing by the two American editors. Assisting them were Peter Arnesen, James McClain, and Adrianne V. Suddard. This editorial team worked over the manuscripts carefully to assure consistency of style and terminology. The editors are most appreciative of the work of the three editorial assistants in preparing the edited English manuscript. The editors also wish to thank Shōgakkan Publishers of Tokyo for providing the illustrations appearing in this volume.

Japan
Before
Tokugawa

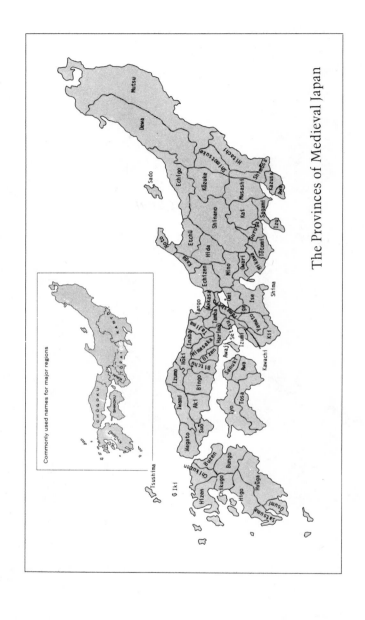

The Provinces of Medieval Japan

Commonly used names for major regions

The Ōuchi Domain (ca. 1550)

IWAMI

AKI

SUŌ

NAGATO

Yamaguchi

IYO

BUNGO

BUZEN

CHIKUZEN

CHIKUGO

HIGO

HIZEN

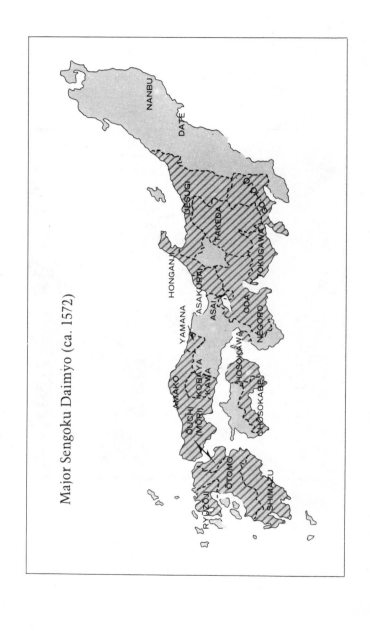

Major Sengoku Daimyo (ca. 1572)

Cities and Major Transportation Routes (ca. 1600)

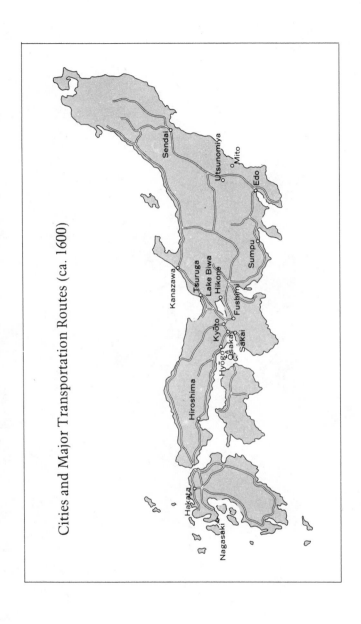

Introduction

DURING THE CENTURY and a half from roughly 1500 to 1650 that forms the time span of this volume, Japan emerged from the period of its greatest political fragmentation into what was to be its most successful centralization prior to modern times. As of 1500, the country had entered a time of protracted military competition among the fast-growing local military lords, or daimyo, who had sprung up throughout the provinces. Although both the emperor (*tennō*) and his military delegate (the Ashikaga shogun) remained in their palaces in the capital city of Kyoto, neither possessed the power to affect events outside the capital. The daimyo, especially the large regional hegemons, were in nearly all respects locally autonomous. They asserted full proprietary rights over their domains, enfeoffing their retainers within their borders in return for military service. They had begun to build at the strategic center of their domains defensive castles and living quarters for samurai retainers and their men at arms. To these castle headquarters there flocked merchants, artisans, and provisioners of all sorts, and also the local branch temples of the major Buddhist sects. The daimyo issued their own laws and spoke of their domains as *kokka* (states or countries). By 1550 this process of fragmentation had run its course and was about to be reversed. The "unification" of Japan that took place in the second half of the sixteenth century is better understood as a unification, or pacification, of the daimyo, for while the country was brought under the command of a strong military hegemony imposed by the Tokugawa House—the new shogunal line— the daimyo and their locally self-administered domains remained.

The unification of the daimyo (some 160 in 1590) was

the work of three military leaders: Oda Nobunaga (1534-1582), Toyotomi Hideyoshi (1535-1598), and Tokugawa Ieyasu (1542-1616). Hideyoshi completed the conquest of the daimyo in 1590, reducing all daimyo not destroyed to a state of vassalage. But his hegemony did not long outlast his death. Ieyasu succeeded to the hegemony in 1600 at the battle of Sekigahara, and became shogun in 1603. He destroyed Osaka Castle, the last Toyotomi stronghold, in 1615. The result was the formation of what is now called the *bakuhan* system, an extremely stable government in which the country was governed at the local level by daimyo (a daimyo domain was called a *han*) under the national overlordship of the shogun (the shogun's government was known as the *bakufu*).

The stabilization of daimyo rule and the creation of a national military hegemony was accompanied by a series of legal and administrative changes that literally transformed Japanese society. These changes were not the result of a sudden and purposeful political act by some interest group or a single all-powerful military leader, nor were they the result of a massive social upheaval. Rather they resulted from a number of deep and pervasive movements that had been slowly modifying Japan's political power structure and social organization, its agricultural and commercial economies, and its balance between city and country over the course of several centuries. Among the culminating developments that took place during the sixteenth century were the separation of the samurai from the land and their movement into the daimyo's castle towns, the reorganization of the rural communities into self-governing villages (*mura*)—a phenomenon achieved by a cadastral survey of all the arable land of Japan—the disarming of everyone except the samurai class, and the beginning of class legislation on a national basis. Added together, these changes constituted a revolution in the basic conditions under which the Japanese were to live for the next two and a half centuries. For it was then that the mechanisms of national law and order that assured the remarkable stability of the Tokugawa regime, from 1600 to 1868, were fashioned. In the words of the modern historian, Japan moved out of its middle ages and into its early modern condition.

Traditionally, the period of a century and a half to which this volume is devoted has been treated under three particular concepts. The first is *Sengoku*, translatable as "the country at war" or "the warring states." This reference to widespread civil warfare applies to the period between the outbreak of the Ōnin War in 1467 and the pacification of the daimyo under Toyotomi Hideyoshi in 1590. The second concept, *Taihei* or "Great Peace," stands for the condition of peaceful order eventually achieved under the Tokugawa shoguns as a result of their military ascendancy, their repression of Christianity, and the enforcement of a policy of national closure. Between these contrasting conditions that stood at the opposite ends of our time scale the course of military-political events has been explained in terms of a third concept: the continuous play of the forces of *gekokujō* or "rebellion from below," when inferiors attacked their betters and when vassals usurped the status of their lords. Unification came as a result of human ambition, forcefulness, and daring. The concept of gekokujō focuses attention on the individual and the idiosyncratic in the historical process: on military and religious leaders, on merchant princes and militant spokesmen at the head of village uprisings.

It is understandable that the period between the start of the turbulent Sengoku era and the eventual consolidation of the Tokugawa "Great Peace" should be treated in terms of battles won or lost and the rise and fall of local military powers. This was an era when truly heroic figures strode the stage of Japanese history. Regional lords—the Sengoku daimyo—having acquired by military force domains the size of provinces, or even larger, now fell upon each other to battle for national supremacy. Such were Hōjō Sōun of southwest Kantō, Takeda Shingen of Kai and Shinano,

Uesugi Kenshin of Echigo in eastern Japan, and of Ukita Naoie of Bizen, Ōuchi Yoshitaka of Suō, and Shimazu Takahisa of Satsuma in the west. These were battle-tested leaders, men around whom legends could be built. And the battles between them for national supremacy lent themselves to dramatic description. It was in this milieu that the "Three Unifiers"—men of strong character and fierce ambition—rose from comparative obscurity to put their stamp on three generations of military struggle. Oda Nobunaga began his rise from a relatively minor domainal base in Owari; Toyotomi Hideyoshi started as a footsoldier in Nobunaga's service to become national hegemon; Tokugawa Ieyasu succeeded to a holding in Mikawa precariously placed between rival daimyo, little suspecting that he would one day be shogun. All three were self-made in the extreme. To the chroniclers of their time and to modern historians alike, these men were exemplars of their age; their motivations and deeds were accepted as sufficient explanations of the meaning of their times.

It is surprising, therefore, that the only satisfactory biographies of the three unifiers have been in Japanese. Probably the most sophisticated and reasonably extended treatment in English of the three so far is to be found in G. B. Sansom's *A History of Japan, 1334-1615* (1961). Sansom's coverage of the period 1560-1615 is skillfully handled at a level of detail that brings all three unifiers into view as individuals. He also devotes attention to the political and economic changes effected by these figures, describing the land surveys, sword hunts, class-separation measures, and the new village tax provisions that were the hallmarks of their domestic policies. Since Sansom's writing, Japanese scholarship on the period from 1500 to 1650 has added a great deal to our understanding of the linkage between the exploits of the Sengoku warlords and the political, social, and economic changes that accompanied the unification of the country under the Edo shogunal regime.

The current state of scholarship on the sixteenth century

in Japan acknowledges its debt to two studies published just before the outbreak of World War II by Nakamura Kichiji. These were his *Kinsei shoki nōseishi kenkyū* (Studies on the agricultural policies of the early Kinsei period) (1938) and *Nihon hōkensei saihenseishi* (A history of the restructuring of the Japanese feudal system) (1939). In the first work Nakamura applied himself to the problem of explaining the changing nature of daimyo powers of lordship, particularly as these increased the capacity of daimyo to control large masses of the peasant population. In the second he analyzed the differences in structural form between the "feudalism" of the Sengoku age and that of the Edo period, concluding that Tokugawa Japan, though still feudal in certain respects, was not so in many others. The shift in emphasis from daimyo exploits to daimyo governance was critical, for it led to the current preoccupation of Japanese historians with questions about the nature of daimyo rule, the changing basis of daimyo power, the emergence of new classes—samurai, peasant, and merchant—the formation of new class interests, and the creation of the Edo political order—what Japanese call the *bakuhan sei kokka* (the bakuhan state).

As more has become known of the deep-running currents of institutional change in sixteenth- and seventeenth-century Japan, historians have been obliged to face difficult problems of interpretation. What was the significance of these changes within the total context of the historical development of the Japanese people? Granted that it can be said that a revolution did take place, what should it be called? And what were the forces that brought it into existence? For answers to such questions scholars have had to devise first a satisfactory conception of historical change. The most common convention used by Japanese historians in general, and also within this volume, are the periodizing terms Chūsei (medieval) and Kinsei (early modern). Hideyoshi, under this approach, is commonly described as having led Japan out of the Chūsei into the Kinsei age. A difficulty with terms of this sort is obvious: they have no generally agreed-upon definition. As long as they are used by professional historians who share a common understanding of what they were meant to stand for, there is no problem. But even professionals are not in agreement over the precise definition of such terms.[1] And this is true of the contributors to this volume.

Generally speaking, there have been three different approaches to the problem of interpreting Japan's transition from Chūsei to Kinsei conditions. The first to be commonly used by modern historians has been the analogy with Western European history. In the works of historians, both Japanese and Western, one frequently finds an implied, if not explicit, comparison of sixteenth-century Japan with Europe during its passage from its feudal age to the appearance of the early monarchal states. Often, too, this is done with the added judgment that Japan's movement out of feudalism was "delayed" by the "immaturity" of Japanese society and the conservative policies of Hideyoshi and Ieyasu. The Western analogy has provided the Japanese historian with a ready-made set of indicators by which to measure the passage of their society from medieval to early modern times. These were the familiar list of antifeudal developments that presumably marked the beginning of Europe's early modern transformation: the rise of the ab-

---

[1] The complexity of trying to define the meaning of Chūsei is well illustrated in Professor Nagahara's introduction to Nagahara Keiji, Nuki Tatsuto, and Yasuda Motohisa, eds., *Chūsei-shi hando-bukku* (Tokyo: Kondō Shuppansha, 1973), pp. 1-3. One of many works that attempt to grapple with the meaning of Kinsei is Shōda Ken'ichirō and Hayami Akira, *Nihon keizaishi* (Tokyo: Sekai Shoin, 1965), pp. 85-88. The authors argue the inconsistency of putting the feudal label on Tokugawa society in view of the centralizing powers of the shogunate. Bito Masahide sees the problem as one of defining for Japan a period that apparently falls in between the recognized concepts of "medieval" and "modern." He is left with the task of identifying what is "distinctively Kinsei" about the period from the rise of Nobunaga to the end of the Tokugawa regime. Bito Masahide, "Kinsei shi josetsu," in *Iwanami kōza Nihon rekishi* 8 (*Kinsei* 1) (Tokyo: Iwanami Shoten, 1975), 2-5.

solute monarchy and its encroachment on the landed aristocracy, the breakdown of medieval social divisions, the
growth of the city, of the merchant class and commercial
economy, the spread of secular thought, and so forth.
Some of these same phenomena were indeed visible in
sixteenth-century Japan, but comparisons with Europe,
while informative and suggestive, have needed to be handled cautiously and systematically and with full awareness
of the noncomparability of many aspects of Japanese and
European society. And few historians have managed this.

The second, and more common approach to the problem of periodization, comes from Marxist theory. This line
of reasoning has played an important role in opening up
the study of medieval Japan to social and economic analysis
and in directing attention to the substructure of the political process. In particular, Marxist-oriented historians have
focused their attention on the land-working class, seeking
to identify the point at which this class changed from being
predominantly unfree, bound under the patriarchal controls exerted by the leading village family heads, to being
free. In other words, in Marxist terms, when did the Japanese peasant change from slave to serf? The postwar debate over problems of this sort is acknowledged to have
started with the publication in 1946 of Ishimoda Shō's
Chūsei-teki sekai no keisei (The formation of the medieval
world). It was his assertion that in Japan, between the late
Heian and the end of the Kamakura period, the "ancient
patriarchal slave system" broke down with the transformation of various unfree and bound groups into the more independent status of serf. Thus to him the Kamakura era
saw the establishment of feudalism, and hence the beginning of Chūsei. This thesis is accepted by most Japanese
medievalists, though some, like Nagahara Keiji, would
move the point at which the "patriarchal slave system" was
dissolved down into the Nanboku (1336-1392) period.[2]

[2] See his *Nihon hōken shakai ron* (Tokyo: Tōkyō Daigaku Shuppankai,
1955).

How differently the evidence can be read, however, is demonstrated in the work of Araki Moriaki. Araki published in 1953 a preview of his study of the *Taikō kenchi* (Hideyoshi's nationwide cadastral survey) in which he claimed that only as a byproduct of these surveys, which were carried out between 1583 and 1594, did the Japanese peasantry change from slavelike bondage to powerful land holders into the freer, more nearly "feudal," condition of serf.[3] Thus the early Kinsei era was for him the high point of feudalism in Japan. There is no need to go into further detail either on Araki's thesis or the vast literature that has come out for or, in large part, against it. The point to be made is that the concepts of Chūsei and Kinsei are subject to contradictory interpretations, particularly as they become dependent on equally slippery concepts like feudalism and serfdom.[4]

This brings us to the third approach, which is essentially empirical. While paying lip service to some general scheme of periodization, historians often in practice have conducted their research and analysis in terms of observable differences, and hence suspected changes, in basic institutions between roughly 1500 and 1650. What they have done is to take the institutional features that stood out in 1500 or so as characteristic of the late Chūsei society, and those that stood out in 1650 as the defining features of Kinsei society. With such an approach, each historian is apt to have his own check list, or at least priority list, of critical features that differentiated these two periods.

Since the authors represented in this volume are not necessarily in full agreement on what the essential defining features of Chūsei and Kinsei society should be, there is lit-

[3] Araki Moriaki, "Taikō kenchi no rekishiteki zentei," in *Rekishigaku kenkyū* 163 (1953), 1-17; 164 (1953), 1-21.

[4] See Hall's "Feudalism in Japan—a Reassessment," in John W. Hall and Marius B. Jansen, eds., *Studies in the Institutional History of Early Modern Japan* (Princeton: Princeton University Press, 1968), pp. 15-57, for an effort to treat the problems of comparative analysis of feudal institutions.

Introduction

tle point in attempting to arrive at some common understanding in the details.[5] In a very general sense, however,
they are all talking about the shift in the power structure
from a fragmented to a centralized polity, the transformation of the samurai class from locally enfeoffed military
proprietors to urban-dwelling stipendiaries, the change
among the peasantry from a condition of being directly
managed by village samurai and patriarchal family heads
to one in which the vast majority of cultivators lived in villages under their own headmen, secure in their holdings
by virtue of their inclusion in the village cadastral registers.
One of the best illustrations of what is meant by the difference between Chūsei and Kinsei political organization is
seen in the contrast between daimyo of the Sengoku period
and those of the Kinsei period. The Sengoku daimyo was
very much the local military magnate, leading a vassal band
of privately enfeoffed warriors in the military defence of
his composite domain. The Kinsei daimyo, on the other
hand, was more the political administrator using legal and
bureaucratic organizations to govern his domain. His retainers had been pulled out of their fief villages into castle-
town headquarters, where they were paid in rice stipends
for their services. Most of the institutional end products of
the sixteenth-century revolution—the bakuhan polity, the
kokudaka system, the samurai stipendiary system, and the
autonomous village (mura) system—were idiosyncratic to

[5] Several of the authors in this volume have explained their own working assumptions of what they consider to be the critical differences between "Sengoku practices" and "Kinsei practices" as these apply to their
particular subfields. Sasaki Gin'ya and Wakita Osamu are agreed that the
key indicator in the field of commerce was the dissolution of the *za* (medieval guilds) and the establishment of daimyo control over commerce.
Sasaki Junnosuke places his emphasis on the successful assertion of
ideological legitimation by exploiting the concept of *kōgi* (public authority). Sasaki also exemplifies the tendency of historians to debate the dividing points in the sequence of periods. Hence he uses the term "early Kinsei" for the period 1582 to 1636, and reserves the label "Kinsei" for the
period after 1636.

the point that the use of the European analogy or any general model based on European data for analytical purposes is more apt to distort than to assist the historian in his effort to understand their meaning.

The 1977 Conference on Sengoku Japan, from which the essays brought together in this book are derived, was conceived of in part as a sequel to the Conference on Muromachi Japan held in Kyoto in 1973. It brought together equal numbers of Japanese and American historians specialized in Sengoku to early Edo history, with a somewhat different format from the earlier conference. The principal difference is that out of eleven papers, all but two were prepared by Japanese scholars. The greater number of Japanese contributors was necessitated by the nature of the subject under study and the availability of talent. The Conference on Muromachi Japan had dealt broadly with a variety of cultural fields in addition to political and economic history, and so it proved possible to call on a larger number of American authors. The Conference on Sengoku Japan was purposely restricted to political and economic subjects. This narrowing of range was decided upon to attempt a greater depth of analysis, and also because of recent attention given to the cultural aspects of the Azuchi-Momoyama period. The 1975 exhibition of art treasures of the Momoyama age at the Metropolitan Museum of Art provided direct visual evidence of the artistic achievements of the period, and the 1974 Carleton College lecture series, "The Momoyama Era, Japan in the Sixteenth Century," has become the basis of a publication covering the art, literature, and religion of the period by recognized American scholars.[6] When it was decided to cover a more limited range of inquiry, it became evident

[6] *Momoyama, Japanese Art in the Age of Grandeur* (New York, Metropolitan Museum of Art, 1975). The Carleton symposium has resulted in George Elison and Bardwell L. Smith, eds., *Warlords, Artists, and Commoners: Japan in the Sixteenth Century* (Honolulu: University Press of Hawaii, 1980).

that the pool of American scholars working on sixteenth-century Japanese political and economic institutional history was limited. Moreover, it was quite clear that the major breakthroughs in these fields were the work of Japanese historians; hence the preponderance of Japanese contributors.

As explained above, Japanese historians of the postwar period see the sixteenth century as a period of major constitutional change, and particularly as a time during which most of Japan's Kinsei institutions first emerged. The essays in this volume are in some ways the final product of this line of approach, the capstone of a whole set of inquiries that have called new attention to the sixteenth century and redefined its importance to the entire sweep of Japanese history. In this limited sense, the general thrust of the essays is not entirely new. Their value lies in the fact that they recapitulate the findings of the postwar period and for the first time make them available in English. Second, like all good articles, they raise new questions and suggest agendas for future research. Having established the general importance of the sixteenth century, the authors present different ideas about where to place the emphasis: on the administration of Hideyoshi, for example, or the long-range changes at the village level. Some see changes as coming from the top via new concepts of governance, while others see it as the result of actions taken by hundreds of lesser figures on the local level, through the building of new networks of commercial exchange, or through the application of new agricultural technology. Some see it as engineered change, others as spontaneous. Some see it as resulting in new, more absolute forces of political dominance by a military elite, others as a working out of a series of compromises that contained advantages for all levels of society. The importance of these contrasts is that they provide a whole new set of questions that will have to be dealt with in the years to come.

The eleven essays prepared for the Sengoku Conference

fall into five natural groupings. The two lead essays, by
Nagahara Keiji and Matsuoka Hisato, provide insight into
how two great Sengoku daimyo came into existence and
held on to their extensive domains. Nagahara, in his study
of the *kandaka* system, whereby cultivators paid their taxes
in cash, inquires into the political and fiscal structure of
one type of Sengoku domain. The kandaka system, which
was eventually displaced by the kokudaka (rice payment)
system, has been inadequately studied. Nagahara's analysis
of the system as implemented by the Go-Hōjō reveals not
only the manner in which this practice worked, but also
how it differed from the earlier *shōen* (estate) system, and
how the historical power of the court nobility over the land
was taken over by the local warrior houses and the rising
class of peasant landlords (or *myōshu*). If asked to choose
between these developments, Nagahara would undoubtedly place the emphasis on changes among the peasantry
as being the prime motive force behind them. It was pressure from below that continuously goaded the daimyo into
creating the means of orderly administration and taxation
and into pressing forward with cadastral surveys. As
Nagahara points out, the kandaka system also became the
basis for a more systematic method of exacting military
service from vassals. But the main point to be gleaned from
this article is not the facts about kandaka system, but a better general understanding of how the daimyo of the sixteenth century were forced into greater and greater systemization or rationalization of their local administration.

Matsuoka Hisato's essay provides a close-up view of local
conditions in western Japan and how one Sengoku daimyo,
the Ōuchi, while relying heavily on the remnants of the
earlier provincial administrative system for purposes of
land management and vassal organization, managed to
maintain control over a domain that extended over the
three provinces of Aki, Suō, and Nagato well into the Sengoku age. This domain was taken over by the Mōri in 1558.
But there is little cause to believe that the Mōri, whose

holdings lasted into and throughout the Edo period, succeeded where the Ōuchi failed simply because of a more systematic administrative and tax system. The crucial factor in the Mōri takeover was military prowess. Matsuoka's article provides new insight into the elements of local power available to the daimyo who had the courage to take advantage of military opportunities.

The next two essays, by Katsumata Shizuo and Sasaki Gin'ya, take up two special aspects of Sengoku daimyo rule. The first studies the house laws issued by Sengoku daimyo in their domains as a means of extending control over both samurai vassals and the general domain inhabitants. The second provides additional detail on the subject of daimyo regulation of trade, which was briefly touched on by Nagahara Keiji.

Katsumata's essay is particularly valuable for its revelation of the sophisticated conceptions of legitimation developed by the daimyo to justify their power and authority. Daimyo house laws, though often issued as simple "wall writings," reveal a mature sense of political and social order. They show also that the large daimyo, during their periods of greatest local autonomy, successfully projected an image of legitimation that satisfied both their vassals and the people of their domains. If the daimyo's domain (*ryōgoku*) was conceived as a kokka (a country), the daimyo could lay claim to being its hegemon endowed with public authority (*kōgi*). This claim was made in principle on the basis of "succession" to local offices created under imperial provincial administration and on personal ability (*kiryō*): the capacity to maintain law and order. This theme, which has been developed only recently by Japanese historians, is followed out in several of the other essays in this volume. The message from these studies is that Sengoku daimyo had to rely much more on ideological legitimation than previously supposed, and that despite the warfare and the gekokujō atmosphere, orderly process was not completely abandoned to the sword.

Sasaki Gin'ya's essay touches on an entirely different aspect of Sengoku daimyo rule, namely, the practices of economic regulation that were the economic imperatives of secure daimyo governance. Sengoku daimyo had to build up the economic resources of their domains, and in so doing competed with their own locally enfeoffed vassals and with the merchant community. Just as the Sengoku daimyo had to conceive of themselves as politically self-sufficient in their kokka, so they also needed to struggle for economic security. The problem was that such daimyo did not have the means to achieve economic controls on their own. For this they had to rely on the powers of a national hegemon. As this essay concludes: "No Sengoku daimyo, attempting to create a politically stable and economically self-sufficient domain, could have succeeded on his own. It was only within the framework of the bakuhan system . . . that the daimyo succeeded in forcing or enticing the kokujin to live in castle towns, thus depriving them of their power base, and in establishing full control over merchants and market activities." But by that time they had surrendered many features of their earlier local autonomy to the national hegemon.

Three essays deal with Oda Nobunaga and Toyotomi Hideyoshi. Fujiki Hisashi treats the political side of Nobunaga's career between 1568 and 1582, dealing in particular with problems of legitimacy. Again the concepts of kōgi and *tenka* (the realm) are introduced in reference to the legitimation of supreme authority. Fujiki's essay raises more clearly than in any other English language study the question of whether Nobunaga aspired to replace the emperor, and whether he could have done so if he had tried. Was Nobunaga, who claimed the status of "tenka," attempting to substitute his tenka for the emperor's? His early death makes any suggested answer moot. Of secondary importance is the question of whether Nobunaga coveted the title of shogun. In this masterful treatment of Nobunaga in Kyoto we are given an intimate look at the

internal workings of Japanese politics at the top. The overall impression is that, although powerless, neither tennō
nor Ashikaga shogun could be treated casually. Nor could
they be swept aside easily, even by a man who without hesi-
tation could order the destruction of the great Enryakuji
monastic establishment on Mt. Hiei. Hideyoshi's return to
the use of imperial court sanctions to support his hegemony must indicate that Nobunaga would have had a hard
time in displacing these traditional repositories of symbolic
authority.

John Hall's essay is a synthetic analysis of Hideyoshi's
domestic policies, chiefly in the political and social spheres.
Coming midway in this volume, it looks both backward and
forward in the effort to single out the most significant institutional changes of the sixteenth-century revolution, and
to judge the impact of the Hideyoshi era on these. The
conclusion is that while Hideyoshi was neither the sole instigator nor the final actor in the many transformations of
the period, he was the principal mover in creating the new
national order inherited by the Tokugawa and institutionalized as the bakuhan polity.

The third article dealing with the exercise of hegemonic
power is Wakita Osamu's analysis of the economic policies
of Nobunaga and Hideyoshi. As in the political sphere,
Nobunaga, in particular, was obliged to move with caution
against the established court families and religious institutions, as well as the merchant organizations that served and
were protected by them. Not until the military ascendancy
of Hideyoshi could the national hegemon dissolve the independent merchant guilds, bring all cities under the rule
of military authority (giving rise to the typical castle town),
and push through the national cadastral survey that established the kokudaka system of taxation.

The two essays that follow deal with the maturation of
the bakuhan system under the Tokugawa shogunate and
the measures required to assure the Great Peace. Asao
Naohiro deals with the problem of legitimacy still encoun-

tered by the Tokugawa shoguns following Ieyasu's demise. For, despite the overwhelming military power possessed by the Tokugawa House, and despite the political and economic measures for control inherited from the Hideyoshi administration, Ieyasu's successors could not count automatically on national recognition of their supreme authority. Without a general war that would give the succeeding shoguns the opportunity to demonstrate their military powers, other means to routinize their supreme status had to be pursued. Control of the imperial symbol was critical, and so was the image of national protector gained through the suppression of Christianity and enforcement of the *sakoku* (national closure) policy. But as Asao points out, there remained weaknesses in the Tokugawa claim to absolute national authority. Above all, it depended upon a continuation of good government, a requirement that became increasingly difficult to fulfill.

Sasaki Junnosuke treats the post-Hideyoshi problem of daimyo legitimation in a more theoretical manner. If the shogunate had to strive to perfect its institutions of national command, so also did the several daimyo need time to perfect what Sasaki calls "the mature Kinsei daimyo domain, or han." The requirements were two: control of vassal retainers, and control of the peasant class. Sasaki argues that in order for the daimyo to gain recognition as local "princes," in other words to acquire the status of local "kōgi," they were obliged to pose as protectors of "the people." In the process, daimyo worked to reduce the independence of their retainers in their dealings with the peasantry. They also acknowledged the responsibility of daimyo administrators to maintain the welfare of the domain. The day of arbitrary rule by military force, if indeed there had ever been one, was over.

The last two essays inquire into the nature of urban and economic growth that accompanied the transformation of the political order from Sengoku to Kinsei times. Wakita Haruko describes the evolution of the urban community from its medieval origins to the highly regulated conditions of the Edo period. Kozo Yamamura closes the volume with an analysis from the point of view of neoclassical economic theory of the causes and effects of Japan's agricultural revolution and of the accelerated growth of commerce during the same period. This is, like Hall's, a synthetic study that comments on recent Japanese scholarship and its Marxist methodology.

As in the Muromachi conference, papers written by Japanese contributors were translated and adapted by American scholars who in their own right are knowledgeable about the subject of the papers they were asked to translate. This arrangement was adopted to assure maximum communication between the Japanese author and the nonspecialist English reading audience. This in turn necessitated various degrees of adaptation. The fact that more than simple translation was involved is indicated by the notation that the papers have been prepared by the Japanese author with the assistance of the American translator-adaptor. The American participants were in contact with their Japanese counterparts before the conference meeting to suggest textual changes; they met during the conference in individual sessions to discuss points requiring clarification or elaboration, and they played an active role, along with the editors, in the final revision of the essays in the months following the conference.

One problem common to all papers and all efforts at communication through translation is that of nomenclature. As generations of Japanese historians have worked over the data of this period, several sets of vocabularies have come into common use, not always clearly defined or mutually exclusive so as to prevent overlap or inconsistency. In some cases, it would seem that each new generation of scholars has coined new names for phenomena already adequately named, simply to avoid unnecessary debate. Simple terms like daimyo or *jitō* present little problem when used with precision; but even these are often used to carry idiosyncratic meanings, or are combined with other terms to cover new objects of reference—for example, *shugo daimyō*. Moreover, there are whole sets of terms coined by modern historians, which in themselves may carry contradictory explanatory implications. Such are *zaichi ryōshu, kokujin, jizamurai, dogō, gōshi, myōshu, kajishimyōshu, dorei, nōdo, reinō, fudai, hikan, nago, sakunin, hyakushō, nauke-hyakushō*. Many such terms overlap in meaning, and few are capable of precise definition even in Japanese. This problem is multiplied when it comes to translation into English.

As the translators, and especially the editors, of the English-language version of the Conference symposium are acutely aware, many of the above terms that are of such critical importance to the analysis of medieval Japanese history have no exact equivalent in English. Moreover, a translation that works in one context may not be satisfactory in another. To take as examples the terms listed above, ryōshu presents a particularly difficult problem. The term in Japanese refers to the possessor (*shu*) of certain superior rights over land and its workers conveyed by the term *ryō*. English provides a number of possible equivalencies for ryōshu, such as "proprietor," "lord," "proprietary lord," "fief holder," "land holder," "local magnate," and others. By the middle of the Muromachi age, the fact that ryōshu could be used to refer to powerful daimyo-size magnates as well as small village-based fief holders will often make the use of an English equivalent such as "lord" quite inappropriate. In cases in which the size of the ryō-holder is purposely left ambiguous or unstated in Japanese, the fact that the translator into English has no alternative but to select an English equivalent that infers size is apt to distort the meaning intended by the Japanese author. Often the only safe procedure has been to leave the term in its original untranslated form.

Kokujin is a graphic term literally translated as "man of the province," "a provincial," or "a local." But Japanese usage implies that such locals are also ryōshu, either large or small. This additional meaning can only be conveyed by such inadequate English equivalencies as "local magnate," "local proprietor," "local lord," or even "baron." Jizamurai is another graphic term translatable as "warrior of the soil," "local samurai," "village warrior." But then there is the term dogō, which in certain contexts seems to refer to the same type of local land holder. The term dogō is generally applied to the village leader who possesses landed wealth and thereby local political (and even military) power. Depending on the period of reference, the dogō would be more or less militarized, and hence more or less similar to the jizamurai or kokujin. One is tempted to use the term "gentry" for this type, except for misconceptions that would arise from the English side of the equivalence.

Myōshu is another term for which there is no single meaning that will hold throughout medieval Japanese history, because the object of reference underwent several changes over the course of time. The original reference is to the possessor of rights to collect dues over a specific piece of land under the shōen system from the middle of the Heian period and into the Kamakura period. By Sengoku times it becomes hard to differentiate myōshu from dogō or even jizamurai as one reads the works of Japanese historians.

The whole range of subordinate statuses among the peasantry defined by terms like dorei, nōdo, reinō, fudai, hikan, and nago are extremely hard to differentiate and therefore to translate. In fact, there is not a perfect English equivalent for any one of these terms, let alone enough English terms to give each its particular Japanese nuance. Dorei is uniformly translated "slave," but the reference is to slavery in the Marxist sense rather than to the slave in pre-Civil War America. Nōdo is a term coined by modern Japanese historians to carry the Marxist concept of serf. Reinō is an even more recently coined term referring to the status of small cultivators—often emancipated nōdo—during the early Edo period.

The three remaining terms in the above list refer to various types of "bound" or "unfree" personal status among the agricultural population. The implication of each of these terms is that the status is defined within the context of the extended land-cultivating family organized under the authority of a patriarchal head. The resort to such inadequate English equivalents as "agricultural servants," "hereditary servants," "indentured servants" gives evidence of the difficulty of finding appropriate translations.

Finally, even the term hyakushō presents problems. First, the point of reference for the term changed its nature in the course of history so that the Kamakura type of hyakusho differs appreciably from the Edo type. The English equivalent, "peasant," may be applied appropriately to the earlier type, but not necessarily to the latter, for which "farmer" frequently seems more suited. The English connotations applying to the words "peasant" and "farmer" are not found in Japanese, since hyakushō is more generally applicable. Thus the translator is sometimes obliged to use the more neutral terms "cultivator" or "agriculturalist." But even this is no adequate solution, since hyakushō can be used to refer to the dogō type of villagers, who themselves may not have cultivated the soil directly.

Many of the problems of terminology and translation are avoidable, of course, simply by leaving the Japanese words transliterated and untranslated, and this is what has been done in certain cases in the essays that compose this volume. Yet for the sake of readability in English, it has seemed desirable to limit as much as possible the number of untranslated Japanese terms. And this is the policy adopted by the editors. The reader should understand, however, that each essay has been handled differently with respect to the problem of translation. For reasons both of style and subject matter no two essays presented identical translation problems or required identical solutions.

JOHN WHITNEY HALL
NAGAHARA KEIJI
KOZO YAMAMURA

Chapter 1

The Sengoku Daimyo and the Kandaka System

Nagahara Keiji
with Kozo Yamamura

WHEN WE THINK of the history of sixteenth-century Japan, it is generally the warfare and social disruption of the Sengoku period that spring first to our minds. Yet although the existence of a profound degree of disorder during this period is beyond dispute, it is also true that in the midst of this turmoil the Sengoku daimyo managed to institute a number of policies that gave their rule a considerable degree of stability, among the most important of which were those related to land tenure and taxation. The changes in existing patterns of land tenure and taxation were, on the surface, relatively simple. What the daimyo sought to do was to register all land within their territory in terms of its *kandaka* (the cash equivalent of the yield in goods and services to a vassal from his holdings), and to levy military service from each vassal in proportion to the kandaka figure. Simple though these changes may appear, however, it was this registration of all landholdings in terms that allowed the immediate calculation of both the level of dues owed by the peasant cultivators and the level of military service owed by the warrior seigniors that formed the basis of the land-tax system upon which the power of the greatest daimyo of the Sengoku period was based. This vitally important new technique, which historians refer to as the kandaka system, will be examined here from a number of points of view.[1]

[1] Among the best recent discussions of the kandaka system are Fujiki

To place the development of the kandaka system in historical perspective, we will first consider the nature of the contrast between the kandaka system itself and the *shōen* (estate) system that had preceded it as the fundamental framework upon which land tenure and taxation were ordered. Next, we will examine the impact that the kandaka system had upon each of the three fundamental classes of Sengoku society—the daimyo himself, his vassals, and the peasantry. Finally, we will conclude by discussing the eventual disappearance of the kandaka system in the context of the economic and monetary conditions that underlay the system, and the social and economic problems to which the system itself gave rise.

Before embarking upon this analysis, a word must be said about the great differences that existed in regional patterns of land tenure and administration during the Sengoku period. With the effective collapse of central authority, each daimyo tended to develop his own system of local administration in response to particular social and economic conditions within his domain. But although local conditions produced considerable variation in the details of daimyo administration from domain to domain, it is possible to distinguish three general patterns for the inception of the kandaka system and to relate these to differences in the strength and stability of the ancient shōen system in each of three geographical regions.

The first of these regions is the Kantō-Tōkaidō section of eastern Japan, an area whose most important daimyo included the Go-Hōjō, Takeda, Imagawa, Oda, and To-

---

Hisashi, "Kandakasei ron no kadai: Murata, Miyagawa, Sasaki (Jun) sanshi no setsu o megutte," in *Sengoku shakaishi ron*, by Fujiki Hisashi (Tokyo: Tōkyō Daigaku Shuppankai, 1974), pp. 355-95 (originally published as "Kandakasei to Sengokuteki kenryoku hensei: Murata, Miyagawa, Sasaki (Jun) no sanshi no shoron ni manabu," in *Nihonshi kenkyū* 93 [1967]); and Katsumata Shizuo, "Sengoku daimyō kenchi ni kansuru ichi kōsatsu: Erinji ryō 'kenchichō' no bunseki," in *Sengokuki no kenryoku to shakai*, edited by Nagahara Keiji (Tokyo: Tōkyō Daigaku Shuppankai, 1976), pp. 3-34.

kugawa. Here the daimyo were able to register and tax virtually all land in terms of its kandaka, and it is therefore upon the daimyo of this region that most discussions of the kandaka system are focused. Probably the best explanation for the rapid spread of the kandaka system in this region lies in the fact that this was an area in which the power of noble shōen proprietors had long been extremely weak, and that of local warrior proprietors (*zaichi ryoshū*) quite strong. Furthermore, the difficulties of transporting rice and other products from this region to the capital had resulted in the early commutation of most shōen dues to payments in cash, a practice that would have facilitated the registration of all land in terms of its kandaka.[2]

The second region is the Chūgoku-Shikoku-Kyūshū section of western Japan, whose major daimyo included the Mōri, the Chōsokabe, and the Ōtomo. While the kandaka system was widely used in this region, there were also significant stretches of land that the daimyo never succeeded in registering or taxing in terms of their putative cash yield. The reason for this latter phenomenon seems to have been that the shōen system and the rights of shōen proprietors had not been entirely supplanted here, and that a high proportion of agricultural dues had traditionally been paid in rice.

Third and last, there is the so-called capital region, here construed to include the five Kinai provinces plus the province of Ōmi. In this region, the rights of noble shōen proprietors remained strong throughout the Sengoku period, and the practice of commuting shōen dues to cash never

[2] On the issue of geographical patterns in the commutation of shōen dues to payments in cash, see Sasaki Gin'ya, "Shōen ni okeru daisennō no seiritsu to tenkai," in *Chūsei no shakai to keizai*, edited by Nagahara Keiji and Inagaki Yasuhiko (Tokyo: Tōkyō Daigaku Shuppankai, 1962). The precise relationship between such payments and the emergence of the kandaka system is likely, however, to have been extremely complex. See Nagahara Keiji, "Daimyō ryōgokusei no kōzō," in *Iwanami kōza Nihon rekishi* 8 (*Chūsei* 4), 3rd ed. (Tokyo: Iwanami Shoten, 1976), pp. 211-60.

took hold. Resistance to the kandaka system was so great within this region that even Oda Nobunaga could not impose it upon Ōmi. Instead, he registered the land of Ōmi province in terms of the rice it yielded to its holders (this rice yield being referred to as the *komedaka*) rather than of cash.

Given the existence of three such distinct patterns in the development of the kandaka system, generalizations about land tenure and taxation in Sengoku Japan are hazardous, all the more so because the study of the kandaka system has been far less systematically pursued in the cases of central and western daimyo than it has in the cases of daimyo like the Imagawa, Takeda, and Go-Hōjō. While it is clearly necessary, therefore, that we not assume that the kandaka system developed by a small number of well-known eastern daimyo was characteristic of patterns of land tenure and taxation throughout sixteenth-century Japan, it is in fact with the system of the Kantō-Tōkaidō region—and particularly with the kandaka system of the Go-Hōjō—that the remainder of this essay will be concerned. There are two advantages in thus limiting our focus: it is in this region alone that the foundation for studies of the kandaka system has been particularly well laid, and the very dominance of the kandaka system within this region allows us to examine it in a context in which it was least colored by the remnants of an earlier tenurial order.

THE LATTER DAYS OF THE SHŌEN SYSTEM

The first point to be recognized in our examination of the kandaka system is that the growth of daimyo power was by no means the only cause of changes in the nature of land tenure and taxation during the Sengoku period. Long before the Sengoku daimyo's emergence, the structure of land tenure within Japan had been in a state of profound flux, and to a large extent the kandaka system may be viewed as an attempt by the Sengoku daimyo to bring order out of the complex tenurial situation that had developed by the late fifteenth century from the progressive collapse of the ancient shōen system.

Under the shōen system, from perhaps the middle of the eleventh century, proprietary interests in land had been vested for the most part either in important religious institutions or in nobles of extremely high rank. The right to manage the land, as well as to rule and tax the peasants who inhabited and tilled it, belonged entirely to these proprietors, and was delegated to local figures with whom the proprietors maintained patron-client relationships of varying degrees of commitment.

By the early fifteenth century, this monopoly by the nobility and clergy of proprietary control over land had been reduced significantly, and a much more complex tenurial picture had begun to emerge. One new element was the provincial warrior as independent proprietor. The vast majority of these warrior-proprietors were so-called *kokujin*—powerful provincial figures whose families had in the past served either as relatively high-ranking local functionaries of absentee shōen proprietors or as military stewards (*jitō*) appointed to noble estates by the Kamakura bakufu. Warrior lordship over land had begun within the formal confines of the shōen system as the shōen proprietors' effective authority over their landholdings had, during the course of the Kamakura period, become greatly circumscribed by custom. Specifically, while the shōen proprietor was entitled both to manage and to tax all lands within his holdings that had traditionally been under cultivation, it became the common rule that land which had remained waste, or which had been brought under cultivation more recently, should be left in the hands of the local figures who served on his estates either as officials of the proprietor himself or as jitō appointed by the Kamakura bakufu. By the late Kamakura period, then, it was quite possible for a significant proportion of the land within any given shōen to be under the de facto proprietary control of local warriors.[3]

The most spectacular growth of kokujin lordship, however, occurred under the radically new provincial order forged during the prolonged civil wars of the fourteenth century. By the mid-thirteenth century, authority relationships within the cultivating class had begun to change dramatically and, while the precise nature of these changes need not concern us for the moment, one of their effects was to make it increasingly difficult to collect the dues traditionally rendered by the peasantry to absentee shōen proprietors. By the fifteenth century, this problem, combined with the difficulties already inherent in having a part of their estates controlled by local warriors, had produced a situation in which shōen proprietors saw less and less point in their struggle to retain direct control of their properties. Seeking to salvage what income they could, many such proprietors granted contracts to local kokujin to manage their holdings for them. So complete was the transfer of authority that such contracts embodied, however, that many of the kokujin who entered into them ended by taking complete control of the land under their management. By the end of the century, many such warriors were conducting their own surveys of these lands and enrolling the lands' inhabitants as their own vassals. For all intents and purposes, the warriors themselves were proprietors of the land, and the shōen proprietors gradually became a powerless class of noble pensioners.

A second major complication in the tenurial picture of

[3] I have argued at some length in an earlier study that the lands that remained fully subject to the shōen proprietor's authority were generally limited to those lands within his shōen which had been subject to government taxation in the period before the shōen was created. See the discussion of *kōden* in Nagahara Keiji, "Landownership under the *Shōen-Kokugaryō* System," *Journal of Japanese Studies* 1:2 (1975), 269-96. Hereafter cited as Nagahara, "Landownership."

fifteenth-century Japan was the advent of the shugo daimyo. The shugo's impact upon land tenure was twofold. First, the shugo were powerful warriors who were themselves legally capable of assuming proprietary control over a significant body of land. Second, in addition to their authority over the lands of which they themselves had become proprietors, the shugo assumed virtually all functions of the ancient civil provincial government, which enabled them as early as the first decade of the fifteenth century to subject all landholdings within their provinces to levies of *tansen*—a sort of extraordinary provincial land tax. By the middle of the century, these once extraordinary levies were being collected on an annual or even semiannual basis, and shugo tansen had given the daimyo a significant claim to income against every landholding within the territories to which they were assigned.

The dispersal of seigniorial prerogatives once vested exclusively in shōen proprietors among a large number of locally powerful kokujin and a much smaller number of shugo daimyo was only one feature of the changing tenurial order in the second half of the fifteenth century. Another phenomenon, whose roots went back to the late Kamakura and the Muromachi periods, was a pronounced social and economic cleavage within the cultivating class. Throughout the early medieval period, shōen proprietors had governed the peasantry of their estates by dealing directly only with the *myōshu*—members of a select group of peasants who had been accorded hereditary control over certain bodies of land and the peasants tilling them, with the responsibility for overseeing cultivation as well as assembling the various imposts incumbent upon the land and the peasantry. By the early Muromachi period, however, the structure of relationships within the peasantry was undergoing a critical change. During the thirteenth century, rapid increases in agricultural productivity and the diffusion of a new agrarian technology had made it possible for an increasing number of peasants to acquire relatively secure rights of tenure over the fields they cultivated, and to escape their subjection to the myōshu class. The myōshu, for their part, became in effect a class of peasant land-lords—men who no longer attempted to administer and tax the inhabitants of a given sector of some shōen for the proprietor but, rather, were content to extract a "supple-mental land rent" (*kajishi*) from whoever cultivated the lands to which they could claim superior title as myōshu. By the fifteenth century, the kajishi that such a man might earn frequently outweighed the traditional land rent that shōen proprietors had been accustomed to levy from the same land, and the right to collect kajishi had become so far divorced from the necessity to fulfill any real role within the shōen administration that the myōshu's kajishi rights were the object of an active trade.

This fundamental change in the structure of peasant so-ciety represented a grave threat to the integrity of the shōen system. To the extent that the myōshu became mere landlords, it was impossible to use them to administer the remainder of the peasantry; and shōen proprietors made every effort to prohibit both the imposition of kajishi and the brisk trade in kajishi rights. But their efforts were largely futile; by the late fifteenth century the shōen system was in ruins. Not only had the exclusive seigniorial pre-rogatives that the shōen proprietors had once enjoyed over a subject peasantry been fragmented among proprietors, kokujin, and shugo daimyo, but the subject peasantry was no longer as easily controlled as it once had been; the myōshu had ceased to function as the proprietors' agents in controlling their fellow cultivators, and had instead be-come contenders for proprietary control. The significance of these developments completely transcends the end of noble and clerical dominance. With the collapse of the shōen system, there ceased to be a single legal order defin-ing the relationships among the various groups—whether noble, warrior, or peasant—which might conceivably enjoy a species of proprietary claim against a single parcel of land. The consequent insecurity of the proprietary rights that had superseded those of the shōen system was a major source of the local violence that characterized the Sengoku period, and it was partly in an attempt to recreate a unified method of collecting dues that the kandaka system was devised.

THE KANDAKA SYSTEM AND THE REGISTRATION OF LAND

As noted at the outset of this essay, the kandaka system draws its name from the Sengoku daimyo's practice of registering land in terms of the cash value of the goods and services that it afforded its holders—in terms, that is to say, of its kandaka. While this rather limited definition has thus far been sufficient for our purposes, the full impact of the kandaka system upon land tenure and taxation during the Sengoku period can only be understood if we specify with much greater detail just what the kandaka was. In pursuit of this greater precision, we will henceforth be devoting most of our attention to the daimyo of the Kantō-Tōkaidō region—particularly the Go-Hōjō of Odawara.

At the outset it should be emphasized that there were two essential differences between the kandaka-based valuation of land that was used during the Sengoku period, and the kokudaka-based valuation of land used during the succeeding early modern period. The most obvious one, of course, is that one valuation was expressed in terms of *kan* (a unit of 1,000 copper coins) of cash, and the other in terms of *koku* (approximately 4.5 bushels) of rice. Far more interesting is the difference between the bases of the two systems of valuation. The early modern kokudaka was an estimate of the total value of the land's yield, and the *nengu* (annual land rent) due from the land was calculated as a certain percentage of the kokudaka. The Sengoku-period kandaka was itself the direct expression of the nengu due from the land rather than of the land's total yield.[4]

[4] For an English-language treatment of the kokudaka system, see Wakita Osamu, "The *Kokudaka* System: A Device for Unification," *Journal of Japanese Studies* 1:2 (1975), 297-320.

The fact that the Sengoku daimyo registered land in terms of the nengu may give rise to a certain amount of confusion. Nengu, after all, was the name given to the basic annual land rent that shōen proprietors had extracted from the cultivators of their estates, and it may therefore appear that the kandaka system amounted to little more than an attempt by the Sengoku daimyo to register all land in terms of the cash value of the rent that it had traditionally yielded its noble proprietors. In fact, the nengu defined by the shōen system was quite different from that defined by the kandaka system. While the former had referred only to the land rent due to shōen proprietors, or to the kokujin proprietors who had supplanted them, the latter was defined to include not only the income going to the shōen proprietor and the kokujin, but also as much as possible of that going to the kajishi myōshu. The nengu of the kandaka system, in other words, included under a single rubric all the proprietary and quasi-proprietary imposts that had sprung up with the decay of the shōen system. This relationship of the kandaka-system nengu to changing patterns of the distribution of landed income is represented graphically in Figure 1.1.

It was precisely the Sengoku daimyo's ability to acquire a knowledge of tenurial rights and income distribution detailed enough for him to redefine nengu, and to register each parcel of land in terms of the amount of this newly defined impost, that made the daimyo a pivotal figure in the land law of the Sengoku period. Underlying this extraordinary ability was a phenomenon that was among the most striking in the history of late medieval Japan—the administration of extensive cadastral surveys—and an understanding of their purpose is crucial to our understanding of the kandaka system as a whole. The precise details of these surveys differed considerably from one daimyo domain to another, making it impossible to discuss anything like a typical Sengoku-period survey. But we can examine those of the Go-Hōjō, which are generally acknowledged to

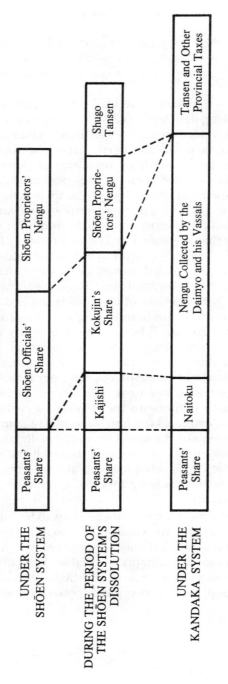

FIGURE 1.1

UNDER THE
SHŌEN SYSTEM

Peasants' Share	Shōen Officials' Share	Shōen Proprietors' Nengu

DURING THE PERIOD OF
THE SHŌEN SYSTEM'S
DISSOLUTION

Peasants' Share	Kajishi	Kokujin's Share	Shōen Proprietors' Nengu	Shugo Tansen

UNDER THE
KANDAKA SYSTEM

Peasants' Share	Naitoku	Nengu Collected by the Daimyo and his Vassals	Tansen and Other Provincial Taxes

have been the most thoroughgoing cadastral surveys conducted by any Sengoku daimyo, and attempt to discover in these the common concerns of daimyo throughout the country.

The Go-Hōjō family of Odawara are known to have begun making detailed surveys of territory they conquered as early as 1506, when they had barely emerged as a significant power in the southern part of the Kantō. By the middle of the sixteenth century, systematic resurveys of their territories were being conducted at the succession of each new head of the family. In their fully developed form, these surveys had three important characteristics. First, the basic territorial unit was the administrative village (*gō*) rather than the individual proprietorship. The respective claims of each proprietor to individual fields within the village were recognized, but all fields were listed within a single village register, and the village itself was registered in terms of total kandaka of all its fields. Second, nengu was assessed on a uniform basis throughout the provinces subject to Go-Hōjō rule. The area of each field was carefully determined, and nengu was then assessed against all paddy, at a rate most often of 500 *mon* per *tan*, and against uplands usually at a rate of 165 mon per tan. At least initially, no provision was made for exempting fields that had hitherto been immune to the imposts of civil or military proprietors, or for taking into account past complexities in the distribution of the land's income. Finally, the principle was maintained that in any case in which the surveys resulted in the land's being assessed at a higher rate than in the past, the surplus nengu was to be rendered to the Go-Hōjō themselves.

One of the most important questions to be considered in our examination of the kandaka system is that of the extent to which the Sengoku daimyo's surveys may have raised the level of nengu assessments. Available data show that the figure of 500 mon per tan which the Go-Hōjō used in assessing nengu against rice paddy was extremely common during the Muromachi period. Among other Sengoku daimyo, the Go-Hōjō's rivals, the Imagawa, used a sliding scale of 600, 500, and 400 mon per tan in assessing nengu against paddies of various grades; and it is possible to demonstrate that a rate of assessment of close to 500 mon per tan had been common in eastern Japan even under the shōen system (see Table 1.1).[5] This seeming continuity between assessment rates in the shōen and the kandaka sys-

TABLE 1.1
NENGU ASSESSMENTS AND RATES 15th-16th CENTURIES

Year	Province	Area in Paddy (tan)	Total Assessment (A)	Assessment Rate (B)	Sources
1519	Mutsu	5	1,800	360	Date-ke monjo, No. 86
1519	Mutsu	2	1,000	500	Date-ke monjo, No. 86
1519	Mutsu	1	400	400	Date-ke monjo, No. 86
1534	Mutsu	2	750	375	Date-ke monjo, No. 131
1534	Mutsu	2	800	400	Date-ke monjo, No. 131
1400	Hitachi	30	15,000	500	Yoshida jinja monjo
1418	Hitachi	1	650	650	Yoshida jinja monjo
1418	Hitachi	1	400	400	Yoshida jinja monjo
1471	Hitachi	1	600	600	Konponji monjo
1482	Shimozuke	3	1,500	500	Motegi monjo
1482	Shimozuke	2	800	400	Motegi monjo
1555	Suruga	5	2,360	472	Senshōji monjo
1549	Mikawa	3	1,800	600	Taiheiji jiryō mokuroku

[5] On the Imagawa's assessments, see *Kashiwagi monjo*, in *Shizuoka-ken shiryō* 1 (Tokyo: Kadokawa Shoten, 1965), 636-37.

TABLE 1.1 (cont.)
NENGU ASSESSMENTS AND RATES 15th-16th CENTURIES

Year	Province	Area in Paddy (tan)	Total Assess- ment (A)	Assess- ment Rate (B)	Sources
1549	Mikawa	2	1,300	650	Taiheiji jiryō mokuroku
1549	Mikawa	2	1,400	700	Taiheiji jiryō mokuroku
1498	Owari	7½	2,925	390	Myōkōji monjo, No. 435
1498	Owari	5	1,950	390	Myōkōji monjo, No. 435
1516	Mino	1	500	500	Ryūseiji monjo, No. 3
1518	Mino	3	1,300	433	Ryūseiji monjo, No. 4
1521	Mino	1	357	357	Ryūseiji monjo, No. 5
1530	Mino	1⅓	500	375	Ryūseiji monjo, No. 7
1351	Mino	1⅓	1,100	827	Ryūtokuji monjo, No. 1
1436	Mino	1⅓	300	225	Ryūtokuji monjo, No. 6
1472	Mino	1⅓	500	375	Ryūtokuji monjo, No. 13

NOTE: All monetary data in columns A and B are in kan and mon. 1,800 is 1 kan 800 mon, and 360 is 360 mon. 1 kan is 1,000 mon.

tems may seem at first glance to demonstrate that the kandaka figures used by the Sengoku daimyo sprang directly from nengu assessments used by the land's former proprietors. There are at least two points, however, that militate against such a view. The first is that there can be little doubt that it was extremely difficult for shōen proprietors to collect as much as 500 mon per tan from their holdings, as illustrated in the case of Ryūtokuji's holdings in Mino (Table 1.1). It is apparent that Ryūtokuji was forced to vary its rate of assessment considerably, and it is known from other evidence that it was seldom possible for this proprietor to collect nengu at the formally constituted rate. It seems likely that even on those fields against which proprietors may traditionally have levied nengu, the daimyo's assessment of 500 mon per tan must have represented a de facto increase over the amount of nengu that the proprietors had been able to realize.

The second point is that the nengu levied under the kandaka system was levied against all arable land, not simply those fields that had traditionally been subject to the shōen proprietors' authority. The resultant increase in the amount of nengu levied against a given village following the daimyo's surveys was enormous, frequently more than double, as the figures for some villages within the Go-Hōjō's territories show (see Table 1.2).

Increases of this magnitude, which were among the most striking consequences of surveys conducted under the kandaka system, seem to have resulted from a combination of two factors: the assessment of nengu against fields that hitherto had escaped this burden, to which we have already alluded, and the incorporation into the nengu assessment of at least part of the kajishi that the upper stratum of the peasantry was collecting from its lesser fellows. This dramatic growth in the level of nengu assessment was a reflection of the degree to which the cadastral surveys had enabled the Go-Hōjō to achieve a better grasp of the total flow of income from the land than had been possible under the shōen system. Since the daimyo maintained the right to any new nengu, he stood to increase his wealth substantially.

Though the survey techniques of other daimyo could

TABLE 1.2

THE INCREASES IN TAX REVENUES ACHIEVED AS A RESULT OF THE CADASTRAL SURVEY IN THE HŌJŌ DOMAIN

Year of the Cadastral Survey	Province	Adminis- trative Unit (gō)	Assess- ment prior to the Survey (A)	Increase in Assess- ment (B)	Assess- ment after the Survey	(B) (A)
1506	Sagami	Miyaji	57,600	23,300	80,900	0.404
1542	Musashi	Iwama	120,000	16,734	136,734	0.136
1542	Sagami	Nukumizu	23,000	30,600	53,600	1.330
1543	Sagami	Ishida	83,000	167,900	250,900	2.022
1543	Sagami	Funago	50,512	51,440	101,952	1.018
1543	Sagami	Hase	63,000	127,230	190,230	2.019
1543	Sagami	Nakahara	17,017	50,350	67,367	2.958
1543	Sagami	Ono	45,010	96,602	141,612	2.146
1543	Sagami	Aina	7,000	39,125	46,125	5.589
1543	Sagami	Asō	35,300	47,200	82,500	1.337
1543	Izu	Nagamizo	30,000	5,150	35,150	0.171
1543	Musashi	Ōta	120,000	16,734	136,734	0.139
1555	Musashi	Imanari	109,065	91,400	200,465	0.838

NOTE: All assessments are in mon.

SOURCE: The figures in this table are drawn from the *Odawara-shū shoryō yakuchō*, edited by Sugiyama Hiroshi (Tokyo: Kondō Shuppansha, 1969). For a discussion of similar increases effected by the Imagawa, see Arimitsu Yūgaku, "Sengoku daimyō Imagawa-shi no rekishiteki seikaku," *Nihonshi kenkyū* 138 (1974).

vary considerably from those of the Go-Hōjō, such daimyo houses as the Imagawa, Takeda, and Tokugawa also used their surveys to increase the amount of income to be drawn from the peasantry and the land. The case of the Imagawa is particularly interesting in this regard. Unlike the Go-Hōjō, the Imagawa seem to have relied almost entirely upon reports from the peasantry for information about the extent of the imposts incumbent upon the land, and only rarely to have surveyed the fields themselves. In this sense, the Imagawa's perception of the realities of land tenure within their territories was certainly far less systematic than was the Go-Hōjō's. Nevertheless, the Imagawa's law codes provided that if any peasant undertook to cultivate the land of another person and to render a higher level of nengu than in the past, the land was to be taken from its current holder and granted to the peasant who was willing to render the greater nengu.[6] Whatever the inadequacy of their survey techniques, the Imagawa were clearly capable of increasing the amount of nengu drawn from the land; and the prevalence of this sort of concern among the daimyo of the Sengoku period suggests that an increase in the level of nengu assessment must have been among the key objectives of the kandaka system and of the cadastral surveys underlying it.

Nengu Collection under the Kandaka System

Having analyzed changes in land registration and assessment under the Go-Hōjō, we must now turn to an examination of the impact that the kandaka system had upon the

[6] This provision is set forth in the first clause of the *Imagawa kana mokuroku*, a law code that was adopted in 1526. (See *Imagawa kana mokuroku*, in *Chūsei hōsei shiryōshū* 3 [*Buke kahō* 1], edited by Satō Shin'ichi, Ikeuchi Yoshisuke, and Momose Kesao [Tokyo: Iwanami Shoten, 1965].) it should be noted, however, that the transfer of the land to the man promising to render more nengu was not automatic; if the original holder of the land agreed to render as much nengu as the new man offered, he could keep the land himself.

imposition of taxes and services in Sengoku Japan. This
will be done by focusing on each of three distinct categories
of imposts—the nengu rendered by peasants to the proprietors of their lands, the military services owed the daimyo
by his vassals, and the various provincial taxes the daimyo
levied from the territories subject to his rule. In virtually all
discussions of the kandaka system, it is suggested that
among this system's most important characteristics were
the collection of nengu at a higher rate than had been possible under the shōen system, and the collection of nengu
in cash rather than in kind. It can scarcely be doubted that
the Sengoku daimyo's surveys resulted in enormous increases in the rate of nengu assessment, and that the
daimyo, as we shall see below, made vigorous attempts to
collect their taxes in cash. It is important to recognize,
however, that the differential between the rates at which
nengu was levied under the kandaka and shōen systems
was not always as great as the raw kandaka figures would
seem to indicate, and, furthermore, that the expression of
nengu assessments in cash terms did not necessarily require that the nengu actually be paid in cash.

The danger of reading too much into the raw kandaka
figures produced by the Sengoku period surveys is particularly apparent in the case of the Go-Hōjō. In their system,
the total kandaka assigned to a village by the formal assessment of 500 mon per tan against paddy and 165 mon
per tan against uplands was a purely fictive figure referred
to as the *kenchi takatsuji*, or "survey-based total." While this
fictive figure was carefully recorded in the Go-Hōjō's
cadastral registers, the amount of nengu actually drawn
from the village was shown by a rather different figure
known as the *jōnō takatsuji*, or "total actually rendered."

The sort of deductions that were made from the formal
assessment in arriving at the actual assessment are best
seen in a specific example, such as those that the Go-Hōjō
allowed for the village of Madarame-no-gō in Sagami province (see Table 1.3). From the total formal assessment

TABLE 1.3

DEDUCTIONS ALLOWED IN COMPUTING THE ACTUAL TAX
LIABILITY OF MADARAME-NO-GŌ IN SAGAMI

Survey-based total assessment of the village (*kenchi takatsuji*)		211 kan 252 mon
Deductions allowed		74 kan 604 mon
special exemption granted in the year of the survey (1569)	18 kan 295 mon	
stipend for the daimyo's agent (*jōshi*)	1 kan 200 mon	
stipend of the myōshu	1 kan 500 mon	
costs of the festival of the local shrine	1 kan 200 mon	
miscellaneous taxes	50 kan 409 mon	
other	2 kan	
Actual tax liability of the village (*jōnō takatsuji*)		136 kan 604 mon

SOURCE: *Ashigara Kami-gun monjo*, no. 72, in *Kaitei shinpen Sōshū komonjo* 1 (Tokyo: Kadokawa Shoten, 1965), 70-71.

against this village of 211 kan 252 mon, deductions of
more than 74 kan were made, leaving the village with an
actual assessment of only 136 kan 604 mon. Included were
an ad hoc exemption granted on the occasion of the most
recent cadastral survey, exemptions covering the stipends
of village officials, an exemption to cover the costs of a local
festival, and a considerable exemption to cover the amount
of other taxes rendered. Though not seen in this case, it
was common in other villages for further exemptions to be
made for the costs of maintaining irrigation facilities.
Given the daimyo's practice of taking for himself any increase in nengu resulting from his cadastral surveys, these
exemptions amounted to a rebate from the daimyo to the
peasantry of at least part of the increased income gener-

ated by his surveys. Similar extensions of beneficence to the peasantry were practiced by the Imagawa and Takeda.

Particularly interesting is the conscious use by the Takeda of exemptions as a basis for the extraction of alternative services from the upper stratum of the peasantry. Under the Takeda, all rice paddy was classified as either "peasant land" (*hyakushō-chi*) or "myōshu land" (*myōden-chi*), with the latter being assessed nengu at a lower rate than the former. In return for their lower nengu assessments, the peasants whose land was registered as myōden-chi were enrolled in the lower ranks of the Takeda's military structure, and were liable to mobilization in time of warfare.[7]

Aside from the question of the level at which nengu was actually collected, there is the matter of the form that such collections took. It is well known that the military exigencies of the Sengoku period created an extraordinary demand for cash on the part of the daimyo, and it is generally argued that one goal of the kandaka system was to provide this cash. Although there can be little doubt that the daimyo made considerable efforts to collect as much taxation as possible in cash, the hard evidence available to us makes it quite clear that nengu was rendered in a variety of forms under the kandaka system, and that the particular form of paying varied tremendously with changes in time, daimyo domain, or even in different regions within a single daimyo's territory. A few examples drawn from the histories of the Imagawa and the Takeda will serve to illustrate this point. According to a 1569 patent by which Imagawa Ujizane invested the Okuyama family with a new fief, the grant was expressed as an annuity of 60 kan in cash from an area called Kaminagao and 200 *hyō* (bales) of rice from Tomonaga. This document indicates that nengu was levied in rice within the Imagawa's territory even ex-

[7] Nagahara Keiji, "Daimyō ryōgokusei-ka no nōmin shihai gensoku," in *Sengokuki no kenryoku to shakai*, edited by Nagahara Keiji (Tokyo: Tōkyō Daigaku Shuppankai, 1976), pp. 112-25.

tremely late in the Sengoku period.[8] In the case of the
Takeda, it is known that part of the rice paddy within their
domain was classified as *kokumaichi*, or lands for which
nengu was normally to be paid in rice rather than in cash.
Moreover, on lands that were held by temples or local warriors, the variety of forms of nengu payments in kind could
be extensive. We know, for instance, that while the dues
that the temple of Erinji was entitled to extract from its
holdings were formally expressed in cash, a number of
miscellaneous imposts (*zatsu kuji*) carried over from the
shōen period continued to be levied in maize, charcoal,
straw mats, and thatching.[9] Yet, although the daimyo
probably had little interest in insisting that nengu be rendered to others in cash—if the land's proprietor preferred
payment in kind, his preference could scarcely have adversely affected the daimyo—the situation on the daimyo's
own holdings might easily have been quite different.
There, the daimyo's demand for cash ought theoretically
to have induced him to insist that the nengu be paid in
coin. To judge from the case of the Takeda, however, such
considerations cannot have been quite so overriding as we
sometimes tend to assume. One document describing lands
that the Takeda granted Erinji refers to the nengu on a
portion of these lands as "24 *koku* 2 *to* 4 *shō* 5 *gō* [of rice],
equivalent to 121 *hyō* 3 *shō* 5 *gō*, this equivalent to a cash
payment of 34 kan 620 mon." It is clear from this notation
that the nengu due from this land must normally have
been collected in bales of rice, for hyō was the unit used to
count bales.[10]

[8] *Okuyama monjo*, no. 2, in *Shizuoka-ken shiryō* 4 (Tokyo: Kadokawa Shoten, 1968), 796.

[9] For an outstanding analysis of the Erinji documents from which this
and the following example are drawn, see Katsumata, "Sengoku daimyō
kenchi ni kansuru ichi kōsatsu."

[10] In measuring the volume of rice, the units normally used were *koku*,
to, *shō*, and *gō*, with 1 *koku* = 10 *to* = 100 *shō* = 1,000 *gō*. It was also possible,
however, to measure rice in bales, or *hyō*, each of which normally contained either 2 or 4 *to*.

If we may conclude that the collection of nengu in both rice and cash was a formal feature of the Imagawa's and Takeda's kandaka systems, the evidence available in the case of the Go-Hōjō is rather more ambiguous. In general, the Go-Hōjō demanded that the nengu due from their own holdings be paid in cash, but there were many exceptions. A 1583 document concerning the nengu to be rendered from Shirahama-no-gō in Izu reveals that, of a total of 86 kan 104 mon due from this village, 43 kan 906 mon were to be paid in rice, 10 kan 250 mon in 41 hyō of unbaled rice, 1 kan 650 mon in dried abalone, and 10 kan 143 mon in salt. An addendum to this listing states that since salt was not needed this year, rice was to be substituted for it.[11] Another document reveals that in 1570 the village of Igusa-no-gō in Musashi rendered its nengu in the form of 5 kan of cash and 2 kan 470 mon worth of unhulled rice, soybeans, and barley.[12]

The problem with the Go-Hōjō evidence is that it is unclear whether the payment of nengu in kind rather than in cash was a practice that had always been allowed, or whether it was merely a reflection of the difficulties that the Go-Hōjō are known to have experienced in collecting their taxes in cash by the end of the Sengoku period. For the moment the distinction is unimportant; what matters is that neither the Go-Hōjō nor their Imagawa and Takeda rivals had achieved a system of taxation in which all nengu was rendered in cash.

Nevertheless, the impact of the kandaka system upon the levying of nengu from the peasantry should not be minimized. The great cadastral surveys of this period had the effect of imposing a uniform, cash-expressed index for the assessment of all nengu within the daimyo's territories, and of allowing the daimyo to become the sole judges of

[11] *Ikonahiko no Mikoto Jinja monjo*, in *Shizuoka-ken shiryō* 1, 85-87.
[12] *Hiki-gun monjo*, no. 4, in *Shinpen Bushū komonjo* 1 (Tokyo: Kadokawa Shoten, 1975), 524.

48

whether the peasants of certain areas should be allowed to render less nengu than was formally assessed against them. If the system did not necessarily insure that the peasants' taxes would be paid in cash, it nevertheless helped insure that the daimyo would enjoy a greater degree of authority over the peasants of their territories than had any provincial rulers since the decay of the ancient imperial state.

MILITARY SERVICE UNDER THE KANDAKA SYSTEM

Thus far our discussion has centered upon the nature of the dues extracted from the peasantry under the kandaka system, but the kandaka figures that were so carefully recorded by the Sengoku daimyo also served as the basis for the extraction of military services from the daimyo's vassals. As in the case of nengu, the formal kandaka figures yielded by the cadastral surveys did not necessarily coincide with the assessment figures upon which the actual levies of military service were based. The Go-Hōjō used a "military assessment" (*gun'yaku takatsuji* or *chigyōyaku takatsuji*) of a vassal's holdings, a figure that frequently differed both from the survey-based formal assessment of those fields and from the modified assessment upon which the peasant's nengu obligations were based.

Let us consider, for the moment, the case of one of the Go-Hōjō's major vassals, Matsuda Samanosuke. According to the *Odawara-shū shoryō yakuchō*, a register of vassals' landholdings, Matsuda held lands whose formal assessment was 1,277 kan 200 mon. Of this total assessment, 277 kan 200 mon were excluded from his "taxable income," and he was obliged to render military service for only 1,000 kan. Furthermore, although a 1555 survey had rated new lands granted to him at 150 kan per year, his military obligation with respect to these holdings was levied against only 75 kan. Because exemptions of this sort were based upon the particular relationship obtaining between the daimyo and each of his vassals, it is impossible to specify just what may have produced any given level of military assessment.

It is also impossible to determine exactly how the kandaka-based "military assessments" listed against each of the Go-Hōjō's vassals were translated into specific demands for military service. At least something of the principles involved can be guessed at, however, from surviving examples of the nature of services provided by individual retainers. In 1581, for instance, Ikeda Sōzaemon of Sagami was ordered to serve the Go-Hōjō with a force of twenty-seven men that included, besides Sōzaemon himself, six mounted warriors and twenty foot soldiers (a musketeer, twelve pikemen, an archer, and six others). The holdings against which this service was levied were rated at 191 kan 600 mon.[13] Another Go-Hōjō vassal, Miyagi Shirōbeinojō of Musashi, was obliged to lead forth seven mounted warriors and twenty-eight foot soldiers (two musketeers, seventeen pikemen, one archer, and eight others) from holdings rated at 284 kan 84 mon.[14] A quick comparison of these examples reveals that the ratio of the kandaka of these vassals' holdings to the level of military service demanded was roughly the same.

Considering that in 1559 the Go-Hōjō had 500 vassals whose holdings were carefully registered in the *Odawara-shū shoryō yakuchō*, it must have been a relatively simple matter to calculate the extent of the military power available to them. Other daimyo had developed similar formulas for the assessment of military service. The Takeda vassal Ōi Samanojō, for example, was obliged in 1564 to provide four mounted warriors and thirty-four foot soldiers from holdings whose military service assessment was 228 kan.[15] As we shall see in somewhat greater detail below, this ra-

[13] *Ōsumi-gun monjo*, no. 60, in *Kaitei shinpen Sōshū komonjo* 1, 209-11.

[14] *Miyagi monjo*, edited by Nerima Kyōdoshi Kenkyūkai (Tokyo: Nerima Kyōdoshi Kenkyūkai, 1956), mimeo., pp. 24-26.

[15] *Toshima-gun monjo*, no. 38, in *Shinpen Bushū komonjo* 1, 38.

tionalized pattern of military assessments was just as significant a step in the reorganization of military service as
the restructuring of nengu assessments was in rationalizing
the obligations of the peasantry. The kandaka system, in
other words, represented as much an advance in the
daimyo's control of his vassals as it did in his control of the
peasantry.

The Kandaka System and Provincial Taxation

The last category of imposts we need to examine is that of
provincial taxation. Unlike nengu, which was owed by the
peasantry to a large number of individual proprietors,
provincial taxation was a "public" impost levied by the
daimyo against the lands and peasantry of his entire territory. The best known examples of these taxes were tansen,
a cash tax levied against rice paddies in proportion to their
area, and *munebechisen*, a cash tax levied against peasant
households in proportion to the number of buildings in
their possession. Both taxes had been levied by the shugo
daimyo of the earlier Muromachi period, but their collection was put on a more systematic basis as a result of the
cadastral surveys and household censuses carried out by
the more powerful daimyo of the Sengoku period.

Once again, the Go-Hōjō provide the most clearcut
example of the sort of rationalization that was effected.
Under the terms of the new tax system that they adopted in
1550, the Go-Hōjō collected three varieties of provincial
taxes—munebechisen, tansen, and *kakesen*. Of these,
munebechisen continued to be collected on the basis of the
number of buildings the peasantry possessed. Tansen,
however, was divorced from considerations of land area as
such, and was linked instead to the kandaka system; tansen
became an impost that was collected from each village at
the rate of 6 mon for every 100 mon of the village's total
formal assessment (kenchi takatsuji). Kakesen, which
seems to have been a cash levy designed to replace a num-

ber of miscellaneous imposts (zatsu kuji) under the shōen system, was levied at the rate of 4 mon per 100 mon of formal assessment.[16]

The daimyo's determination to wring substantial sums of cash from the territories subject to his rule is particularly obvious in the collection of these provincial taxes. The daimyo's need to act in this way arose essentially from three causes. First, the purchase of arms and provisions for his vast armies frequently required payments in cash rather than in kind. Second, large numbers of the daimyo's lower-ranking retainers were granted cash stipends (*okuradashi*) rather than landed fiefs.[17] Finally, cash was necessary in order to pay the increasingly large numbers of artisans and coolie laborers whom the daimyo were obliged to employ.

Since the daimyo himself received nengu only from his sometimes small amount of directly held land, his attempts to force the peasantry to render this particular impost in the form of cash were apt to be relatively restrained. The same cannot be said of his attitude toward the collection of provincial taxes. On the contrary, it is known that the daimyo not only insisted that provincial taxes be rendered exclusively in cash, but also imposed strict limits on the extent to which inferior coins could be used for their payment. For a time provincial taxation became a major source of the cash the daimyo needed so desperately.[18] In the long run, however, the Sengoku daimyo's insistence upon the payment of all provincial taxes in cash proved to be profoundly disruptive for the rural economy, and the collec-

---

[16] Sawaki Eichi, "Go-Hōjō-shi no zeisei kaikaku ni tsuite," in *Go-Hōjō-shi no kiso kenkyū*, by Sawaki Eichi (Tokyo: Yoshikawa Kōbunkan, 1976), pp. 1-22.

[17] For examples of the Imagawa family's granting of cash stipends rather than of land see *Nakamura monjo*, no. 6, in *Shizuoka-ken shiryō* 5, 585-97.

[18] On this issue as it relates to the Hōjō see Sawaki Eichi, "Go-Hōjō-shi no kahei seisaku ni tsuite," in *Go-Hōjō-shi no kiso kenkyū*, by Sawaki Eichi (Tokyo: Yoshikawa Kōbunkan, 1976), pp. 175-96.

tion of cash taxes came to be largely abandoned during the
early modern period.

THE SOCIOECONOMIC EFFECTS OF THE KANDAKA SYSTEM

Inevitably, the sweeping changes in land registration introduced under the kandaka system had an immense impact upon the socioeconomic structure of Sengoku-period
Japan and upon all people inhabiting the daimyo domains.
Among the phenomena already referred to, one ought to
note that the success of daimyo such as the Takeda in creating a fief system that incorporated even upper-class peasants into the daimyo's military structure constituted a
major advance over the far less comprehensive *shiki* structure of the shōen system.[19] The daimyo's ability to extract a
much higher level of revenue and services than had been
possible in the past also reflected a major change in the socioeconomic conditions that had obtained in the early medieval period. The latter phenomenon, however, turned
out to have rather unfortunate consequences, for the
rigorous collection of the level of dues and services provided for by the kandaka system imposed such extreme
hardships upon the peasantry and the daimyo's vassals as
to damage the viability of the kandaka system itself. It is to
the nature of these defects in the kandaka system that we
must now turn our attention.

[19] Because the concept of *shiki* was rooted in the idea that rights to income from a given shōen derived from the official functions (shiki) that
one performed within that shōen, the only tenurial rights capable of incorporation within the shiki structure were those of shōen officials such as
the jitō and *geshi*. Upper-class peasants held no officially sanctioned posts,
and their claims were incapable of expression within the shōen system's
shiki-rationalized tenurial hierarchy. Under the kandaka system, however, one's tenure or fief (*chigyō*) was expressed solely in terms of a given
kandaka, with no reference being made to one's official position. It was
therefore entirely possible for the daimyo to create a tenurial hierarchy in
which the rights of upper-class peasants were explicitly recognized. For a
further discussion of the limitations inherent in the shiki structure, see
Nagahara, "Landownership."

While the evidence adduced earlier has demonstrated that by no means all taxation was levied in the form of cash under the kandaka system, there can be no real doubt that the Sengoku daimyo's need for cash led him to use the kandaka system in such a way as to realize as much cash as possible. In doing so, however, the daimyo was faced with a difficult problem: the total volume of money in Sengoku Japan was extremely limited, and what cash there was was of uneven quality. The daimyo's response to these difficulties took two forms—regulation of the amount of less desirable currencies which the peasantry might use in paying their dues, and promotion of the flow of cash into his own territories.

The daimyo's resort to these policies, and the problems encountered in doing so, are clearly evident in the case of the Go-Hōjō, a chronology of whose major attempts at fiscal reform may be found in Table 1.4. The Go-Hōjō, it will be recalled, completed a major reorganization of their tax system in 1550. Eight years later they began to issue decrees specifying the proportion of inferior to superior coins that they were prepared to accept in payment of taxes. As of 1558, 20 mon of "base money" (*akusen*) to 80 of "good money" (*seisen*) was acceptable in payment of each 100 mon of taxes.[20] By 1559 the proportion had been changed to 25 mon of base money for every 75 of good, and in 1560 was changed again to 30 mon of base money for only 70 of good. This fairly rapid liberalization of the terms of payment suggests that the peasantry found it extremely difficult to make payments in the high-quality coins that the Go-Hōjō preferred to receive. The difficulty the Go-Hōjō experienced in securing cash in payment of taxes does not seem to have been much alleviated thereafter; from the 1560s on we begin to discover what was referred to as *daimotsu hatto*, that is, regulations specifying the exchange rates between cash and a variety of goods that

[20] Sawaki, "Go-Hōjō-shi no kahei seisaku ni tsuite."

TABLE 1.4
MAJOR FISCAL REFORMS INSTITUTED BY THE GO-HŌJŌ

1506	First cadastral survey; beginnings of the kandaka system
1542-43	Large-scale cadastral survey conducted by Hōjō Ujiyasu upon succeeding Ujitsuna; basis established for periodic resurveys of Hōjō territories
1550	Perfection of a kandaka-based system of taxation; assessment of tansen, munebechisen, and kakesen placed on uniform basis throughout Hōjō's lands
1558-60	Promulgation of series of edicts establishing the proportion of less desirable coins the Hōjō would accept in payment of taxes
1562	Appearance of regulations establishing the rates at which commodities could be substituted for cash in payment of taxes
1564	First establishment of rokusai ichi. These markets begin to be established at a much greater rate around 1578

the daimyo was occasionally prepared to accept in payment of taxes. Clearly, the way was being opened for the increased payment of taxes in kind rather than in cash.[21]

At about the same time, the Go-Hōjō began to establish what were called *rokusai ichi* (periodic markets), open six days a month.[22] This trend, which became far more pronounced after 1578, was also a reflection of the Go-Hōjō's

[21] The *daimotsu hatto* issued in 1586 for Tana-no-gō in Sagami, for example, established exchange rates between copper cash and gold, rice, sumac lacquer, and silk batting. One to four shō of rice, for instance, were valued at 100 mon. See *Kōza-gun monjo*, no. 91, in *Kaitei shinpen Sōshū komonjo* 1, 295.

[22] On the timing of the Hōjō's creation of rokusai ichi, see Fujiki Hisashi, "Daimyō ryōgoku no keizai kōzō," in *Sengoku shakaishi ron*, by Fujiki Hisashi (Tokyo: Tōkyō Daigaku Shuppankai, 1974), pp. 287-325.

difficulties in maintaining a steady flow of cash into their treasury. Since the money economy of the sixteenth century was still not very highly developed, the peasantry's opportunities to obtain the cash the daimyo was demanding from them were extremely limited. To deal with this problem in a somewhat more positive way than by relaxing their insistence that taxes be paid in cash, daimyo such as the Go-Hōjō sought to manipulate the market economy.[23] But many of the existing market places in Sengoku Japan were the private possessions of the daimyo's vassals, and therefore largely outside his effective control. It was in order to escape the limitations inherent in this situation that rokusai ichi were established. By creating an extensive network of new markets and post towns, daimyo such as the Go-Hōjō were able to assume direct control over much of the trade taking place within their territories, and thereby stimulate the flow of cash into the local economy.[24]

While such attempts to manipulate the market economy may fairly be said to have represented a policy that was forced upon the daimyo by the problems arising from his earlier attempts to raise large amounts of cash through the kandaka system, it is important to recognize that the daimyo's difficulties were themselves only part of rather more severe problems faced by other elements of provincial society—his vassals and the peasantry. Furthermore, the policies through which the daimyo sought to overcome his difficulties frequently had the effect of accentuating the problems of others.

The kandaka system had imposed a twofold burden on the daimyo's vassals, placing limits upon their income while substantially increasing their military obligation. As noted earlier, the level of nengu that individual proprietors were

[23] For a fuller discussion of these points, see Professor Sasaki Gin'ya's study in this volume.

[24] Ōishi Shinzaburō, *Nihon kinsei shakai no shijō kōzō* (Tokyo: Iwanami Shoten, 1975), chapters 1 and 2; and Fujiki, "Daimyō ryōgoku no keizai kōzō."

allowed to extract from the peasants' tilling their land was set by the daimyo's cadastral surveys rather than by the proprietors themselves. Lest one of their vassals presume to ignore the rate of assessment sanctioned by these surveys, many daimyo encouraged peasants to report to the daimyo's own officials any excessive—and therefore illegal—levies of nengu or corvée that a vassal might make. This restriction of the vassals' freedom to enhance their income was made the more galling by the fact that the rationalization of military service under the kandaka system had resulted in far heavier obligations than in the past. Throughout the Kamakura and early Muromachi periods, military power had been based primarily upon lineage groups, with the level of military service owed by vassals to their lords rarely spelled out. Now the daimyo's vassals were obliged to maintain a precisely specified body of both related and unrelated retainers in readiness for war, and to mobilize and provision these men at their own expense in the event that fighting broke out.

To these basic problems imposed by the kandaka system itself, the daimyo's attempts to mitigate the chronic shortage of cash within the local economy added yet another difficulty. Unfortunately for his vassals, his establishment of an extensive network of new markets meant a substantial reduction in the income that his vassals could realize from taxes on their privately owned markets, and from private arrangements with merchants who wished to trade there. The economic straits to which some vassals were driven are dramatically evident in the fact that many were obliged to sell their lands. Although the sale of fiefs was ultimately forbidden during the Tokugawa period, such sales were explicitly sanctioned in the house laws of such Sengoku daimyo as the Imagawa, Takeda, and Date, and are known to have been allowed by the Uesugi, Satake, Asakura, and Go-Hōjō. This expedient seems to have been particularly common under the Date (see Table 1.5). Impoverishment among the Go-Hōjō's vassals did not reach

TABLE 1.5

SALES OF FIEFS AMONG VASSALS OF THE DATE FAMILY

	Date monjo	Sources Harumune-kō saichi kashiroku [a]	Totals
Number of transactions (based upon the number of *andojō* surviving in the sources cited at the left)	40	85 (125)[b]	125 (165)
Number of vassals selling fiefs	140	185 (275)	325 (415)
Number of vassals purchasing fiefs	40	100 (150)	140 (190)

[a] The *Harumune-kō saichi kashiroku* is a roster of the enfeoffments made by Date Harumune.

[b] The *Harumune-kō saichi kashiroku* was compiled in three volumes, of which one is now missing. The figures appearing within parentheses in this table are estimates of the figures we would obtain if all volumes were still extant.

such proportions, though some thirty entries in the *Odawara-shū shoryō yakuchō* indicate similar dispositions, and there can be little doubt that vassals in financial distress were a fairly widespread phenomenon.[25]

The kandaka system's economic burdens fell most heavily, however, upon the peasantry. Although the peasantry may have benefited to the extent of getting protection against arbitrary levies of nengu and corvée by the daimyo's vassals, overall the exaction of nengu was greater under the kandaka system than it had been under shōen proprietors. Compounding their woes was the requirement that the peasants pay their taxes in coins of high quality. As discussed earlier, the cash basis of the kandaka system was in no sense the outgrowth of any growing involvement of the peasantry in the market economy. In-

[25] Fujiki, "Kandakasei ron no kadai," p. 330.

stead, the daimyo in his desperate need for cash made the peasants' participation their only chance for survival. For many peasants, this forced entry into the market economy was profoundly upsetting, and the daimyo increasingly found themselves faced with peasant protests whose goal was a reduction in the level of nengu. The most common countermeasures were: 1. to prohibit the buying and selling of peasant land (this being a practice by which peasants sought to escape the burden of tilling and paying dues on their holdings); 2. to forbid peasant desertion and to direct that absconding peasants be forcibly returned to their holdings; 3. to prohibit the sale of grain before the date at which nengu payments were due;[26] and 4. to prohibit the practice of leaving land fallow in an attempt to avoid paying any taxes on it.

One point requiring emphasis is that the impact of the kandaka system varied considerably according to position within the peasantry. Upper-class peasants were frequently so powerful that they could force the daimyo to concede to them a portion of the increased nengu assessments that had resulted from the cadastral surveys. The threat of the abandonment of their holdings by men who controlled as much land as did these kokujin conjured a degree of disruption too great for the local economy to bear; and such a threat was often sufficient to extort considerable concessions from the daimyo. Beyond this, there was a much more positive inducement for the daimyo to maintain close ties with the upper peasantry. This lay in the fact that, as upper-class peasants were generally the leaders of the village communities of late medieval Japan, the daimyo might reasonably hope that by enrolling upper-class peasants within his vassalage organization he would be able to govern the peasantry as a whole.

For upper-class peasants, therefore, life under the kan-

[26] Izumi Seiji, "Sengoku daimyō Go-Hōjō-shi ni okeru chigyōsei," in *Kantō Sengokushi no kenkyū*, edited by Go-Hōjō-shi Kenkyūkai (Tokyo: Meichō Shuppan, 1976).

daka system was not likely to be too difficult. Their nengu assessments were lower than those of the peasantry at large, and at least a part of the kajishi they had been accustomed to collect in the past might be confirmed to them as *naitoku*, a sort of private rent. The remainder of the peasantry was not so fortunate. As a matter of fact, the misery of the lower peasantry, who constituted the vast majority of individuals who were driven to flee their holdings during the Sengoku period, was accentuated by the activities of their more fortunate fellows. In many cases, peasants who were unable to meet their tax obligations to the daimyo fell heavily into debt to upper-class peasants who, having been enrolled as local officials of the daimyo's administration, had sufficient resources to pay the taxes of their less fortunate fellows. The gravity of the situation may be readily sensed from the fact that by the end of the Sengoku period more and more daimyo were forced to issue decrees canceling peasant debts entirely. In 1566, for instance, the Imagawa issued such a decree, a *tokusei rei*, in favor of the peasants living on the holdings of one of their vassals in Tōtōmi province, though the resistance of the usurer class and of the vassal family was so great that the Imagawa had trouble enforcing the decree.[27]

Such problems at the village level reveal a developing weakness in the daimyo's ability to govern the peasantry. The upper-class peasants were favored because they seemed to offer the daimyo the best means of controlling their fellows; yet the privileges that they were granted enabled the upper peasantry to become a usurer class whose interests were in conflict with those of the people they were supposed to lead. It was this sort of fundamental defect in the operation of the kandaka system which, together with the difficulties inherent in trying to collect all dues in cash,

[27] For an example of this particular sort, see *Nakamura monjo*, no. 7, in *Shizuoka-ken shiryō* 5, 587-88.

would ultimately lead the daimyo who survived the Sengoku period to seek more satisfactory means of administering their territories.

THE KANDAKA SYSTEM AND SENGOKU DAIMYO GOVERNANCE

To the extent that one's assessment of the kandaka system is colored by an awareness of the considerably more sophisticated institutions of the early modern period, problems of the sort just examined loom extremely large. Much can be made, for instance, of the fact that the monumental cadastral surveys carried out under Hideyoshi and his Tokugawa successors resulted in the complete elimination of the upper peasantry's rights to collect such imposts as naitoku, and in the daimyo's assumption of direct control over every cultivator within their territories. Yet while the epoch-making significance of the reforms of the late sixteenth century is beyond dispute, the historical significance of the kandaka system must also be assessed in light of the conditions that had obtained before it was instituted.

The most significant of these conditions, as we have seen, was the complete collapse of the social and economic order embodied in the shōen system. For all the defects it may have had, the kandaka system did bring a reasonable degree of order out of the chaos that had arisen within tenurial relationships by the late fifteenth century, and to that extent its institution must be accounted a considerable achievement. Beyond this, moreover, the kandaka system played a major role in the creation of the unified domain economies that would characterize the early modern period. Under the shōen system, no single estate had been economically self-sufficient, and thus no shōen proprietor had been able to establish an economic base extensive enough to give him complete control of any given region. His control over the land and peasantry of his own estates may have been unquestioned, but it was impossible for him to secure exclusive control over all the merchants and artisans whose activities were essential to the economic health of his shōen.

In contrast, the territory subject to a major Sengoku daimyo's rule covered a considerable area, and the kandaka system constituted a powerful tool for converting that territory into a fully integrated economic unit. By adopting a uniform system of taxation and a set rate of exchange between rice and cash, and also by creating a domainal economy that stimulated economic specialization, a growth of trade, and the wider use of cash, the Sengoku daimyo achieved a far greater control of the economy of his region than any shōen proprietor could have hoped to do. This is a topic that has received careful treatment elsewhere in this volume, and it need not detain us further here. The one point that should be emphasized, however, is that while the Sengoku daimyo's economic control was far from complete, the kandaka system still represented a major advance over early medieval institutions in the degree to which it made it possible to govern the peasants, administer the economy, and mobilize the resources of an extensive area.

The problem, as we have already seen, is that the kandaka system constituted such a drastic reworking of existing economic and political institutions that it quickly gave rise to profound difficulties. So great was the emphasis placed upon meeting the needs of the daimyo himself that his vassals and the peasantry were subjected to severe economic burdens. Furthermore, the daimyo's insistence that taxes be paid in coins of the highest quality placed such a strain upon the market that the difficulties faced by his subordinates were increased substantially. According to the records of the Myōhōji temple in Kai, for instance, the Takeda's demand that taxes be paid in superior coins resulted in the total disappearance of such coins from the market and in a drastic drop in economic activity.[28]

[28] *Hachisaki Jinja monjo*, nos. 14, 17, and 18, in *Shizuoka-ken shiryō* 5, 904-11.

By the end of the Sengoku period, then, the kandaka system was producing severe dislocations in the various daimyo domains. Even the Go-Hōjō, who must be adjudged to have been among the most powerful and successful daimyo of the Sengoku period, had begun to experience serious trouble in the collection of taxes by the 1570s. While some scholars have suggested that the Go-Hōjō's increasing willingness to allow the payment of taxes in kind rather than in cash should be seen as an indication that the Go-Hōjō were moving toward the kokudaka system of the early modern period, this is not a suggestion that bears up under close examination. The kokudaka system, after all, involved far more than the collection of nengu in rice rather than in cash. The development of the early modern kokudaka system required not only the creation of an economy in which nengu rice was so readily marketable as to constitute a quasi money, but also the complete separation of the military and farming classes (*hei-nō-bunri*) and destruction of the proprietary lordship of the daimyo's vassals.[29]

[29] Nagahara, "Daimyō ryōgokusei no kōzō."

Chapter 2

The Sengoku Daimyo of Western Japan: The Case of the Ōuchi

MATSUOKA HISATO
WITH PETER J. ARNESEN

THOUGH THE LOCAL AUTONOMY that became so pronounced during the Sengoku period had been foreshadowed to some extent by the degree of local power concentrated in the hands of the *shugo* of the late fourteenth and early fifteenth centuries, the so-called *Sengoku daimyo* of the sixteenth century differed significantly from their shugo daimyo predecessors. One of the more obvious differences was that a large proportion of Sengoku daimyo had not been particularly important figures before their emergence as regional lords. Typical was the Go-Hōjō family of Odawara, who were the subject of the previous chapter. No more than military commanders in the service of the Imagawa daimyo house of Suruga in the late fifteenth century, the Go-Hōjō managed in the short span of fifty years to carve out their own sphere of authority in the southern Kantō and to establish themselves as one of the ten most powerful daimyo in the country.

Not all Sengoku daimyo rose to power so precipitously, however, and the subject of the current study is a case in point. The Ōuchi family of Suō, already the most powerful warrior family in that western Honshu province by the early Kamakura period, succeeded during the 1350s in destroying the *bakufu*-appointed shugo of both their home province and the neighboring province of Nagato. In 1363 the Muromachi bakufu found it expedient to appoint the Ōuchi shugo of these two provinces, and by the 1420s the Ōuchi had been appointed shugo of the northern Kyushu provinces of Buzen and Chikuzen, as well. Their control of this extensive territory was weakened somewhat during the Ōnin war by Ōuchi Masahiro's preoccupation with Kyoto-centered campaigns, but after 1477 Masahiro and his retainers set about consolidating the Ōuchi's dominance over an increasingly large section of western Japan. At his death in 1495, the Ōuchi controlled not only the four provinces to whose rule Masahiro had succeeded some thirty years earlier, but also the provinces of Iwami and Aki. Though the attempts between 1520 and 1540 by the Amako family of Izumo to seize Aki severely tested the Ōuchi's authority over Iwami and Aki, all six provinces would remain Ōuchi territory until Masahiro's grandson, Ōuchi Yoshitaka, was overthrown by a rebellion of his vassals in 1551.

The Ōuchi's shugo heritage, however, was a characteristic shared by a number of other powerful Sengoku daimyo houses. The special interest of the Ōuchi case lies in the fact that although the Ōuchi as Sengoku daimyo carried out a number of innovations that are generally thought to have been characteristic of the new daimyo of the Sengoku period, it is also evident that the Ōuchi were far less concerned with restructuring the social and economic relationships within their territories than were such contemporary eastern daimyo as the Go-Hōjō, the Imagawa, and the Takeda. In order fully to understand the significance of this contrast, we must begin by devoting some attention to the local problems that the daimyo of the Sengoku period faced.

CHANGES IN THE LOCAL ORDER DURING THE SENGOKU PERIOD

It has been apparent for some time that among the most important factors in the history of the Sengoku period was the profound change that occurred during the fifteenth and sixteenth centuries in the structure of relationships within the cultivating class. For much of the medieval period, the main body of the peasantry had been subject to the patriarchal control of a stratum of somewhat more powerful individuals whom historians of the Muromachi and Sengoku periods generally refer to as *dogō*—a term literally meaning something like "powerful rustics." (As explained in the Introduction, dogō is one of many terms used to refer to this "middle stratum" of rural society. The term applies broadly to what in other contexts can be referred to more specifically as *shōryōshu, jizamurai,* or *myōshu*.) These dogō frequently occupied a position more or less intermediate between that of the bulk of the peasantry and that of the ruling warrior class, and for most of the early Muromachi period the dogō had been the dominant figures within the peasant village communities that had begun to emerge during the mid-thirteenth century.

By the beginning of the Sengoku period, however, the authority of the dogō over the mass of the peasantry had become weak enough to make their economic position extremely unstable. To use an example from the Ōuchi's province of Buzen, ever since the beginning of the Kamakura period the Takamure family had served as *dokichō* (hereditary overseers of the production of sacred earthenware) for Usa shrine, and had enjoyed hereditary control over the land in Takamure-myō.[1] The history of the Takamure's rights over that land is extremely difficult to determine, but there is evidence that by the early fifteenth century, Takemure-myō had been divided into the subsidiary myō of Jirōmaru, Aritsugu, Arinobu, Arinaga, Tanaka, and Hirano,[2] and that the Takamure family's

---

[1] *Takamure monjo*, nos. 2-3, in *Ōita-ken shiryō* 2, edited by Ōita-ken Shiryō Kankōkai (Ōita: Ōita Kenritsu Kyōiku Kenkyūjo, 1952-1964). Hereafter cited as *OKS*, followed by volume number, section title, and number of the document within the section.

[2] *OKS* 2, *Karashima monjo*, nos. 2, 5, and 19.

rights over the land as a whole included the enforcement of criminal justice.[3]

Something of the state at which the Takamure's rights had arrived by the Sengoku period emerges in a field register (*tsubotsuke*) of Takamure-myō that was drawn up when Takamure Nobuuji succeeded his father Ujimori in 1521.[4] According to this, the Takamure family's holdings had been divided into three portions, known as the Chō-bun, the Tokinaga-bun, and the Gakutō-bun—a division likely to have arisen at some point in the past through a partition of the management of the holdings among three sub-groups within the Takamure lineage. Under this arrangement, the *sōryō* (head of the main line of the lineage) presumably retained direct management of the dokichō share—the Chō-bun—as well as a less direct jurisdiction of the Tokinaga-bun and Gakutō-bun, as lineage chief of the subgroups which managed them. By 1521, however, the three parts of Takamure-myō appear no longer to have been managed as distinct entities.

The rights that the Takamure family exercised over these lands were a heterogeneous body of prerogatives referred to in the idiom of the times as the *shitaji-shiki* (lit. "administration of the land"). These rights were most comprehensive over some two *chō* of paddy and dryfield (one chō was something less than three acres at the time) and eight yardlands (*yashiki*) which were referred to as the *jisakubun*, or demesne. The internal structure of this demesne emerges in a second field register dating from 1535,[5] at which time some nine parcels of land (two yardlands, four paddies, three dryfields) were worked by retainers (*fuchinin*), nine more (four yardlands, one paddy, four dryfields) by cultivators (*sakunin*), and ten had reverted to waste (*arefu*). While the evidence available to us on these points is extremely fragmentary, it does appear

[3] *OKS* 2, *Takamure monjo*, no. 21.
[4] *OKS* 2, *Takamure monjo hoi*, no. 6.
[5] *OKS* 2, *Takamure monjo*, no. 23.

that the dokichō had originally worked the entire demesne by parceling it out among retainers who were hereditarily bound to serve the Takamure lineage. As it became increasingly difficult to control these subordinate peasants, however, the dokichō was forced to contract with outsiders for the cultivation of much of the demesne, thus giving rise to the appearance of cultivators (sakunin) alongside the retainers (fuchinin) in the 1535 field register. The reversion of a third portion of the demesne to waste was probably due to the difficulty of finding men willing to work this land.

Aside from this demesne, for which the *gesakushiki* (formal rights of cultivation) were clearly the Takamure's either to enjoy themselves or to let out, as they saw fit, there were a number of other sorts of land with whose gesakushiki the Takamure had no business interfering. The first of these was land which was referred to as the *kakaechi* (holdings) of one or another of eleven nearby temples. Such lands, whose gesakushiki was subject to the temples' disposition, came to something under two and a half chō of paddy and dryfield, and two yardlands—an area greater than that of the demesne and comprising a sixth of the total area of Takamure-myō. Another category of land was that registered as the *kyūchi, katsubun*, or *kakae* of some individual. The *kyūchi* were lands granted to free artisans in compensation for their production of sacred earthenware. The *katsubun* were lands from the demesne that had been permanently settled upon some individual other than the sōryō; and the *kakae* were simply lands held by individuals to which they had gesakushiki rights. These lands had a total area of 1 chō and 1 *tan* (a tan being a tenth of a chō). Finally, some two-thirds of all land in Takamure seems to have been *hyakushōchi*, or lands over which peasants enjoyed de facto possession and at least an informal right to cultivate.[6]

[6] It should be noted here that a *gesakushiki* was a cultivation right to which at least some formal recognition was frequently given. The ques-

The Takamure's land rights, then, reflected the complexity of the tenures they held—with the gesushiki of some lands belonging to the Takamure themselves, the gesushiki of some others to various temples or nonpeasant individuals, but the gesushiki of most lands being under de facto control of the peasantry. The problems associated during the sixteenth century with such an ambiguous body of rights may be guessed from the history we have hypothesized for the Takamure's demesne. The major basis for the family's rights over Takamure-myō lay in the traditional authority which the Takamure, as dokichō, held within the religious hierarchy of Usa shrine; and, though the Takamure did their utmost to maintain their traditional authority, the mass of peasants saw this authority as imposing a species of bondage upon them. As the peasantry grew restive, the Takamure found it ever more difficult to work their demesne, and some areas fell into disuse. Dogō from neighboring areas took advantage of the situation to negotiate contractual relations with the Takamure for the cultivation of this land, and thereafter, confident of their own power, proceeded to ignore the Takamure's traditional authority. The peasantry soon followed the dogō's example in ignoring their erstwhile masters, and the proprietary authority of the Takamure—as embodied in their shitaji-shiki—became increasingly meaningless.

The deterioration of the traditional authority of the dogō class was in fact a widespread phenomenon during this period, and the dogō reacted in at least two ways. The first can be detected, for instance, in two clauses from a set of instructions that Motoshige Shizuyori, another Buzen dogō, left to his descendants in 1574:

ITEM: The gesakushiki both of this and of other myō must assiduously be sought after.

ITEM: It must be realized that if one is negligent and

---

tion of whether peasants' rights in *hyakushōchi* amounted to *gesakushiki* is obscure.

relies solely upon *yakushiki-myōden*, one will become powerless.[7]

The yakushiki-myōden here referred to were lands over which the Motoshige enjoyed a loose shitaji-shiki like that of the Takamure over most of their holdings. What these clauses imply is that Motoshige Shizuyori had become aware of the growing weakness of the traditional authority of his class, and was advising his heirs that securing direct control over the rights of cultivation was the only means by which the well-being of the family could be maintained.

Motoshige Shizuyori was, essentially, urging his descendants to buy up large quantities of land and become peasant landlords (*jinushi*). While this sort of policy was fairly common among dogō who were confronted with a decrease in the number of their dependent cultivators and with a growing resistance to the traditional authority of their class, it was not the only option available. It was also possible to attempt to preserve one's dominance over the bulk of the peasantry by suppressing disunity within one's own lineage and allying oneself to powerful warriors in the vicinity of one's holdings. This is, for example, the course that the Buzen dogō Yoshimura Jōkin set forth for his heirs in 1554.[8] In contrast to the Motoshige's policy of consolidating a position as peasant landlords, the Yoshimura sought to consolidate a seigneurial (*ryōshu*) position as at least minor members of the warrior class. In both cases, however, the important point to be noted is that policies adopted by the dogō reflected the fundamental instability of their traditional position by the sixteenth century, and this suggests the presence of profound changes in the whole local social and economic order of the Ōuchi's territories.

[7] *OKS* 8, *Motoshige Jitsu monjo*, no. 20.
[8] *OKS* 8, *Yoshimura Kanta monjo*, no. 7.

Peasant Struggle during the Sengoku Period

The peasantry's refusal to accept the traditional authority of the dogō class led ultimately to their disinclination to accept the authority of any of their superiors, and peasant recalcitrance became a persistent problem for most Sengoku daimyo. The Ōuchi came face to face with the problem, for instance, following their imposition of *hanzei* (the obligation to render half a holding's income to the daimyo) upon the Dazaifu Tenmangū shrine's holdings in Chikuzen. In a petition submitted to the Ōuchi in 1518, the shrine made explicit reference in the last seven of eleven articles to peasant defiance of the shrine's authority, listing 1. default in rendering *nengu* (annual land rent) and various other payments (*seimotsu*) due the shrine, 2. a proposal by the peasants of one village that they henceforth pay no dues but nengu, 3. the payment of less than the stipulated nengu on the grounds that the harvest was bad, 4. the nonperformance of the routine corvée (*jōfu*) due from the villages, 5. a decrease in the amount of nengu and *yashikisen* (duty levied in cash against yardlands) rendered, 6. the defiance of the jitō by the peasants of both villages, and 7. trafficking in cultivation rights (*sakushiki*) to lands in these villages.[9]

Some of these acts of defiance may have been provoked by the hanzei ruling itself, but quite probably the daimyo's imposition of hanzei merely galvanized an attitude of resistance to the shrine's authority which was already present among the peasants. This seems particularly likely to be true given the fairly predictable nature of the peasants' goals—essentially the reduction of their corvée and nengu obligations, and the freedom to sell certain of their land rights. It is also interesting to note, in light of the discussion that we shall take up at the end of this section, that the lan-

---

[9] *Manseiin monjo.* See *Fukuoka Kenshi shiryo* 7, edited by Fukuoka-ken (Tokyo: Fukuoka-ken, 1937), 197-98.

guage of a number of these clauses makes it clear that the inhabitants of the villages comprised both peasants (hyakushō) and a dogō stratum, referred to as *myōto* or *myōzu*, and that the latter had joined the hyakushō in resisting the shrine.

In the above case, peasant resistance occurred within the sphere of authority of both a shōen proprietor and of the daimyo, but was directed specifically against the proprietor. The Ōuchi themselves, however, were scarcely immune to overt peasant resistance. Individual peasants and townsmen frequently sought to escape the authority of a superior by securing the support of another powerful individual. Such an attempt might take two general forms. First, a peasant might become a retainer of a new lord in order to avoid personal subjection and the obligation to render various dues to the lord (ryōshu) of his own holdings.[10] As such, the act did not necessarily entail defiance of the Ōuchi's authority. More serious was the second form, in which a peasant might become the retainer of a powerful warrior or temple in an effort to avoid public levies due the daimyo. It is apparent from the Ōuchi house laws (*Ōuchi-shi okitegaki*) that activity of this sort had begun to be a problem for the Ōuchi as early as Norihiro's tenure as shugo (1441-1465), and remained a problem under Masahiro, as well.[11]

In addition to such individual acts of resistance, it was not uncommon for groups of peasants to band together to circumvent Ōuchi authority. Such a conspiracy is evident in a document regarding the Nagasoe region of Buzen, an area lying near the frontier between the Ōuchi and Ōtomo territories. This land had originally been listed in the Ōuchi's *tansen* registers as containing 55 chō 5 tan of taxable land, but after the Ōuchi's defeat by the Ōtomo at

---

[10] *Ōuchi-shi okitegaki*, no. 172, in *Chūsei hōsei shiryōshū* 3 (*Buke kahō* 1), edited by Satō Shin'ichi, Ikeuchi Yoshisuke, and Momose Kesao (Tokyo: Iwanami Shoten, 1965), hereafter cited as *Ōuchi-shi okitegaki*; and *OKS* 5, *Nagahiro monjo*, no. 1544.

[11] *Ōuchi-shi okitegaki*, no. 145.

Uma-ga-take in 1501, the peasants of the area rendered tansen and nengu on only 13 chō. While the land was held by the powerful Ōuchi retainer Sue Nagafusa, his agents were occasionally able to force the peasants to render dues on 26 chō, but never on the full amount listed in the Ōuchi registers. When in 1555 the land was granted to one Eda Hidemori, Ōuchi officials made a determined effort to find out what had happened to the "missing" 42 chō 5 tan of land. No matter how closely the daimyo's envoy questioned the peasant league about this, however, the peasants maintained that they knew about no more than 13 chō.[12] It is clear from this account that the peasants of Nagasoe had taken advantage of the fact that their lands lay in an unstable frontier region to misrepresent the amount of land subject to either nengu or tansen, and had adopted a flexible policy under which the degree of their misrepresentation was tailored to the degree of force that the authorities might bring to bear.

There are, moreover, several examples of cooperative resistance transcending the village in scale. This was the case in the Saba River area of the Ōuchi's home province of Suō, where the inhabitants were obliged by law to sell their firewood and charcoal at Miyaichi and to pay a tax on the sale to the market's owner, one of the temples associated with the Matsuzaki shrine. In the early 1520s, it became necessary for the Ōuchi to issue a series of orders directing the peasants of this region to desist from selling their products in Mitajiri so as to avoid the customs at Miyaichi. When the shrine complained to the Ōuchi in 1528 that the peasants were still selling at Mitajiri, the Ōuchi issued a new prohibition and forced the leaders of each village to signify their full understanding of the order.[13]

---

[12] *OKS* 8, *Era monjo*, no. 28.

[13] *Hōfu Tenmangū komonjo no utsushi*, nos. 17, 19-21, and 28, in *Bōchō fūdo chūshin'an* 10 (*Mitajiri saihan* 2), edited by Yamaguchi-ken Monjokan, 23 vols. (Yamaguchi: Yamaguchi-ken Monjokan, 1961-1964). Hereafter cited as *BFC*, followed by volume number, section title, and either document number or, if a document number is lacking, page number.

Another incident involving the villagers of the same region occurred in 1531 when the Ōuchi forgave the debts of Tōdaiji's officials in the temple's holdings in the Suō *kokugaryō* (the ancient provincial domain). Irritated that Tōdaiji officials alone benefited from this dispensation, the inhabitants of five villages banded together to demand a general cancellation of debts. It would appear from the fact that it was necessary for the Ōuchi to send their major retainer, Sue Okifusa, to suppress this uprising that the scale of the incident was considerable;[14] and although there is little evidence of similar incidents elsewhere within the Ōuchi's territories, it should be noted that every time the Ōuchi cancelled the debts of a major temple or shrine they manifested considerable anxiety that their action might call forth a general demand for the cancellation of debts. We would probably be safe in concluding, therefore, that the conditions for such uprisings were always present, and that the Ōuchi were genuinely worried about them.[15]

One significant aspect of peasant resistance on this scale is that, in resisting the authority of shōen proprietors or of the daimyo, the peasant and dogō classes were frequently able to transcend their own differences and work together. The most probable explanation is that the dogō, forced to act as intermediaries between superior authority and the peasants, were often squeezed by the same daimyo and proprietors that were squeezing the peasantry at large.

A concrete example of a dogō caught in this position emerges in the documentation surrounding a 1537 suit between the Naritsune and Tsuzu families. The Naritsune were myōshu of the two *myō* of Jittoku Tokimoto and Daisekiji in Buzen, over which superior proprietary rights had been granted the Tsuzu family by the Ōuchi at some point before 1506. As of 1523, the Naritsune and Tsuzu were still cooperating well enough to prepare jointly a register of fields in the two myō,[16] but two years later the

[14] *BFC* 10, *Hōfu Tōdaiji ryō komonjo no utsushi*, nos. 4 and 88-89.

[15] *Ōuchi-shi okitegaki*, nos. 45, 166, 175, etc.

[16] *OKS* 8, *Naritsune monjo* 8, nos. 1-2.

Tsuzu dispatched a *daikan* (personal agent) to assume direct management of these myō on the Tsuzu's behalf. The reaction of the Naritsune to this blatant attempt to negate their rights as myōshu was so fierce that the Tsuzu initiated a preventive suit against the Naritsune for their "unlawful" behavior. Investigators for the Ōuchi court concluded, however, that the Tsuzu had not only tried to assume the Naritsune's prerogatives as myōshu but had, as friction between the two families increased, even tried to deny the Naritsune's right to cultivate the land. In the end the suit was decided in the Naritsune's favor.[17] Though the Ōuchi had thus preserved the rights of the Naritsune in their two myō, it was the Ōuchi's grant of superior proprietary rights to one of their vassals that had placed the Naritsune's rights in danger. The Naritsune's ability to prevail over the Tsuzu in the dispute may also have been due in large part to the fact that the Naritsune had become vassals of the Sugi family, who were the Ōuchi's *shugodai* (deputy shugo) for Buzen, and could have obtained the Sugi's intercession before the Ōuchi.[18]

That dogō placed in a position like that of the Naritsune should have shared an interest with the peasants and occasionally acted in concert with them against the daimyo and his powerful vassals is scarcely surprising. While it is true that a great many dogō became vassals of the daimyo and were granted land for their services, the fact remains that as holders of myōshu-shiki and gesakushiki in their ancestral holdings, the dogō often found themselves in opposition to superior authority.

CADASTRAL SURVEYS UNDER THE ŌUCHI

The problems of a disintegrating local order and of growing peasant unrest, which we have touched upon in the preceding sections, were common throughout Japan by the

---

[17] *OKS* 8, *Naritsune monjo* 4, no. 9.
[18] *OKS* 8, *Naritsune monjo* 4, nos. 4 and 10.

early sixteenth century, and they presented the Sengoku daimyo with grave difficulties in maintaining a stable local rule. In eastern Japan, these problems had a profound effect upon the institutions by which the daimyo sought to control their territories. In particular, it would appear from the examples of such daimyo houses as the Go-Hōjō, the Takeda, and the Imagawa that the practices by which the daimyo of this period sought to conduct cadastral surveys (*kenchi*) of their territories, and to register all land according to its putative yield in cash (*kandaka*), were designed in part to establish a new tenurial structure in which the resistance of the peasantry to warrior authority could be held to a minimum. Yet in western Japan, while the Ōuchi can be shown to have conducted cadastral surveys and to have adopted a kandaka system of sorts, the evidence available to us suggests that neither the surveys nor the kandaka system of the Ōuchi was designed to meet the challenge presented by the disintegration of the local order. The examination of this evidence is the concern of this and the following sections.

The first point to be noted is that the total number of Sengoku-period surveys that it is possible to document for the Ōuchi's territories is quite limited. Table 2.1 lists all instances in which surviving documents refer specifically to surveys conducted either by the Ōuchi or by the Sue—the latter being an Ōuchi branch family who were the Ōuchi's most important retainers up until 1551, when Sue Takafusa (Harukata) destroyed Ōuchi Yoshitaka and assumed control of the Ōuchi's territories. Of the ten surveys thus recorded, one was conducted during Ōuchi Masahiro's tenure as shugo (1467-1495), four during Ōuchi Yoshioki's tenure (1495-1528), and five under either Ōuchi Yoshitaka or Sue Takafusa.

The reasons for which any of these surveys were undertaken emerge only indistinctly from the documents. In cases B and H, the Sue ordered surveys of Rurikōji's maintenance holdings in Odakano because of the financial dif-

Case of the Ōuchi

TABLE 2.1

CADASTRAL SURVEYS CONDUCTED UNDER THE ŌUCHI

Case	Date	Ordered by	Area Surveyed
A	1480	Ōuchi	Chōkōji's holdings in Hōtō-gun, Nagato
B	1508	Sue	Odakano, Niho-no-shō, Suō
C	Eishō era (1503-21)	Ōuchi	Kōryūji temple's and Nagahiro family's lands in Buzen
D	Eishō era	Ōuchi	Shōi-no-shō, Suō
E	1523	Ōuchi	Yamashiro region, Kuga-gun, Suō
F	1538	Sue	Holdings of Kō-no-ue Shrine and Miyabō in Tsuno-gun, Suō
G	1539	Ōuchi	Yamato-no-shō, Sawara-gun, Chikuzen
H	1540	Sue	Odakano, Niho-no-shō, Suō
I	1543	Ōuchi	Kanpei Shrine's lands in Satō-gun, Aki
J	1552	Sue	Sasai-gun, Aki

SOURCES: A in *Bōchō jisha yurai* (in the collection of the Yamaguchi-ken Monjokan), *Saikōji monjo*; B in *BFC 13, Kami Uno-ryō 8*, pp. 181-83; C in *OKS 5, Nagahiro monjo*, no. 1738; D in *BFC 10, Hōfu Tōdaiji ryō komonjo no utsushi*, no. 87; E in *BFC 3, Hongō-mura*, p. 238; F in *BFC 8, Suetake Shimo-mura*, p. 67; G in *BFC 13, Kami Uno-ryō 5*, pp. 136-38; H in *BFC 13, Kami Uno-ryō 8*, pp. 181-83; I in *Hiroshima-kenshi, Kodai-Chūsei shiryō hen 2, Itsukushima monjo hen 1, Itsukushima Nosaka monjo*, edited by Hiroshima-ken (Hiroshima: Hiroshima-ken, 1976), no. 190; J in *Nosaka monjo*, Dai 2 katsu. The *Nosaka monjo* are in the collection of Nosaka Motosada, Miyajima-chō, Hiroshima-ken.

ficulties of this Sue-patronized temple. As a result of the surveys, there was a 50 percent increase in the registered area of these holdings, and a 70 percent increase in the amount of nengu drawn from them. The Sue-ordered survey of Kō-no-ue shrine's and Miyabō's holdings in case F

77

also resulted in the discovery of a considerable amount of unregistered paddy. In these examples, then, it would appear that the Sue-ordered surveys had as their primary goal the increased collection of nengu, and that this was accomplished largely through the measurement of field area and the determination of field type (that is, whether the land was paddy or dryfield, as dryfield was not normally subject to nengu) as the basis for the rate of nengu assessment (*todai*). Of the Ōuchi surveys, case C alone yields even vague evidence of their purposes. It is apparent from the document recording this survey that among the consequences of this particular investigation was that both Nagahiro Ujisuke's shiki-based authority over certain lands and the lands themselves (shitaji) were confiscated and bestowed upon another retainer, Ikenaga Yajirō. We may perhaps infer that in this instance the survey accompanied a readjustment of old land rights and an investigation of gesakushiki.

The last case in which the motivation emerges is J, a survey of some of Itsukushima shrine's lands that was conducted shortly after the Sue overthrew the Ōuchi. As soon as this survey began, several vassals of the former *kannushi* (chief priest) of the shrine came before the Sue and asked that the survey be put off. They were told, however, that the survey would continue and that any of their holdings found to be in excess of the amount registered in their names would be confiscated and dedicated to the shrine's own use. What this incident suggests is that the men who appeared before the Sue to request the postponement of the survey had, at some point in the past, obtained control of lands that the Sue were determined to return to the direct control of Itsukushima shrine. Apparently this survey, like those of the Rurikōji and Kō-no-ue shrine holdings treated above, was made in order to increase the income of a religious proprietor.

The evidence derived from the documents listed in Table 2.1 seems to indicate that the surveys conducted by

the Ōuchi and Sue were designed to do little more than increase the amount of nengu obtainable from the land, and
that they were conducted primarily through the examination of field area, field type, and nengu assessment. Case C,
however, suggests that they may also have occasionally
been intended to determine the actual cultivators of the
land and to readjust the relationship among shifting tenurial rights.

While our discussion thus far has been based upon documents in which the word survey (kenchi) actually appears,
there is plenty of other evidence that surveys or survey-like
investigations were being conducted in the Ōuchi's provinces during the Sengoku period. One might cite, for instance, the 1523 field register drawn up by the Tsuzu and
Naritsune that was mentioned in the previous section, or
the field registers of Ichihara-mura to be discussed below.
Even if cases of this nature are included in our discussion,
however, the extent of the surveys conducted by the Ōuchi
during the Sengoku period remains extremely limited. Indeed, the Ōuchi house laws themselves reveal that the
Ōuchi's surveys are unlikely to have been systematically
conducted. Specifically, clause 142 of these laws provided
that whatever unregistered land or yield therefrom was
discovered during the course of the routine surveys conducted by Ōuchi officials on the occasion of boundary disputes should be confiscated. The very promulgation of
such an edict presupposes the widespread existence within
the Ōuchi's territories of holdings whose extent and yield
was greater than what was registered.

In point of fact, there is other evidence as well to suggest
that the entire tenurial system over which the Ōuchi presided was strongly colored by the daimyo's lack of information on the details of the land tenure of the Ōuchi's vassals
and of other proprietors. A document in the possession of
the Ōuchi's ancestral temple of Kōryūji states that "although Kōdo is listed as 130 *kanmon* land [that is, land
whose annual yield is 130 *kan* of cash], its actual yield is said

to be much higher."[19] Nevertheless, there is almost no evidence to sustain the proposition that the Ōuchi's surveys were designed to overcome this lack; they appear, on the contrary, to have been extremely limited investigations carried out on a piecemeal basis in disputed land, land that had recently been transferred to Ōuchi control, or newly conquered land. In light of this, it seems all but impossible to suggest—as is generally done in the case of eastern daimyo—that the Ōuchi's surveys represented a positive response to problems posed by the decay of the traditional local order.

THE KANDAKA SYSTEM OF THE ŌUCHI

The ad hoc nature of the Ōuchi's surveys notwithstanding, the Ōuchi did in fact make substantial efforts to develop a systematic registration of their vassals' holdings, and it was a holding's kandaka that increasingly became the basis for this registration. As Nagahara Keiji notes in his essay above, the registration of all landholdings in terms of their putative yield in cash, or their kandaka, was one of the signal accomplishments of the Go-Hōjō daimyo house, and allowed the Go-Hōjō to make at least some progress toward establishing a new and fairly stable local order within their territories. The Ōuchi kandaka system was considerably less ambitious in its conception.

The registration of landholdings in terms of their kandaka had been known in western Japan ever since the Nanbokuchō period, when the bakufu had used the kandaka as the basis for levying cash in lieu of military service. There are, however, many ambiguous points about such issues as how the bakufu arrived at its kandaka figures, and the relationship of these figures to the kandaka systems of the Sengoku period is obscure.[20] Be that as it may, it is

[19] *Higami-san Kōryūji monjo*, no. 67, in *Bōchō komonjo Dai 1-shū-Dai 5-shū*, *Higami-san Kōryūji monjo*, edited by Bōchōshi Dankai, appended to *Bōchō shigaku* 1-5 (1930-1932).
[20] Kishida Hiroyuki, "Shugo Yamana-shi no Bingo no kuni shihai no

quite clear that by the Sengoku period the Ōuchi themselves had developed a profound interest in the extent of their vassals' landed wealth. As early as the 1450s, for instance, Ōuchi Norihiro sent two envoys to determine the extent of the holdings of his vassal Niho Hiroari. In response to the envoys' questions, Hiroari submitted a statement of his holdings (*bungen chūmon*), together with an oath that the statement was accurate. Subsequently, Hiroari was obliged to write a letter explaining discrepancies between his statement and the figures for his holdings that the Ōuchi had found within their own registers, and this letter survives.[21]

It is apparent from this letter that the Ōuchi had raised two questions concerning Hiroari's earlier statement. The first of these was whether or not the 350-kan figure he gave for Niho-no-shō included his interests in the *ryōke-shiki* (proprietary rights) as well as in the *jitō-shiki* (land steward rights), and the second was whether the kandaka figure for his holdings in Shibuki-gō ought not really to be 300 kan. Hiroari's response to the first question was that his interest in the ryōke-shiki was indeed included within the 350-kan figure for Niho-no-shō. To the second question he replied that while there had been a time when the correct figure for his Shibuki holdings had been 300 kan, there had been numerous changes since then, and he now held but 150 kan. This afforded him an actual income of 115 *koku* of rice, and of this some 30 kan had been granted in exchange for his *honryō* (ancestral holdings) in Tatara.

To judge from this document, it would appear that the primary objectives of the investigations conducted during Norihiro's tenure as shugo (1441-1465) were the verification of a holding's kandaka, the determination of whether

tenkai to chigyōsei," in *Nihon chūseishi ronshū*, edited by Fukuo Kyōju Taikan Kinen Jigyōkai (Tokyo: Yoshikawa Kōbunkan, 1972), pp. 114-26.

[21] *Miura-ke monjo*, no. 53, in *Dai Nihon komonjo, Iewake 14, Kumagai-, Miura-, Hiraga-ke monjo*, edited by Tōkyō Teikoku Daigaku Shiryō Hensanjo (Tokyo: Shiryō Hensanjo, 1937). Hereafter cited as *DNK, Miura-ke monjo*.

land was a purely military tenure—and thus fully subject to military levies—or also contained tenures belonging to or derived from civil proprietary interests, and of whether the holding was honryō or *kyūchi* (land granted by the daimyo). An extremely revealing picture of the extent to which the Ōuchi's grasp of the dimension of their vassals' holdings had progressed by the time Masahiro had become shugo (1465-1495) is provided by a document drawn up by another of the Ōuchi's vassals, and this particular document is worth quoting in full.

A Statement of the Holdings of
Yasutomi Bingo nyūdō Munesada

These total as follows

[1] One place, 30 koku—This lies in Mitsui-mura, Kumage-gun, Suō.

This was granted in Chōshōji-dono's [Ōuchi Mochiyo's] generation, and we have his patent.

[2] One place, 20 koku—This lies in Ogawa-gō, Abu-gun, Nagato.

This was granted in Chōshōji-dono's generation, and thus we have an official directive.

[3] One place, 30 koku—This lies in Sogabe, Usagi-mura, Sawara-gun, Chikuzen.

This was granted in Chōshōji-dono's generation, and thus we have an official directive.

[4] One place, 50 koku—This lies in Takamizu-no-shō, Kumage-gun, Suō.

For this we have Tsukiyama-dono's [Ōuchi Norihiro's] patent.

[5] One place in Kumage-gun, Suō—30 koku of the jitō-shiki of Niiya Kawachi belonging to Hachiman Shrine; 30 is my fief.

For this we have Tsukiyama-dono's patent.

[6] One place, 100 koku—This lies in Hara-mura, Sawara-gun, Chikuzen.

For this we have Tsukiyama-dono's patent.

[7] One place in Suō's Nakaryō-mura—The proprietor (*honke*) is Saishitsu-dono.

This was granted in Tsukiyama-dono's generation.

[8] One place, 10 koku (Migita Shōgen's former holding)—This lies in Suō's Omata-mura.

For this we have Chōshōji-dono's patent.

[9] One place, 30 koku—Iwafuchi in Omata-mura, Suō.

For this we have Tsukiyama-dono's patent.

[My holdings are] as above

[10] The *daikanshiki* of Onga-no-shō in Chikuzen was also granted me as a fief.

Tsukiyama-dono's generation.

My report is as above

1470/2/9   Munesada

[On the reverse of this document, and in a different hand, is written:]

[11] One place, 30 koku—Sogabe-mura, Sawara-gun, Chikuzen.

When my superiors checked this listing against the 1469/2/3 fief registry, it was there listed as "some 28 chō 6 tan of land—the former holding of Shinkai Shinzaemon no jō." Thus, further evidence must be provided.[22]

The changing basis of land registration that this document reflects is best understood by comparing clause 6 in the above document with the language of the 1459 document by which the land in Hara-mura was bestowed upon Yasutomi Munesada's family. According to the original grant, this land was "28 chō 6 tan 2 jō of land in Hara-mura, Sawara-gun, Chikuzen." Within just eleven years the Yasutomi's holdings in Hara-mura had come to be expressed in terms of their kokudaka (annual yield as ex-

---

[22] *Yasutomi-ke shōmon*, in *Nagata hitsuroku*, in the collection of the Yamaguchi-ken Monjokan.

pressed in koku of rice) of 100 koku, rather than in terms of their area. Similarly, the 1434 grant of the holding listed in clause 3 above was originally expressed as being "half of Sogabe-mura in Sawara-gun," but by 1470 had come to be expressed in terms of a kokudaka of 30 koku.[23]

Perhaps the most interesting feature of the conversion from area to kokudaka is illustrated by the surprising mix-up, evident in the notation added to Munesada's statement by an Ōuchi official (clause 11), that arose when the Ōuchi *bugyō* (administrators) compared his statement with a registry of vassals' holdings compiled the year before. Unable to find evidence there for a 30-koku holding in Sogabe-mura, the bugyō mistakenly concluded that the 28 chō 6 tan holding that the Yasutomi enjoyed in Chikuzen—a holding that we have already seen corresponded to that listed in clause 6—must correspond to the Sogabe holding listed in clause 3.

What this document suggests, then, is that between Norihiro's and Masahiro's generation, the Ōuchi had begun to register their vassals' holdings in terms of their kokudaka, but that the readjustment of the official registers had not always kept pace with the conversion. We must conclude either that the Ōuchi's bureaucracy lacked the administrative competence to keep track of vassals' holdings extending over several provinces, or that the conversion of the means of registration was simply proceeding too rapidly for the bugyō to keep up.

Another point to be noted is that no matter how rapidly this conversion may have proceeded in some instances, a policy of listing holdings in terms of their kokudaka had not been uniformly imposed. As of 1470, the civil proprietors of Nakaryō-mura (clause 7 of the Yasutomi document) and Onga-no-shō (clause 10) each seem to have retained an interest in their ancient holdings, and it is apparent that in neither case had the Ōuchi or the Yasutomi contrived to assign a kokudaka to those holdings. But soon even civil

[23] *Yasutomi-ke shōmon.*

holdings of this type would go through stages in which any excess above a specifically determined proprietor's share was treated as the warrior's fief,[24] and then in which this excess was treated as a taxable base (*kujiashi*) of so many koku on which the warrior was obliged to render military service.[25] In other words, the shares of civil proprietors were being carefully distinguished, and the military service due from the warriors was being linked to the kokudaka of their holdings. As this happened, the amount of land registered as ambiguously as were Nakaryō-mura and Ongano-shō above must steadily have diminished.

While kokudaka figures were presumably based on the amount of nengu drawn from paddy fields, a new valuation of land in terms of its kandaka began to emerge during Ōuchi Yoshioki's tenure as shugo (1495-1528). The intensity of Yoshioki's interest in the details of land tenure is clearly evident as early as 1499, in a policy that the Ōuchi maintained toward temple and shrine land. In that year, all religious proprietors were told to submit reports of the extent of their holdings, and any who failed to do so were punished by being obliged to accept warrior tenants for their land.[26] Furthermore, while the Ōuchi's interest was directed in this case toward religious property, there is some reason to suspect that they were also beginning to show considerable interest in the details of their vassals' tenures.

The most interesting evidence of this sort pertains to a

[24] For instance, a 1501 appointment of a certain warrior as *daikan* on a civil holding stated that "the stipulated *shōzei* [nengu] must be faithfully rendered to the capital; any excess is to be treated as a military grant (*buon*)." *Kodama onsaishū monjo*, in the collection of the Tōkyō Daigaku Shiryō Hensanjo.

[25] For instance, a 1523/2 *kudashibumi* issued by Yoshioki stated that "with regard to the *shōzei* rice of 5 koku—to be measured as paid at the capital—this must be paid to the shrine each year. As regards the remaining (proceeds of this holding), this is a 30-koku *kujiashi* land, and you shall hold all of it, rendering the military service thereon." *Sugi Shinshirō Hidekatsu-ke shōmon*, in *Nagata hitsuroku*.

[26] *Bōchō jisha yurai*, *Shūzenji monjo*. See Source A, Table 2.1.

grant of 45 kan in land within Ichihara-mura, Kuri-gō, Iwami, which Yoshioki made to Kikkawa Tsunenori in 1515. Yoshioki's order and his bugyō's directive confirming the grant were sent to the Iwami shugodai in 1515/4, and the shugodai then ordered one Hesaka Tango no kami to deliver the land to the Kikkawa. It was some sixteen months, however, before the Kikkawa were seized of the land by one Kokubu Shigeyori, who at the same time delivered a number of newly prepared field registers and registers of dues owed the Kikkawa from their new holding.[27] The major events that seem to have transpired between the time when Yoshioki granted the land and the Kikkawa received it were: 1. the submission by the peasantry of a detailed report (*sashidashi*) that recorded the lands pertaining to the holding, the cultivators working them, and the dues incumbent upon them, 2. the verification of the peasants' report by the daimyo's officials, and 3. the partition of the Kikkawa's 45 kan in land from the remaining land in Ichihara-mura. The details of the peasants' preparation of their report are unknown, but it is apparent that the Ōuchi's officials spent considerable time checking the reliability of the peasants' statements concerning lands allegedly purchased by nearby temples, shrines, and village communities (*sōson*). A partition of the land was then necessary because the Kikkawa were to be granted only half of the 90 kan per year which could be collected from Ichihara-mura. The variety of sources from which the dues were supposed to be extracted was considerable, and it was the task of the Ōuchi's county intendant, or *gundai*, meticulously to halve each of these assets.

The register of dues that the gundai prepared for the Kikkawa in this process had two categories of assets: those precisely quantifiable in terms of cash and those not so

[27] *Iwami Kikkawa-ke monjo*, nos. 33, 42-44, 51, 64, and 74, in *Dai Nihon komonjo, Iewake* 9, *Kikkawa-ke monjo besshū, Furoku, Iwami Kikkawa-ke monjo*, edited by Tōkyō Teikoku Daigaku Shiryō Hensanjo (Tokyo: Shiryō Hensanjo, 1932).

quantifiable, such as corvée, the chief residence of the holding, and hidden fields that it was anticipated that the Kikkawa would turn up. While the existence of this second category of assets obviously demonstrates that the kandaka for this holding was not a completely accurate statement of its value to the Kikkawa, the fact remains that the Ōuchi's gundai was able to calculate a kandaka that included not only the nengu and tansen due from land not held by temples, but also tansen and *yashikisen* (dues from yardlands) incumbent upon land that was so held. This kandaka was presumably transcribed in the county registers and in the Ōuchi's central registers, as well, and in this sense the case under analysis would seem to demonstrate the advanced nature of the Ōuchi's knowledge of the extent of their vassals' holdings.

The Ōuchi's land registration system as a whole, however, was not nearly as advanced as this example might lead one to believe. For instance, while the fact that the tansen collected from Ichihara-mura was included within that holding's kandaka suggests a degree of tax rationalization comparable to that achieved by the Go-Hōjō when they linked tansen directly to a holding's kandaka, the inclusion of tansen within the kandaka in this instance was due to the fact that the right to collect tansen had been granted to the daimyo's vassal at some point.[28] The situation revealed in a number of other instances is quite different.

As our first example, let us consider the case of Jittoku Tokimoto- and Daisekiji-myō in Buzen. According to a 1523 field register drawn up by the Tsuzu and Naritsune families, these myō had a total paddy area of some 9 chō 6 tan, of which 2 chō 6 tan 10 shiro were *honden* (lands recognized since the Kamakura period as being subject to tansen and related imposts), dryfields of some 3 chō 4 tan, and 9 yardlands. For each parcel of land the nengu in rice or

---

[28] See Matsuoka Hisato, "Sengokuki Ōuchi, Mōri ryōshi no chigyōsei no shinten," *Shigaku kenkyū* 82 (1961), 1-20.

cash were listed in the case of paddy, the nengu in barley or cash for dryfields, and duties in cash for yardlands. There was, therefore, a fairly detailed statement of the income to be derived from these myō, and the Ōuchi's vassal's share as based on this register was calculated as 15 koku of rice and barley, all to be rendered by the myōshu. Tansen, however, was levied only against the honden of 2 chō 6 tan 10 shiro, and was supposed to be rendered to the daimyo's own officials.[29] Both the basis and the recipient of the tansen differed clearly from the Ichihara case, and tansen was not included in any kandaka or kokudaka figure.

Our second example relates to Kanpei shrine's holdings in Satō-gun, Aki. A 1545/12 nengu account for these holdings has been cited in a number of earlier studies as showing markedly different land policies from those adopted by the Mōri in later years,[30] and it is possible to deduce that the calculations in that account are based upon a field register for these holdings which was drawn up by Ōuchi officials in 1543.[31] In this register, the tansen is excluded from the kandaka, which does, however, include nengu drawn from both paddy and dryfield. Thus the registration of this holding is similar to that for Jittoku Tokimoto- and Daisekiji-myō above.

Finally, let us consider the case of Itsukushima shrine's Miyauchi holding in Saeki-gun, Aki. The documentation for this item has been cited by Murata as providing evidence for the Mōri's kandaka system,[32] but there is no

[29] *OKS* 8, *Naritsune monjo* 8, nos. 1-2; *Naritsune monjo* 5, no. 4; and *Naritsune monjo* 4, no. 13.

[30] Murata Shūzō, "Sengoku daimyō Mōri-shi no kenryoku kōzō," *Nihonshi kenkyū* 73 (1964), 9, and 16 n. 6; and Fujiki Hisashi, "Kandaka-sei to sengokuteki kenryoku hensei," *Nihonshi kenkyū* 93 (1967), reissued as "Kandakasei no kadai—Murata, Miyagawa, Sasaki (Jun) sanshi no setsu o megutte," in *Sengoku shakaishi ron*, by Fujiki Hisashi (Tokyo: Tōkyō Daigaku Shuppankai, 1974), at pp. 357 ff.

[31] *Hiroshima Kenshi, Kodai-chūsei shiryō hen* 2, *Itsukushima monjo hen* 1, *Itsukushima Nosaka monjo*, edited by Hiroshima-ken (Hiroshima: Hiroshima-ken, 1976), no. 190.

[32] Murata, "Sengoku daimyō," pp. 9-10; 15-16 nn. 8, 10-11, 13.

proof that the listing of this holding in terms of its kandaka originated with the Mōri. There are, in fact, a variety of rent registers surviving from the period 1558 to 1580 for this holding, and it is apparent that all are based upon an earlier land register. To state merely the author's own conclusions concerning the origins of the now vanished land register, it was apparently drawn up by the Itsukushima kannushi family, which the Ōuchi destroyed in 1541. This suggests that neither the Ōuchi nor the Mōri bothered to resurvey these lands after gaining authority over them, but rather continued to rely upon yield figures calculated by an earlier holder.

To summarize the evidence treated in this and the preceding section, it is apparent first of all that the Ōuchi had begun moving toward a systematic grasp of the extent of their vassals' landed wealth and toward a system in which the registered yield of their vassals' holdings would serve as the basis for levying services. A vassal's holding was increasingly designated in terms either of its kandaka or of its kokudaka;[33] land subject to military service was distinguished from land that was not; and military service was specified as being due upon a holding of such-and-such a yield. Yet the Ōuchi had come nowhere near unifying and systematizing the disparate patterns for the collection of nengu, tansen, corvée, and other dues in holdings that had wildly divergent histories. In Jittoku Tokimoto-myō, Daisekiji-myō, and the Kanpei shrine's holdings, nengu was extracted from both paddy and dryfield, but in Ichihara-mura only from paddy. In Ichihara, tansen was levied against every parcel of dryfield and paddy, and was included in the vassal's kandaka, but tansen in Jittoku Tokimoto- and Daisekiji-myō remained a daimyo impost levied against a limited amount of paddy. Furthermore, there is little indication that the Ōuchi were making substantial attempts to unify land registration through surveys. After consolidating their control over all of Aki in the

---

[33] The Ōuchi generally used an exchange rate of 1 koku = 1 kan.

1540s, for instance, the Ōuchi surveyed the holdings of the Kanpei shrine but continued to use old registers in the Miyauchi holdings.

Unlike the Go-Hōjō, the Ōuchi had not established a kandaka system that, by systematizing and limiting the imposts extracted from the peasantry, was capable of controlling the tension between warrior and village. This slowness in the establishment of a new local order is also visible in one of the aspects of the Ōuchi's authority structure, which we will discuss in the following section.

THE ŌUCHI'S AUTHORITY STRUCTURE

In attempting to understand the mechanisms by which the Ōuchi sought to govern their provinces, it is useful to begin by examining the *Ōuchi-dono yūmeishū*, a list of major vassals drawn up during Ōuchi Yoshitaka's tenure as shugo (1528-1551).[34] The most important vassals included: 5 *kunishū* (major kokujin allies, roughly analogous to *tozama*), 11 *shinzoku kerai* (kinsmen vassals), 3 *bugyō sankarō* ("the three bugyō elders"), 12 *kobugyō* (lesser bugyō), 25 *kozashiki* (men of sufficient standing to be seated in a chamber known as the kozashiki), and 125 *samurai taishō* (captains) and *sakiteshū* (vanguard). This body of 200 or so men can scarcely have encompassed the Ōuchi's entire *kashindan* (vassal force), but is probably about the right size for the Ōuchi's direct *gokenin*. These gokenin enjoyed a lord-vassal relationship with the daimyo sustained by the confirmation of their ancestral holdings and the grant of new lands, and it goes without saying that the authority structure of the Ōuchi as Sengoku daimyo was grounded in the military power afforded by these men.

Above this power base, however, rose an extremely complex authority structure comprising a composite of lord-vassal ties, differentiations in status among their vas-

[34] See Kondō Seiseki, *Ōuchi-shi jitsuroku* (1887; reprinted Tokuyama: Matsuno Shoten, 1974), pp. 374-82.

sals, and administrative networks through which the Ōuchi
ran both a central government at their capital of Yamaguchi and a number of local offices throughout their provinces. To begin with the differentiations in status that
existed among the Ōuchi's gokenin, we note that aside
from the Ōuchi themselves, some forty-eight men are
known to have served at one point or another as chief patrons of the Kōryūji *Nigatsu-e*, an important religious
ceremony held during the second lunar month at the
Ōuchi's ancestral temple of Kōryūji. There can be no
doubt that the privilege of serving in this capacity was very
highly esteemed. A check of the *Ōuchi-dono yūmeishū* dis-
closes that all of these families were shinzoku kerai, sankarō, kozashiki, or kunishū. We may safely conclude that
these particular groups enjoyed the very highest status
within the Ōuchi's vassal band, and that membership
within them must have been restricted to an extremely
small group of families. It is important to recognize, however, that the relationship between ascriptive status, as represented by the rank that one's family may traditionally
have enjoyed among the gokenin, and the official status
that any given warrior enjoyed within the Ōuchi's governmental administration was not static. If we contrast membership within the group of the Ōuchi's most senior officials in Yamaguchi—within, that is to say, the *jūshin* (major
retainers) or *hyōjōshū* (daimyo's council)—with membership
in their kobugyō (general administrative corps), the relatively open nature of membership in the latter group is
readily discernible. Among the men who signed their
names to the Ōuchi's administrative edicts (*bugyō hōsho*)
around 1486 were the jūshin Toida Hirotsuna, Sugi
Shigetaka, Sugi Shigechika, Sugi Takemichi, Naitō
Hironori, and Yasutomi Fusayuki, while among the bugyō
we find Tomoda Hirooki, Mishima Hiroyasu, Sugi Hiro-
teru, Owa Takechika, Moji Yoshihide, Sugi Takeaki, Iida
Sadaie, Sagara Masatō, Uno Hirotaka, and Takaishi
Shigeyuki. Every one of the jūshin belonged to extremely

high-ranking families that had served the Ōuchi for generations; but among the ten bugyō, four came from
families—the Mishima, Owa, Moji, and Sagara—that had
hitherto been outside the Ōuchi's vassalage organization.
Three decades later, around 1518, the Ōuchi's administrative edicts carried the signatures of Sue Okifusa, Sue
Hiroakira, Toida Okiyuki, Sugi Shigenori, Sugi Okinaga,
and Naitō Okimori among the jūshin, together with a fairly
diverse group of some ten bugyō. The latter included
members of the Kōjiro (three individuals), Asō (the Asō
were numbered among the kunishū a generation later),
and Ryūzaki families, none of which had had members
among the bugyō before. Similarly, in the period around
1547, members of the Ida, Nuki, Ohara, and Aokage
families appeared as bugyō for the first time.[35]

The implications of these findings are very important.
To begin with, it is clear that membership within the
policy-making hyōjōshū (or jūshin) was limited to such
Ōuchi branch families as the Sue and Toida, to hereditary
retainers of long standing like the Sugi, and to the Naitō
family, which had been extremely important as Kamakura
gokenin. This select group of families—of which the Sue,
Naitō, and Sugi constituted the sankarō, or three
elders—made up the central nucleus of the Ōuchi's authority structure. Membership within the kobugyō was not
nearly as restricted, and this flexibility in according routine
administrative authority to their vassals was an important
characteristic of the Ōuchi's administration. By constantly
adding new gokenin to their administration as the territory
subject to their rule expanded, the Ōuchi gave the acts of
that administration a much more strongly public character
than they would have had if membership among the bugyō
had been restricted to the Ōuchi's kinsmen and to the
gokenin families of Suō and Nagato.

The Ōuchi's authority structure was also profoundly af-

[35] The names of these jūshin and bugyō are drawn from the *Ōuchi-shi
okitegaki*, and from surviving documents.

fected by the mechanism through which each of the provinces subject to the Ōuchi's rule was placed under a shugodai (deputy shugo), who functioned in organic relationship to the Ōuchi's central administration in Yamaguchi. While the shugodai had originally been appointed as deputies who carried out the Ōuchi's responsibilities as shugo appointed by the bakufu, the Ōuchi's emergence as virtually autonomous lords of six provinces during the Sengoku period had converted the shugodai into local representatives of the Ōuchi's own authority as daimyo. Their most common function was the execution of the daimyo's judgments concerning disputes within their respective provinces, and in fulfilling this function the shugodai might issue their own orders either to personal deputies (known as *shō-shugodai*) or to the daimyo's county-level magistrates (the so-called *gundai* or *gun bugyō*).

By the Sengoku period, the local power the shugodai held by the authority vested in them by the daimyo might be presumed to have been considerably enhanced by the fact that the post of shugodai had become hereditary within certain powerful families—the Sue for Suō, the Naitō for Nagato, the Sugi Hōki no kami family for Buzen, the Sugi Bungo no kami family for Chikuzen, and the Toida for Iwami. Actually, the authority of individual shugodai varied throughout the Ōuchi's territories. The ancestral holdings of most of the Ōuchi's retainers were heavily concentrated in Suō, and this fact, together with the presence of the Ōuchi's Yamaguchi headquarters within the province, left the shugodai little freedom for independent activity. Nagato was fairly tightly under central control, as well. Buzen and Chikuzen, however, which had been Ōuchi territory for a much shorter time than had Suō and Nagato, retained a strong flavor of front-line, frontier territory. In these provinces the shugodai's independent power was considerable, and there was a marked tendency for the kokujin and dogō classes to become vassals of the shugodai Sugi houses.

Indeed, the military instability of these provinces, and their distance from the effective authority of Yamaguchi, led not only to the enrollment of kokujin and dogō as vassals of the shugodai, but also to their enrollment as the vassals of other powerful Ōuchi retainers, or even of such low-ranking Ouchi functionaries as the gundai.[36] The effect of these diverse vassalage ties is not at all easy to determine. If the overlord chosen by a given kokujin or dogō happened to be a warrior from outside the district in which his new retainer's holdings lay, the creation of the vassalage tie must certainly have cut across the lines of the Ōuchi's own political authority, and been at least potentially disruptive of it; on the other hand, to the extent that the lord one chose was the shugodai or gundai of one's district, then the vassalage tie thus created must have strengthened the Ōuchi's regional administration.

With regard to the latter of these possibilities, it is at least conceivable that the existence of vassalage organizations centering upon the gundai and shugodai is related to a striking difference between the authority structure of the Ōuchi and that of some of their well-known eastern contemporaries. Like most Sengoku daimyo, the Ōuchi had only a relatively small group of men who were constantly garrisoned and under arms. These were the daimyo's own guard forces in Yamaguchi and the various castle garrisons set up in the frontier regions of western Chikuzen, eastern Buzen, the borders of Iwami, and Tōsaijō in Aki. The rest, making up the majority of warriors, lived in their own villages except during actual warfare. Under some Sengoku daimyo, the dogō-class warriors who were normally resident in the countryside were organized into village or regional groupings called *isshoshū*, and these were bound by fictional father-son (*yorioya-yoriko*) ties to the daimyo's greater vassals. The so-called yorioya-yoriko system pro-

---

[36] On the tendency of kokujin and dogō to become vassals of shugodai and of gundai-level retainers, see *Ōuchi-shi okitegaki*, no. 144; and *OKS* 5, *Nagahiro monjo*, no. 1544.

vided the daimyo with an important means for mobilizing the dogō and peasant classes in time of war, and may also have enabled the daimyo to begin to control the frequently restive peasantry of this period.[37] In the case of the Ōuchi, however, it is quite difficult to find evidence of such a system, though the fact that Niho Morisato numbered isshoshū among the forces he led in 1501 may suggest that it was at least beginning to emerge.[38]

The slowness with which a yorioya-yoriko system developed within the Ōuchi's territories may well be due to the fact that in many regions the dogō and lesser kokujin warriors had been enrolled instead in the gundai- and shugodai-centered vassalage organizations mentioned above. Whatever the reason, the Ōuchi's authority structure, like their kandaka system, did not extend to the close control of the dogō class that some of the Sengoku daimyo of the east had developed. Yet, although this fact may seem to bespeak a fatal weakness in the Ōuchi's rule of their territory, it is important to recognize that even after the Mōri had succeeded to control of the Ōuchi's provinces, a direct response to the problems of an embattled dogō class and a restive peasantry was slow to emerge. While it is beyond the province of this study to discuss the Mōri in any detail, our understanding of the nature of Sengoku daimyo rule in western Honshu will benefit considerably from at least a brief discussion of the Mōri's evolution as Sengoku daimyo.

A COMPARATIVE VIEW OF THE ŌUCHI AND THE MŌRI AS SENGOKU DAIMYO

The Mōri family, which won control of the Ōuchi's former territories in 1558 and controlled at least Suō and Nagato until the Meiji era, entered the Sengoku period as an unusually powerful kokujin family in Yoshida-no-shō in Aki.

---

[37] The classic exposition of this thesis is Kikuchi Takeo, "Sengoku daimyō no kenryoku kōzō," *Rekishigaku kenkyū* 166 (1953), 1-17.

[38] *DNK, Miura-ke monjo*, no. 87.

The basis of their power had been assured during the
1470s, when the main line of the family succeeded in subjecting both its branch families and the Mōri's fudai to the
direct authority of the sōryō of the entire Mōri lineage.
From that point on, even powerful members of Mōri
branch lineages were treated essentially as retainers of the
sōryō, and began to serve as officials of his household.[39]
Even with the consolidation of the sōryō's power, however,
there were distinct gaps in the Mōri's authority for much of
the Sengoku period. The relations between the Mōri and
their retainers remained personal ones colored by individual circumstances. In particular, because the Mōri lacked
both a well-developed fief system and a uniform standard
for the assessment of military service from their vassals, the
level of service they could extract from those vassals was
dependent upon variations in personal and family status
rather than upon the size of one's holdings. Furthermore,
administration of the peasantry continued to be an exercise
of personal lordship by individual vassals over the inhabitants of their holdings rather than of any authority vested
in the Mōri themselves.

The point at which the Mōri may be considered to have
overcome these disadvantages enough to become daimyo
came in 1550, when Mōri Motonari's son Takakage, who
had been adopted as head of the Takehara branch of the
powerful Kobayakawa family, became the head of a unified
Kobayakawa house by succeeding to the headship of the
Nuta branch of the family, as well. In 1550/2, moreover,
Mōri Motoharu, another of Motonari's sons, succeeded to
the headship of the powerful Kikkawa family after nearly
five years of negotiations with the Kikkawa's retainers. The
basis of the Mōri's famous Ryōsen or "Twin Rivers" system—so named because the character *kawa* (river) was an
element of the names of the two families to whose headship

[39] Kawai Masaharu, "Sengoku daimyō to shite no Mōri-shi no seikaku,"
Shigaku kenkyū 54 (1954); reprinted in *Chūsei buke shakai no kenkyū*, by
Kawai Masaharu (Tokyo: Yoshikawa Kōbunkan, 1973), pp. 387-403.

Motonari's sons had succeeded—was thereby established. The Mōri now constituted a political and military force capable of dominating the entire province of Aki, and in 1550/7 Mōri Motonari suppressed the independent power of the overmighty fudai house of Inoue to consolidate his authority as daimyo.[40]

The authority structure that the Mōri maintained as Sengoku daimyo had much in common with their earlier authority structure as leaders of an alliance of the kokujin of Aki. The various warrior houses that had subordinated themselves to the Mōri retained much the same individual property rights and authority structures as before, making it nearly impossible for the Mōri to inject their own authority into the holdings of any of these houses. The most important advance in the Mōri's authority over these warriors lay in the greater degree of coercive power the Mōri now commanded both because of the support of numerous warrior houses from the area surrounding their ancient base in Yoshida-no-shō—a support that the Mōri took care to foster through judiciously arranged marriages—and because of the strength provided by the Ryōsen alliance. The central administrative structure of the Mōri, like that of the Ōuchi, may be thought of as the union of a policy-making group of jūshin and a somewhat less important group of executive bugyō. In deciding any major issue, Motonari relied first of all upon his sons Takamoto, Kobayakawa Takakage, and Kikkawa Motoharu, as well as upon his vassal kinsmen Fukuhara Sadatoshi, Katsura Motosumi, Kuchiha Michiyoshi, and Shiji Hiroyoshi. These *ichizoku* (related retainers) formed the nucleus of a policy-making body whose meetings were held in secret, and which in its fuller form might include such unrelated jūshin as

---

[40] Sankō-den Hensanjo, ed., *Mōri Motonari-kō den* (Tokyo: Rokumeikan, 1944), Dai 2-shō: Dai 2-, 3-, 6-setsu. The earlier establishment of cooperation between the Mōri and Shishido families, and Mōri and Kumagai families, was significant as well, but does not really seem to have marked the Mōri's transition to daimyo status.

Shishido Takeie, Kumagai Nobunao, Amano Takashige, and Yamanouchi Takamichi. The more routine affairs of governance were assigned to a group known as the *gonin bugyō* (five administrators) which was made up of three of Takamoto's bugyō chosen from among his highest ranking fudai, and two bugyō chosen by Motonari from among his most intimate associates, with little attention being paid to their family status. Together, the gonin bugyō constituted a distinct organ that enjoyed considerable independence from the individual wills of Motonari and Takamoto, and which, by means of mutual discussions and restraints, was able to determine and enforce a sort of public will of the Mōri. The emergence of this sytem marked the full consolidation of the Mōri's central administrative structure.[41]

For all the sophistication of their central administration, the Mōri were not successful in establishing an independent regional administration for the whole of Aki. In most areas of the province, they had confirmed the ancient administrative rights of individual kokujin lords, and thus had a limited prerogative to establish a regional administration of their own. Their conquest of Suō and Nagato, however, gave them considerably more scope in this respect. At first, they appended a number of former Ōuchi bugyō to their own gonin bugyō system to help with the task of reorganizing the governance of these provinces. Once this reorganization was effected, Suō and Nagato were placed under the overall administrative control of organs referred to as the *Yamaguchi bugyō* and the *Suō shigundansen bugyō* ("magistrates in charge of tansen for the four counties of Suō"). Beneath these bodies, the Mōri's regional administration of these provinces simply continued to use the Ōuchi's gundai (or *gunji*) system.

If we compare the general outlines of the Mōri's authority structure with those of the Ōuchi's, the following points

[41] Matsuura Yoshinori, "Sengoku daimyō Mōri-shi no ryōgoku shihai kikō no shinten," *Nihonshi kenkyū* 168 (1976), 33-48.

emerge. First, although both families had at the center of their power structure a policy-making council of both related and unrelated retainers, the nucleus of the Ōuchi's council included such unrelated jūshin as the Sugi and Naitō, while the central members of the Mōri's council included only ichizoku. Second, the Ōuchi's corps of bugyō numbered some ten or more members, and always included newly enrolled gokenin, while the Mōri's numbered only five, each of whom was a fudai. Third, the Ōuchi had a well-ordered regional administration in which major retainers were assigned hereditarily as shugodai of each province and presided over county-level magistrates known as gundai. The Mōri, on the other hand, had no regional administration in Aki, and only began to create such an administration after conquering Suō and Nagato in 1558. The administration that they came up with continued the use of the Ōuchi's gundai-gunji system, but placed each province under the overall supervision of a large number of bugyō rather than of a single shugodai.

It is evident that in building their own authority structure the Mōri should have been able quite readily to consult the example afforded by their Ōuchi overlords, and it seems quite possible that the pattern of rule that the Mōri developed resulted from a conscious reworking of Ōuchi practices. While this reworking is particularly clear in the sort of regional administration that the Mōri developed for Suō and Nagato, it is also worth noting that at each major point of divergence of the Mōri from Ōuchi patterns of administration, the Mōri can be seen to have simplified the central administration and its subsidiary organs, monopolizing control of these entities in the hands of ichizoku and fudai so as to reduce the possibility of fragmentation and decentralization.

Viewed simply from this perspective, the Mōri would appear clearly to have achieved significant advances over the patterns of rule maintained by their Ōuchi predecessors. It is essential to recognize, however, that there were a number of areas in which the Mōri had not advanced at all beyond the stages reached by the Ōuchi before them. As discussed above, the Mōri were unable for some time to conduct unified cadastral surveys of their territories, to erect a kandaka system that was any more sophisticated than that of the Ōuchi, or to mobilize the dogō class through a well-articulated yorioya-yoriko system.[42] Furthermore, while the compilation of the Ōuchi house laws show that the Ōuchi were at least attempting to impose a rule of law upon their territories, no such intention can be detected on the part of the Mōri. Indeed, the extremely narrow base of the Mōri's bugyō system suggests that they were content that their rule should have only a limited public (*kōgi*) character.

   The value of noting these points lies in the fact that it is frequently suggested that the Mōri's success in emerging as the most powerful daimyo in the far west of Japan in the period from roughly 1560 to 1600 derived from the fact that they were much more nearly like the great Sengoku daimyo houses of the east than were the Ōuchi before them. In point of fact, however, the area in which the Ōuchi's divergence from eastern patterns of daimyo rule was most pronounced—that of the daimyo's ability to deal with the problems of decaying dogō authority and of a restive peasantry—was also an area in which the Mōri failed to make any substantial progress until long after the Ōuchi's passing. The Mōri's eventual success in creating a stable domain in Suō and Nagato, in other words, appears to have owed little to any inherent superiority of the patterns of daimyo rule that they maintained as of the 1550s; the crucial factor appears rather to have been the benefits they derived from adherence to Toyotomi Hideyoshi in the 1580s and 1590s.

[42] This thesis is developed at some length in Matsuoka, "Sengokuki Ōuchi, Mōri ryōshi no chigyōsei no shinten."

Chapter 3

The Development of Sengoku Law

KATSUMATA SHIZUO
WITH MARTIN COLLCUTT

THIS PAPER seeks to reveal through analysis of the laws issued by *Sengoku daimyo* the concept of ruling authority
held by such daimyo during the sixteenth century, and also
to define the character and historical significance of Sengoku law in relation to that concept of rule. The adoption
of this approach derives initially from an interest in the
problem of why the laws issued by Sengoku daimyo
should have been so confidently authoritarian when the
political authority of Sengoku daimyo was so unstable and
was poised on such a weak base. Since the characteristics of
Sengoku law seem to have been intertwined with the conception of ruling authority developed by Sengoku daimyo,
the problem does not lend itself readily to solution by a
straightforward historical approach. I must state at the
outset, therefore, that this paper does not offer a detailed
itemization of the provisions of Sengoku legal codes. It focuses, rather, on the basic thrust of the rationale and
policies of rule that are revealed in Sengoku laws, and the
relationship between law and the concept of ruling authority that supported it.

Before launching into a more detailed analysis it would,
perhaps, be helpful to remind ourselves of some of the
general characteristics of Sengoku house laws.[1] As the

---

[1] All the *kahō* cited in this paper are included in Sato Shin'ichi, Ikeuchi
Yoshisuke, and Momose Kesao, eds., *Chūsei hōsei shiryōshū* 3 (Tokyo:
Iwanami Shoten, 1965). For a recent article setting Sengoku kahō in the

fundamental laws enacted by Sengoku daimyo to control
the daimyo house (*ie*) and domain (*ryōgoku*), Sengoku
house laws (*kahō*) were intended to have enduring valid-
ity. Thus they addressed crucial domain problems, and
were generally issued in the form of legal codes (see Table
3.1). Looking first at the process by which Sengoku law developed, we see that the regulations included in these codes
display two quite distinct aspects. One aspect is that of
"house law" in the narrow sense, laws for the regulation of
the band of housemen, or retainers, the *kashindan*. The

TABLE 3.1

MAJOR SENGOKU HOUSE CODES

Title of Code	Province	Year	Daimyo
		1493	Sagara Tametsugu
Sagara-shi hatto	Higo *pre*	1518	Sagara Nagatsune
		1555	Sagara Haruhiro
Ōuchi-shi okitegaki	Suō	c.1492	?
		-1560	
Imagawa kana mokuroku	Suruga	1526	Imagawa Ujichika
Imagawa kana mokuroku			
tsuika	Suruga	1553	Imagawa Yoshimoto
Jinkaishū	Mutsu	1536	Daté Tanemune
Kōshū hatto no shidai	Kai	1547	Takeda Harunobu
Yūki-shi shin hatto	Shimōsa	1556	Yūki Masakatsu
Rokkaku-shi shikimoku	Ōmi	1567	Rokkaku Yoshikata
			Rokkaku Yoshiharu
Shinkasei shiki	Awa	?	Miyoshi family
Chōsokabe-shi okitegaki	Tosa	1596	Chōsokabe Motochika
			Chōsokabe Morichika
Kikkawa-shi hatto	Aki	1617	Kikkawa Hiroie

context of the development of *buke* law and indicating the level of postwar
research, see Ishimoda Tadashi, "Kaisetsu" in Ishii Susumu, Ishimoda
Tadashi, Kasamatsu Hiroshi, Katsumata Shizuo, and Sato Shin'ichi, eds.,
Chūsei seiji shakai shisō 1 (Tokyo: Iwanami Shoten, 1972), 565-646.

laws directed specifically at the daimyo household are thought to have had their origin in the regulations (*okibumi*) imposed upon the various houses by their warrior founders, and thus to share a common source with the moral injunctions known as "house precepts" (*kakun*) bequeathed by warrior dynasts to their successors as guides to ensure the continued dignity and prosperity of the house. Although the distinction between law and moral exhortation is clearly defined in Sengoku house codes, the moral tinge had not been completely eradicated. A second aspect clearly apparent in Sengoku house codes is that of domain law, which was directed at the general populace of the domain. This element had its immediate origins in the laws issued by the provincial military governors, *shugo*, to control their provinces. And it was probably via the jurisdictional authority of the shugo that the heavy deposit of influence from the *Goseibai shikimoku*, issued in 1232 by the Kamakura *bakufu*, and of Muromachi bakufu law found its way into Sengoku law. The fact that many of the Sengoku daimyo who issued house codes had held the office of shugo under the Muromachi bakufu reflected the historical situation in which the right of the shugo to issue laws for their domains although limited, had been recognized by the bakufu.

Although the origins and foundations of Sengoku law can be located in okibumi, kakun, and shugo and bakufu law, it is important to remember that Sengoku law also included novel features, and differed in certain significant respects from earlier warrior class law and moral precept. One important new development was the reflection in Sengoku legal codes of the influence of the written pacts (*ikki keijō*) drawn up by the members of the leagues of local warrior proprietors (*zaichi ryōshu*) that emerged in many parts of Japan in the unsettled years between the fourteenth and sixteenth centuries. Behind numerous articles in Sengoku house codes we can glimpse the collective will of local proprietors who had delegated proprietary authority to the daimyo.

The most striking characteristic of Sengoku house codes, however, was that each went unchallenged as the supreme legal norm within the boundaries of its particular domain. Although Sengoku codes were influenced by the *Goseibai shikimoku*, the supreme legal authority in medieval warrior society, and in some cases even included articles from bakufu codes, within the daimyo domain, it was the house law, rather than the *Goseibai shikimoku*, that held ultimate sway. If articles from bakufu codes were employed, this was done at the volition of the Sengoku daimyo and to enhance his authority, not out of deference to any external authority. Moreover, only those articles that seemed useful were given renewed force within the domain. Seen in this light, Sengoku house laws can be said to have terminated the absolute supremacy of the *Goseibai shikimoku* as the fundamental law of warrior society, to have been directly harnessed to Sengoku daimyo efforts to build new political control structures, and to have been, in effect, the declarations of independence of Sengoku daimyo.

THE RATIONALE FOR KASHINDAN CONTROL

As already suggested, Sengoku laws can be divided into two broad categories, according to their primary object: those for the regulation of the band of retainers or housemen, which we shall call kashindan control laws, and those for the regulation of domain inhabitants in general, which we shall describe as ryōgoku control laws. Of these, laws in the first category constitute the bulk of Sengoku kahō. By analyzing kashindan control laws from the standpoint of the enforcement of loyalty to the daimyo, it is possible to expose the underlying logic or rationale for daimyo control over their retainers.

Two imperatives for Sengoku daimyo, whose common ambition was to survive and triumph in the violent society of post-Ōnin Japan, were to gather as many warriors as possible about themselves and to forge them into a unified military organization. The extension and consolidation of military power by Sengoku daimyo, however, was impossible without the establishment of new lord-vassal ties with large numbers of hitherto uncommitted *bushi* in addition to the older bonds with the established retainers known as *fudai*. These newly forged lord-vassal relations were, unfortunately, extremely unstable. In the general social perception of medieval bushi, a high degree of loyalty was required of fudai retainers, who were expected, if need be, to follow their lord in death as well as in life. Less was expected of those retainers known as *tozama*, whose ties with their lords were of more recent origin. It was generally accepted that they were free to repudiate their allegiance if they had a serious grievance against their lord or if he failed them in battle. This right of repudiation has been described as "freedom of movement" (*kyoshū no jiyū*).[2] Especially in the unstable conditions of the Sengoku period, rebellion against overlords by their followers was so common as hardly to warrant particular condemnation.[3]

In these circumstances, the first priority for any Sengoku daimyo was to extract unquestioning loyalty from all his retainers. Before discussing the means by which daimyo enforced loyalty we should, perhaps, identify those bonds of loyalty that were perceived of as taking precedence over loyalty to the daimyo.

Maruyama Masao has observed that "both loyalty (*chūsei*) and rebellion (*hangyaku*) can be regarded as objective principles centering on the self but transcending it, and as expressions of the self in contrast tó the superior, group, or system to which one belongs."[4] Sakata Yoshio, discussing the ethic sustaining the rebelliousness of medieval bushi,

[2] Satō Shin'ichi, *Nanbokuchō no dōran* (Tokyo: Chūōkōronsha, 1965), p. 175.

[3] Sugiyama Hiroshi, *Sengoku daimyō* (Tokyo: Chūōkōronsha, 1965), p. 407.

[4] Maruyama Masao, "Chūsei to hangyaku," *Kindai Nihon shisō-shi kōza* 6, *Jiga to kankyō* (Tokyo: Chikuma Shobō, 1960), p. 379.

has pointed to the prevalence of the idea that in cases where the overlord lacked ability (*kiryō*)—in this context a combination of moral virtue with powers of military and political leadership—his followers could assume the right to dissolve the lord-vassal relationship in rebellion.[5] Sugiyama Hiroshi agrees with Sakata that the spirited independence of Sengoku warriors could quickly spark rebellion. For Sugiyama, the right to repudiate one's lord was implied in the medieval ideal of the "Manly Way" (*otoko-dō*), defined as "the way of life a bushi should follow, the basic archetype of manliness."[6] If a bushi were disgraced, even at the hands of his overlord, pursuit of the Manly Way prescribed the cleansing of that dishonor. Accepting this ideal of the Manly Way as a vital component of the ethic that sustained rebellion, we can redefine it in more general terms as one form of the ideal of securing the redress of grievances by one's own power (*jiriki kyūsai kannen*).

Self-redress was a very strong and deeply rooted ethical norm in medieval Japanese bushi society, and was manifested in the frequent quarrels and vendettas for the recovery of honor and authority. Though the public authorities of the day, including the bakufu, were only partially successful in curbing such private initiatives, the ideal did not mean that warriors would necessarily act alone, nor did the "self-power" (*jiriki*) used in this context imply an ethic of individualism. Efforts at self-redress were made by öne of the groups to which the individual belonged— groups based on such various ties (*en*), as kinship (*ketsuen*), locality (*chien*), or vassalage (*shujū no en*). Bushi in the Sengoku period were fully aware that their survival and security were linked to that of the group, and for this reason the highest norm of action was their loyalty toward the group.

[5] Sakata Yoshio, *Sengoku bushi* (Tokyo: Fukumura Shoten, 1969), pp. 29-44.
[6] Sugiyama Hiroshi, *Sengoku daimyō*, pp. 411, 433.

In the context of such a perception of group loyalties, the obligations of the lord-vassal relationship were regarded as relative ones, the product of choice based on prevailing social and political circumstances. From the point of view of the lord, ready recourse to self-help by vassals on the basis of such competing ties tended both to frustrate the strengthening of lord-vassal relations and to exacerbate rivalries among retainers, the pillars of daimyo power. Thus, for a Sengoku daimyo to build a unified and powerful kashindan whose exclusive loyalty was to him, the most vital task was the dissolution or transference of competing loyalties.

When we examine the kashindan control as enacted by Sengoku daimyo, we find that most of them attempted to meet this agenda. One of their basic principles was the prevention of recourse to acts of self-redress on the part of retainers by bringing the settlement of every kind of dispute under daimyo jurisdiction. A second basic principle common to Sengoku legal codes was the assertion of standards of loyalty to the daimyo that would have priority over the ties of group loyalty.

The first of these principles is most powerfully expressed in the laws punishing both parties to a dispute (*kenka ryōseibai-hō*), which are frequently cited as typifying the basic principles of Sengoku law. For example, Article 8 of the *Imagawa kana mokuroku* states:

> In dealing with those who have quarreled, both parties should be sentenced to death, irrespective of who is in the right or in the wrong. In cases where one party to the dispute, although provoked and attacked, controls himself, makes no defense and, as a result, is wounded his appeal should be granted. While it is reprehensible that he should have been a party to the dispute and perhaps contributed to its outbreak, his respect for the law in not returning the attack merits consideration. However, in cases where warriors come to the aid of

one or other parties to a dispute and then claim to be an injured party, their claims shall not be entertained, even if they should be wounded or killed.[7]

Elsewhere, I have discussed at greater length how kenka ryōseibai-hō rejected recourse to self-redress in disputes involving honor or rights and subjected them to the daimyo's jurisdiction.[8] Regulations to this effect, though some do not stipulate the punishment of both parties, can be found in almost every Sengoku house law. In the Date family domain law, the *Jinkaishū*, for instance, almost a third of the 171 articles were penal laws setting the standards for judicial decisions in a wide variety of individual situations.[9] And since articles like these forbidding private feuds are always accompanied by articles forbidding association with, or assistance by, allies and relatives, it is clear that the daimyo aim of reducing competing loyalties was closely related to the effort to eliminate acts of self-redress.

We can gauge the importance attached to the second principle, that of replacing loyalty to rival groups with absolute loyalty to the daimyo, from a number of Sengoku house laws. In the Yūki house code (*Yūki-shi shin hatto*), for instance, which can be described as having been compiled to stress this principle, there are strict prohibitions against the formation of private subgroups within the kashindan. The preamble to the *Yūki-shi shin hatto* explains that the code was enacted to prevent kashin from trying to exert undue influence over the daimyo on behalf of relatives or others to whom they had private ties.[10] The Takeda family code, the *Kōshū hatto no shidai*, states emphatically that the mere formation of any groups on the basis of private pledges among kashin would in itself be construed as an act of treachery against the overlord.[11] Laws of this kind were

[7] *Chūsei hōsei shiryōshū* 3, 117.

[8] Katsumata Shizuo, "Sengoku-hō," *Iwanami kōza Nihon rekishi* 8 (Tokyo: Iwanami Shoten, 1976), 189.

[9] *Chūsei hōsei shiryōshū* 3, 135-90.

[10] Ibid., p. 227.   [11] Ibid., pp. 227-58.

aimed at preventing the formation among retainers of any lateral relationships, such as ikki, that might serve as the basis for independent action on the part of retainers, and at breaking down ikki-like structures within the kashindan, where these had developed. Laws restricting freedom of matrimonial alliance among members of the kashindan were intended to give the daimyo similar control over kinship groupings. Article 4 of the *Rokkaku-shi shikimoku* provides one of many similar instances in house laws in which it is evident that only by rejecting the actions of retainers that were based on private ties could the laws of daimyo achieve full realization:

> Taking and keeping the landholdings of others is the worst kind of unlawful act. Those who have taken by force the domains of others should return them immediately to the lawful proprietor. When such domains are not returned voluntarily, the daimyo shall order their return. If an order of this kind by the daimyo is not complied with, he shall order his retainers to expel the offender by force. In such cases the retainers must act cooperatively together as a single group in aid of the daimyo. Even though the offender may be someone with whom they have close ties, a relative, or someone whom it is difficult to ignore, retainers are forbidden to go to the aid of the lawbreaker. On the other hand, even if the one whose domains have been taken is disliked by the retainers, insofar as the daimyo orders, they must put aside their resentment and cooperate fully and actively in chastising the offender.[12]

We have so far been considering the preconditions for the articulation of a concept of loyalty to Sengoku daimyo in terms of the efforts made by daimyo to redirect the prevailing ethical attitudes of medieval bushi. Let us next ex-

---

[12] Ibid., p. 259.

amine the nature of that loyalty and the limitations under which it operated.

The character of loyalty to daimyo revealed in Sengoku house codes differed significantly from the ideal of loyalty as self-abnegating service that was inculcated under the later Tokugawa *bakuhan* political structure. During the Sengoku period, the service (*hōkō*) expected of retainers was limited and directly proportionate to the amount of favor (*onkyū*) provided by the daimyo. In concrete terms, loyalty was expressed in the fixed amount of military service levy (*gun'yaku*) paid by the retainer, as exemplified in the provisions of the *Kōshū hatto no shidai* and other house codes.[13] This type of loyalty, a kind of strongly reciprocal relationship, was, of course, restricted by the prevailing conception of lord-vassal ties, providing the daimyo with only a limited basis for its enforcement and little hope of forging from it a rationale of absolute loyalty.

Although the concept of loyalty expressed in Sengoku house codes was very circumscribed, the concept of disloyalty was comprehensive. Under the lord-vassal laws of the Kamakura bakufu, the scope of disloyalty was virtually restricted to failure to render gun'yaku. By the Sengoku period, however, the concept had been broadened to include, in extreme cases, any transgression against kashindan control laws. This implies that the daimyo's assertion of authority had transcended the limited reciprocal concept of loyalty derived simply from the feudal claims of an overlord upon his vassals, and now involved also the claim to a different, more extensive kind of authority. It was accepted as a general principle under Sengoku law that, just as daimyo would not recognize litigation by children against parents, so too they would not accept litigation involving claims by vassals against their overlord. This, of course, was a reflection of the powerful seignorial authority of feudal lords over their retainers. The Imagawa, however, enacted exceptional regulations which stipulated that

[13] Ibid., p. 202.

in the case of such acts as consorting with enemies of the
domain, engaging in rebellion, robbery, gambling, or any
other transgression threatening the security of the polity or
state (*kokka*), litigation involving retainers should be heard,
even if the overlord himself were a party to the dispute.[14]
These regulations posit the existence of a broadly conceived principle of loyalty to the kokka, one that transcended the strong lord-vassal bond and differed in character from the loyalty owed to the daimyo. When this was
reinforced by the concept expressed clearly in the *Asakura
Eirin kabegaki* (the legacy of Asakura Eirin, 1474-1555) that
only by preserving the kokka was the security of the
daimyo and his kashindan assured, it provided a rationale
for daimyo absolutism. This *kabegaki* (lit. wall writing) took
the form of a list of precepts that Asakura descendants
should observe. Although it might be described as a kakun,
the contents of the kabegaki display many of the features
of Sengoku house codes, and it can fairly be accepted as
such. In the conclusion it states quite explicitly that "if the
kuni (domain) can be preserved, then the Asakura house
can continue to survive and flourish."[15] Thus the daimyo,
using their retainers' traditional consciousness of subordination to the group, transmuted the obligations of loyalty
felt by retainers toward the various groups to which they
belonged into obligations of loyalty toward the kokka.[16]
The ultimate goal was the inculcation of absolute loyalty to
the daimyo and the establishment of an authoritarian
power structure.

[14] Although no author or date of compilation is given for the *Imagawa-
shi sosho jōmoku*, it is thought to have been enacted by Imagawa Yoshimoto,
who led the Imagawa between 1536 and 1560. The *Jōmoku* is in thirteen
articles, most of which were intended to provide standards for the domain
officials who were responsible for judging appeals and litigation. For the
text of the *Jōmoku*, see *Chūsei hōsei shiryōshū* 3, 134.

[15] *Chūsei hōsei shiryōshū* 3, 338.

[16] The *Shimazu nisshin kyōkun, Shimazu-ke monjo*, no. 1403, provides an
example of a typical call for loyalty to the "kokka."

THE RATIONALE FOR CONTROL OF THE RYŌGOKU

In view of the strong influence of the concept of the kokka
on the lord-vassal system of daimyo and *kashin*, it is hardly
surprising that the laws enacted to regulate the domain
(ryōgoku) and its inhabitants should have reflected the
same influence. In this section we shall try to clarify the nature and significance of ryōgoku control laws by analyzing
the character of this Sengoku kokka in greater depth.

The word kokka appears in many documents of the
Sengoku and early Kinsei period. In use from ancient
times, of course, as a term for Japan as a whole, the word
had gained new overtones by the end of the Sengoku period. In reference to daimyo—for instance, in cases where
daimyo ordered temples and shrines within their domain
to offer prayers and ceremonies for the safety of the
kokka—the word did not imply all of Japan but only the
consolidated sphere of a daimyo's political control. For
daimyo under the early bakuhan system, it corresponded
to the larger han, those whose boundaries embraced a
whole province and hence were referred to as *kunimochi
daimyō*. The Japanese-Portuguese Dictionary, *Nippo jisho*,
offers this definition: "Cocca. Cuni, iye. Reinos, & casas, ou
familias."[17] Pertinent here is the association under the
heading of kokka of the concepts of kingdom (kuni) and
house (ie). As is evident from such contemporary expressions as "for the sake of province (kingdom) and house"
(*okuni, oie no tame*) the basic components of the word kokka,
that is, kuni and ie, were frequently used separately in the
Sengoku period and were conceived of as being conceptu-
ally distinct from each other. The word kokka, however,
expressed the idea of the union of the daimyo house (the ie
broadly conceived of as including all the retainers under
the daimyo's control) and the kuni that served as the
sphere of political control. Satō Shin'ichi has shown that
the authority of the Ashikaga shoguns comprised two as-

[17] See folio 53.

pects: a private or personal feudal authority and a public, territorial, governing authority.[18] It is significant that the word kokka, which embraced both the private aspect of control over the ie and the public aspect of rule over the kuni, should have been used in the age of the Sengoku daimyo to describe the composite object of their political control.

Among the major characteristics of this Sengoku kokka, a very important one was the autonomy or complete integrity of the sphere of political control. In Sengoku legal codes there are numerous prohibitions against the formation of ties with other domains or their inhabitants. Implicit in all these regulations is the consciousness of a sharp distinction between other kuni and the daimyo's own. Thus, alongside the frequent daimyo assertions that inhabitants of other kuni were subject to domain law while they were visiting his domain, there were also explicit regulations putting the residents of other kuni outside the scope of domain law. The obverse of this consciousness of the separateness of other kuni was the assertion of the integrity of the daimyo's own kuni and a self-awareness on the part of the daimyo that he was building an autonomous sphere of political control. The concrete realization of this awareness was to be seen in the imposition of unified standards applicable only to the home kuni. Among the ryōgoku control laws of the Sengoku daimyo we find numerous laws regulating weights and measures, transportation, religious institutions, markets, guilds, and commodities. Among the most typical expressions of this policy were coin selection edicts (*erizeni-rei*). The fact that almost every Sengoku daimyo attempted to control the selection of the coins circulating within his domain and regulate their basic exchange rates is one of the clearest expressions of this sense of the autonomy and integrity of the domain.

---

[18] Satō Shin'ichi, "Muromachi bakufu ron," *Iwanami kōza Nihon rekishi* 7 (Tokyo: Iwanami Shoten, 1963), 5-7.

A second striking characteristic of the Sengoku kokka is the fact that all the inhabitants of the domain, not merely the daimyo's direct retainers, were seen by the daimyo as constituent members of the kokka, understood by Sengoku daimyo to be made up of a sphere of territorial authority (*kokudo*) and of the people who resided within that sphere (*kokumin*). For this reason the laws regulating the kokka were conceived of, unless their subject was specifically defined otherwise, as applying equally to all inhabitants of the domain and as offering the protection of law to the whole populace.[19]

The third, and most important, characteristic of the Sengoku kokka, and one that derived from the second characteristic, was the use by the daimyo of the kokka as an ideology of political control for the purpose of legitimizing their authority over the ryōgoku. Daimyo assessment of their regimes as having been established in order to preserve the kokka was predicated on the political value of the concept. From the activities of such daimyo as the Asakura, Mōri, and Shimazu, it is clear that this conception of kokka was widely held in the Sengoku period; it was probably most fully articulated by the Go-Hōjō, generally regarded as the most mature Sengoku daimyo. For the Go-Hōjō, the kokka transcended daimyo authority, being not only responsible for protecting its constituent populace but also, at the same time, invested with independent authority over them. Daimyo authority was therefore interpreted by the Go-Hōjō leaders to have been entrusted to them for the purpose of maintaining the peace, security, and social order of this kokka.[20] Thus, Sengoku daimyo, who had

---

[19] *Rokkaku-shi shikimoku kishōmon*.

[20] Katsumata Shizuo, "Sengoku-hō," pp. 202-203. In this context it should be mentioned that Sasaki Junnosuke denies the existence of this kokka, so clearly evident in the documentary record of the period. He discusses this issue in "Futatsu no monjo kara," *U.P. 42* (Tokyo: Tōkyō Daigaku Shuppankai, 1976), but the grounds for his objections are far from clear.

carved out their domains and enforced their authority over the inhabitants of these domains by force of arms and with little heed to legitimacy, were able to claim legitimacy for their rule as a "public" or "official" authority (*kōgi*) or *kubō* under the shield of a concept of kokka they had themselves created.[21]

Although the articulation by Sengoku daimyo of this ideology of political control, which can be regarded as an embryonic concept of the sovereign state, and the forging of a rationale for the legitimation of daimyo authority, which can be described as a theory of delegation of ruling authority, mark an important epoch in the history of the development of political thought in Japan, they were not entirely without antecedents. Satō Shin'ichi has pointed out that in the fifteenth century the offices (*shiki*) of shogun and shugo, as well as the holdings of land stewards and retainers, were not regarded simply as the private possessions of the holder of the shiki. Rather, shiki holders bore the responsibility for maintaining peace and order within their respective spheres of authority, whether these embraced the whole of Japan, a single ryōgoku, or even one small holding. Moreover, holders of shiki were expected to demonstrate their ability (kiryō) to discharge this responsibility. Satō suggests that what helped to guarantee the discharge of this responsibility was the fact that the Confucian philosophy of revolution, comprising the ideal of virtuous government that could only be achieved with the

---

[21] Reflecting the diversity of medieval political and social life, there existed several concepts of *kō* (public or official). In the political realm, shōen proprietors and land stewards, like shoguns, were referred to as *kubō* (public or official authorities). At the same time, in the sphere of everyday life, people's actions were strongly affected by the pressures of the "public world" (*kugai*), of public opinion. And people of the day also thought of this opinion as kō (public or official). The historical significance of the establishment of "public" or "official" (kōgi) ruling authority by Sengoku daimyo lay in the fact that they created a single, indivisible "public" world which embraced the latter concept of kō as well as unifying the former.

support of the people, and its obverse, the punitive re-moval from office of a ruler who proved to have neither the virtue nor the ability to rule justly, had taken root as a political principle.[22] Behind the creation of the kokka as an ideology of political control, then, lay consciousness by Sengoku daimyo of distinct spheres of political control, ac-knowledgment of the Confucian philosophy of revolution, awareness of the extremely tense political circumstances that kept their domains always in danger, and the convic-tion that they had created and protected their kokka by their own efforts. Instead of seeking authority to rule their domains through the possession of shiki, the expression of authority of the old political order, they located the basis of their authority in a political ideology forged by themselves, which incorporated newly formulated political principles and rested on their military power.

The ryōgoku control laws, which aimed at the preserva-tion of the security, peace, and social order of the domain, were the paramount expressions of the will of such daimyo-created kokka. In the disturbed conditions of the Sengoku period, when warfare constantly threatened the existence of the kokka and the lives of the kokumin, the survival of the kokka was made the highest imperative, and the idea was born that the kokka stood above all restraint. As the expressions of the will of the kokka, laws (*kokuhō*) were invested with sovereign authority and endowed with unrestricted powers of interference into the social struc-ture, customs, and private rights of the people. In all the varieties of law that embodied the basic policies of the Sen-goku daimyo, we can detect the priority given to the kokka and its requirements—in the cadastral regulations that broke down the old shōen system and laid the foundations for a new ryōgoku system; in new tax regulations institut-ing such domain-wide levies as *tansen* and *munebechisen*, which established the economic basis of daimyo authority;

[22] "Muromachi bakufu ron," p. 29.

in laws enforcing the return of absconders, which were a major step in limiting the control hitherto exerted by various individual proprietors over the inhabitants of the domain; and, finally, in registration edicts which, by requiring that all inhabitants of the domain be registered, allowed for the mobilization of the whole populace in times of danger to the kokka.

Another important characteristic of Sengoku law was an almost excessive respect for law. Sengoku daimyo stressed that the dictates of law were superior to the customs and moral principles (*dōri*) that regulated social life. Article 39 of the *Jinkaishū* provides one of many similar examples of, to use the contemporary phrase, the kind of "law that overrides principle" (*ri o yaburu hō*):

> ITEM: Wounding with a sword cut. It is forbidden for anyone wounded by a sword cut in a quarrel to take private measures of retaliation and not wait for the action of the daimyo's court of appeal as he should. Although such acts of revenge may be in keeping with the principles (*riun*) of a bushi, because they break the law [forbidding private vendettas], those guilty of such illegal acts should be punished.[23]

We can assume that this assertion of the primacy of law derived from the heightened status that Sengoku daimyo accorded to law as the expression of the will of the kokka. A corollary was the insistence by the retainers that the daimyo should also be subject to law. The classic documentary expression of this was the *Rokkaku-shi shikimoku*, which was explicitly intended to curb arbitrary rule by daimyo. At least half the articles in this code, compiled on the basis of a written agreement between the Rokkaku-shi daimyo and twenty senior retainers that they would carefully observe the provisions of the code, were directed to the daimyo, such as article 37:

[23] *Chūsei hōsei shiryōshū* 3, 145.

ITEM: It is forbidden for the daimyo to hand down and enforce a judgment in a trial without a full enquiry or without allowing the defendants an opportunity to explain the circumstances.[24]

Logically, at least, Sengoku law also regulated the daimyo who conceived and enacted it.

Using the new laws as powerful levers, Sengoku daimyo were able to achieve the structural transformation of their domains. The concept of delegated authority, however, which provided a foundation for these policies, was sustained by the related theory of virtuous government (*tokuji shugi*). Consequently, daimyo could hardly fail to recognize that in order to maintain that peace in the kokka which would guarantee the legitimacy of their rule, they had not only to win the support of their retainers, the principal basis for daimyo power, but also to earn the support of the common inhabitants (kokumin), who were naturally reluctant to accept as their overlord anybody who could not protect their lives and property, and who were prone to vent their anger in violent group action. It is in this awareness that we can find the roots of the concern for, or mollification of, the people (*bumin shisō*) that is also apparent in many laws.[25] Probably most typical were the debt moratoria edicts (*tokusei-rei*). Whereas the tokusei edicts of the Muromachi bakufu were almost exclusively concerned with controlling the social abuses arising from usury, the tokusei edicts issued by Sengoku daimyo, while they still had debt amelioration as a central theme, broadened the general connotation of tokusei to one of "good government" (*zensei*). And when we note that these edicts were issued by daimyo only during such periods of confusion within the domain as defeat in battle, civil war, or maladministration, it is clear that they were seen by the daimyo as

[24] Ibid., p. 265.
[25] Fujiki Hisashi, "Daimyō ryōgoku-sei ron," *Taikei Nihon kokka-shi* 2 (Tokyo: Tōkyō Daigaku Shuppankai, 1975), 251-89.

a means of winning the support of the general populace of the domain.

In this section we have examined the nature and significance of the laws issued by Sengoku daimyo to regulate their domains, viewing these laws as expressions of the kokka that Sengoku daimyo had created as a rationale for political control. The influence of this concept of kokka was not, however, restricted to domain regulations. It was also manifest in the laws aimed specifically at the regulation of the band of retainers. Two significant developments in the relationship between lord and retainer during the Sengoku period were the enforcement of very much tighter, more authoritarian, ties between lord and vassal, and the assertion of daimyo authority over those inhabitants of the domain who were under the control of individual proprietors, many of whom still preserved a large measure of independence within their holdings. Both these developments can be said to have been shaped by the articulation of the kokka as an ideology of control and by the primacy accorded to the laws promulgated by Sengoku daimyo as expressions of the will of the kokka.

KOKKA AND TENKA: THE SIGNIFICANCE OF SENGOKU POLITICAL IDEOLOGIES

Any useful answer to the question of the "development" of Sengoku law raised in the title of this essay must be sought in the relationship between the rationale for political control developed by Sengoku daimyo and the rationale for centralizing, unifying political authority asserted by Oda Nobunaga and Toyotomi Hideyoshi.

Oda Nobunaga emerged from among the ranks of the Sengoku daimyo and took the first major strides toward the formation of a unified political regime in late medieval Japan. For Nobunaga the equivalent of the Sengoku daimyo concept of kokka was undoubtedly the ideal of "*tenka*." Nobunaga's concept of tenka has been defined by

Asao Naohiro in these terms: "Nobunaga conceived of 'tenka' both as a sphere of political control and as a universal principle (dōri) transcending social status, and he sought to instill in his followers the recognition that he was the tenka. For their part, subordinate daimyo were well aware that this assertion of 'tenka' by Nobunaga served their own interests, and they were therefore willing to accept him as the 'official ruling authority' (kōgi)."[26] From this definition, if we allow for the greater scale on which Nobunaga was operating, we can understand Nobunaga's tenka as being intrinsically similar in character to that of the Sengoku daimyo kokka. By comparing tenka with kokka, we can hope to attain deeper insight into the historical significance of Nobunaga's tenka as a rationale for the governance of the unified political structure he sought to establish.

As a political concept, the word tenka was already in use in the fourteenth century to designate the object of the political authority that had been vested in the Ashikaga shoguns.[27] And just as the authority to rule their domains ceded to shugo by the shogun had served as the premise for the conception of kokka by the Sengoku daimyo, so the authority to rule the tenka claimed by the holders of the shogunal office served as the premise for Nobunaga's conception of tenka. Nobunaga, however, very quickly rejected shogunal authority over the tenka and demonstrated the ambition to seize that authority for himself. In 1565, according to Satō Shin'ichi, Nobunaga, taking advantage of the incident in which Matsunaga Hisahide assassinated Shogun Ashikaga Yoshiteru, began to use the ciper (kaō) based on the character rin from the name of the legendary Chinese creature kirin that was believed to bring

[26] Asao Naohiro, "Shōgun kenryoku no sōshutsu" 3, *Rekishi hyōron*, no. 293 (1975), p. 34.
[27] Satō Shin'ichi, "Muromachi bakufu ron," pp. 6-7.

peace to the world.[28] This may well have marked the point at which Nobunaga, aware that shogunal authority over the tenka had ebbed irreversibly, decided to create his own tenka by force of arms. Two years later Nobunaga began publicly to use the famous seal bearing the inscription *tenka fubu*, which implied control over the tenka by military power.

In 1568 Nobunaga entered Kyoto in support of Shogun Ashikaga Yoshiaki. This action reflected an ambiguous, or at least two-layered, attitude on the part of Nobunaga toward ruling authority over the tenka. While acknowledging that authority to govern the tenka had been delegated to Yoshiaki as holder of the shogunal office, Nobunaga was also asserting that this authority was being delegated to himself, without whom the shogun was helpless. If this was an attitude of compromise on Nobunaga's part, it did little to impede his march to power. Underlying Nobunaga's rationale for the final expulsion of Yoshiaki from Kyoto in 1573 lay the criticism that Yoshiaki lacked the ability (kiryō) to rule the tenka, and the assertion that only someone like Nobunaga who could maintain peace in the land should have the authority to rule. This assertion by Nobunaga that the legitimacy of his control over the country rested in the ability to enforce order by his own military power paralleled the earlier use by Sengoku daimyo of the concept of kokka that they had carved out for themselves as instruments for legitimizing their rule over their domains. For Nobunaga, therefore, the reinstallation of the shogun was merely a political expedient. It was to the concept of tenka, not to Shogun Yoshiaki, that he consistently looked for the source of his political authority. Nobunaga's evasion in 1582 of the proposal by the imperial court to appoint him to the offices of *daijōdaijin, kanpaku,* and

---

[28] Satō Shin'ichi, "Nihon kaō-shi no issetsu," *Nagoya Daigaku Nihonshi ronshū* (Tokyo: Yoshikawa Kōbunkan, 1975), p. 8.

seiitaishōgun demonstrated his conviction that his authority over the country was sustained by the tenka he was trying to create for himself and not by any imperial court or shogunal office.[29] That the ancestry of Nobunaga's rationale for control over the country was to be found in the Sengoku daimyo rationale for control over their domains is evident from the following quotation: "The basis for rule over the kuni is not attained by being appointed shugo by the shogun. Control [of the kokka] is achieved when the daimyo, by his own efforts, brings peace to the kokka by establishing the laws of the kuni."[30]

The concept that it was the support of the inhabitants of the tenka that guaranteed the legitimacy of political control (*tenka o kō to nasu*), a concept that was frequently brought into play in Japanese political history as a normative restriction transcending both the transformations of political form and concrete control relationships,[31] was also called upon by Sengoku daimyo and Nobunaga to justify their challenge to the traditional system of political authority. As a unifier extending paths first beaten by Sengoku daimyo, Nobunaga sought to consolidate his authority by attempting to legitimize rebellion against the old political order on the basis of loyalty to this political principle. Nobunaga's initial justification for his authority to rule was based on the political principle that "the tenka is the common property of all men" (*tenka wa tenka no tenka nari*).[32] As he extended his control, Nobunaga attributed to tenka the status of an absolute, all-transcendent political principle. He proceeded to develop the rationale that, because only he was capable of bringing peace to the tenka, ruling authority

[29] Iwasawa Yoshihiko, "Honnō-ji no hen shūi," *Rekishi chiri*, nos. 91-94 (1968).

[30] "Imagawa kana mokuroku, tsuika," article 20. *Chūsei hōsei shiryōshū*.

[31] Maruyama Masao, "Chūsei to hangyaku."

[32] In the Chinese text *Lu-t'ao* of the Chou dynasty we find the statement: "The *t'ien-hsia* (tenka) does not belong to any one individual, but is the common property of all those who live 'under heaven' (*t'ien-hsia*)."

had been delegated to him by the tenka. Ultimately, there-fore, his final justification for the legitimacy of his absolute control over the country rested on the assertion that "tenka belongs to the individual" (*tenka wa hitori no tenka nari*).[33]

Like Nobunaga, Hideyoshi stressed the idea of tenka, and even went so far as to refer to himself as "tenka." The role played by the concept of tenka in their respective jus-tifications for their exercise of political authority was, how-ever, very different. Nobunaga's tenka was a rationale for rule created as the sole source for the legitimation of his authority over the country. Hideyoshi based his claim to rule the country on his appointment to the office of kan-paku by the emperor. Thus, in form, at least, tenka became the object of the authority exercised by the kanpaku. As a self-appointed kanpaku, Hideyoshi was, of course, very different from the nobles who were the traditional incum-bents of that office. Moreover, as we can see from his asser-tions that only somebody who could take and pacify the tenka by force of arms should be appointed kanpaku, in practice Hideyoshi pursued the same course as Nobu-naga.[34] Yet, in the final analysis, Hideyoshi shifted back from the rebels' rationale of control articulated by Sengoku daimyo and Nobunaga to a rationale of rule based upon the traditional political order, one that acknowledged del-egation by the emperor. This was to have profound im-portance in the subsequent development of Japanese polit-ical thought.

As kanpaku, Hideyoshi declared in 1585 that continua-tion of fighting in Kyushu against the "imperial will" was disgraceful, and that he personally would crush anyone

[33] The concept of "tenka" was sustained intellectually by ideas of "the heavenly way" (*tentō shisō*). The great influence exerted by tentō shisō on the lives of Sengoku bushi is discussed in detail by Ishige Tadashi, "Sen-goku, Azuchi-Momoyama jidai no shisō," *Taikei Nihonshi sōsho* 23 (*Shisō-shi* 2) (Tokyo: Yamakawa Shuppansha, 1976).

[34] Asao Naohiro, "Toyotomi seiken ron," *Iwanami kōza Nihon rekishi* 9 (Tokyo: Iwanami Shoten, 1963), 208.

who disregarded the imperial command to cease fighting. He thus designated himself the enforcing agent of the imperial will. Furthermore, two years later he asserted that he had been given the authority by the emperor to rule all sixty-odd provinces of Japan.[35] Hideyoshi's justification for his rule, which consistently sought legitimation for his unification of the tenka in authority entrusted to him by the *tennō*, was thus very different from Nobunaga's logic of pacification of the tenka, which asserted that to support him was to sustain the tenka.[36] With the basic source of authority to rule the country, which supported any rationale for political control, located once again in the historical precedent of the traditional order instead of in political principle, the wheel had turned full circle.

[35] *Shimazu-ke monjo* 1, nos. 344 and 345. My attention was directed to these by Akizawa Shigeru.

[36] Asao Naohiro, "Shogun kenryoku no sōshutsu" 2, 23.

Chapter 4

Sengoku Daimyo Rule
and Commerce

SASAKI GIN'YA
WITH WILLIAM B. HAUSER

THE CONTROL of commerce, which had been of relatively minor concern to the *shōen* proprietors, *shugo* daimyo, and local *kokujin*, became an economic and military necessity for the Sengoku daimyo struggling to establish a firm hold over their domains during the sixteenth century. The study of Sengoku daimyo commercial policies has produced a considerable body of research, and I would like to offer some new perspectives on the subject. First, the tendency up to now has been to focus on separate elements like the *kenchi*, the *kandaka* system, controls over various handicraft industries, or urban policies. I will try here to take a broader approach, examining Sengoku daimyo commercial policies for their basic premises and for their foundations in historical precedent. Second, while acknowledging the general restraints imposed by conditions inherent in medieval society, I will emphasize what I see as the originality and novelty of the commercial policies of the Sengoku daimyo by comparison with those of the shōen *ryōshu* (proprietors) and shugo daimyo. Third, my analysis will show the ultimate dependence of the Sengoku daimyo for the final solution to their economic problems on the strong central authority that Nobunaga, Hideyoshi, and the Tokugawa shoguns alone were to establish.

A fundamental problem faced by the Sengoku daimyo in seeking to extend their control over commerce was that, in the sixteenth century, domain trade had become closely interrelated with two other types of trade, namely, the Kinai trade and intervillage trade within the domains. The Kinai trade, centered in the cities of Kyoto, Nara, and Sakai, had been in existence from the early medieval period and had flourished as *dosō* (pawnbrokers) and *sakaya* (*sake* dealers) became affluent suppliers of capital to commerce and money lenders. Foreign trade with Ming China and, later, Europe was conducted by the Kinai merchants, foreign imports being paid for by exports of goods from the countryside, where in isolated areas craftsmen had developed high levels of technical skill in metalwork, silk weaving, and various other arts and crafts. The intervillage trade within domains had grown up between self-governing village communities (like the *sōmura*), and emerged as agriculture and handicraft production increased and specialization of production proceeded in these communities. All three types of trade—Kinai, village, and daimyo domain—had originated well before the Sengoku period, and so must be understood in the context of the lengthy evolution of land-tax procedures and commodity trade practices in medieval Japan. Their successful development was heavily interdependent, and from time to time had been intensely competitive. Any realistic discussion of control over domain trade therefore must take the interaction of these types of trade into consideration.

A major problem for most Sengoku daimyo was that their effort to assert local political autonomy was often hindered by the absence of a sound economic base. Inadequate supplies of various commodities made their domains neither self-sufficient nor self-supporting. The underlying causes of economic deficiency ranged from adverse geographical or climatic conditions, to scarcity of natural resources, to the legacy of the medieval shōen system, which because of its effect on land tax practices, the division of labor, and commodity circulation, had led to economic distortions in the regional economies. In addition, the cultivation of rice, the staple grain, was still a precarious matter in the sixteenth century. Even in the domains of powerful daimyo like the Go-Hōjō and the Imagawa in southern Kantō and the Tōkaidō region, self-sufficiency in rice was difficult to maintain. One important means for coping with this critical problem was to develop reliable sources of rice outside the domain. This, of necessity, became the first priority in the trade policies of the Sengoku daimyo.

Finally, the Sengoku daimyo domains were still in political flux. Domains included lands held directly by the daimyo (*honryō*),[1] fiefs (*shoryō*) held by many members of the vassal band (*kashindan*), as well as newly conquered territory where the assertion of local authority and territorial control changed continually according to the balance of power. Stabilization of the domain economy required the subjugation of local authority. Or to put it another way, the success or failure of the Sengoku daimyo's control over commerce and his political control of his domain amounted to one and the same thing.

PATRONAGE AND CONTROL OF TRADE IN REMOTE AREAS

Several factors in addition to the natural and systemic limitations noted above conspired to keep most sixteenth-century daimyo domains economically deficient in one aspect or another, and thus made them dependent on the central markets of the Kinai region for some commodities. Daimyo whose domains were located inland had to purchase salt, fish, and other marine products.[2] Many daimyo had to import rice and other grains periodically to cover

---

[1] *Honryō* is a term applied to the historically established private holdings of a local proprietor. Within a daimyo domain, the lands administered directly by the daimyo, in contrast to those held in fief by his vassals, were generally called *chokkatsu-ryō*.

[2] Sasaki Gin'ya, *Chūsei shōhin ryūtsūshi no kenkyū* (Tokyo: Hōsei Daigaku Shuppankyoku, 1972), pp. 172-74.

domain shortages. After the 1540s, all daimyo were to feel
the need to acquire the new firearms that were rapidly rev-
olutionizing the technology of warfare.

Following the introduction of firearms to Japan, which
came with the arrival of Portuguese ships at the island of
Tanegashima off southern Kyushu in 1543, most daimyo,
unable to manufacture their own because of the scarcity of
iron and the low level of production technology, turned to
the merchants of Sakai and other central areas for the new
weapons. For example, Anayama Nobukimi, a retainer of
the Takeda house in the province of Kai, in the 1570s ordered ten wealthy merchants from the town of Suruga
Imajuku, including the Tomono and Matsuki houses, to
buy guns and iron from other domains, even those of Anayama enemies. In return, the Anayama guaranteed these
merchants other special trading rights.[3]

One would normally expect that rice, the most important
grain in Japan, would be a commodity for which all areas
of the country were comparatively self-sufficient, but in the
sixteenth century rice production was never fully depend-
able. Even daimyo like the Go-Hōjō and the Imagawa, both
of whom controlled highly productive domains, were
forced in years of poor harvests to purchase rice grown in
the province of Ise—the shipping merchant Kadoya of
Ōminato and the wealthy merchant house of Tomono
from Suruga Imajuku being two traders known to have
engaged in such sales. This condition continued into the
first quarter of the seventeenth century, when domains like
Tsugaru, located in what would be the future rice granary
of the Tōhoku region, still occasionally had to import rice
from Echigo.[4]

As we will discuss later, during the sixteenth-century

[3] See document 11 in the section "Tomono monjo," in *Shizuoka-ken*,
ed., *Shizuoka-ken shiryō* 3 (Tokyo: Kadokawa Shoten, 1966), 261-62. The
document bears the seal of Anayama Nobukimi.
[4] Yamaguchi Tōru, "Obama-Tsuruga ni okeru kinsei shoki gōshō no
sonzai keitai," *Rekishigaku kenkyū* 248 (December 1960), 1-16.

period of warfare, various eastern daimyo instituted restrictions on trade such as *komedome* (rice prohibitions) or
tawaradome (baled-goods prohibitions) as a tactic of war.[5]
These prohibitions made self-sufficiency in rice a major
goal for daimyo. Irrespective of whether it was a time of
peace or a time of war, one of the most important commodities traded between daimyo domains and the central
markets became the rice that was essential to military and
economic security.

In the case of daimyo with landlocked domains, it goes
without saying that fish, salt, and other marine products
had to come from outside the domain. The Takeda house
in the mountainous province of Kai maintained a stable
supply of fish by an arrangement with the Sakata merchant
house from the town of Kofu Yōkaichi. In Aizu Wakamatsu, during the rule of the Ashina house, there were, in
addition to usual domain merchants, many merchants
from Kyoto, Ise, and the Kantō region, as well. These outside merchants had been granted a reduction in shipping
charges and exemptions from barrier taxes in exchange
for goods supplied to the Ashina domain. During the
1590s, in the landlocked castle town of Mito, the Satake
house welcomed itinerant merchants from such trading
centers as Kyoto, Sakai, Ise, and Utsunomiya. Itinerant
merchants were also given permission to conduct business
in the stores of special merchants in service to the Satake
house—like the Fukaya, Tōyama, and Ogawa—and there
sold high-quality goods not produced in the domain, such
as dyestuffs, textiles including silks and crepe, red dye,
ceremonial robes (*kataginu*), *hakama, obi,* and the nationally
famous Uji tea.[6]

In their concern for assuring a steady supply of essential
commodities, the Sengoku daimyo went beyond simple tol-

[5] Toyoda Takeshi, *Zōtei chūsei Nihon shōgyōshi no kenkyū* (Tokyo:
Iwanami Shoten, 1954), pp. 340-47.

[6] Mito Shishi Hensan Iinkai, ed., *Mito-shishi* 1 (Mito: Mito Shiyakusho,
1963), 708.

erance of outside merchants, as was the case with the shugō
daimyo, to actively encourage long-distance trade. Specific
policies varied, but the following examples illustrate characteristic provisions for the protection and control of
long-distance trade. The Date house of Mutsu in their *Jinkaishū* house laws included regulations designed to protect
merchants who came from outside their domain. Many
daimyo appointed powerful merchants within their domains who were active in long-distance trade as agents or
supervisory merchants (*shōnin tsukasa, shōnin kashira*, or
daikan), granting them special status and prestige within
the local merchant community. The Date did this with the
Yanada, the Imagawa with the Tomono, and the Takeda
and Asano with the Sakata. Other daimyo used their public
authority to support long-distance trade, and granted
powerful guild (*za*) merchants special trade rights to protect their power and position: the Uesugi did this for the
Kurata house of the hemp za, the Takeda for the Suruga
fish za, and the Imagawa for the Tomono za. The Ashina
granted exemptions from shipping and barrier taxes to
merchants who came to their domain of Aizu from Kyoto,
Ise, and the Kantō region.[7] Many other examples could be
cited, but whatever their particular inducements, all these
policies were designed to encourage outside merchants to
bring essential commodities into the domains.

To pay for imports, the domains had to have exports,
and the daimyo used their authority to facilitate and assure
the flow of domain surplus commodities and products to
the central markets. Taxes on exports provided an important source of cash for the daimyo, as well. A famous
example of this process was the export of hemp from the
Uesugi domain in Echigo. The major markets for this
hemp were in Kyoto and Shitennōji (Osaka), where it was
used as a special raw material for clothing manufacture.
Hemp was a rich source of income for the Uesugi, and this

[7] Ibid., p. 709.

is underlined by the fact that when in 1564 Uesugi Kenshin had decided, as part of the program for the revival of the major seaport of Kashiwazaki in Echigo, to waive a variety of taxes on merchants and artisans, he retained the levies on hemp alone.[8] His successor, Uesugi Kagekatsu, appointed the Kurata house (heads of the hemp za) to serve as *goyō* (officially sponsored) merchants to the Uesugi, and to ensure, by the inspection of vessels and strict application of all tax levies on hemp, that only licensed vessels engaged in hemp exporting.[9]

In the Suruga domain of the Imagawa, a similar situation developed around a special red dye made from *akane*, a domain specialty much in demand among the producers of high-quality clothing in Kyoto. Sales of the dye were monopolized by the Tomono house, who served as magistrates in charge of merchants (shōnin tsukasa) to the Imagawa. For some time exports of akane and other special products from the domain had been subject to strict official examination by the Imagawa as well as to standardized tax levies. When in 1566 the Imagawa fixed transit taxes on exports to Kyoto at three strings of cash (*kanmon*) per horseload, the Tomono were put in charge of examining all exports and issuing certificates of authorization for each shipment. The important Imagawa retainer, Asahina, lord of Shimotsuke, officially stamped the shipping documents and certified them.[10] The inspection system devised by the Imagawa, an important departure from the trade practices up to that time, achieved two simultaneous results. It guaranteed through taxation a sizable income from long-

[8] See document 496 in the section "Uesugi Ke monjo" in Tōkyō Teikoku Daigaku Shiryō Hensanjo, ed., *Dai Nihon komonjo iewake* 12 (Tokyo: Tōkyō Teikoku Daigaku, 1931), part 1, 485-86.

[9] Ono Kōji, "Sanjō Nishi Ke to Echigo aosoza no katsudō," *Rekishi chiri* 63:2 (1934).

[10] See document 5 in the section "Tomono monjo" in *Shizuoka-ken shiryō* 3, 253-54. This bears the seal of Imagawa Ujizane and was issued 1566/10/26.

distance trade, while preventing the uncontrolled export of key commodities.

To summarize, the Sengoku daimyo engaged where possible in the direct protection and control of long-distance trade in order to assure supplies of goods in which their domains were not self-sufficient and to secure the cash necessary to purchase them. First, they guaranteed the safety and status of merchants from within and outside the domain who engaged in long-distance trade. Second, they protected and reassured the long-time holders of guild-style special business rights. Third, they created conditions favorable to business for certain merchants by reducing or eliminating transport and enterprise taxes. Fourth, they enforced an inspection system for all types of export goods.

These policies adopted by Sengoku daimyo must be regarded, at the very least, as evidence of their strong desire to change the course and conduct of commerce to an extent that had not been attempted by the political powers that preceded them. However, if we compare their performance with that of the early modern bakuhan daimyo, certain limitations are readily apparent. For instance, the inspection system for export goods, if we exclude the Imagawa example, did not normally involve the daimyo's direct interference in commercial control. At the most, we can assume that it was generally carried out by goyō shōnin appointed from among the merchants and was intended as a supervisory check on domain imports and exports. This is clearly a lesser stage of development than the monopoly system that operated in various domains during the Tokugawa period.

In addition, the effective reach of the commercial policies adopted by the Sengoku daimyo was limited to the confines of their domains, and did not extend to other daimyo or other domains. It goes without saying that long-distance trade meant dealing with markets in distant domains and in the Kinai region, and the continuation and safety of such trade depended on the maintenance of agreements with other daimyo. However, in the sixteenth century, particularly in the latter half, when conditions of warfare were chronic, it was almost impossible to maintain peaceful ties with the many daimyo who might have economic interests in any particular trade agreement. Thus the domains of the Sengoku daimyo that were not self-sufficient were economically dependent on the growth of long-distance trade between cooperating domains. But, to assure this, it was necessary that a stable national order be established under a strong and unified national authority.

THE STRENGTHENING OF THE COMMERCIAL TAX SYSTEM

The private house economies and the public economies of the Sengoku daimyo overlapped at many points, making it extremely difficult to identify income and expenditure on a domain basis. Therefore I will limit my discussion to the general features of domain economies as these relate to the commercial tax system.

The most important expenditures of the Sengoku daimyo included: castle building; the construction of wells, ditches, and embankments; mine development and other kinds of engineering projects; the acquisition of firearms, gunpowder, spears, swords, and other military equipment; purchases of everyday consumer goods as well as imported Chinese and other luxury goods appropriate to the prestige of the daimyo; visits to temples and shrines, gifts to the nobility, and other obligations to civil and religious authorities.

From the fifteenth century on, monetary payments increased with the rapid development of a monetized commodity economy and the gradual increase in the proportion of monetary disbursements. The needed corresponding increase in monetary income necessarily came from the following sources: 1. taxes on exports of special products from the domain; 2. land taxes, provincial taxes (*tansen*), commercial frontage taxes, land rents, house rents, and other forms of monetized feudal levies; 3. commercial taxes on influential merchants whose wealth came from trade and usury capitalism; 4. barrier taxes, ship taxes, road taxes, and other forms of transport taxes.

The export taxes listed in category 1 have already been covered in the discussion of policies for the protection of long-distance trade, and will be omitted here. The daimyo could obtain cash from the taxes mentioned in 2 above. Either the peasants had to pay them in cash or the daimyo had to sell the taxes delivered in kind (for the most part rice) for cash. In either case, the amount of cash the daimyo could obtain was limited by the degree of development of *rokusai ichi* (markets held six times monthly) and the castle town, and the demand for rice both within and outside of the domain. The fact that, at the end of the sixteenth century, the Go-Hōjō changed from the kandaka system (which required that the taxes were, in principle, to be paid in cash) to the *kokudaka* system (which required tax payment in rice) reflects the relatively underdeveloped state of the market as well as the still limited and unstable demand for rice.[11]

Transport taxes were a new source of income for the Sengoku daimyo, and their appeal was undeniable. However, as we will touch on later, to guarantee these taxes the daimyo had to be able to assert his authority over the fief holders among his vassals whose fiefs were sometimes situated near highways or rivers and thereby presented the opportunity to set up private barriers. Transport taxes could also be in conflict with the Sengoku daimyo's policies designed to facilitate the domain's internal and external

---

[11] For two opposing views concerning the relationships between the Go-Hōjō protection policies for the six-day markets and the kandaka and kokudaka systems, see Nakamaru Kazunori, "Go-Hōjō-shi no hatten to shōgyō," *Rekishigaku kenkyū* 229 (March 1959), 34-42; and Fujiki Hisashi, *Sengoku shakai shiron* (Tokyo: Tōkyō Daigaku Shuppankai, 1974), pp. 287-96.

Daimyo Rule and Commerce

trade. From the time of Nobunaga, many daimyo chose to abolish toll barriers (*sekisho*) and rely rather on increased trade to bolster domain income.[12]

Among the new revenue sources that were developed in response to the expanded cash expenditures of the Sengoku daimyo, one predictably came in for special emphasis: the various forms of business or enterprise taxes that were levied on merchants and pawnbrokers (*dosō*). For example, the Date of the province of Mutsu in 1533 issued a thirteen-article code, the *Kurakata no okite no koto*, of detailed regulations for the business procedures of dosō and warehouse keepers.[13] Three years later, in 1536, the well-known Date *Jinkaishū* house laws included regulations on pawnbroker activities.[14] These regulations indicate that by the first half of the sixteenth century a monetized commodity economy had developed, and that pawnbrokers were active in the Date domain. Indeed, many of the retainers of the Date house had accumulated sizable debts because they grew more dependent on the market in meeting their needs.[15] Under the circumstances, the Date house could not overlook the wealth being amassed by the pawnbrokers at the expense of their retainers. Thus, the Date began regulating and taxing the pawnbrokers, creating thereby a new revenue source under daimyo control.

The Imagawa house of Suruga offers another example of daimyo policy to levy various taxes on commerce. In 1561, in the laws promulgated in the aftermath of Imagawa Yoshimoto's defeat by Oda Nobunaga at the battle of Okehazama, grants of exemptions from pawnbroker, sake, and other commercial taxes were apparently used as a means of controlling sales of red dye (the domain specialty)

[12] Toyoda, *Zōtei chūsei Nihon shōgyōshi*, pp. 403-406.

[13] See vol. 3 of Satō Shin'ichi and Ikeuchi Yoshisuke, eds., *Chūsei hōsei shiryōshū* (Tokyo: Iwanami Shoten, 1969).

[14] Ibid.

[15] Fujiki Hisashi, "Sengoku daimyō seika ni okeru baichi andosei," *Chihōshi kenkyū* 16 (April 1966): 1-10.

by the Matsuki, the wealthy merchant house that served as the special representative of the Imagawa in Kyoto.[16] It appears that pawnbroker taxes were commonly levied by the Imagawa within their domain and, we can assume, this practice had been effectively systematized. As early as 1526, in the *Imagawa kanamokuroku* house laws, there were articles on goods left as security for loans—clear evidence that economic activity by pawnbrokers was lively enough to require regulation. The systemization of enterprise taxes on pawnbrokers by the Sengoku daimyo at first infringed upon and then replaced the rights to tax pawnbrokers in Kyoto and the surrounding region, which had been exercised by the Muromachi bakufu in the fifteenth century.

Closely related to enterprise taxes were the commercial taxes that had their origin in the taxes on periodic markets during the shōen period. Four types had become common in daimyo domains during the Sengoku period: 1. *dabetsusen* (packhorse taxes), as imposed by the Ashina and Imagawa, in which the quantity of goods was the basis of taxation; 2. enterprise taxes, levied by type of merchant or business; 3. guild taxes (*zayakusen*) on specific goods to protect special guild rights or privileged business activity, such as the taxes instituted by the Uesugi, Takeda, and Imagawa; 4. transport taxes, like those levied on packhorses by the Takeda, on ships by the Ōuchi, and on coolies by other daimyo, in which the form of transport was the basis of taxation.

Analysis of the commercial tax systems of individual daimyo is outside the scope of this essay, but some general observations can be offered on how medieval conditions kept commercial taxes from reaching their full income potential during the Sengoku period. One limitation was that the basis of taxation varied from domain to domain as well as within domains. As indicated earlier, taxes were levied

---

[16] See document 1 in the section "Yairi monjo" in *Shizuoka-ken shiryō* 3, 233. This is dated 1561/11/28 and carries the seal of Imagawa Ujizane. See also document 2, p. 234, dated 1565/7/3.

on such diverse bases as the volume of goods traded, merchant population, and the means of transport, or they were designed to protect special business rights. The existence of so many different forms of tax base suggests that the Sengoku daimyo had not fully grasped the significance of the growing commercial trade or the great possibilities commercial taxes offered as a source of cash income. Their use of commercial taxes remained arbitrary.

Another inhibiting factor was that most Sengoku daimyo still had not perfected their own system for collecting commercial tax revenues. For example, in the Imagawa domain, to obtain tax revenues from traders in cotton and sesame oil, the daimyo had to rely upon the Tomono house, head of the Tomono-za in the Imagawa castle town of Suruga Imajuku. The Tomono held special trade rights for cotton and sesame oil sales, and were able to exploit them by virtue of their special za privileges.[17] In the Takeda domain, to take another example, the Sakata house of Kofu Yōkaichi paid taxes to the daimyo for various types of fish imports. After the fall of the Takeda and their replacement as daimyo by the Katō, the Sakata were made responsible for the collection of tribute from all fish merchants trading in the domain for a total of forty gold *ryō*.[18] The Sakata's appointment as tax collection agents derived from their earlier role as powerful za merchants. Such ad hoc arrangements for tax collection differed from the consolidated and systemized structure for making land surveys and enforcing land tax collections that had been established in most Sengoku daimyo domains by this time. Thus, as these examples testify, the Sengoku daimyo had not developed their own bureaucracy for the efficient collection of commercial taxes.

[17] See document 1 in the section "Tomono monjo" in *Shizuoka-ken shiryō* 3, 250-51. This is dated 1553/2/14 and bears the seal of Imagawa Yoshimoto. Also see document 3, p. 252; dated 1561/8/2 and sealed by Imagawa Ujizane.

[18] For more on the Sakata house see Toyoda, *Zōtei chūsei Nihon shōgyōshi*, pp. 435-54.

Nidome Policies of Trade Restriction

To assure that supplies of essential military and everyday commodities were available in their domains, the Sengoku daimyo combined an aggressive policy of promoting imports of essential goods from outside the domain with a defensive policy involving the regulation of exports from the domain. In those daimyo domains where economic self-sufficiency was difficult or impossible to maintain, export controls and export prohibitions (*nidome*) provided the only effective means of keeping essential internally produced goods within the domain.

Protectionist policies based on nidome, which became common in the Sengoku period, can be traced to the 1540s, when Oda Nobunaga and Imagawa Yoshimoto interdicted rice and leather exports. There followed, during the height of warfare between the 1560s and the 1580s, many instances of nidome being used to weaken an enemy by economic blockade. Shimomura Fujio has suggested that nidome policies in the peaceful early modern period necessarily had economic objectives, but that in the Sengoku period such policies were chiefly military in purpose.[19] However, as we will explain below, nidome policies based on purely economic considerations were far from rare during the Sengoku period.

Whether or not efforts to restrict exports of domain commodities were successful depended in the first analysis on the extent to which the Sengoku daimyo could control water and land transport within their domains. Water transport was, of course, considerably harder to police than land transport, with the result that in the western provinces of Japan, where most trade was by sea, efforts at nidome were relatively ineffective. Thus the medieval examples of nidome are found principally in eastern Japan, where most goods were transported overland.

[19] Shimomura Fujio, "Kinsei no bōeki tōsei no ichi kōsatsu—iwayuru tsudome ni tsuite," *Shakai keizai shigaku* 3 (1933), 339-61.

Among the examples of nidome practice in the Kantō, where presumably the policy had a strong military character, is the case of the Yūki house of Shimofusa. The *Yūki-shi shinhatto* house laws issued in 1556 contain nidome restrictions on exports from the domain for clearly economic objectives.[20] Moreover, these laws were designed to regulate not only the economy of the Yūki domain but also the economies of their vassals. Pertinent articles on nidome prescribed that: 1. the determination of nidome policy would be reserved to the Yūki house; 2. the nidome policy, while in the interest of the Yūki house, would be enforced primarily in response to demands from the vassals; 3. the nidome would apply to shipment of goods: a. from other domains to the Yūki domain; b. from the fiefs of powerful Yūki retainers to other domains or to the private Yūki demesne; and c. from the Yūki demesne to vassal fiefs and other daimyo domains. Shippers whose goods did not have transport authorization documents for their cargoes were to be subject to a penalty varying according to the status and residence of the shippers. The most severe penalties were to go to those who shipped goods from the Yūki daimyo's direct holdings without permission; somewhat less onerous were those imposed on shippers of goods from vassal fiefs; the lightest penalties applied to merchants who shipped goods to the Yūki domain from other domains without authorization. The near exemption of traders from outside reflected the need to attract goods from other areas and was similar to the preferential treatment accorded outside traders in most other Sengoku daimyo domains.[21]

Several aspects of the Yūki case are of interest here. First, the nidome policy was applied under certain circumstances to the entire domain, and under other conditions to the domains of the Yūki vassals. That is, local proprietors, as long as they had permission from the Yūki, could adopt

[20] Satō and Ikeuchi, *Chūsei hōsei* 3.
[21] Toyoda, *Zōtei chūsei Nihon shōgyōshi*, p. 343.

their own nidome regulations. Moreover, such policies were motivated more by economic than by military objectives. Second, there was a strong sense of expediency in the Yūki regulations, which seemed to be directed largely to those who did not possess proper authorization. Even when the nidome policy was in force, trade in the controlled commodities could continue if transport documents had been obtained, and ordinary commodity exchanges within the domain are thought to have been relatively free from controls. Third, an intent to influence domain commercial structure is clearly evident in the *Yūki-shi shinhatto* house laws. In it are articles concerning the tranquillity of market towns, the freedom and safety of commercial transactions (articles 8, 17, and 35), the establishment of uniform measures of quantity for rice and sake as well as for the length of textiles (articles 91 and 93), and the standardization of currency rules, the so-called *erizeni* (coin selection) regulations (article 83). The Yūki house thus tried through nidome policies to develop trade within and outside their territory. This, of course, is not meant to deny the military character of many nidome policies of the Sengoku period, namely, to restrict the efforts of retainers to assert their independence and local autonomy within the daimyo domain. However, in my opinion, we must assume that a very few daimyo were able to enforce effectively a nidome policy throughout their domains.

CONTROLS ON MERCHANTS

Historical precedents can be found for some features of merchant control in the commercial policies of the Sengoku daimyo. For example, in the Kamakura period the *jitō ryōshu* (local military land stewards) used merchants as well as *kashiage* and *sansō*—both of whom engaged in money lending—to serve as tax agents.[22] However, it is

---

[22] The various provincial jitō appointed money lenders (sansō and

clear that the Sengoku daimyo were the first to regulate
large numbers of merchants and to go so far as to fix their
social status, as well.

A typical example of the control exerted by a daimyo
over merchants was the appointment of powerful za merchants from within their domains as magistrates or supervisory merchants in charge of commerce (shōnin tsukasa or
shōnin kashira). Similarly, to oversee the activities of artisans within the domain, influential artisans were given positions as supervising artisans such as head carpenter
(*sōkanshiki* and *sōdaikushiki*).[23] This practice is evident in the
appointments of the Tomono as shōnin kashira by the
Imagawa, the Yanada as shōnin tsukasa by the Date, and
the Itō as shōnin tsukasa over the provinces of Owari and
Mino by Oda Nobunaga.[24]

The particular duties assigned to these merchants indicate the central role such merchant houses played in the
commercial policies of the Sengoku daimyo. Thus the
Yanada were to oversee outside merchants active in the
Date domain, set up markets (*ichidate*), and take care of
disputes that occurred between merchants and bandits.[25]
The Tomono were to supervise merchants from other
provinces who resided in or stayed the night in one of the
cities located in the Imagawa domain, examine goods ex-
ported from the domain, and collect the various commercial taxes levied by the Imagawa. The Kurata were to
supervise the za that controlled trade in hemp, which was
the special product of the domain, supervise exports of

kashiage) and merchants as agents (*jitō daikan*), but since they customarily
used the position for profit, the bakufu repeatedly issued edicts prohibiting the practice. See, for example, Satō and Ikeuchi, *Chūsei hōsei* 1, doc.
116, pp. 113-14, and doc. 120, p. 116.

[23] Toyoda, *Zōtei chūsei Nihon shōgyōshi*, p. 87.

[24] Ibid., pp. 436-54.

[25] "Yanada monjo" item 7 (1589/7/13) in Fukushima Ken, ed.,
Fukushima Kenshi (Fukushima. Fukushima Kenchō Bunsho Kōhōka,
1966), vol. 7.

hemp, superintend all residents of the Uesugi castle town of Kasugayama, and guard Funai and Kasugayama.

One special characteristic of the Sengoku daimyo's efforts to oversee the activities of merchants was that the powerful merchants of the above variety performed functions within the apparatus of feudal control and in some instances were themselves given warrior status. In exchange for their services to the daimyo, these merchants were guaranteed special business rights, given exemptions from their individual land and service taxes, and granted other favors. For instance, when castle towns were constructed or periodic markets established, or when *rakuichi-rakuza* (free market) orders were issued, the merchants in service to the daimyo might be exempted from all tax levies imposed on other merchants and artisans. Their exemptions from commercial and residence taxes were, in principle, granted in exchange for the service they rendered to the daimyo. Thus, such exemptions were analogous to the exemption from dues that local village ryōshu received on the supplemental income (kajishi) that the daimyo knew, through the cadastral survey, they had been receiving from the villagers. That is, in this case, the daimyo was waiving dues on the income of these village ryōshu in order to define the lord-vassal relationship between himself and these ryōshu. As the merchants owed services to the daimyo for receiving the tax exemptions, these ryōshu owed military services to the daimyo by becoming vassals. In either case, the principle was the same: the status of both the merchants and the ryōshu was being defined within a feudal polity that was being created by the daimyo.

As noted above, the powerful merchants in daimyo domains—like the Yanada, Tomono, Itō, and Kurata—often had surnames and bushi ancestry, as did the dogō and jizamurai. Some, like the Kurata, even had military forces at their disposal. One could almost say that, under the rule of the Sengoku daimyo, these powerful merchants were a part of the ruling class, both in status and in function. The Matsuki, who served under the Imagawa, in addition to commercial service also loaned funds to the Imagawa and their retainers, and together with the Tomono held the special status of merchants by appointment. Subsequently those who entered service as members of the Imagawa kashindan were exempted from all payments except their rice and monetary debts to the Matsuki.[26]

Relations between the Sengoku period daimyo and powerful merchants who, like the property holding artisans in the Go-Hōjō *Odawarashū shoryō yakuchō* (Duty roster of domains in the Odawara group), were listed in the same manner as other members of the kashindan, should not be compared to the relations between bushi and merchants and artisans in early modern society under the bakuhan system, where important status differences existed. In the Sengoku period, when the four-class system of samurai, peasant, artisan, and merchant had not yet been established, it is possible that not only bushi but also powerful merchants and artisans, being granted warrior status, were included in the ruling structure. This is one of the most intriguing questions still to be studied regarding the character of Sengoku daimyo authority.

KOKUJIN RYŌSHU CONTROLS ON TRADE AND THEIR ELIMINATION

A serious obstacle to more effective control by the Sengoku daimyo over trade within their domains was the independent local authority of the kokujin ryōshu, dogō, jizamurai, and other small village proprietors within their domains, each of whom had entrenched local interests over commerce that were in competition with or in opposition to those of the daimyo. Local ryōshu historically retained authority over the operation of periodic markets within their

---

[26] See document 2 (1565/7/13) of "Yairi monjo" in *Shizuoka-ken shiryō* 3, 234.

fiefs, assigning certain village merchants from within or
without their fiefs to subordinate roles, much like protégés.
Such local proprietors held independent tax rights over
markets, merchants, and goods traded, as well as the right
to regulate transit on major roads and to erect toll gates.
To cite two examples, vassals of the Yūki as well as the
Kuchiki house, a powerful landed proprietor in the province of Ōmi, both held the authority to enforce nidome
policy on their own initiative.[27]

Though the elimination of the local authority of the
kokujin ryōshu was an obvious prerequisite to the assertion
of their own full authority over commerce, the Sengoku
daimyo could not always afford to eliminate the independent authority of their vassals. A policy of coexistence and
compromise was often required by local circumstances.
This condition is well illustrated in the changing relations
between the Rokkaku house, a Sengoku daimyo of the
province of Ōmi, and the kokujin ryōshu, who later became vassals of the daimyo. In Ōmi during the fifteenth
century the great Enryakuji on Mt. Hiei, as the largest
shōen proprietor in the area, arbitrated and settled any
disputes among merchants in the village markets, and the
Rokkaku as shugo enforced the settlements. By the beginning of the sixteenth century, however, disputes that
erupted in the periodic markets of Mabuchi, Yōkaichi, and
Shimagō on the eastern shore of Lake Biwa were being
settled directly by kokujin, vassals of the Rokkaku, who
controlled the area and had established the markets. These
proprietors—the Iba, Kuri, Takebe, Shimagō, and others
—issued documents prescribing the settlements.

This development, which challenged the authority of
both the Enryakuji and the Rokkaku, reflected the fact that
the local proprietors were strengthening their rights to
administer their fiefs and the periodic markets located

[27] Suzuki Atsuko, "Kokujin ryōshu Kuchiki-shi no sangyō-ryūtsū
shihai," *Shisō* 17 (Tokyo: Nihon Joshidai, 1976).

within them. In 1549, however, in the *Rokkaku bugyōnin rensho hōshoan*, the Rokkaku ordered that the new Ishidera market established in the castle town of Kannonji become a free market.[28] The Rokkaku, at least in form, were asserting their superior authority over that of local proprietors to award special business rights and monopolies in new markets. Many documents concerning this effort survive, including those giving evidence that many local proprietors in Ōmi successfully resisted the elimination of all of their rights to exercise their authority over markets.[29] On the other hand, documents issued by the Go-Hōjō and other daimyo in the 1560s and 1580s establishing periodic markets and fixing the days of operation within their domains would seem to indicate a greater concentration of power in daimyo hands.

The same is true for commercial taxes. Article 25 of the 1526 *Imagawa kana mokuroku* house laws ordered vassals to stop collecting transport taxes in the provinces of Suruga and Tōtōmi on merchants and on goods shipped by water, and in Tōtōmi on goods transported by pack animals. This is an early example of a daimyo's effort to divest his retainers of the right to levy commercial taxes.

Another impediment to full Sengoku daimyo control over domain commerce was the local authority of the kokujin ryōshu type of vassals to maintain toll barriers. To return to Ōmi province as an example, from the late fifteenth through the sixteenth centuries kokujin ryōshu erected toll barriers at Norisaka, Oiwake, Ōsugi, and elsewhere along the major road, the famous Kurihan kaidō, linking the

[28] *Imabori Hie Jinja monjo* (Shiga-ken, Yōkaichi-shi, Hie Monjo Kankō-kai, 1975), no. 112 (1549/12/11), "Shugo Rokkaku-shi hōkōnin rensho hōshoan."

[29] Sasaki Gin'ya, "Ryōiki shōgyō keisei katei no shōgyō seisaku," *Rekishi kōron* 3 (April 1977), 106-15; Wakita Haruko, *Nihon chūsei shōgyō hattatsushi no kenkyū* (Tokyo: Ochanomizu Shobō, 1969), pp. 578-79. Although the Rokkaku house held the right to settle these market disputes within their domain, in fact they could not afford to ignore the influence of the kokujin ryōshu in each region.

provinces of Ōmi and Wakasa.[30] Here again the Rokkaku had to use the settlements of disputes among Ōmi merchants who traveled the Kurihan kaidō as opportunities to assert their rights to control transit and toll barrier construction throughout the province. The extent to which the Sengoku daimyo were effective in assuming rights traditionally held by the kokujin ryōshu cannot be generalized. Success or failure, however, had a profound impact on the cash deficit and troubled economies of the Sengoku daimyo.

CONCLUSIONS

A number of questions require further study before the full story of Sengoku daimyo commercial policies becomes clear. There remain, for example, such matters as the relationship between commerce and the kandaka system; the promotion and construction of castle towns, cities, and markets as the nucleus of the domain economy; the practice of erizeni, which resulted from the use of numerous kinds of coins; the needs to deal with serious problems caused by an increasing indebtedness among the bushi, merchants, and peasants; and one effort at solution, the promulgation of debt cancellation (*tokusei*) edicts. In addition, we need more research on commercial development by western daimyo. The fact that the specific examples cited in this essay are biased toward the daimyo of eastern Japan is attributable entirely to their preponderance in the surviving documents. In western Japan, the development of waterborne transport centered on the Inland Sea and the impact of foreign trade with Korea, China, and Europeans led to more rapid growth of trade than that in eastern Japan. The question of what kinds of commercial policies were used by the western daimyo, as well as the

---

[30] Suzuki Atsuko, "Kokujin ryōshu." In this paper Suzuki discusses in detail the establishment of Kuchiki authority in the region north of Lake Biwa.

question of what kinds of economic and commercial policies were common to both eastern and western daimyo, are important issues that remain to be pursued in the future.

To the extent that generalizations can be justified at this point, I should like to offer a hypothesis concerning the historical development of commercial policies adopted by the Sengoku daimyo. I believe that there were three relatively distinct stages of development. A first stage occurred during the period from the Ōnin War of the late fifteenth century through the first half of the sixteenth, when the productive capacity of peasants within the domain increased, the upper level of peasants gained a degree of independence, and the social differentiation of commerce and the specialization of the handicraft industry progressed. By this time the framework of the shōen-shugo daimyo system had given way to a condition of political fragmentation under the local authority of kokujin. The emerging Sengoku daimyo had to overcome competition from the kokujin ryōshu and establish sound economies, and to do so required further military conquest within their domains. This period should therefore be assessed as a preliminary stage in which the pains of developing the domain economies were first experienced.

In the second period, roughly the last half of the sixteenth century, the Sengoku daimyo were able to assert control over the kokujin ryōshu, and began to conduct cadastral surveys and to exert more influence over commerce. While not all of these political and economic policies fully realized the goals of the Sengoku daimyo, this was a distinct stage during which the power of the Sengoku daimyo over kokujin and commerce rose perceptibly.

The third period, from around 1620 to 1660, was a time during which the previous efforts of Nobunaga and Hideyoshi to unify the nation continued to have an effect and the Tokugawa bakuhan system reached its first stabilization. Though by this time the Sengoku daimyo as such and their domain economies had disappeared, the pattern of development of agriculture and commerce had not changed fundamentally since the mid-sixteenth century. In fact, this continuity was a special characteristic of this third period. The promotion of long-distance trade and enforcement of nidome policies during the sixteenth century had contributed to making the domain economies more self-sufficient. However, no Sengoku daimyo, attempting to create a politically stable and economically self-sufficient domain, could have succeeded on his own. It was only within the framework of the bakuhan system, based on a strong central authority, that the daimyo finally succeeded in forcing or enticing the kokujin to live in castle towns, thus depriving them of their power base, and in establishing full control over merchants and market activities, that is, over all aspects of commerce.

1. Portrait of Oda Nobunaga dating from shortly after his death.

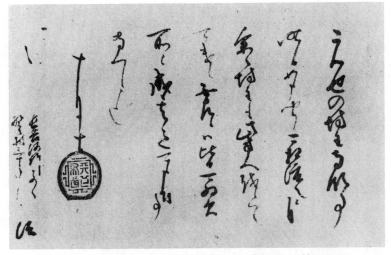

2. *Oda Nobunaga's "Tenka Fubu" seal affixed to an order to two of his retainers.*

3. *The battle of Nagashino, 1575, showing Nobunaga's early use of firearms.*

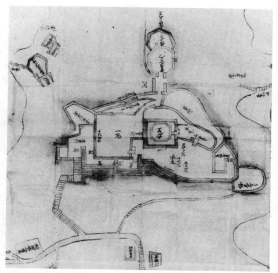

4. *Sketch map of the base plan of Azuchi castle showing moats, walls, and the main keep.*

5. *Hikone castle retains today many features of Oda-Toyotomi era castle architecture.*

6. *Portrait of Toyotomi Hideyoshi in court robes.*

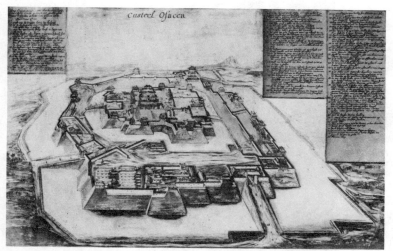

7. *Osaka castle before its destruction, sketched by a Dutch resident in Japan.*

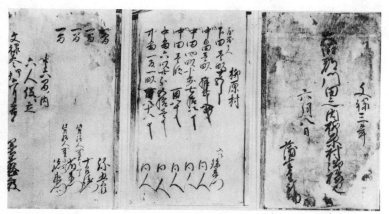

8. *Example of a* kenchi-chō *dated 1594. In this instance assessment is still stated in kandaka terms.*

9. *Officials surveying rice fields.*

10. *The storming of Osaka castle in 1615.*

11. Nijō castle, Tokugawa headquarters in Kyoto, begun in 1603 by Ieyasu.

12. Horses laden with bales of rice.

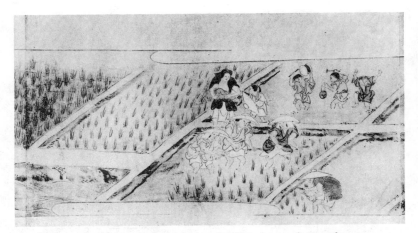

13. Women transplanting rice to the rhythm of children beating drum and gong.

14. Improved irrigation techniques were among the technological features that increased agricultural production during the sixteenth century.

Chapter 5

The Political Posture
of Oda Nobunaga

Fujiki Hisashi
with George Elison

ODA NOBUNAGA's entry into the capital city of Kyoto in
1568 marked the coming of a new era in Japanese history.
Most modern chronologies give this date as the terminal
point of the Sengoku period, and Nobunaga's advent to
national prominence is considered the first step in the establishment of the regime of unification that restored
order to Japan after a century of war. But contemporary
observers who perceived the epochal nature of the event
were surely rare. Nobunaga's march on Kyoto seemed to
have traditional objectives: he was a daimyo who cham-
pioned the cause of one pretender to the Ashikaga shogunate against a claimant who had been emplaced in the
bakufu by other daimyo; in the history of Sengoku this was
nothing new. To be sure, Nobunaga's candidate Ashikaga
Yoshiaki had a better claim to succeed the murdered Shogun Yoshiteru than his cousin Yoshihide, who owed his position to the assassins, the so-called Miyoshi Triumvirs.
More pertinent to the outcome, however, was that
Nobunaga had the bigger battalions. The Miyoshi offered
only token resistance to his forces and withdrew from
Kyoto, Yoshihide died in flight even as the brief campaign
was ending, and Yoshiaki was consequently installed in the
shogunate without much trouble. These facts would have
passed into chronicles as the details of an ordinary Sengoku affair—being attributed perhaps to *tentō* (fortune)—

save for one thing: soon enough, it became apparent that Nobunaga was no ordinary Sengoku daimyo, and was pursuing policies that were anything but traditional.

What was the nature of those policies and of Nobunaga's statecraft? What, in short, was his political posture? Recent studies of the foundations of early modern Japan (Kinsei) have sought to shed light on the political character of Nobunaga's regime as an emergent national governmental system by inquiring into its relations with the traditional centers of authority—the emperor, the civil and religious elite, and the shogunate.[1] This approach has contributed much to our understanding of Nobunaga, and the present essay follows the same direction. By "political posture," therefore, is meant especially the regime's governmental and legal relationship with the traditional structure of authority, that fusion of imperial and military hierarchies which for some four hundred years had constituted central government in Japan.

Nobunaga's relations with both the imperial court and the shogunate antedate 1568. Although the year is not absolutely certain, it appears that official envoys were dispatched to Nobunaga by Emperor Ōgimachi and by Shogun Yoshiteru in the winter of Eiroku 7 (1564-1565); in other words, the highest central authorities, imperial and military, made political overtures to Nobunaga as he was trying to expand his control from Owari province westward into Mino.[2] Yoshiteru was assassinated in the summer

[1] See particularly the following works: Asao Naohiro, "Bakuhansei to tennō," *Taikei Nihon kokka shi,* edited by Hara Hidesaburō et al. 3 (*Kinsei*) (Tokyo: Tōkyō Daigaku Shuppankai, 1975), 187-222; Miki Seiichirō, "Nobunaga no kuni-okite o megutte," *Shinano* 28:5 (1976), 24-34; Miki Seiichirō, "Sengoku-Kinsei shoki ni okeru kokka to tennō," *Rekishi hyōron* 320 (1976), 15-30; Okuno Takahiro, "Oda seiken no kihon rosen," *Kokushigaku* 100 (1976), 29-58; Sasaki Junnosuke, "Nobunaga ni okeru 'gaibun' to 'Tenka' ni tsuite," *Niigata shigaku* 8 (1975), 1-11; Wakita Osamu, *Oda seiken no kiso kōzō, Shokuhō seiken no bunseki* 1 (Tokyo: Tōkyō Daigaku Shuppankai, 1975); Wakita Osamu, *Kinsei hōkensei seiritsushi ron, Shokuhō seiken no bunseki* 2 (Tōkyō: Tōkyō Daigaku Shuppankai, 1977).

[2] See Okuno Takahiro, *Oda Nobunaga monjo no kenkyū,* no. 52, vol. 1

of 1565 and we know that, as the year drew to a close, Nobunaga expressed the positive ambition to install the murdered shogun's younger brother Kakukei—the future Yoshiaki—in power in Kyoto, and responded to Kakukei's request for support with the assurance that he was "absolutely determined to accompany His Highness to the Capital whenever so ordered."[3] When Nobunaga completed his conquest of Mino in 1567, destroying Saitō Tatsuoki and moving his headquarters to Gifu, he received imperial approval for his "unparalleled designs."[4] Also dating from this time was his adoption for his seal of the slogan *Tenka fubu*, "the realm subjected to the military."[5] It expressed publicly his confidence in his plans. By now these had a solid goal: to advance upon the capital in the name of the emperor and in the cause of Ashikaga Yoshiaki.

This aspiration may have been shared by other Sengoku daimyo—indeed, the goal was within easier reach of

---

(2nd ed., Tokyo: Yoshikawa Kōbunkan, 1971), 93-94. This is the copy of a letter dated-/12/20, signed Oda Sansuke Nobunaga, and addressed to the Bakufu official Ōdachi Saemon no Suke; in it, Nobunaga expresses his gratitude for the receipt of a direct message (*gonaisho*) from the shogun. Okuno places the letter in the year Eiroku 7 because there is no instance of Nobunaga's using the name Sansuke after that date.

On the mission of Tateri Sōkei (Munetsugu), the imperial court's envoy to Nobunaga, see Takao Kazuhiko, "Nobunaga nyūkyō," *Kyōto no rekishi* 4, edited by Kyōto-shi (Tokyo: Gakugei Shorin, 1969), 47-50.

[3] Okuno, *Monjo*, no. 60, vol. 1, 112. The earliest extant example of Nobunaga's use of the character *rin* (for the mythological beast camelopard) as his signature cypher occurs in this letter. Since the camelopard is the rarest of prodigies and the possessor of sublime virtues, Nobunaga's adoption of this cypher is supposed by some historians to express a new and positive political concept, symbolizing a vow to bring about peace and order in the realm. See Satō Shin'ichi, "Nihon kaōshi no issetsu: 16-seiki no buke no kaō," *Nagoya Daigaku Nihonshi ronshū* 2 (Tokyo: Yoshikawa Kōbunkan, 1975), 8; cf. Satō, "Kaō shōshi," *Sho no Nihonshi* 9 (Tokyo: Heibonsha, 1976), 72-73 and 246.

[4] See Okuno, *Monjo* 1, 126-27.

[5] The earliest extant documents that bear the *Tenka fubu* seal are dated Eiroku 10/11/-; see Okuno, *Monjo*, nos. 77 and 79-81, vol. 1, 139-40 and 142-45, and supp. no. 10, 2nd ed., vol. 2 (1973), 842; cf. 2, 944.

some—but Nobunaga was the one who transformed it into an actual policy. Let us have a look at one or two contrary examples. From the time of his escape from the Ichijōin, the Nara monastery whose abbot he was, Kakukei sent repeated requests for assistance to the great daimyo of Echigo, Uesugi Kenshin, and several times received promises of support from him.[6] In the end, however, Kenshin undertook nothing; he was too distant from Kyoto and too involved with other conflicts to be a realistic hope for the would-be shogun. That, however, was not the case with Asakura Yoshikage of Echizen, under whose protection Yoshiaki put himself in 1566; but beyond his hospitality and sympathy, Yoshikage offered the exile nothing. Nobunaga alone had the vision to act. To be sure, the resurrection of the old regime was not Nobunaga's objective; rather, he used Yoshiaki for the purpose of legitimating his own aspirations.

On the seventh day of the ninth month, Eiroku 11 (1568), Nobunaga began his march on Kyoto, leading a "four-province host" composed of his vassals from Owari, Mino, and Ise, and his ally Tokugawa Ieyasu's Mikawa samurai.[7] The army swept aside the opposition mounted

[6] The earliest extant announcement of Kakukei's intention to compete for the shogunate is the letter he addressed to Uesugi Danjō no Shōhitsu [Kenshin] on [Eiroku 8 (1565)]/8/5, one week after his escape from the Ichijōin monastery to Wata Koremasa's fort in Ōmi; see *Dai Nihon komonjo, Iewake* 12: *Uesugi-ke monjo*, no. 506, vol. 1, compiled by Tōkyō Teikoku Daigaku Bungakubu Shiryō Hensanjo (Tokyo: Shiryō Hensanjo, 1931), 498. The matter occasioned a fairly copious correspondence: ibid., pp. 495-509, documents dated from [Eiroku 8]/6/16 to [Eiroku 9]/7/1; vol. 3, compiled by Tōkyō Daigaku Shiryō Hensanjo (Tokyo: Tōkyō Daigaku Shuppankai, 1963), 177-81, documents dated from [Eiroku 9]/9/13 to Eiroku 10/7/1; and no. 1187, vol. 3, 235, Yoshiaki to Uesugi Danjō no Shōhitsu, dated Eiroku 10/2/24.
A handy summary of Yoshiaki's activities from his escape from Nara to his installation as shogun in Kyoto will be found in Okuno Takahiro, *Ashikaga Yoshiaki*, Jinbutsu Sōsho 55 (Tokyo: Yoshikawa Kōbunkan, 1974), 99-139.
[7] Details of the campaign in Ōta Izumi no Kami Gyūichi, *Shinchō kōki*

by Rokkaku Shōtei in Ōmi province, and on the twenty-sixth of the same month Nobunaga and Yoshiaki entered the capital. On the eighteenth day of the tenth month, Emperor Ōgimachi formally invested Yoshiaki with the title of shogun. But it is clear that from the very beginning the emperor did not view the newly revived bakufu as a unitary organism with the shogun in command. For that matter, neither did people in general.

The emperor gave Yoshiaki and Nobunaga simultaneous orders for the imperial court's estates to be restored, expecting Nobunaga to use his actual power in the execution of directives nominally issued by the shogunate. Ordinary petitioners also sought to obtain the double assurance of a shogunal disposition (*gogeji*) and also one with Nobunaga's vermilion seal (*goshuin*). There are quite a few instances of governmental ordinances put into effect by the parallel issuance of that typical bakufu administrative directive, the *bugyōnin rensho hōsho* (jointly signed by more than one of the shogunate's administrative officers, *bugyōnin*), along with orders issued over Nobunaga's goshuin.[8] Apparently it was assumed that a disposition was apt to have little effect unless it was made by the bakufu with the full sanction of its powerful protector. This was the actual state of affairs in the central government. At the very least, the fact that the shogunate's administrative directives and Nobunaga's vermilion-seal letters were issued in parallel means that Nobunaga did not function as the shogun's subordinate in the capacity of a bakufu official, but occupied a position independent of the shogunate's corps of administrators. This independence Nobunaga meant to preserve.

Shinchō kōki, the chronicle of Nobunaga's exploits, tells us that Yoshiaki, immediately after becoming shogun, sought

(c. 1610), edited by Okuno Takahiro and Iwasawa Yoshihiko, Kadokawa Bunko 2541 (Tokyo: Kadokawa Shoten, 1970), pt. 1, secs. 3-4, pp. 84-89.

[8] Examples of such parallel issuance from the year 1568 are: Okuno, *Monjo*, no. 124, vol. 1, 211-13; ibid., nos. 126-27, pp. 214-21.

to have Nobunaga accept a post equivalent to vice-shogun or *kanrei* (the bakufu's chief executive officer, sometimes rendered "deputy shogun").[9] This story is of interest as an indication of Yoshiaki's early discomfort at Nobunaga's independent posture, and as evidence of a plan on his part to shut in Nobunaga within the confines of the shogunate's structure. The following year the emperor also urged Nobunaga to assume the position of vice-shogun.[10] This manner of handling the obvious problem posed by the hegemon's presence at the fulcrum of political power was evidently a notion held by the imperial and the shogunal establishments alike. There is, however, a delicate point to consider: the post of vice-shogun as such had no precedent in the history of the shogunate's organization. Here we may perceive some measure of the perplexity into which the Kyoto authorities were thrown by Nobunaga. The man who refused to accept appointment as vice-shogun despite an imperial command to do so showed a remarkable political determination. This resoluteness could only lead to an intensified antagonism between Nobunaga, on the one hand, and both the shogun and the emperor, on the other.

Amidst the gala atmosphere of Nō performances and courtly entertainments that prevailed in Kyoto after Yoshiaki's proclamation as shogun, potential antagonisms were obscured and happy concord seemed to prevail. On the twenty-fourth of the tenth month, Nobunaga took his leave of Yoshiaki, and the next day received from the shogun a letter lavish with words of praise and gratitude. This letter was addressed to "My Father, Lord Oda Danjō no Jō," and offered Nobunaga the use of the Ashikaga family's armorial bearings.[11] Freshly become the fifteenth Ashikaga shogun, Yoshiaki did not yet suspect that he would also be the last.

[9] *Shinchō kōki*, 1.5, p. 89.
[10] *Dai Nihon shiryō*, ser. 10, vol. 2, compiled by Tōkyō Teikoku Daigaku Bungakubu Shiryō Hensanjo (Tokyo: Shiryō Hensanjo, 1928), 7; extract from *Tokitsugu-kyō ki*, entry for Eiroku 12/3/2.
[11] *Shinchō kōki* 1.6, pp. 91-92.

Nobunaga's Relations with the Shogun

For all the pious tones of address to "My Father," written in the early days of his advent to power, Shogun Yoshiaki's manner with regard to Nobunaga was destined to be anything but filial. Before the year 1569 was over, Yoshiaki had quarreled with his protector so severely that the emperor had to intercede.[12] Before another year had passed, Nobunaga was fighting a war with a coalition of religious and secular lords who aimed at his encirclement and destruction; some historians believe that the shogun was an accomplice in that league from an early date. Naturally enough, Nobunaga's attitude toward the man he had installed as shogun and nominal head of the military hierarchy was never one of perfect deference. Eventually it became one of overt hostility.

The development of a public confrontation between Nobunaga and Yoshiaki is expressed intensely in three political documents dating from early 1569, right after the shogunate's restoration, to late 1572, when its fall was near at hand. These documents illustrate how thoroughly Nobunaga intruded himself into the shogunate's routine business, and how free he felt to criticize Yoshiaki's administration of affairs.

The background of the first one is, however, not a conflict between Nobunaga and Yoshiaki, but quite the reverse.[13] In the first days of the New Year, Eiroku 12 (1569), forces mobilized by the Three Miyoshi, taking advantage of Nobunaga's absence from Kyoto, attacked the Honkokuji, where Yoshiaki was staying. Only the determined resistance of his own bodyguard and of Nobunaga's vassals

---

[12] See *Tamon'in nikki*, edited by Tsuji Zennosuke 2, *Zōho Zoku shiryō taisei*, edited by Takeuchi Rizō 39 (Kyoto: Rinsen Shoten, 1978), 152, entry for Eiroku 12/10/19. On the emperor's efforts to placate the hegemon, see Okuno Takahiro, *Ashikaga Yoshiaki*, pp. 158-59. The nature of the quarrel is unclear.

[13] On these events, see *Shinchō kōki* 2.1-3, pp. 93-96, and cf. Okuno, *Monjo* 1, 236, where a slightly different chronology is given.

in the area prevented the shogun's residence from being overwhelmed. When a courier brought news of the attack to Nobunaga's castle town of Gifu, Nobunaga dropped everything and hurried to the rescue, completing the three days' journey in two, although he had to ride through a fierce snowstorm that cost the lives of several attendants. By the time he reached Kyoto, the episode was over, but the crisis had evidently given him substantial leverage over Yoshiaki. Fearing a repetition of the attack, Nobunaga gave orders that Nijō castle, where Yoshiteru had met his end, be made into a safe residence for the shogun. But even before work on the fortifications had started, Nobunaga—only a few days after his arrival in the capital—presented Yoshiaki with a set of "regulations for the shogunal residence" (*Denchū On'okite*).

The *Denchū On'okite* is a document in nine articles dated Eiroku 12/1/14 (30 January 1569), with a supplement in seven articles dated two days later.[14] The document, issued over Nobunaga's cypher, was acknowledged with Shogun Yoshiaki's seal at the head of the text; it had a public character and a legal force, regulating the activities of the shogun's entourage. Nobunaga, we recall, held no bakufu post; hence the very fact that he put his name to such a document must be considered extraordinary. In effect, the shogun was from the very beginning of his term in office forced to accept an outsider's control over his administration.

What could Nobunaga have intended to accomplish by thus imposing his will upon the shogun? He apparently wanted to prevent the tightening of private bonds between Yoshiaki and his shogunal retainers, the mainstays of the bakufu. In the body of the regulations, he therefore dic-

[14] Okuno, *Monjo*, no. 142, vol. 1, 239-43. From the fact that these regulations have been transmitted to the present day in two collections of documents as disparate as the Ninnaji Monjo and the Mōri-ke Komonjo, we may deduce that they were indeed made public, probably for the purposes of propaganda.

tated to the shogun what types of persons were to be permitted entry into his residence, and who would be denied access to him. Moreover, he evidently thought it wise to keep a close eye on the shogun's involvement in jurisdiction, intending to make sure that the bakufu's judicial processes were fair and impartial.

The supplement makes it clear why Nobunaga should have considered the regulations necessary. Its first four articles address themselves to a major problem, the abuse of the shogun's authority by shogunal vassals; here Nobunaga condemns the illegal actions that were in fact being undertaken by persons directly subject to Yoshiaki. The first article enjoins the shogun's entourage from usurping temple and shrine domains; the second prohibits arbitrary delegation of authority; the third proscribes fights and quarrels; the fourth orders a stop to unreasonable extortions. There follow three articles that clearly demonstrate Nobunaga's intent to keep the shogun's judicial authority from being used to abet and justify his intimates' circumventions of legality. The fifth article prohibits direct petitions to the shogun, and the sixth orders petitioners to go through the proper channels, that is, bugyōnin, in bringing suit; the seventh and last specifies that shogunal dispositions (gogeji) regarding current holdings of land (*tōchigyō*) shall be made according to the documentary evidence. Surely these were not hortatory statements of general principle but rather the opposite—determinate approaches to actual problems.

After the shogunate's "restoration," Yoshiaki was able to draw on a significant force of household troops in the central area around Kyoto. How to bring the independent activities of this shogunal bodyguard's leading members under control was one of Nobunaga's main political problems. Propaganda was one possible way. By making his criticism of Yoshiaki public, Nobunaga would not only broadcast his own political preeminence but would also expose the shogun's regime to opprobrium throughout the realm.

We may regard the fact that he twice refused the post of vice-shogun as inseparable from his design to draw a sharp line between his own regime and that of Yoshiaki.

One year after the *Denchū On'okite*, Nobunaga again sought to impose his will on Yoshiaki with respect to the shogunate's conduct of its own affairs. He did so by forcing yet another formal compact on the shogun. This is the second of our three illustrative documents, a five-item set of "capitulations" (*Jōjō*) issued over Nobunaga's vermilion seal, dated Eiroku 13/1/23 (27 February 1570) and addressed to Nichijō Shōnin and Akechi Jūbyōe no Jō (Mitsuhide), Nobunaga's intermediaries in Kyoto.[15] This document, too, was acknowledged with Yoshiaki's seal at the head of the text and assumed a legal form. We may consider the shogun's acceptance of these capitulations as having been the precondition for restoring amity between him and Nobunaga after their quarrel of the previous year's tenth month.

Item [1] of the capitulations states: "Should there be occasion for [the shogun] to send orders to the provinces in the form of letters issued over his own signature [*gonaisho*], he shall inform Nobunaga, who will append his letter of endorsement." Item [2] then declares that all prior shogunal directives (gogeji) are void and that Yoshiaki sought to make new dispositions only after careful consideration. The significance of this order can only be understood when one recognizes that the word gogeji had a precise legal meaning.[16] Unlike the shogun's gonaisho (ordinary

---

[15] Okuno, *Monjo*, no. 209, vol. 1, 343-45.

[16] *Gogeji* is the contemporary reading attested by João Rodrigues S.J., for a term that had been read *ongechi* during the earlier middle ages. See Rodrigues' *Arte da lingoa de Iapam* (Em Nangasaqui [Nagasaki] no Collegio de Iapão da Companhia de IESV, 1604), f. 190; facsimile published by Shima Shōzō, *Rodorigesu Nihon daibunten* (Tokyo: Bunka Shobō Hakubunsha, 1969), p. 379: "Goguengi. *Carta em nome do* Cubŏ sama, *ou por ordem sua por algum seu* Buguiŏ." Rodrigues' elaborate treatment of the language and the types of Japanese correspondence is highly instructive and fully worth reading, either in the original, *Arte*, ff. 189-206v (Shima,

correspondence), circumscribed by the preceding item [1], gogeji referred specifically to the shogun's most important legal dicta. It is clear from the usage of the term in article [7] of the previously discussed supplement to the regulations of 1569, moreover, that the usual connotation of gogeji was that of documents issued to guarantee landholdings. Hence it is clear that the gogeji were part of the shogun's exercise of his authority to grant and confirm proprietorships, and that item [2] of the capitulations demanded the invalidation and revision of the confirmatory titles to land issued in the shogun's name. This point corresponds directly to one of the major objectives of the previous year's regulations: Nobunaga's claim to disciplinary control over the shogun's direct subordinates and their unlawful activities.

The capitulations were forced on Yoshiaki at a time when disputes over rights to proprietorship were proliferating. These disputes between the shogunal regime and shōen proprietors, brought on in the main by the way the shogun's power to confirm or withdraw such rights was exercised, occasioned considerable litigation, in which Nobunaga could not help being involved. The extant documents make it appear that much of the trouble was caused by the misuse of the shogun's authority on the part of subordinates, who at times made dispositions in regard to property on their own initiative and in their own interests. The objective of item [2] of the capitulations was to invalidate such baseless and unfair dispositions, have them reevaluated under Nobunaga's supervision, and thereby eliminate the cause of widespread discontent.

A good illustrative case is Nobunaga's defense of the interests that the Zen nunnery Dongein had in Ōzumi-no-shō, an estate in Yamashiro province. On Eiroku 12 (1569)/4/20, Nobunaga issued a vermilion-seal document

pp. 377-412), or in the nicely edited Japanese translation by Doi Tadao, *Nihon daibunten* (Tokyo: Sanseidō, 1967), pp. 678-739.

to the convent's estate administrator (*zasshō*) in which he
noted that the Dongein had since the previous year's wars
and upheavals failed to receive certain land rents due it
from Ōzumi-no-shō, ruled that it should have full and
direct control over those dues hereafter, and assured the
Dongein that he would not tolerate interference with its
rights.[17] Within a year, however, Nobunaga was forced to
renew his assurance because one of Shogun Yoshiaki's
closest associates, Isshiki Fujinaga, was making illegal pre-
tensions to the property.[18] The matter dragged on incon-
clusively for several more months,[19] and on Genki 2
(1571)/7/5, Nobunaga wrote to Yoshiaki's attendant Ueno
Hidemasa and his own agent Akechi Mitsuhide, asking
them to bring the case of the Dongein to the shogun's personal attention: not only had the convent's rights been
guaranteed in the past by the shogun, he reminded them,
but this was a matter in which Nobunaga's reputation was
at stake as well.[20] Two weeks later, Nobunaga felt compelled to write the shogun's attendants yet again. On this
occasion he expressed astonishment that the bakufu should
have installed its own manager (*gokyūnin*) in the estate, and
once again warned that this was a matter affecting his own
honor.[21] He then had his agents inform the yeomanry
(*myōshu*) of Ōzumi-no-shō that the assignment of a shogunal retainer to the estate was undoubtedly something of
which the shogun himself was unaware; in any event, the
Dongein would henceforth manage its income from the estate directly.[22]

As we can see, the settlement of proprietorship disputes
was a complex problem made no easier by the resistance of

[17] Okuno, *Monjo*, no. 171, vol. 1, 288-89.
[18] Ibid., no. 215, pp. 356-59.
[19] Ibid., no. 219, pp. 365-67. Also see ibid., nos. 217 and 218, pp. 361-65.
[20] Ibid., no. 289, 470-71.   [21] Ibid., no. 290, pp. 471-72.
[22] Ibid., no. 290 supp., pp. 472-73; dated [Genki 2]/7/20.

the shogunal intimates to all efforts to curb their questionable activities. Nobunaga was intent on settling this problem, but he also aimed beyond it at a more ambitious objective. The next important point of the capitulations of 1570
is Nobunaga's arrogation of the shogun's powers of jurisdiction. This is spelled out in item [4]: "Since the affairs of
the realm have in fact been put in Nobunaga's hands, he
may take measures against anyone whatsoever according to
his own discretion and without the need to obtain the
shogun's agreement."[23] The sentence clearly shows that
Nobunaga was intent on curbing the shogun's jurisdictional powers and forcing him to recognize Nobunaga's
personal authority over the administration of justice. And
that is not yet the full significance of this statement. Its first
words—that the affairs of the realm have "in fact" (*nani-
sama nimo*) been left in Nobunaga's hands—encompass the
two principal prerogatives of a ruler: his supremacy over
his subordinates and his competency to govern. Assuming
that to deny Yoshiaki these rights was indeed the purport
of this dictate, what we have here is nothing less than a
forced agreement to transfer the shogun's powers almost
in toto to Nobunaga.

The third point we note in the capitulations of 1570 is
Nobunaga's insistence that the shogun attend properly to
the affairs of the imperial court. It is an early indication of
the way in which Nobunaga used the question of the emperor as a means of discrediting the shogun, an expression
of a new political posture on the part of Nobunaga, and a
foretoken of his subsequent concept of the Tenka, his
realm. Nobunaga was to return to this point in the last of
the three documents that illustrate the mounting tension
between him and Yoshiaki.

This document is a "remonstrance" (*iken*) in seventeen
articles, which apparently was being circulated by the ninth

[23] Ibid., no. 209, p. 344.

month of Genki 3 (ca. October 1572).[24] This is a public indictment of the shogun, and its appearance was the prelude to Yoshiaki's fall. Its background was the atmosphere
of a gathering storm, brought on by the evident readiness
of the great eastern daimyo Takeda Shingen, the very in-
carnation of the Sengoku spirit, to enter the stakes against
Nobunaga.

As the year 1572 progressed, Nobunaga found himself
increasingly in difficulty. The coalition that had formed
against him in 1570—bloodied but not vanquished in the
intervening years—confronted him with undiminished
force, entangling him in campaigns on several fronts. He
was harassed in southern Ōmi by the armed confederates
of the True Pure Land sect (*Ikkō ikki*) and by the remnants
of his old enemy, the Rokkaku family; in the northern part
of the same province, he had to contend with the bitter resistance of Asai Nagamasa; the powerful daimyo of Echizen, Asakura Yoshikage, although slow to move, was an
ever-present threat to his northern flank; trouble festered
in Settsu and Kawachi, toward the south; and Matsunaga
Hisahide of Yamato adopted an inimical posture. Nobunaga spent the two months after Genki 3/7/19 in the
weary effort to reduce Asai's fortress of Odani, but the
siege failed, in large part because Asakura did come to the
relief with an army of fifteen thousand men.[25] In short,
Nobunaga and the coalition ranged against him were
stalemated for the time being. If Shingen were now to
move westward, the threat to Nobunaga would be immense.

To bring about such an offensive was the cherished goal

---

[24] Ibid., no. 340, pp. 565-78, extract from *Jinkenki* (the diary of the imperial abbot of the Daijōin in Nara); cf. the variant in *Shinchō kōki* 6.2, pp.
141-46. Other contemporary sources allude to this document, which is
commonly known as the Seventeen-Article Remonstrance (*Iken
jūshichikajō*). Hence we may assume that it was also made public for prop-
agandistic purposes.
[25] *Shinchō kōki* 5.3, pp. 134-37.

of Nobunaga's enemies. The worst of these, the pontiff Kennyo Kōsa of the True Pure Land sect, operated directly, asking Shingen to fall on Nobunaga's back.[26] Shogun Yoshiaki played a subtler game in the year 1572. It would appear that, not yet ready to turn on his erstwhile benefactor openly, he nonetheless was tugging at the strings of the cordon that threatened to strangle Nobunaga.

Historians have repeatedly told us that Yoshiaki was the actual manipulator of the anti-Nobunaga coalition; some have even asserted that he was secretly involved in it from the time of its inception.[27] Documentary evidence for this supposition is, however, next to nonexistent. But we do have for the year 1572 the striking coincidence in the timing of two letters that deal, each in its own way, with Takeda Shingen. The first is a message sent by Rokkaku Shōtei to three of the shogun's close intimates on Genki 3/5/7, reporting that Shingen was about to go on the march and stressing that the shogun ought to urge him onward.[28] The other is the letter that Yoshiaki addressed to Shingen a week later, on 5/13, acknowledging the receipt of Shingen's oath of allegiance and urging him to "take action so that the realm be set at peace."[29] The shogun's language is ambiguous. We cannot say for certain that the message constitutes proof of his active complicity

We know that Nobunaga himself, as late as 7/27 of the same year, wrote to Shingen's great enemy Uesugi Kenshin of Echigo that he should make peace with Shingen in adherence to the shogun's repeated wishes. Okuno Takahiro explains Yoshiaki's "peace initiative" as nothing more

[26] *Dai Nihon shiryō*, ser. 10, vol. 8, 178-79.

[27] For example, Nagahara Keiji, *Sengoku no dōran, Nihon no rekishi* 14 (Tokyo: Shōgakkan, 1975), 308, speculating that Yoshiaki was intriguing with the Asai, Asakura, Takeda, and the Honganji against Nobunaga as early as 1569, and that this intrigue formed the background of that year's quarrel between Nobunaga and the shogun.

[28] *Dai Nihon shiryō*, ser. 10, vol. 9 (1957), 37.

[29] Ibid., pp. 196-97.

than another device meant to hasten Shingen's march on
Kyoto.[30] No doubt an air of suspicion prevailed among the
major actors of this drama. In any event, Nobunaga soon
enough made it clear that he distrusted Yoshiaki. On 9/16
he broke off his campaign in northern Ōmi and returned
to Gifu in order to prepare himself for an encounter with
Shingen. That same month the remonstrance was made
public.

The content of the remonstrance of 1572 is closely related to that of the capitulations of 1570. Indeed, in the
second of its seventeen articles Nobunaga refers directly to
the previous document as he castigates the shogun doubly
for making overtures to the daimyo:

> You have sent letters over your signature [gonaisho] to
> various provinces, requesting horses and such. You
> should have had the foresight to consider what would
> be thought of such behavior. In cases absolutely re-
> quiring the issuance of orders, however, I had stated
> that Your Highness should let Nobunaga know and
> that I would add my endorsement. You agreed, but
> did not act so: instead, you have been sending such let-
> ters and issuing instructions to distant provinces. This
> is contrary to the previous arrangement. I stated a
> long time ago that, if Your Highness heard of suitable
> horses and so forth, Nobunaga would arrange to have
> them presented to you from wherever. You have not
> acted accordingly, but have instead been issuing in-
> structions in secret. I find this improper.[31]

Whether or not this is an unsubtle allusion to the famous
steeds (*Kiso-goma*) to be found in Takeda Shingen's domains, it is obvious that Nobunaga suspected the shogun of
diplomatic activity injurious to him. Beyond that, we find

[30] Okuno, *Monjo*, no. 331, vol. 1, 551-53, with detailed explanatory
note. Other documents relevant to this matter will be found in *Dai Nihon
shiryō*, ser. 10, vol. 9, 288-90.
[31] Okuno, *Monjo* 1, 566 (cf. *Shinchō kōki*, p. 142).

that the remonstrance repeats and elaborates all the major points of the capitulations, and that it adds a new one.

The question of the authority to grant landholdings is treated in four articles of the remonstrance; the issue of jurisdiction occupies six; and relations with the emperor are discussed in greater detail than before, with two articles devoted to the subject. Five are lavished on the new point, the censure of Yoshiaki's private conduct. Nobunaga's criticism of the shogun takes on an even more severe and concrete form than before.

The right to grant proprietorships, one might think, is of its nature the private prerogative of the feudal ruler, and is a part of his lordship over his vassals; as such it ought to be outside the sphere of criticism on the part of others. In order to get around this problem, Nobunaga had to avoid giving the impression that he was speaking as an individual when he denounced the shogun. Instead, he invoked the slogan of *chū-fuchū* (loyalty vs. disloyalty), that old common standard of the medieval *bushi*—the notion that those who serve their lord with singular loyalty must be rewarded, while those who do not exert themselves in faithful service deserve no recognition.[32] Had the shogun exercised his prerogative fairly, or had he not? In order to demonstrate that he had not, Nobunaga applied a universal standard, citing "people's opinion" (*shonin no omowaku*), and alleging that Yoshiaki had earned an "outrageous notoriety throughout the realm" for his reckless favoritism and disregard of true merit.[33]

The question of jurisdiction is pursued in detail through six articles that itemize the shogun's unjust actions. Again appealing to "what people are apt to think" (*sejō ni zonzubeku sōrō koto*),[34] Nobunaga stresses that Yoshiaki has lost the ability to govern and no longer has the competency of a ruler. Scathing criticism of Yoshiaki's private conduct rein-

[32] Item [3], ibid.
[33] Item [15], *Monjo*, p. 568 (cf. *Shinchō*, p. 145).
[34] Item [9], *Monjo*, p. 567 (cf. *Shinchō*, p. 144).

forces this contention. Why, Nobunaga asks, has Yoshiaki emptied his Nijō castle's storehouse of rice and converted it to cash? "That a shogun should engage in trade is something unknown until now!"[35] Why had he had his treasures removed from the castle, built for him with so much toil and sweat, a safe and splendid residence?[36] "These appear to be preparations for exile. . . . Even the populace will note that your intention is to abandon Kyoto."[37] The inference is clear: Yoshiaki is planning to throw down the gauntlet to Nobunaga.

Needless to say, Nobunaga continues, the people of the capital are distraught at Yoshiaki's misdeeds; even the nameless peasants call him the "evil shogun."[38] Thus the indictment concludes with an iniquitous comparison. "Evil shogun," Nobunaga does not forget to remind Yoshiaki, is a name once applied to his predecessor Ashikaga Yoshinori, who was assassinated by a slighted vassal in the Kakitsu Disturbance of 1441. This allusion to the ill fate that sometimes befalls even shoguns surely was nothing but a threat.[39]

It ought to be clear by now that this remonstrance, justified by references to "public opinion," invited a comparison between the manner in which Yoshiaki presided over the "public order"—*kōgi*, the traditional body politic[40]—and the way Nobunaga administered his "realm," the Tenka. Malfeasance is the gravamen of the charge against the shogun.

But what did Nobunaga mean by Tenka? Let us look at the text of a document drafted for Nobunaga's signature in

[35] Item [14], *Monjo*, p. 568 (cf. *Shinchō*, p. 145).
[36] Item [4], *Monjo*, p. 566 (cf. *Shinchō*, pp. 142-43).
[37] Item [16], *Monjo*, p. 568 (cf. *Shinchō*, p. 145).
[38] Item [17], ibid.
[39] Cf. Takao Kazuhiko, "Nobunaga no Kyōto shihai," *Kyōto no rekishi* 4, 86-87.
[40] On the wider implications of the term *kōgi*, see Fukaya Katsumi, "Kōgi to mibunsei," *Taikei Nihon kokka shi* 3, 147-85; and cf. Asao Naohiro, "Bakuhansei to tennō," ibid., pp. 201-205.

the first month of Eiroku 13 (exactly contemporary with the capitulations) to be sent to a long list of daimyo and representative provincial samurai: "In the middle of the next month, I shall be in the capital to attend to the repairs of the imperial palace (*kinchū goshūri*), to the service of the military (*buke goyō*), as well as to the increase of the realm's tranquillity (*sono hoka tenka iyoiyo seihitsu no tame*). You are to come to the capital and present your compliments. Your cooperation is expected, and there are to be no delays. Yrs, etc."[41] The phrasing clearly distinguishes the Tenka from both the imperial and the shogunal hierarchies. Tenka is a broader concept than the other two; it is a polity that encompasses and controls those other spheres of politics; it is the common weal over which Nobunaga intends to preside. The word is one that he increasingly used to impress upon others the designs of his regime, to rally loyalties, and to justify extraordinary actions. From 1570 onward, we note that documents issued by Nobunaga repeatedly invoke the two phrases *Tenka no tame* and *Nobunaga no tame* in close association.[42] This coupling of the abstract idea, "for the sake of the realm," with the personal slogan, "for the sake of Nobunaga," was a clever political device. Nobunaga recognized the ideological potential of such an identification, and he used it consciously in his efforts to draw the allegiances of the samurai class toward himself. This was a ruler with a good sense of raison d'état.

Such a ruler could not tolerate the competing presence in the military hierarchy of a figure who was—if only nominally—superior to him. Hence the shogun had to be impeached. One way of doing so was to condemn him for his neglect of the emperor, the sovereign who had invested him with his office. The very first article of the remon-

[41] Copy of Nobunaga's draft orders, extract from *Nijō Enjō nikki*, entry for Eiroku 13/1/15; Okuno, *Monjo*, no. 210, 1, 346-48.

[42] The *locus classicus* is Nobunaga's vermilion-seal letter, dated [Genki 1 (1570)]/5/25, ordering the Endō family of Mino to mobilize its forces for a campaign against Asai Nagamasa; *Monjo*, no. 233, 1, 388-90.

strance of 1572 takes up this issue and elaborates on it:
"The imperial court was neglected by Lord Kōgen'in [Sho-
gun Yoshiteru], so that in the end he met misfortune; this
is an old story. Accordingly, from the time of your entry
into the capital, I have advised Your Highness never to be
remiss in your attention to His Majesty's affairs. Nevertheless, you quickly forgot your resolution, and there has been
a decline in recent years. I find this inexcusable." Here the
emperor is the pretext for the shogun's derogation. And
Yoshiaki's impeachment is further pressed on the basis of a
related but more concrete reason specified in item [10] of
the remonstrance: "That the era name Genki is unpropitious and ought to be changed was the talk of the entire
realm. Accordingly, the imperial court made the arrangements necessary to change it, but you failed to provide the
mere pittance required, and the delay continues. This is a
matter that concerns the realm's [Tenka] interests, so that I
find this sort of negligence on your part improper."[43] The
uncooperative shogun has turned his back on the interests
of the realm, disregarding the realm's consensus, and spit-
ing the emperor himself. How could the realm's protector
not find this improper?

Changing an era name was part of the imperial prerogative. The actual procedure, however, was for the shogun to
petition the emperor for a change. The imperial court's
councils then deliberated over the choices, and the
emperor selected a new name. The ceremony that announced the change would then be held with funds provided by the shogun. This customary procedure was followed even in the Sengoku period,[44] and the shogun's role
in it was by no means a minor one. Hence Nobunaga was
engaging in no mere pettifoggery when he indicted
Yoshiaki for his failure to perform his part.

[43] Item [1], *Monjo*, 1, 565 (cf. *Shinchō kōki*, pp. 141-42); Item [10],
Monjo, p. 567 (cf. *Shinchō*, p. 144).

[44] Imatani Akira, *Sengoku-ki no Muromachi bakufu*, Kikan Ronsō Nihon
Bunka 2 (Tokyo: Kadokawa Shoten, 1975), 166-78.

One can understand the shogun's reluctance to do so, for the name was intimately associated with Yoshiaki's ascent to the shogunate. The era name in effect when Yoshiaki entered Kyoto was Eiroku. As early as the winter of 1568, immediately after he became shogun, Yoshiaki began his effort to have this name changed. He formally petitioned the emperor in the fourth month of the following year, Eiroku 12, and a private agreement was reached in the seventh month of that year. Within the imperial court, however, there was opposition to a change, and the era name Eiroku was not abolished in favor of Genki until 4/23 of the following year, twelve and a half months after Yoshiaki had submitted his petition.[45] He had provided much more than the ordinary amount of funds for the ceremony. Genki was to be his era, its name a symbol of his rulership.

In that case, "the era name Genki is unpropitious" are code words for "the shogun is unfit to rule." No wonder Yoshiaki opposed Nobunaga's efforts to have that name abolished, sabotaged his approaches to the emperor, and refused to listen to "the talk of the entire realm." But this opposition meant that Yoshiaki would be isolated and branded an enemy of the emperor and the Tenka.

After the remonstrance, the only choices left to Yoshiaki were total subservience to Nobunaga or military action against him. The shogun took the latter course. In the second month of Genki 4 (1573), Yoshiaki sent messages to Asai Nagamasa, Asakura Yoshikage, and Takeda Shingen that he was taking up arms, took steps to fortify Nijō castle, and ordered the forces available to him into the field.[46]

---

[45] *Oyudono no Ue no nikki*, edited by Ōta Tōshirō, 3rd ed., 7 (Tokyo: Zoku Gunsho Ruijū Kanseikai, 1958), 20; entry for Eiroku 13/4/22. For the wider background, see *Dai Nihon shiryō*, ser. 10, vol. 4 (1934), 312-34, particularly pp. 313-14, extract from *Tokitsugu-kyō ki*, entry for Eiroku 12/4/8, specifying that the request for a change of the era name was made "the previous winter," that is, in the last three months of Eiroku 11.

[46] Rich documentation appears in *Dai Nihon shiryō*, ser. 10, vol. 14

Nobunaga called this the shogunal regime's treason—*kōgi ongyakushin*—against the Tenka, but for the moment was conciliatory.[47] Apart from ordering the reduction of Yoshiaki's uncompleted forts at the southern end of Lake Biwa,[48] Nobunaga for the time being avoided armed conflict with the shogun, still hoping for a rapprochement with him. That Nobunaga, for all his violent criticism of the shogun, should for the purposes of obtaining such an agreement have been willing to acknowledge that he was subordinated to Yoshiaki as a vassal to his lord indicates that his Tenka, after all, was not yet established firmly as an independent entity; indeed, the momentary weakness of his position is indicated best of all by his lament that the Tenka might yet be "restored," if only the shogun changed his mind![49] To be sure, his seemingly weak pliancy was to prove temporary; conciliatory is not the word that best describes his nature; his apparent willingness to subordinate himself to Yoshiaki had only external reasons.

The démarche toward Yoshiaki was forced on Nobunaga by the threat of Takeda Shingen's advance on the eastern flank of his domain. Shingen had taken the field on

---

(1971), 141-88. See particularly Asai Nagamasa's letter to the Shōkōji in Etchū Province, dated [Genki 4]/2/26, stating that the shogun had sent gonaisho to him and to Yoshikage on 2/13 and that he was appending copies (pp. 145-46); Asai's letter to Takeda Saemon no Daibu (Shingen's captain Anayama Nobukimi), dated 2/24, forwarding Yoshiaki's gonaisho to Shingen (p. 146); and Yoshiaki's own letter to an unidentified member of the Asakura family, dated 2/19, asking for the dispatch of five or six thousand troops to the Kyoto area (pp. 143-44). An interesting account of the sequence of events leading up to the showdown, written from the standpoint of a shogunal retainer who went over to Nobunaga's side, Hosokawa Fujitaka, will be found in the extracts from *Hosokawa-ke ki*, pp. 162-67.

[47] Okuno, *Monjo*, no. 360, vol. 1, 606-10.

[48] *Shinchō kōki* 6.2-3, pp. 146-47.

[49] See letters recorded in *Monjo*, no. 364, p. 614; no. 362, p. 611; and no. 363, p. 613. Along with ibid., no. 360, these three make up a truly extraordinary series; nowhere else do we find Nobunaga adopting such compliant tones. These letters are all addressed to Hosokawa Fujitaka.

Genki 3/10/3 and had swept all before him, two months later dealing Ieyasu's and Nobunaga's allied army a sharp blow at Mikatagahara in Tōtōmi province. Indeed, it was Shingen's successes that had enticed Yoshiaki to break openly with Nobunaga in the first place; and Nobunaga's expressions of peaceful sentiments toward the shogun were written in the knowledge that Shingen's forces had advanced farther westward and taken the important fortress of Noda in Mikawa on the seventeenth of the second month, Genki 4. But this offensive was Shingen's last foray. He was mortally ill even as his troops laid siege to the castle, and he had to withdraw from the scene before it fell. His death came on Genki 4/4/12; even prior to it, Nobunaga had acted, in the knowledge that it was expected. Yoshiaki had gambled all on a card that could not come up.

In the first days of the fourth month, Genki 4, Nobunaga's huge army surrounded the capital city of Kyoto and methodically burned down some ninety villages of its periphery. On the night of Genki 4/4/3-4, Kamigyō, the "Upper Capital," was burned by his troops. Yoshiaki, who had intended to make a stand in Nijō castle, "now thought it would be difficult to hold and expressed the desire to begin peace talks."[50] The shogun was saved by the emperor's intercession, but his period of grace was to be of short duration.

A the end of the fourth month the two sides exchanged oaths of friendliness, but surely—for all their sacred char-

---

[50] *Shinchō kōki* 6.4, p. 148. On these events, further see *Kanemi-kyō ki*, edited by Saiki Kazuma and Someya Mitsuhiro 1 (Tokyo: Zoku Gunsho Ruijū Kanseikai, 1971; Shiryō Sanshū, 1st ser.), 65-69, entries for the fourth month, Genki 4; cf. P. Luis Frois, S.J., to P. Francisco Cabral, S.J., Miyako, 27 May 1573, *Cartas qve os Padres e Irmãos da Companhia de Iesus escreuerão dos Reynos de Iapão & China aos da mesma Companhia da India, & Europa, des do anno de 1549. atè o de 1580.* 1 (Em Euora por Manoel de Lyra, 1598), 343-50. Nobunaga reported the conclusion of peace to Ieyasu in a black-seal letter dated 4/6, averring that he could not remember the reasons for the shogun's odd and unexpected attitude! Okuno, *Monjo*, no. 367, vol. 1, 624-26.

acter, gruesome anathema clauses, and seals of blood—
neither expected that peace would last.[51] On the second
day of the seventh month, the shogun again cast down the
gauntlet to Nobunaga, left Nijō castle in charge of
Mizubuchi Fujihide, and himself departed for what he
thought was an impregnable fort, the water fastness of
Makinoshima south of Kyoto. Sixteen days later—after
Nobunaga, having forced a crossing of the Uji River, had
reduced the outer defenses and was about to carry the castle by storm—Yoshiaki pleaded pardon.[52] His life was
spared, but he was driven from the central arena of politics. Although he continued to posture as shogun for years
thereafter, he was henceforth a king without a kingdom.
The Ashikaga shogunate was finished.

Nobunaga adjudged Yoshiaki's departure from his capital to be an "abandonment of the realm,"[53] which now
clearly was Nobunaga's to govern. On Genki 4/7/21, the
hegemon returned to the imperial city in triumph and ordered its ravaged upper half to be rebuilt. With the elimination of the shogun, the city now belonged to Nobunaga's
realm; in view of that fact, he appointed his vassal Murai
Sadakatsu as the governor of Kyoto. The police powers of
the shogunate's *samurai-dokoro* were assumed by Nobunaga's official.[54] Having thus put the capital under his con-

[51] Takikawa Sakon [Ichimasu], Sakuma Uemon no Jō [Nobumori] et al.
for Nobunaga, to Isshiki Shikibu no Shō [Fujinaga], Ueno Nakatsukasa no
Daibu [Hidemasa] et al., dated 4/27; Isshiki, Ueno et al. for the Bakufu, to
Hanawa Kurozaemon no Jō, Takikawa, and Sakuma, dated 4/28; standard *Goō-fuda* formula; Okuno, *Monjo*, no. 371, vol. 1, 629-35 with supple-
ments. On the very day his vassals signed this *kishōmon*, Yoshiaki was busily
repairing the moats of Nijō Castle; *Kanemi-kyō ki* 1, 69.
[52] *Monjo*, no. 385, pp. 660-63. Details in *Shinchō kōki* 6.7-8, pp. 149-53.
Cf. Okuno, *Ashikaga Yoshiaki*, pp. 216-27.
[53] *Monjo*, no. 377, p. 648.
[54] *Shinchō kōki* 6.8, p. 153. Further see Asao Naohiro, "Kyōto shoshidai,"
Kyōto no rekishi 4, 510-14. Imatani Akira, *Sengoku-ki no Muromachi bakufu*,
p. 211, suggests a connection between the power to order remissions of
debts and dues (*tokusei*) and the assumption of imperative control; following that criterion, we may say that the critical date in the establishment of

trol, Nobunaga on the twenty-sixth departed the city. Two days later, on 7/28, the era name was changed from Genki to Tenshō.

NOBUNAGA'S RELATIONS WITH THE EMPEROR

Having expelled the shogun from Kyoto and taken over the shogunate's powers in the capital city, Nobunaga also assumed the shogun's customary role of petitioning the emperor for a change in the era name. The diary of an office in the imperial palace, *Oyudono no Ue no nikki*, tells us that the matter was brought up by Nobunaga "suddenly."[55] Indeed, no time was wasted: not three days had passed since Yoshiaki's fall before Nobunaga was urging upon the emperor the abolition of the era name Genki; and he evidently did impress him with the gravity of the need for a change, because the new era Tenshō was proclaimed a week later. The great dispatch with which the procedure was completed indicates that there was a strong political purpose behind this seeming formality. When he insisted on the proclamation of a new era, Nobunaga meant to avail himself of a powerful symbol. By showing all the world that a word from him to the emperor (not to speak of his financial support) sufficed to bring about immediately a procedural change that was binding throughout Japan, Nobunaga would make it clear that political authority had passed conclusively from the shogun Yoshiaki to him.

Moreover, there are indications that Nobunaga used the foothold he thereby obtained in the imperial court's affairs for the purposes of an effort to force Emperor Ōgimachi from the throne. The diary of the imperial noble Nakayama Takachika gives us a good picture of the pressure

---

the Oda regime's control of Kyoto was the third month of Tenshō 3 (1575), when Nobunaga ordered Murai Sadakatsu to put a *tokusei* in effect in Kyoto. On the significance of this event, see Wakita Osamu, *Oda seiken no kiso kōzō*, pp. 165-70.

[55] See *Oyudono no Ue no nikki* 7, 138, entry for Genki 4/7/21.

that Nobunaga applied as the first year of the new Tenshō era drew to a close.[56] According to Takachika, Nobunaga subjected the emperor to repeated requests that he abdicate. An imperial message was sent to Nobunaga through the *kanpaku* (regent) Nijō Haruyoshi, indicating consent. Nobunaga expressed his gratitude for its contents; there was, however, little left of the year, so that it was agreed to defer the matter until the following spring. The rest of the interview was spent in discussing the procedures of imperial abdication and enthronement.

Takachika is a reliable source, for he was one of the intermediaries in the affair and was present at the kanpaku's meeting with Nobunaga. What he tells us is a story of the hegemon's overt interference in the imperial court's affairs. To be sure, he leaves an interesting puzzle unsolved: did the abdication question arise from the emperor's own initiative or was it forced by Nobunaga's insistence? Historians disagree on this point; there can be little doubt, however, that Nobunaga took the active part in this drama, that he "importunately" (*shikiri ni*) urged the emperor to abdicate, and that he was prepared to assume the expenses for the ceremonies involved. For all that, Emperor Ōgimachi did not abdicate—not in the spring of Tenshō 2, not in Nobunaga's lifetime, and not until 1586.

Instead, in the spring of Tenshō 2 (1574), Nobunaga was raised to the status of an imperial noble, being promoted to the junior third rank (*ju sanmi*) and the post of an imperial adviser (*sangi*).[57] Can his acceptance of these honors be interpreted as a political victory for the emperor? The background is not clear, and the question is not easily answered.

[56] Okuno, "Oda seiken no kihon rosen," pp. 42-43. Okuno cites the *Takachika-kō ki*, entries for Tenshō 1/12/7-8 (30-31 December 1573), and the holograph copy of Emperor Ōgimachi's letter in the form of a *nyōbō hōsho*, addressed to "Danjō no Jō-dono" (that is, Nobunaga), n.d. He speculates that the latter is nothing else than the message sent by the emperor on this occasion.

[57] Tenshō 2/3/18; see *Kugyō bunin* 3, *Kokushi taikei* 55 (Tokyo: Kokushi Taikei Kankōkai, 1936), 471.

We shall merely note that ten days after accepting the appointments, Nobunaga—an avid collector of rarities—was able to add a piece of that legendary imperial heirloom in the Shōsōin, the perfume-wood Ranjatai, to his hoard of treasures.

The Shōsōin storehouse at the Tōdaiji in Nara had preserved the items deposited there in the eighth century so well largely because its doors were kept closed with imperial seals. These seals could be specially opened for the emperor, but aside from him only for the shogun on the occasion of his visit to the Kasuga shrine and through the agency of an imperial envoy.[58] In view of this tradition, it is clear that when Nobunaga had the seals broken and a piece of the Ranjatai cut off for him, he was in effect forcing the emperor to acknowledge that he had claim to privileges equal to a shogun's. The *Shinchō kōki* notes in describing this episode that ever since that other fancier of rare and precious items, Ashikaga Yoshimasa, had in 1465 been granted the boon, "many of the shogunal house had desired it without success, for it was truly extraordinary." Now Nobunaga had obtained what even the shoguns had hoped for in vain; he had excelled the powerholders of the past. As an indication of "fame and honor in our Empire, how could anything compare with this!"[59] Nobunaga's act was indeed a striking demonstration of the power he held over the emperor.[60]

The questions of the emperor's abdication and Nobunaga's court status persisted throughout the subsequent history of relations between the two. Nobunaga was promoted yearly from Tenshō 2 to Tenshō 6; his advancement

[58] See Wada Gun'ichi, "Ranjatai," *Nihon rekishi* 335 (1976), 40-43.

[59] *Shinchō kōki* 7.4, pp. 167-168, entry for Tenshō 2/3/28.

[60] Okuno, "Oda seiken no kihon rosen," p. 43, speculates that Nobunaga's demand for the emperor's abdication was coupled with another demand, that Nobunaga be appointed shogun. When he was refused, Nobunaga vented his spleen by acquiring the piece of Ranjatai. This is an interesting hypothesis, but it needs to be proved.

at court proceeded without a hitch.[61] In the course of this "orderly promotion," he was raised to the junior second rank (*ju nii*) on Tenshō 5/11/16 (25 December 1577), and four days later was made Minister of the Right (*udaijin*). On Tenshō 6/1/6 (12 February 1578), he was raised to the second rank proper (*shō nii*), a step presumptive of his elevation to the highest rungs on the ladder of court posts, Minister of the Left (*sadaijin*) and then grand chancellor of state (*daijō daijin*), the supreme appointment. A scant three months later, however, he suddenly resigned all his imperial offices, pleading that his task of pacifying the country by the conquest of all the "Four Barbarians" had not yet been completed; he would resume his loyal service as the pillar of the throne, he said, once that great endeavor was accomplished; in the meantime he wanted his posts transferred to his son Nobutada.[62]

The emperor appears to have rejected this last request as presumptuous; at any rate, Nobunaga's court posts were not assigned to Nobutada. The next year Nobunaga again went on the political offensive against Emperor Ōgimachi. Having refurbished the residence on Nijō Avenue from which he had chased Shogun Yoshiaki, Nobunaga presented it to Sanehito, the heir to the imperial throne, and presided over the crown prince's festive installation in his new palace.[63] A prominent place in the procession was occupied by the suite of the imperial prince Go no Miya; Nobunaga had received permission to adopt this infant as his own heir.[64] The questions of imperial abdication and

[61] For the chronology of Nobunaga's promotions, see *Kugyō bunin* 3, 471-78.

[62] See *Kanemi-kyō ki* 1, 140; also Okuno, *Monjo*, no. 707, vol. 2, 280-81 (mistakenly entered under Tenshō 5).

[63] For accounts of the crown prince's installation in the New Nijō Palace, see *Shinchō kōki* 12.16, pp. 290-94, entry for Tenshō 7/11/22 (20 December 1579), and *Kanemi-kyō ki* 1, 187-89, entries for Tenshō 7/11/[15]-[22].

[64] See *Tamon'in nikki* 3, *Zōho zoku shiryō taisei* 40, 81, entry for Tenshō 7/11/22.

princely succession were obviously developing a new complexity.

Meanwhile Nobunaga was encroaching bit by bit upon those few powers the emperor and his court still held. The emperor had traditionally exercised the powers of jurisdiction and arbitration over disputes between members of the elite—the court nobility and the religious establishment. We observe a growing tendency on Nobunaga's part to intrude into these traditional rights. A good example is an incident that occurred in the summer of 1576, when a dispute arose in the Kōfukuji at Nara over the directorship of that monastery's administrative headquarters (*bettō-shiki*). The imperial court had reached a decision in the matter, but it had to be reversed on account of Nobunaga's opposition.[65] At this stage Nobunaga was already using four "spokesmen for the military (*buke densō*)"—whom the sources also call *chokushi bugyō* and *yonin no shū*—as his intermediaries in such affairs at court; he had, in other words, succeeded in institutionalizing his material participation in the court's judicial proceedings. He seems to have established a procedure calling for the four in concert to reach a judgment that would, however, not be put in effect until the receipt of Nobunaga's sanction. In short, the imperial court's few remaining discretionary powers were being whittled away by Nobunaga, just as the shogunate's had been before.

This state of affairs may also be noted in the way Nobunaga meddled with the court's handling of the dispute that had broken out in 1575 between priests of the Tendai and Shingon sects in Hitachi province over the right to wear silk robes.[66] (The province, in the distant

[65] See *Tamon'in nikki* 2, 417, entry for Tenshō 4/6/24; *Kanemi-kyō ki* 1, 108, entry for Tenshō 4/7/6, and p. 111, entry for 8/6. Cf. Okuno, "Oda seiken no kihon rosen," pp. 46-47.

[66] See Okuno, *Monjo*, no. 657, vol. 2, 222-25. For the background, see *Mito-shi shi* 1, edited by Itō Tasaburō et al. (Mito: Mito Shiyakusho, 1963), 622-26.

Kantō region, was at the time far from being part of Nobunaga's realm.) It is no less apparent in the famous Azuchi Disputation of 1579. In this disputation, held at the Jōgon'in in Nobunaga's castle town, representatives of the Jōdo sect and the Hokke (Nichiren) sect were pitted against each other in a formal doctrinal debate; the Nichirenists were adjudged the losers and their principals were executed on Nobunaga's orders.[67] The Jesuit missionary Organtino, in reporting this news, drew a self-serving moral: according to him, God had chosen Nobunaga as His instrument to destroy the Buddhists.[68] But the manner in which the disputation was conducted and the verdict reached under Nobunaga's direction affected not only the Buddhists but the imperial court as well. One of the great religious institutions headquartered in the capital received guarantees of protection, another was subjected to persecution—without any reference to the emperor's traditional role as mediator and ultimate juridical authority. What else was this if not an intrusion into the imperial prerogative?

Hence it would appear that Nobunaga had succeeded in arrogating to himself even those functions which the emperor—of all the powers vested in him as sovereign—had until then best managed to retain and exercise. In that case, how do we interpret Nobunaga's use of the imperial court in dealing with yet another powerful religious institution, the Honganji, and its pontiff Kennyo Kōsa? In

[67] On the Azuchi Disputation, which took place on Tenshō 7/5/27 (21 June 1579), see Okuno, *Monjo*, no. 829, vol. 2, 443-45, and ibid., no. 830, pp. 445-47; *Tokitsune-kyō ki* 1, Dai Nippon Kokiroku, edited by Tōkyō Daigaku Shiryō Hensanjo (Tokyo: Iwanami Shoten, 1959), 189, entry for 5/28, and pp. 191-95, containing a record of the disputation and documents signed by Nichirenist priests; *Kanemi-kyō ki* 1, 170, entries for 5/27-28; *Shinchō kōki* 12.4, pp. 272-77. Cf. Nakao Akira, "Azuchi shūron no shiteki igi," *Nihon rekishi* 92 (1957), 48-54, and Fujii Manabu, "Nichiren shūto no katsuyaku," *Kyōto no rekishi* 4, 165-73.

[68] P. Organtino Gnecchi-Soldo S.J. to P. Luis Frois S.J., Miyako, [June] 1579, *Cartas* 1, 450-51 v.

1580, he mobilized court "spokesmen for the military," the former kanpaku Konoe Sakihisa, and Crown Prince Sanehito to bring about peace "by imperial command" with this most persistent of all his enemies, one that had fought him tooth and nail in a ten years' war across widespread areas of Japan and had execrated him as an "enemy of the Buddhist Law (*hōteki*)."[69] We conclude that this approach to solving the problem was entirely Nobunaga's own device.

On 1 April 1581, Nobunaga held a great parade of his military forces on a riding ground prepared especially for the purpose just east of the imperial palace in Kyoto.[70] His vassals—"daimyo, lesser lords, and housemen from the Kinai and the neighboring provinces"—were ordered to take part in this pageant; among the spectators were "the emperor, the nobles, ministers of state, and other courtiers," not to mention an admiring visitor from the West, the Jesuit Padre Alexandro Valignano, who "maintained that never in all his days had he seen such a resplendent and magnificent affair, on account of the great quantity of gold and silks with which [all] were adorned."[71] Nobunaga's own spectacular entry into the parade ground, the *Shinchō kōki* tells us, "gave one and all the uncanny feeling of a deity's presence: surely the appearance of the god of Sumiyoshi must be like this!"[72]

The display evidently made an impression: on the third

[69] See Okuno, *Monjo*, nos. 852-55, vol. 2, 471-80; nos. 858-64, pp. 482-88; nos. 866-67, pp. 490-97; documents dated Tenshō 8/3/17-4/22. Cf. *Shinchō kōki* 13.3, pp. 317-19.

[70] Tenshō 9/2/28, with another parade being held "at the imperial court's request" on 3/5. See *Shinchō kōki* 14.2, pp. 340-47, and cf. *Kanemikyō ki* 1, 248-50.

[71] Luis Frois S.J., *Segunda Parte da Historia de Japam*, edited by João do Amaral Abranches Pinto and Okamoto Yoshitomo (Tokyo: Sociedade Luso-Japonesa, 1938), p. 243. Frois was no less enthusiastic in reporting his own sentiments on the splendor of the feast; see his letter to "another Padre in Japan," Miyako, 14 April 1581, *Cartas* 2, 4-5.

[72] *Shinchō kōki* 14.2, p. 345.

day after the event, the emperor offered Nobunaga the post of Minister of the Left, the second highest of all imperial offices.[73] Nobunaga, however, imposed a condition, responding to the offer with a broad hint: he would accept the appointment (he is reported to have said), but only after the emperor abdicated, once Crown Prince Sanehito was installed in the imperial palace and the enthronement ceremony completed. Hence the plan was undone. Opinions differ as to whether or not to interpret this incident as yet another attempt to force the emperor from the throne against his will; but at the very least it seems clear that the abdication and Nobunaga's willingness once again to accept a court post were inseparable and interdependent questions affecting the central government.

On Tenshō 10 (1582)/4/21, Nobunaga returned to Azuchi from his triumphal campaign in eastern Japan, having destroyed Shingen's son Takeda Katsuyori and incorporated the old Takeda domains—the provinces of Suruga, Kai, Shinano, and Kōzuke—into his realm. Four days later, the imperial court had decided to offer him appointment as daijō daijin, kanpaku, or shogun in recognition of his new conquests; ambassadors were designated to carry this offer to Azuchi. They bore with them a letter from Prince Sanehito that promised to appoint Nobunaga "to any rank at all"; the details, it added, would be settled when Nobunaga came to Kyoto.[74] Was the court's decision indeed to be taken literally, as an offer to give Nobunaga whatever high rank he might choose? What, we may ask, were the precedents? Taira no Kiyomori and Ashikaga Yoshimitsu were the only two members of the military class

[73] Okuno, "Oda seiken no kihon rosen," pp. 49-50. The offer was first made on Tenshō 9/3/1 and repeated on 3/9. See *Oyudono no Ue no nikki* 7, 378, entry for the latter date. That Nobunaga again raised the question of the emperor's abdication is moreover clear from *Kanemi-kyō ki* 1, 251, entry for Tenshō 9/3/11.

[74] Sanehito Shinnō to "the former Minister of the Right," n.d. [Tenshō 10/4/?], reproduced in *Kyōto no rekishi* 4, 230.

who had held the office of daijō daijin; no bushi had ever become kanpaku in the long history of that institution.[75] Was shogun, then, the only real choice? There were procedural difficulties with that, too. There must have been disagreement in court circles. The court's gesture, seemingly so clear, in actuality was equivocal.

The diary of Kanshuji Harutoyo, one of the envoys sent to Azuchi, tells us that when he was questioned on Nobunaga's behalf as to the purpose of his embassy, he responded: "The conquest of the Kantō is a splendid exploit, so that it has been decided to make [Nobunaga] shogun."[76] Hence it would seem that, for all the talk of "any rank at all," appointment to the shogunate was the court's preferred option in this case. An outstanding matter would be settled (court councils or the emperor personally had decided) by granting Nobunaga what was assumed to be his cherished desire.

Historians have told us time and again, however, that a Minamoto lineage was the absolute prerequisite for appointment to the office of shogun. If that idea was indeed commonly held throughout the middle ages, then the emperor ignored ancient precedent and acted contrary to the traditions of his office when he offered the appointment to a man widely identified as a Taira.[77] There was, to be sure,

[75] When Hideyoshi was subsequently made *kanpaku*, the traditionalists were outraged, and spoke of his self-aggrandizement as something "unheard of in previous ages," "unspeakable and unimaginable," and an act of "bushi madness." See *Tamon'in nikki* 3, 431, entries for Tenshō 13 (1585)/7/11, the day Hideyoshi assumed the post, and for the day after.

[76] *Nichinichiki*, entry for Tenshō 10/5/4, reproduced in *Kyōto no rekishi* 4, 231.

[77] E.g., *Tamon'in nikki* 3, 222, entry for Tenshō 10/5/18, with allusions to "the Heike steeped in pride." Nobunaga was indeed considered a member of the Taira or Heike lineage, and figures as such in the *Kugyō bunin*, but he does not appear under that name in his extant epistolary corpus, so that it is difficult to tell when he assumed it. Okuno Takahiro, "Oda seiken no kihon rosen," p. 37, suggests that Nobunaga adopted the style of Taira about 1564, in the course of his Mino campaign, as a way of proclaiming his intent to displace Saitō Tatsuoki, an offshoot of the Fujiwara clan.

sufficient reason for making such an offer to Nobunaga. As the imperial envoy's words clearly indicate, what swayed the emperor to take the step was Nobunaga's "conquest of the Kantō." This accomplishment was proper to and characteristic of a shogun; the man who had subdued the "Eastern Barbarians" deserved to be recognized as "Barbarian-Subduing Generalissimo," *seiitaishōgun*. Nobunaga's "splendid exploit" against the Takeda could not be ignored.

This was the final act of that complex drama in which Nobunaga and Emperor Ōgimachi played the parts of antagonists. The man of power had extended his influence to such a point that the highest traditional authority—imperial sovereignty—was shaken in its foundations. The court's decision to elevate a Taira to the shogunate represents the high point in the development of Nobunaga's political posture. Of no less interest, however, is the anticlimax.

Nobunaga politely declined to meet the imperial envoys, stating through his secretary Kusunoki Chōan that it would be improper to do so unless he were prepared to address himself to the matter with which they were charged. In response to a repeated request, he granted them an interview on the sixth day of the fifth month, but it amounted to nothing more than an exchange of pleasantries as the guests viewed Azuchi castle's splendid lakeside setting; the key matter was not brought up. In short, Nobunaga avoided giving the envoys a direct response.

During the rest of the fifth month of Tenshō 10, Nobunaga busied himself with plans for the conquest of

Okuno's source is the inscription, bearing the date Eiroku 7/11/11, on the bell of the Entokuji in Mino (see *Monjo*, supp. no. 9, vol. 2, 839-41); but there is some question of its reliability because the bell was recast in the seventeenth century, and the suggestion is otherwise unconvincing. Note that the earliest extant document issued over Nobunaga's name, dated Tenmon 18 (1549)/11/-, is signed Fujiwara Nobunaga (*Monjo*, no. 1, vol. 1, 15); but that is the only known instance of his being styled so.

Shikoku and the pursuit of the weary Chūgoku campaign; on the fifteenth, his ally Tokugawa Ieyasu came to Azuchi to be entertained with a five-day feast. On 5/29, the last day of the month, Nobunaga arrived in Kyoto and took up quarters in the Honnōji; the next day, he entertained there some forty of the highest court notables in what one of the participants described as a "most happy" occasion;[78] and in the early hours of the next day, Tenshō 10/6/2 (21 June 1582), he was killed there by Akechi Mitsuhide, a slighted vassal.

How do we interpret Nobunaga's evasiveness vis-à-vis the imperial envoys? Was it tantamount to a refusal of the proffered appointment as shogun? Or did he merely want to put off a definite answer until his visit to Kyoto? Did or did not Nobunaga covet the title of shogun? Whatever the case may be, the fact remains that he did not readily give his agreement to this truly extraordinary resolution of the court. Perhaps high ranks—including the shogunal—far from representing an absolute value and a cherished goal to Nobunaga, simply did not attract him; perhaps he merely pretended that this was so, preferring to play the solipsist. Did he mean thereby to break down another shibboleth, the doctrine of imperial sovereignty? Opinions differ; Nobunaga's abruptly finished drama leaves plenty of room for speculation.

As Iwasawa Yoshihiko has noted, Nobunaga's last visit to Kyoto in a sense represents not the end but the beginning of an epoch.[79] He came to the capital as the head of a regime that had extended its sway over all of central Japan from Kōzuke in the east to Harima in the west; he had taken giant steps toward unifying the country, and a new stage in that process was about to begin. Nobunaga stood at a crossroads. He could give a formal, affirmative answer to the court's proposal, accept appointment as shogun, estab-

---

[78] *Tokitsune-kyō ki* 1, 279, entry for Tenshō 10/6/1.

[79] Iwasawa Yoshihiko, "Honnōji no Hen shūi," *Rekishi chiri* 91.4 (1968), 213-24.

lish a new bakufu, and take the road that Tokugawa Ieyasu was destined to follow two decades later. Or he could spurn the shogunate, refuse the imperial chancery, scorn the regency, throw considerations of precedent to the winds, and open up his own new avenue to rulership. Death robbed Nobunaga of the choice. When Hideyoshi thereupon inherited the Tenka, the regime of the unifiers was again thrown back upon the use of traditional symbols of authority, derived from the imperial throne, for its legitimation.[80]

NOBUNAGA'S POLICIES OF CONTROL OVER THE DAIMYO

We have now seen that Nobunaga countenanced superordinate hierarchies of authority only insofar as they furthered his interests and conformed with his vision of the properly ordered realm. From his subordinates he demanded not only allegiance but the exemplification of the "Way of Arms" (*buhendō*)—or the "Way of the Warrior" (*mushadō*)—by skill in the management of their own vassals no less than by the fighting deed.

To those who gave him total respect and obedience—who were resolved to "do everything as I say"—he promised "enduring good fortune, as befits the proper samurai."[81] But those whom he found remiss in their duty to him, or slack and unfair in dealing with their retainers, he castigated for a failure to "meet the standards of the Way of Arms." The language of his regulations and edicts is even more passionate and harsh than that which he directed at Shogun Yoshiaki in the stern remonstrance. Nobunaga hectors even his oldest vassals and his own son. He accuses Sakuma Nobumori, a retainer of thirty years'

[80] See George Elison, "Hideyoshi, the Bountiful Minister," in *Warlords, Artists, and Commoners: Japan in the Sixteenth Century*, edited by George Elison and Bardwell L. Smith (Honolulu: The University Press of Hawaii, 1980).

[81] Item [9], Regulations for the Province of Echizen (*Okite jōjō: Echizen no kuni*), dated Tenshō 3 (1575)/9/-; *Shinchō kōki* 8.7, p. 199, and Okuno, *Monjo*, no. 549, vol. 2, 89.

standing, of "lacking the stomach to fight," reminds him that "the Way of the Warrior is something else again," condemns him for "blind obstinacy, lack of sense," and "cowardice," dispossesses him and his son, and sends them into exile in the Kōyasan monastery to do penance for their "criminal negligence."[82] (The clincher is in the peroration: "You dared talk back to Nobunaga, who gives the orders to the realm.") His son Nobukatsu he also finds insufficiently aggressive in the pursuit of military exploits and irresolute toward his provincial samurai; he lectures Nobukatsu on the need to "exert yourself now and in the future—first of all for the sake of the realm, in your father's service, as a sign of love for your brother Jōnosuke [Nobutada], and for your own sake," and threatens to disown him unless he changes his disposition.[83] To a commander in the field he does not hesitate to write: "If there is the slightest slip-up on account of some rash action, even if you get away with your life, you will never enter my presence again."[84]

These, too, are more than merely hortatory statements. Having expelled Shogun Yoshiaki from the realm's capital city, Nobunaga himself—whether or not he acquired the title of shogun—assumed the right to speak for the military hierarchy in the name of the realm.[85] There also exists at least one document in which those who do not manifest

[82] *Monjo*, no. 894, vol. 2, 531-39, and *Shinchō kōki* 13.10/11, pp. 330-34, entry for Tenshō 8/8/12. The document exists in several variants, and was apparently made public for the purposes of propaganda. On this matter, also see *Monjo*, no. 892, vol. 2, 529-30; *Monjo*, supp. no. 100, vol. 2, 934. The latter states flatly that the Sakuma deserve death but are spared for the time being in view of their long service.

[83] *Monjo*, no. 843, vol. 2, 460.

[84] *Monjo*, no. 968, vol. 2, 677.

[85] For example, in ordering Shimazu Yoshihisa to make peace with his Kyushu rivals, the Ōtomo—a truly shogunal posture—he also demanded "great loyalty toward the realm" (*Tenka ni taishi taichū tarubeku sōrō*) on the occasion of Nobunaga's forthcoming campaign against the Mōri; copy of a letter to Shimazu Shuri no Daibu [Tenshō 8]/8/12, *Monjo*, no. 886, vol. 2, 520.

"great loyalty" to his Tenka are, remarkably enough, stamped by Nobunaga as "enemies of the imperial court"![86] The Tenka to which he referred again and again was not a haphazard realm; Nobunaga was determined to show that it had strict standards; it was to be governed by firm regimentation (*seitō*).[87] In particular, the repeated invocation of buhendō and mushadō was meant to demonstrate that Nobunaga was engaged in a massive reorganization of the way in which the samurai class exercised dominion over the land. The goal was nothing else than the overthrow of the disjointed Sengoku pattern of allegiances and the creation of a new order in Japan.

Nobunaga's efforts to eradicate Sengoku characteristics among the daimyo who made up his regime became particularly pronounced after the successful conclusion of the conflict that was the greatest challenge of his career, the Ten Years' War against the "religious monarchy" of the Honganji, in 1580. The last years of his life were marked by the pursuit of a comprehensive policy whose key elements were the destruction of provincial forts, the transfer of daimyo from their domains, and cadastral surveys. Let us look at a few concrete examples.

In 1575, having completed the conquest of Echizen by destroying the armed confederations of the True Pure Land sect and thereby eliminating the Honganji's power there, Nobunaga assigned the province to Shibata Katsuie, issuing to him a set of regulations that circumscribed his authority beforehand. In medieval parlance, Shibata would have been termed the shugo of the province. That

---

[86] *Monjo*, no. 1006, vol. 2, 720.

[87] *Seitō*—literally "the way of government"—is no vague abstraction but means prohibitions and other governmental ordinances and laws; a "proper way of government" (*tadashii seitō*) means rigorous laws. This specific contemporary meaning is clear from *Vocabvlario da lingoa de Iapam com adeclaração em Portugues* (Em Nangasaqui no Collegio de Iapam da Companhia de Iesvs, 1603), f. 294v; facsimile published by Doi Tadao, *Nippo jisho* (Tokyo: Iwanami Shoten, 1960), p. 588: "Xeitǒ. Matçurigotono michi. *Prohibições, & ordenações, ou leis de gouerno*."

Nobunaga meant him to have far less than a medieval shugo's autonomy in the governance of this domain is, however, absolutely clear—not least from the document's supplement, which is addressed to Fuwa Mitsuharu, Sassa Narimasa, and Maeda Toshiie:

> The province of Echizen is for the most part left at Shibata's disposal. You three, however, shall act as Shibata's overseers and are assigned two districts. Hence you shall report without duplicity on the good and bad points of his conduct, and Shibata shall report on the good and bad points of yours. Above all, act with due care that you sharpen each other's efficiency. If you are negligent, you will be held in contumely.[88]

These "overseers" (*metsuke*) are also known as the "Echizen Triumvirs" (*sanninshū*). Fuwa died in early 1581; Maeda and Sassa themselves became daimyo over entire provinces, and their cases are important illustrations of Nobunaga's policy in his last years.

In the autumn of 1581, Nobunaga sent Maeda orders informing him that he was being assigned the newly conquered province of Noto and that the holdings granted him in Echizen were to be transferred to Suganoya Kuemon.[89] Maeda's wife and children, the orders stressed, "are without fail to move to [Noto] province immediately." Kuemon, the text pointed out, "will shortly proceed to Echizen." A postscript added: "It is important that your fort in Fuchū and the private residences of your retainers be handed over in good order."

Maeda Toshiie had been a direct vassal and an intimate of Nobunaga since 1551, that is to say from the very first

---

[88] *Shinchō kōki* 8.7, p. 199; *Monjo*, vol. 2, 89. The regulations are discussed in greater detail by George Elison, "The Cross and the Sword: Patterns of Momoyama History," in *Warlords, Artists, and Commoners*, pp. 73-75.

[89] *Monjo*, no. 954, vol. 2, 640-42. What follows below is essentially a reprise of Fujiki Hisashi, "Tōitsu seiken no seiritsu," *Iwanami kōza: Nihon rekishi* 9 (Tokyo: Iwanami Shoten, 1975), 72-75.

year of his lordship, even before Nobunaga had secured his hold over his corner of Owari province.[90] By 1581, however, Toshiie had been settled in Echizen for six years, had developed a local military organization known as the Echizen-shū, and was showing signs of independence in his provincial domain. As Iwasawa Yoshihiko has shown, the mainstays of Maeda's domanial organization included not only members of his family (*ichizoku*) and hereditary vassals (*fudai*), but also many local Echizen samurai, former vassals of the Sengoku daimyo house of Asakura (destroyed by Nobunaga in 1573), who were incorporated into the structures of Toshiie's fief with their old privileges left intact.[91]

Accordingly, the orders to hand over Fuchū castle and "the private residences of your retainers" (*narabi ni shimojimo shitaku tomo*), that is, the estates of the old local landholders, in effect meant the dissolution of Toshiie's power base. This measure could not but affect the entire character of Maeda's territorial rule, which had developed strength by sinking deep roots in the provincial ground, among the local landholders. As a result of the transfer to Noto, the house of Maeda was forced to reorganize its vassalage structure in a mould approximating the early modern model. It is unfortunately not clear just what classes of retainers were encompassed by the term *shimojimo*. One can only hope that further research, especially a comparison with Hideyoshi's policy of daimyo transfers (in the course of which all those of samurai status were forced to move to their lord's new domain), will provide a definitive answer.

Accompanying Maeda Toshiie's transfer to Noto was the transfer of another one of the Echizen Triumvirs, Sassa Narimasa of Komaru castle, to the province of Etchū; the two were thereby posted to hold the Nobunaga regime's front line in the Hokuriku region. Immediately prior to

[90] Iwasawa Yoshihiko, *Maeda Toshiie*, Jinbutsu Sōsho 136 (Tokyo: Yoshikawa Kōbunkan, 1966), p. 15.

[91] Ibid., pp. 47-50.

their installation in their new domains, Nobunaga apparently sent Suganoya Kuemon to Noto and Etchū as a special commissioner charged with the destruction of all the provincial forts save those designated as the daimyo residences.[92] And Sassa Narimasa in advance announced a "province-wide survey" (*kuninami no kyūmei*) to the landholding samurai of Etchū.[93]

But even prior to these events in the Hokuriku region, immediately after the end of the war against the Honganji in 1580, Nobunaga had ordered the transfers of Hosokawa Fujitaka to Tango and Akechi Mitsuhide to Tanba, the immediate hinterland of Kyoto, urging them not to neglect the proper "regimentation" of their provinces.[94] We know from Nobunaga's subsequent pronouncements to the two that his concept of the proper way of governing a province included principally the cadastral survey and a series of judgments made on its basis—the imposition of military levies according to the thereby determined income from the estates granted in fief, the confirmation of fiefs on the basis of the survey, and the confiscation (through absorption into the lord's immediate domain) of holdings beyond those defined by the survey.[95]

It is important to note that the fiefs of local landholders were by no means confirmed as a matter of course and unconditionally when the regime absorbed a new province. The regulations issued to the recipients of domains in Kai and Shinano after the conquest of Takeda Katsuyori in 1582 specify that "the loyal are to be left in place, but [local] samurai of the sort that can cause trouble are to be got rid of either by forced suicide or expulsion"; while stressing

[92] *Shinchō kōki* 14.9, p. 361.

[93] Narimasa to Arisawa Zusho no Suke, Tenshō 9 (1581)/10/13; full text in Kusunose Masaru, "Sassa Narimasa no Etchū e no bunpō o megutte" 1, *Toyama shidan*, 56/57 (1973), 10.

[94] *Monjo*, no. 887, vol. 2, 522. Also see no. 889, pp. 525-26; and no. 90, pp. 526-27.

[95] *Monjo*, nos. 941-42, vol. 2, 622-23; no. 943, p. 623; no. 945, pp. 624-26.

that "provincial samurai are to be treated with courtesy," the regulations also caution their new masters not to let down their guard regarding them.[96] One of the very last documents issued by Nobunaga, the "Regulations concerning your forthcoming mission to Shikoku," which he addressed to his son Kanbe Sanshichirō Nobutaka three weeks before his death, states unequivocally: "Examine the provincial samurai as to their loyalty or lack of it. Leave in place those who ought to be left in place; expel those who ought to be expelled. Apply firm regimentation."[97] The simple procedure of integrating the local samurai into the new lord's vassalage structure by their confirmation in their hereditary domains (*honryō ando*) is going out of use; rather, they are to pass through a strict winnowing before they can be "left in place." The newly prescribed regimen prominently includes a land survey involving the close examination of all holdings, hereditary domains not excluded.

Land surveys immediately preceded by the destruction of forts were also conducted in cases where no large-scale transfer of daimyo from one domain to another occurred. This is what happened in 1580 in three of the five provinces of the Kinai area, where the surrender of the temple-fortress Ishiyama Honganji in Osaka—meaning, for all practical purposes, the end of the Ten Years' War—finally gave Nobunaga a free hand in that region. The reassignment of Akechi Mitsuhide and Hosokawa Fujitaka and the purge of the Sakuma and several other old vassals[98] were two of the measures which Nobunaga

[96] *Kuni-okite: Kō-Shin ryōshū*, dated Tenshō 10/3/-; *Shinchō kōki* 15.19, pp. 398-99, and *Monjo*, no. 985, vol. 2, 702-704.

[97] *Monjo*, no. 1052, vol. 2, 764-65.

[98] Namely, Hayashi Sado no Kami Hidesada, one of his childhood tutors; Niwa Ukon Ujikatsu, another of his oldest Owari retainers; and Andō Iga no Kami Morinari, one of the "Mino Triumvirs" whose defection to Nobunaga's side in 1567 made possible the conquest of that province, and his son. *Shinchō kōki* 13.10/11, pp. 334-35, entry for Tenshō 8/8/17.

took immediately after Osaka's surrender. At least as significant—but until recently not as much noted by historians—was the destruction of castles in the provinces of Settsu and Kawachi that was carried out at the same time; this topic deserves particular attention in future research. Most remarkable of all, however, is the series of events that overtook Yamato in the aftermath of Osaka's fall: this province had to bear the full brunt of Nobunaga's new policies.

We may observe that series of events in detail through the pages of the diary kept by Abbot Eishun of Tamon'in, a priory of the great Nara monastery which was the erstwhile shugo of Yamato province, the Kōfukuji.[99] The entries of interest to us begin on Tenshō 8 (1580)/8/4: Tsutsui Junkei, Nobunaga's governor of Yamato, "went up to the capital on the second [the day on which the Honganji surrendered] and returned last night with orders to destroy castles throughout the province." Before he could set about this task, on the eighth of the month, he was called away on a similar mission to Kawachi: "All the castles in Settsu and Kawachi are going to be destroyed, they say." Eight days later, Junkei returned from the neighboring province to find Yamato in a state of "extraordinary agitation." Those who were afraid and uncertain of what would happen next found out on the following day, the seventeenth, when Nobunaga's special emissaries Takikawa Ichimasu and Yabe Zenshichirō arrived to supervise the destruction on the spot; a labor force was levied from all the households of Nara, and the machinery of castle-demolition in Yamato went into high gear. On the twentieth, Eishun reported: "They say that almost all the forts in the province have been destroyed. Not one is left save for Kōriyama castle, which will supposedly be granted to Tsutsui." That was the first step.

The second—which was to send Eishun into agonies of

---

[99] See *Tamon'in nikki*, entries from Tenshō 8/8/4 to 11/12, vol. 3, 119-33. Also see *Monjo*, no. 898, pp. 545-54.

despair—came on the twenty-fifth of the ninth month, when Takikawa again appeared in Nara as Nobunaga's emissary, accompanied this time by Akechi Mitsuhide. Their purpose became apparent the next day, when they announced that "all the temples, shrines, estate proprietors . . . and provincial samurai [*kunishū*] throughout this province must produce declarations of their income [*sashidashi*]." A form was provided, complete with a rubric declaring that the respondent was aware he faced the confiscation of all his property if he concealed even the slightest portion of his "paddy and dry fields, residential land, and woodlands." Faced with the task of filling out this form, Eishun could only implore divine protection, wondering if "the sun and moon had not yet fallen from the sky." A summary report was not enough for the dour commissioners: they wanted itemization and the attachment of precise schedules (*honchō*). Again and again, they called for greater detail, until they had a complete description of each parcel of dues-producing land—meaning by that the location, square measure, yearly dues, and identity of the person responsible for paying them. Cash income (*zeni-jishi*) was to be converted into its equivalent in rice.

On the twenty-second of the tenth month, the sashidashi for Yamato province were in the hands of the commissioners; on the twenty-fifth came word that the tax levied on the declared income (*sashidashi-sen*) would be ten percent. Three days later, four provincial landholders, who had between them declared income worth 9,000 *koku* in rice, were summoned to Akechi's and Takikawa's field headquarters and sentenced to death, presumably having been found guilty of evasion; troops were sent to confiscate their properties. Having done their work, Akechi and Takikawa on the second of the eleventh month departed Nara, "having spent thirty-eight days here, during which time the anxiety, worry, trouble, toil, suffering, and annoyance of all, high or low, in the province were like the pangs experienced by those fallen into hell." Eishun concluded his laments by blaming all this adversity on the sinful behavior of priests, which had made benevolent deities desert Yamato and demons appear there to bring about "the province's perdition."

The worst did not happen, however. On 11/9, Eishun's despair changed to "joy and happiness," because "last night positive information came from Azuchi that temple and shrine domains would be confirmed without the slightest interference, in accordance with past status; Junkei is to move into Kōriyama castle . . . with the province in its entirety assigned to him." The traditionalist abbot did not perceive the full significance of what had happened. Nobunaga, it is true, had contented himself with establishing his control over Yamato and had not taken the final step to the destruction of the shōen system in the province. But the measures he had undertaken by the survey—most notably the identification of the amount of payment, converted into rice, from each piece of property, as well as of the farmer responsible for the payment—had a great significance for the future. They paved the way for Hideyoshi's subsequent "Taikō survey" and reassessment of incomes in terms of the landholding's putative yield in rice (*kokudaka*), in the course of which the shōen system was indeed destroyed.[100]

What began in Yamato with the demolition of castles in the entire province, climaxed in a province-wide land survey, and was consummated in the execution of prominent provincial landholders was a spectacle that is notable not only for its large scale. What we see here is the prelude to the destruction of the traditional base of local landholding and a foretoken of the Sengoku pattern's dissolution.

[100] Wakita Osamu, *Oda seiken no kiso kōzō*, pp. 197-98. Wakita presents an elaborate discussion of the Yamato survey's significance on pp. 176-202; see especially pp. 186 ff., containing an analysis of new source materials on the sashidashi submitted by the Daijōin, another priory of the Kōfukuji.

Chapter 6

Hideyoshi's Domestic Policies

JOHN WHITNEY HALL

ODA NOBUNAGA's untimely death left to another the task of fulfilling the dream of national unification. Toyotomi Hideyoshi first fought his way into possession of Nobunaga's legacy, and then went on to the final conquest of the daimyo of all Japan in 1590, though it remained for Tokugawa Ieyasu to make that conquest secure. Of the "Three Unifiers," Hideyoshi is clearly the pivotal figure. Not only did he complete the military unification of Japan, but he also presided over vast institutional changes that literally transformed the society of his day.

The specific measures with which Hideyoshi is identified are well known and have been abundantly studied. The land surveys (*kenchi*), confiscation of weapons (*katana gari*), destruction of superfluous castles (*shirowari*), the forcible relocation of daimyo from one domain to another (*kunigae*), the establishment of the *mura* (village) and *kokudaka* (rice tax) systems, and finally the regulations that separated the military and land-cultivating classes (*hei-nō-bunri*), all have been described in great detail. There is less agreement among historians, however, concerning the significance of these measures.

The Toyotomi years witnessed a literal revolution in Japan's governmental and social organization, and it is this transformation that historians have tried to explain by reference to such general concepts as the "transition from Chūsei to Kinsei" or the "movement from feudal to early modern" conditions. If by Chūsei is meant the way things were during the first half of the sixteenth century and Kinsei is defined by what things looked like by 1650, then we have here a tangible continuum to work with. In the analysis that follows, I have tried to give meaning to Hideyoshi's domestic policies by putting them into the context of the historical evolution of Japan's basic political and social institutions. In doing this, I have limited my observations to the changes that took place in five specific fields or levels of national activity over the course of the hundred and fifty-year period recognized in this study. These subjects are roughly in order from top to bottom: national governance, local administration, the samurai class, the land-cultivating class, and the land-tax system that underlay many of the above aspects of sixteenth-century Japanese society.

In reviewing the above five areas in which Hideyoshi's historical impact has been most directly observed, I have drawn heavily from current Japanese scholarly literature, some of which is represented in contributions to this symposium. My own data base, the province of Bizen, is not extensive enough to support by itself a generalized explication of the whole of sixteenth-century Japan.[1] It does, however, suggest an approach that warns against overemphasis either on Hideyoshi's personal influence or the temptation to judge that influence as good or bad, progressive or retrogressive, feudal or nonfeudal. By putting Hideyoshi's policies and their implementation into these contexts it will be clear, first of all, that he was neither the sole instigator nor the final architect of the actual changes that occurred in each sector. Yet he obviously moved each process a considerable distance along the continuum of change, and that is the main conclusion of the following survey.

FORMATION OF A NEW STRUCTURE OF LEGITIMACY

Military force was not the only implement used by Hideyoshi in his creation of a new national hegemony. The

---

[1] See my *Government and Local Power in Japan, 500 to 1700, A Study Based on Bizen Province* (Princeton: Princeton University Press, 1966).

struggle for unification was, of course, a matter of military conquest, and it is demonstrable that there was a progression of increasing military power available to Japan's military leaders from the time of the Ashikaga shoguns through Nobunaga, Hideyoshi, and the Tokugawa shoguns. Armies increased in size. There were important improvements in vassal band (*kashindan*) organization and in military mobilization. And then at the critical moment contact with Europeans revolutionized the technology of warfare through the introduction of firearms. But that was not the whole of it. Acquisition of legal authority and political legitimacy by the military hegemon was also a requirement, if only after the fact.

Neither Nobunaga nor Hideyoshi gained legitimacy through the office of shogun, though it is interesting to note that Asao Naohiro in his essay in this volume uses the term to designate the kind of hegemonic power each acquired. It is frequently forgotten that Yoshiaki, the last Ashikaga shogun, lived on in exile until 1597, so that technically the Ashikaga shogunate ended only then. As Fujiki Hisashi has shown in the previous essay, we cannot know for certain how far Nobunaga might have gone toward establishing a new sovereignty had he lived to preside over the military unification that he had hoped to achieve. Hideyoshi's effort to match his military primacy with tokens of legitimacy was more conservative. But it was persistent and highly visible, so that it stands out as one of the best-documented sides of his career. This effort had four main aspects, most of which followed precedents going back to the earlier Kamakura and Muromachi shogunates.

First, as had previous military leaders from Taira Kiyomori (1118-1181) on, Hideyoshi aspired to high status within the court and, having acquired such status, used it to exploit the symbolism of imperial favor: a private attack upon a daimyo competitor now became a "punitive expedition" for "the good of the state." It should not be assumed that Hideyoshi's "Kyoto orientation" was entirely his own doing. Both the imperial court (*tennō* and *kuge*) and the shogun were in the habit of inviting provincial military leaders to Kyoto to serve as "protectors" or keepers of law and order. And daimyo who showed promise or who emerged victorious in regional struggles were actively courted by the Kyoto nobility, both as a means of protection and in hope of patronage. As we saw in the case of Nobunaga, regional military figures commonly showed their gratitude for favors received from the court by building or rebuilding palaces in Kyoto and by donations of various sorts.

Hideyoshi's "aristocratization," to borrow George Elison's term, was presumably modeled on the precedent of Ashikaga Yoshimitsu (1358-1408).[2] But the highest titles acquired by Hideyoshi, those of *kanpaku* (imperial regent) and *taikō* (retired kanpaku), were unprecedented, in that they moved in upon the private preserve of the Fujiwara family, the most exalted of the court nobility outside the imperial house. The well-known occasion in 1588 when Hideyoshi invited Emperor Go-Yōzei to visit his Kyoto residence (the Jurakutei) was calculated to add luster to Hideyoshi's growing military power. The visit was used symbolically as a way of publicly displaying his superiority over all his vassal daimyo. It also provided an occasion to oblige these vassals to pledge, in the name of the emperor, their loyalty to Hideyoshi. But equally important as the use Hideyoshi made of the emperor was what he did not do: he in no way sought to displace the emperor or diminish his symbolic prestige. Instead of abolishing the court, Hideyoshi assimilated his military organization into the court system, using court titles and ranks—the awards of which he controlled—as a way of rewarding and ranking his own men.

[2] George Elison, "Hideyoshi, the Bountiful Minister," in George Elison and Bardwell L. Smith, eds., *Warlords, Artists, and Commoners: Japan in the Sixteenth Century* (Honolulu: The University Press of Hawaii, 1980), pp. 223-44. See also Nagahara Keiji, "Yoshimitsu to Hideyoshi," in *Chūsei nairanki no shakai to minshū* (Tokyo: Yoshikawa Kōbunkan, 1977), pp. 290-94.

Recently, as is manifest in the essays by Fujiki, Asao, and Katsumata in this volume, Japanese scholars have taken a special interest in probing behind the ceremonial facade of imperial politics to show that both Nobunaga and Hideyoshi were aware of the political, legal, and ideological dimensions of the problems of securing legitimacy. Concepts such as *tenka* (the realm, or the realm's ruler), *kokka* (the state), and *kōgi* (public authority or the possessor of that authority) were consciously used to support hegemonic claims on a public rather than personal basis. Such concepts were useful because they could be pushed to the point of presuming an absolute right of governance not dependent on imperial sanction but rather on the power to perform acts "for the good of the realm."[3]

A second means of gaining legitimacy, particularly in the eyes of the common people, was for the military hegemon to achieve veneration as a *kami* (deity in the Shinto sense), if not for himself then for his lineage after death. According to Asao Naohiro, Oda Nobunaga went farther than his two successors by himself claiming to be a kami.[4] In the case of Hideyoshi, deification came after death with the erection in Kyoto of Toyokuni Jinja and his veneration as the deity Toyokuni Daimyōjin. This precedent was followed by Ieyasu's successors, who enshrined the first Tokugawa shogun at Nikkō as the deity Tōshō-daigongen. Such actions by the military hegemons of the sixteenth century

---

[3] See the essay in this volume by Katsumata Shizuo. For a more extended discussion of the concept of kōgi, see Fukaya Katsumi, "Kōgi to mibunsei," in Sasaki Junnosuke, et al., eds., *Taikei Nihon kokka shi* 3, *Kinsei* (Tokyo: Tōkyō Daigaku Shuppankai, 1975), 149-72; and Nagahara Keiji, "Sengoku daimyō ni okeru 'kōgi' kannen no keisei," in his *Chūsei nairanki*, pp. 295-300, for an application of this concept to daimyo rule.

[4] This subject is thoroughly discussed by Asao Naohiro in "Kinsei hōkensei ron wo megutte," in Fujiki Hisashi and Kitajima Manji, eds., *Shokuhō seiken*, Rōnshū Nihon rekishi, vol. 6 (Tokyo: Yūseidō, 1974), pp. 4-9. A somewhat more cautious handling of the evidence from the Jesuit Luis Frois appears in George Elison, "The Cross and the Sword; Patterns of Momoyama History," in George Elison and Bardwell L. Smith, eds., *Warriors, Artists, Commoners*, pp. 55-85.

and their successors, together with the eventual bans against Christianity, reveal that they realized that more than simple sanctification by the emperor was necessary to safeguard their status.

Several scholars have suggested that yet a third element in the effort to validate his hegemony is evident in Hideyoshi's invasion of Korea.[5] The capacity not only to deal with foreign powers but also to order the fighting forces of all Japan to engage in such an overseas venture was surely a sign of political power of the highest order. Hideyoshi was not the first military leader to assume full command of foreign relations, for the Ashikaga shoguns had also done so. What Hideyoshi did was to assert this authority on a larger scale, even to the supreme acts of sending military forces overseas and of banning on behalf of the entire nation the presence of Christian missionaries in Japan. The Tokugawa shoguns were not to add significantly to this category of hegemonic authority in foreign affairs. Although they did not send troops overseas, they completed the suppression of Christianity and instituted control of foreign trade and foreign relations through a policy of national closure (*sakoku*). The importance of this as a legitimizing device has been pointed out by both Asao Naohiro and Ronald Toby.[6]

The above elements in any assertion of legitimacy, of course, were incidental to the lord-vassal relationship defined between Hideyoshi and the daimyo and *shōmyō* (lesser lords) who accepted his overlordship. Naturally, it had taken force, or the threat of force, to bring all military proprietors to accept Hideyoshi's claim to the status of military hegemon (*bushi no tōryō*). And as Tokugawa Ieyasu's experience was to show, it required a strong balance of power in

[5] Asao, "Kinsei hōkensei ron wo megutte," pp. 10-11.

[6] Asao Naohiro in "Shōgun and Tennō," in this volume; Ronald P. Toby, "Reopening the Question of *Sakoku*: Diplomacy in the Legitimation of the Tokugawa Bakufu," *The Journal of Japanese Studies* 3 (Summer 1977), 323-63.

favor of the central authority to make that status stick. Under Hideyoshi the relationship between ultimate overlord and subordinate local military proprietors became more clearly defined: specific oaths of allegiance were required, hostages were systematically exacted. Perfection of the kokudaka system for assessing land productivity made possible a more accurate determination of the size of daimyo domains. Accordingly, the size of military establishments (men and castles) could be more precisely known and regulated. Vassal daimyo were more easily subject to relocation of fiefs. These techniques, which had grown up within the bushi community over many centuries, were brought to maximum effectiveness by Hideyoshi. The only obvious Tokugawa additions to these methods of daimyo control were the alternate attendance (*sankin-kōtai*), sakoku, and anti-Christian provisions that appear in the Tokugawa code governing military households (*buke shohatto*).

The most tangible feature of Hideyoshi's hegemonic power, and the one that underlay all the above, was the capacity as overlord to control on a national scale the right to hold landed proprietorships. In this case, Hideyoshi completed an ongoing process of consolidation in the locus of proprietary rights. Nobunaga, and in fact all of the great regional daimyo such as the Uesugi, Go-Hōjō, Tokugawa, Mōri, Chōsokabe, and Shimazu, were already in the process of asserting overlord status over regions that contained lesser daimyo who had been coerced into recognizing their superior authority.[7] Each military conquest led to confiscation and reconfirmation or reallotment of proprietary rights by the victorious regional hegemon. The claim to possession of absolute and total proprietary authority over all Japan had been made in the abstract by the Ashikaga

[7] For one example of the "daimyo as lawgiver," see Marius B. Jansen, "Tosa in the Sixteenth Century: The 100 Article Code of Chōsokabe Motochika," in John W. Hall and Marius B. Jansen, eds., *Studies in the Institutional History of Early Modern Japan* (Princeton: Princeton University Press, 1968), pp. 99-114.

shoguns, but the actual enforcement of this authority became possible only after the conquest of all Japan by one of
these competing regional figures. It was Hideyoshi's des-
tiny to be the first to achieve this goal when, in 1590, the
Date, Satake, and other daimyo of northern Japan capitu-
lated after the fall of Odawara castle. By their act, which
completed Hideyoshi's conquest, it became literally true
that all proprietary rights (*ryōshu-ken*) became the possession of the military hegemon, and that all daimyo and
shōmyō (and even court families and religious establishments) could hold territory only as grants (*azukari mono*)
over the vermilion seal (*shuin*) of Hideyoshi.[8] Moreover,
Hideyoshi held sufficient power to preclude any distribution of proprietary rights except at his pleasure or by successful warfare against him. Prior to Hideyoshi's conquest,
civil warfare had led to uncontrolled shifts in territory
among competing daimyo, although such shifts may have
been rationalized after the fact by patents of approval secured from the Muromachi bakufu. After 1590, only on
one occasion did warfare permit the free acquisition of
land rights not sanctioned by the hegemon, and that was at
the climactic battle of Sekigahara (1600), when ultimate
hegemonic power passed from the Toyotomi remnants
into the hands of Tokugawa Ieyasu. The Osaka campaign
fourteen years later, because it did not result in the defeat
of the hegemon, led to no proprietary changes not
sanctioned by Ieyasu.

Hideyoshi's successful acquisition through military conquest of ultimate proprietary rights under his own authority was surely one of his greatest achievements. With this
act he created a new national order, which in its essential
details remained intact until the 1870s. His vulnerable
point was the still precarious balance of actual power between himself and his vassals. This was symbolized by the

[8] See the analysis of this point by Ishii Ryōsuke, "Chiso kaisei to tochi
shoyūken no kindaika," part 7, in *Hōgaku Kyōkai zasshi* 86 (November
1969), 1242.

fact that Tokugawa Ieyasu held a larger territory than did the Toyotomi house. Thus the overlordship vested in the Toyotomi line did not survive the attack of the Tokugawa-led eastern faction of daimyo; but the structure remained. The Tokugawa house simply achieved enduring stability for a system designed by Hideyoshi—though not without effort, as the article in this volume by Asao Naohiro demonstrates.

ESTABLISHMENT OF THE KINSEI DAIMYO SYSTEM

Since Hideyoshi did not become shogun, the national organization he created did not take the precise form of the bakuhan system that characterized the Tokugawa regime. Common to both polities, however, were the daimyo domains that served as the primary units of local administration under hegemonic military authority. The shape of the Tokugawa bakuhan system became inevitable when Hideyoshi did not destroy the daimyo system following his military conquest.

The early history of the emergence of the daimyo domain has been told in local terms, region by region or daimyo house by daimyo house. During the 1950s and 1960s, it became common practice for historians to see a four-stage pattern of evolution in daimyo development as a loosely applied analytical tool.[9] The stages and the rough dates defining them were: shugo daimyo (1338-1467), Sengoku daimyo (1467-1568), *Shokuhō* daimyo (1568-1600), and Kinsei daimyo (1600-1870). Of late this practice of giving special identity to the Shokuhō period (that is, the Oda-Toyotomi years) as a distinct "stage" is less frequently used, and the term has been employed quite sparingly in this volume. Rather, the attention of scholars has focused on the key problems of the shift from Sengoku to Kinsei institutions.

[9] See my "Foundations of the Modern Japanese Daimyō," in Hall and Jansen, *Studies,* pp. 65-77.

We are concerned here with Hideyoshi's influence upon two parallel lines of development: first the evolution of the daimyo domain as a unit of local rule leading to the emergence of the Kinsei daimyo domain or *han*, and second, the evolution of the relationship between daimyo and higher authority, leading eventually to the formation of the bakuhan system.[10] The tendency of recent writing on this subject is to find a closer and more continuous link between developments at the center and in the provinces.[11] It is easy to see that these lines of development—local autonomy versus national control—were mutually dependent but not fully compatible. Unhindered development of the daimyo domain would have produced completely autonomous territories. Central hegemonic power obviously denied this autonomy. Yet it is doubtful whether the daimyo could have achieved full and secure territorial independence on their own. And it is at this point that Hideyoshi comes into the picture. For, as put forcefully by Sasaki Junnosuke in this volume, many of the measures adopted by Hideyoshi to restrict the autonomy of his daimyo vassals were simply the enforcement at a national level of measures necessary to the daimyo's ability to hold his local territory. In other words, the daimyo had to give away some of his potential autonomy in order to safeguard his own authority within his domain. For the daimyo under Hideyoshi, ultimate legitimation and protection came from the investiture they received from him.

Although it leads to some oversimplification, it is useful to reduce the critical aspects of the daimyo problem to two. These are, first, the process by which the daimyo acquired administrative and proprietary possession of their domains, asserting what in legal terms was known as *isshiki*

[10] This process is one of the main subjects of the essay by Sasaki Junnosuke in this volume, "The Establishment of the Bakuhan State."

[11] See Peter J. Arnesen, *The Medieval Japanese Daimyo: The Ōuchi Family's Rule of Suō and Nagato* (New Haven: Yale University Press, 1980).

shihai or *ichien chigyō*, and in ideological terms the right to establish a local *kokka*. The second is the evolution of the process by which the military hegemon acquired the capacity to exert an overlordship over these semiautonomous daimyo.[12]

In recent studies of the daimyo during the Muromachi and Sengoku eras, emphasis on the use of military force to gain local supremacy has been balanced by a greater awareness of the emerging daimyo's reliance on precedents, legal forms, and ideologies. Although military strength was always a necessary ingredient, it alone was not sufficient. Local military houses made use of a number of systems of legitimate authority in order to justify their superior status and their use of force. Remnants of former authority systems from the Heian and Kamakura times were cited to justify the exercise of local authority. The ultimate manifestation of this practice, as apparent in the essay by Katsumata Shizuo in this volume, was the use by daimyo of concepts such as *kokka* and *kōgi*, and the issuance of house laws suggesting the right of the daimyo to assert legitimate judicial and proprietary authority over subdivisions of the state—though eventually such house laws were superseded by the hegemon's edicts.[13] The procedures used by daimyo to support and regularize their local control included the effort to make their vassals totally dependent upon them for their land holdings, the strict registration of land and control of the land-tax system, and the effort to disarm those not enrolled on the daimyo's list of retainers.[14] Each of these measures was picked up and given nationwide application under Hideyoshi, and it is questionable whether any but the

[12] In English see Wakita Osamu, "The Kokudaka System: A Device for Unification," *Journal of Japanese Studies* 1 (Spring 1975), 302-10.

[13] In English, see George Sansom, *A History of Japan 1334-1615* (Stanford: Stanford University Press, 1961), pp. 251-55.

[14] This process is well illustrated by the rise of the Ukita house in Bizen, for which see my *Government and Local Power*, pp. 296-323.

strongest of the daimyo could have enforced these measures on their own. Thus, although the national cadastral survey and the confiscation of weapons were calculated to enhance the hegemon's control, both were to the advantage of the daimyo, as well.

It is difficult to determine whether there was ever a moment in Japanese history when the holders of local power, daimyo of whatever style, could claim to possess independent—or sovereign—lordship rights simply by seizure and without reference to higher authority or precedent.[15] It may well be that only the *ikki* (local confederation) type of organizations, led by either kokujin or religious groups, were capable of doing so.[16] But between Nobunaga and Hideyoshi the religious threat was brutally crushed by force of arms. It has been suggested that the reason for thoroughness and brutality in these instances was the particular nature of the threat the ikki posed. As for the daimyo, military conquest, followed by confiscation and reissuance of all proprietary land grants, permitted Hideyoshi to bring under his absolute control the authority to grant them land rights. He was also able to influence the nature of the rights that daimyo could exercise over their domains.

Although the terms under which Hideyoshi granted or confirmed territories to his vassal daimyo were never spelled out in full legal detail, the weight of precedent was

[15] The question of whether sovereign local autonomy was achieved even by the great regional hegemonic daimyo of the early sixteenth century is moot, since no such situation lasted for long. Nagahara Keiji describes the Tokugawa as ruling a ryōgoku totally separated from central authority in "Chūsei kōki daimyō ryōgokusei ki ni okeru tennō," in his *Chūsei nairan*, pp. 84-92. Katsumata Shizuo refers to the "embryonic concept of the sovereign state" in his treatment of antecedents in Nobunaga's assertion of tenka authority.

[16] Asao Naohiro has suggested that the reason Nobunaga played with the idea of asserting himself to be a living kami was to counter the potential threat from such religious bodies. See his "Kinsei hōkensei ron," pp. 6-7.

always evoked through the technical terms used in documents of award, and also in the general injunctions issued by the hegemon. Ishii Ryōsuke has written to this point, suggesting that under Hideyoshi (and thereafter under the Tokugawa) daimyo received the *ryōchi* and *shioki* rights over a given territory, which in itself was defined not in land-measure terms but by kokudaka (a procedure that will be described below).[17] Ryōchi refers to proprietary rights over land (that is, rights to alienate and to collect dues and labor services), shioki refers to administrative and judicial rights over the inhabitants of that land. While the daimyo themselves were strugging to gain local control of these rights, once they had been forced to capitulate to Hideyoshi and to receive their grants under his vermilion seal, their exercise of these rights became secure although subject to limitations imposed by the hegemon. According to Ishii, these limitations were implied in the concept of precariousness contained in the word *azukaru* (to hold in trust). In other words, the daimyo's domain was considered a trust subject to the hegemon's pleasure. Daimyo were accountable to the overlord's laws, to the expectation of good conduct, good administration, and loyal military support. The idea of azukaru meant that daimyo were obliged to "repudiate" (to use Sasaki Junnosuke's word) the claim that their domains were private possessions. The hegemon could, and did, frequently move daimyo from domain to domain for strategic or other reasons. By Hideyoshi's time there was a conscious policy of reducing the size of daimyo military establishments in terms of men and fortified locations. The relationships between hegemon and vassal daimyo, begun by Nobunaga, were imposed nationally after Hideyoshi's military conquest.[18]

[17] Ishii, "Chiso," pp. 1238-40.

[18] As an example of Hideyoshi's use of the powers of investiture, of marriage arrangement, of taking hostages, and of granting fictional kinship status as a means of cementing close vassalage ties, see his handling of Ukita Hideie of Bizen, as described in my *Government and Local Power*, p. 325.

Thus it appears that, just as daimyo were reaching the height of their local autonomy, Hideyoshi succeeded in imposing upon them the limitations of a kōgi authority (he, in fact, called himself tenka) vested in him as overlord. This relationship became the essence of the Tokugawa bakuhan system at the national level. But the evolution of the local administration within the daimyo domain did not stop at this point. Within the han, relationships between daimyo, samurai retainers (*kashin*), peasants, traders, and religious bodies were yet to reach a stable condition. The differences between what has been referred to as the Shokuhō daimyo and the Kinsei daimyo are to be found primarily in the pattern of internal organization within the han: specifically, the increased bureaucratic "absolutism" of Kinsei daimyo rule and the consequent conversion of the daimyo's vassals to a fully dependent status.[19] This, in turn, was to hinge in large part upon the evolving status of the samurai class as a whole.

FORMATION OF THE KINSEI SAMURAI CLASS

In the century and a half after 1500, the non-daimyo members of the military aristocracy were transformed from rural fief (and sometimes castle) holders to landless, urban-living stipendiaries. The greater part of this transformation came during Hideyoshi's time, resulting from the enforced separation of the military aristocracy from the agricultural class (hei-nō-bunri). Although the stipendiary system (*hōroku-sei*) that distinguished the Kinsei samurai class was not fully extended until the end of the seventeenth century, its institutional base was brought into being by the land registration and weapons confiscation programs enforced nationally by Hideyoshi.

On this subject, there are two primary questions of in-

---

[19] For case examples, see Marius B. Jansen, "Tosa in the Seventeenth Century," in Hall and Jansen, *Studies*, pp. 115-29; Hall, *Government and Local Power*, pp. 375-423. This is one of the main points made by Sasaki in this volume.

terpretation over which historians divide.[20] First, there is
still no agreement on how to characterize the composition
of the lower levels of the rural samurai and potential
samurai families prior to the separation of statuses. Second, there continues to be a strenuous debate over whether
the eventual separation of *hei* from *nō* was spontaneous or
was the result of coercion by the daimyo and by Hideyoshi's hegemonic interests. With respect to the first problem, confusion over how to identify the significant types or
levels of rural military society is reflected in confusion over
terminology. As mentioned in the Introduction, terms like
ryōshu, kokujin, jizamurai, dogō, gōshi, myōshu are applied
loosely to ill-defined types of provincial military figures.
Ryōshu refers to proprietors of any size or form, and
therefore can be used in a broad, unspecific way. With respect to kokujin there is fair agreement that it should be
reserved for local military proprietors who had the potential to become daimyo, or at least high ranking members of
daimyo vassal bands (kashindan). The term jizamurai is
generally applied to part-samurai, part-cultivator types
who functioned as village chiefs by virtue of extensive land
holdings that they managed and, for the most part, cultivated indirectly (that is, by the use of their own bound servants or by letting out to tenants). But the terms dogō and
gōshi are often used in the same context. How many levels
can usefully be distinguished in the rural hierarchy above
the level of simple cultivator is hard to determine, and
probably differs from region to region.[21]

[20] Asao Naohiro explores this problem in his study, "Hei'nō bunri wo
megutte—shō-ryōshu-sō no dōkō wo chūshin ni," *Nihonshi kenkyū* 71
(March 1964), 39-60.
[21] See Miyagawa Mitsuru, "From Shōen to Chigyō" in John W. Hall and
Toyoda Takeshi, *Japan in the Muromachi Age* (Berkeley and Los Angeles:
University of California Press, 1977), pp. 100-103 for a clear description
of the common three-tier social structure prior to hei-nō-bunri from the
point of view of the ruling class. Also in the same volume Nagahara Keiji's
article, "Village Communities and Daimyō Power" (pp. 108-11) offers a
case study of stratification at the village level. Sasaki Junnosuke develops a
four-level model in his essay below.

This uncertainty affects our judgment as to whether the kenchi that drew the line between hei and nō cut across rural society along a ready-made line of separation. In most locations there were in each village families who could have moved either way, to join the local daimyo in the castle headquarters or remain in the village as tax-paying landholders. What determined their choice? Was it, as Sasaki Junnosuke suggests, the restlessness in the next lower level of villagers, who were making the position of partially militarized village leaders precarious? Did it result, as Araki Moriaki maintains, from the breakup of what has been called the patriarchal extended family system, which had characterized rural society up to this point?[22] Did the daimyo simply offer more opportunity for advancement as well as security? Did the daimyo coerce upper-level villagers to move to their headquarters in order to increase the size of their armies? Was it the new technology of warfare based on Western-style firearms and the large castle that demanded a greater concentration of troops at the headquarters castle?[23]

For whatever reason, in Hideyoshi's time, as a result of the cadastral surveys, the class separation edict, and the confiscation of weapons from village residents, a withdrawal from the land was imposed upon the samurai class, and the status of locally based proprietor (zaichi ryōshu) was taken from them. At the same time, as we shall see below, the status of part-samurai zaichi ryōshu was denied any who remained in the village.[24] Two results of hei-nō-bunri are obvious, yet are not sufficiently recognized. Separation had the affect of increasing greatly both the number of samurai (an amazing 5 to 8 percent of the popu-

[22] Araki Moriaki, *Bakuhan taisei shakai no seiritsu to kōzō* (Tokyo: Ochanomizu Shobō, 1964), pp. 187ff.

[23] The evidence from what happened in Bizen under the Ukita and the Ikeda would suggest this. See my *Government and Local Power*, pp. 319-22.

[24] Exceptions did exist, of course, but these were found chiefly in the domains of more distant tozama daimyo. For one exceptional case see Jansen, "Tosa in the Seventeenth Century," pp. 128-29.

lation) and the number of independent villagers secure in their land tenure.

Samurai withdrawal from the land did not necessarily lead to immediate urbanization. There were at first two classes of samurai in the daimyo's vassal band: those who continued to receive their income directly from fiefs (*chigyōchi*) and those who were paid stipends (*hōroku*) by the daimyo out of his domain treasury (granary is the more exact term). Of course, since the kokudaka system of land assessment and tax payment eliminated land and its workers as the direct objects of taxation, the lord-serf relationship between rural samurai and villagers was effectively broken as the kenchi was carried out—not in all areas, to be sure, and not fully within Hideyoshi's lifetime. The most complete separation in this respect was to be found in the economically advanced parts of central Japan.[25] There were many areas in the country in which urban-based retainers of daimyo continued to hold chigyō, which were defined in terms of koku assessed on specific villages. Hence these chigyō holders could continue to interfere in such matters as tax calculation or demands for labor service. But the trend was toward abolition or fictionalization of the chigyō holding and the conversion of these to stipendiary payments, a trend that was complete by the end of the seventeenth century in most han.[26] Hideyoshi had moved this process over its greatest obstacles by enforcement of the kokudaka system and the withdrawal of the samurai from the land.

[25] Shōda Ken'ichirō and Hayami Akira, *Nihon keizaishi* (Tokyo: Sekai Shoin, 1965), pp. 55-67.

[26] The story of how this was accomplished in Bizen under the Ikeda House is told in my "Ikeda Mitsumasa and the Bizen Flood of 1654," in Albert M. Craig and Donald H. Shively, eds., *Personality in Japanese History* (Berkeley and Los Angeles: University of California Press, 1970), pp. 57-84. See Sasaki Junnosuke's comments on this event in his essay below. For him the separation of the daimyo's vassals from the land is the ultimate step toward the creation of the true han.

FORMATION OF THE KINSEI MURA AND
ESTABLISHMENT OF THE HYAKUSHŌ CLASS

More controversy has attended the modern study of the changing structure of the agricultural class than has attended any other aspect of the Toyotomi era. Hideyoshi's policies in this area were quite specific and led to numerous concrete measures, such as the nationwide cadastral surveys, the confiscation of weapons, and the rural census (*hitobarai*). These measures have sometimes been interpreted as the final acts of a victorious military hegemon who sought to stabilize his conquest as efficiently as possible. But the modern historian sees them as a much more complex phenomenon, resulting from three parallel trends: 1. the movement toward local daimyo hegemony, 2. the struggle for village autonomy, and 3. the changing nature of the agricultural household unit. In the Muromachi period rural samurai had lived within the agricultural communities that they held as fiefs, exercising both income rights and judicial authority over the cultivators. Increasingly during the fifteenth and sixteenth centuries, cultivators organized themselves into confederations (ikki) in an effort to gain greater freedom from samurai control. The movement became especially effective as village leaders obtained arms with which to press the demands of their groups. Village communities gradually won free rights over such features of rural life as police enforcement, access to water and communal lands, and even autonomy of dues collection under the practice known as *mura-uke* (village contract). Villages acting as legally constituted communities would agree to deliver to superior authority set quotas of annual dues, thus avoiding the direct interference of samurai collectors.[27] Because this kind of collusion between daimyo and cultivators tended to put the village samurai (jizamurai or dogō) in an increasingly

[27] In English see Nagahara Keiji, "Village Communities and Daimyō Power," pp. 107-23.

precarious position, many jizamurai were only too happy to move out of the countryside and take up residence at the daimyo's headquarters.[28] By the same token, this flow of jizamurai from village to town brought about a revolutionary change in the status and composition of rural society.

The movement of jizamurai onto the daimyo's retainer rolls was a common feature in the domains of Sengoku-period daimyo, and this was apparently a reaction both to village militancy and to the daimyo's effort to gain more complete control over his retainers for military purposes. In this process, as already suggested, the daimyo were assisted by Hideyoshi's country-wide control measures. The most far-reaching and significant of these measures was the series of land surveys by which Hideyoshi enforced on a national scale completely new systems of land registration, tax assessment and payment, and land tenure. The Taikō kenchi was dramatic in its national impact, but it was neither capriciously conceived nor arbitrarily enforced by the hegemon.[29] It was, as were so many other of Hideyoshi's acts, simply the final step in a long-term transformation in land-tax procedures that had been underway for almost four centuries: namely, the final displacement of the shōen institutions of absentee proprietorship by local military lordship and the final passage of the rights of land management (but not proprietorship) from the propri-

[28] But not all. Many Sengoku dogō as Shibata Hajime describes in his article "Sengoku dogō-sō to Taikō kenchi," *Rekishi kyōiku* 8.8 (1960), pp. 52-63, resisted the reduction of their proprietary roles in the village for some time.

[29] Of the vast literature devoted to the Taikō kenchi I can cite only a small selection. A good survey article in French is Guy Morichand, " 'Taiko kenchi' le cadastre de Hideyoshi Toyotomi," in *Bulletin de l'École Française d'Extreme-Orient*, 52.1 (1966), 7-69. Early studies by Japanese scholars which have set the stage for the current controversy over the significance of the Taikō kenchi are: Araki Moriaki, *Bakuhan taisei shakai no seiritsu to kōzō*; Miyagawa Mitsuru, *Taikō kenchi ron*, 3 vols. (Tokyo: Ochanomizu Shobō, 1959-1963).

etary class, whether civil or military, to the peasantry. The more powerful daimyo had, by the sixteenth century, begun to conduct new cadastral surveys in order to systematize their local administration, and to restructure tax collection and labor recruitment on the basis of a full knowledge of the extent and productivity of the domain's lands. This effort was taken over on a hegemonic scale first by Nobunaga and then by Hideyoshi as early as 1583 in Ōmi. Thereafter, a series of orders called for the systematic direct resurvey of all the territory under his control, province by province. By the time of his death all provinces had been resurveyed. Moreover, the practice of conducting kenchi was many times repeated by the Tokugawa authorities.

The Taikō kenchi had three primary features: 1. plot-by-plot measurement of cultivated land; 2. assessment of the quality and productive capacity of each plot, hence its tax potential; and 3. determination of the individual responsible for the tax payment. In actual practice there were several stages in the process, which eventually resulted in the full identification and registration of all cultivated land in Japan. Many early surveys were made indirectly by requiring local authorities to submit their own cadastral documents. But the process was not considered complete until survey teams under orders from Hideyoshi or trusted daimyo actually entered each village, measured each field, whether paddy or dry, recorded its area, noted its quality on the basis of past harvest records, and set down the name of the presumed owner.

The cadastral register (*kenchi-chō*), since it was prepared village by village, became the principal document for defining the membership and land holdings of the village. It established the basic tax assessment for the village as a whole. This must be recognized as the primary institutional result (and surely the intent) of the kenchi from the point of view of the ruling authorities. And because of this, the compilers of the kenchi-chō were more concerned with land and its tax assessment (kokudaka) figure than with the village residents themselves. The new mura were quite different from the older shōen communities. Being autonomous tax-paying units, they represented the ultimate development of the mura-uke nengu system whereby villagers agreed to deliver "contracted quotas" of taxes. As such, the mura also served as basic units for the recruitment of labor service, providing porters in time of military activity (*buyaku*) and corvée in peace.[30] So fundamental was the mura as a basic unit of local administration that Ishii Ryōsuke has suggested that the concept "*han-son* system" be used as a replacement for "bakuhan system."[31]

Among other social byproducts of the kenchi was the definition it gave to the legal status of the cultivator and his relationship to the land. Registration in the kenchi-chō served two purposes: it identified each plot of land with the name of a villager, making him accountable for tax payment on what was registered in his name, and it confirmed his right to cultivate the land. Although the first condition placed a number of restraints upon the villager—such as restriction on alienation—the second served to make more secure his right of tenure. The kenchi thus gave new legal status to a broad sector of land-cultivating villagers, generically referred to as *hyakushō*. This class, by virtue of being recorded in the land registry, became what might be described as copyholders, secure in their tenure as cultivators.

But what were the actual tenure rights afforded the cultivator? This point still evokes conflicting opinions from historians. Both Wakita Osamu and Ishii Ryōsuke emphasize the strength of the concept of "possession" given to registrants. To follow Ishii's argument at this point, the

---

[30] These points are well described in Shōda and Hayami, *Nihon keizaishi*, pp. 73-75.

[31] Ishii Ryōsuke, *Ryakusetsu Nihon kokka shi* (Tokyo: Tōkyō Daigaku Shuppan Kai, 1972), pp. 91, 129. Han, of course, means the daimyo domain; son is another reading for mura (village).

nauke-hyakushō (taxable registrant) status, as it was defined by the Taikō kenchi, combined the previous rights of *myōshu-shiki* (management) and *sakushiki* (cultivation). This added up to a degree of ownership that was very close to what could be called private possession.[32] The proof adduced is that, while proprietary "ownership" over the land was vested in the daimyo and their samurai retainers, such ownership was a political right, and not an economic one. Thus, when the Tokugawa regime came to an end, it was the hyakushō who retained full possession of the cultivated land, not the samurai. Opposed to this reading, Araki Moriaki asserts that the daimyo class obtained both the former ryōshu (proprietary) and myōshu (managerial) rights, leaving to the cultivators only the status of serf.[33] Thus he concludes with a less positive view of the status of the hyakushō following enforcement of the kenchi.

It is of interest as a slight digression here to acknowledge the difficulty historians have had in determining the "intent" of the kenchi as this related to the status of the hyakushō. The current controversy began in 1953 with the publication of Araki Moriaki's studies, later consolidated in his *Bakuhan taisei shakai no seiritsu to kōzō* in 1959. Araki's main argument is that the intent of the kenchi was to create a cultivator class in which the "small peasantry" (*shōnōmin*) was given the chance to establish itself (*jiritsu*). Disagreement focused upon the question of what rural society was like before and after the kenchi was enforced. Were cultivators mainly the slave extensions of large patriarchal families (that is, what are called *kafuchōteki dorei*)? And what was the result of the kenchi upon them? Were they thereby converted to serfs (*nōdo*), as Araki would have it, or to partially dependent small cultivators (*reinō*), as Wakita suggests? Much of this argument (aside from the problem

---

[32] Ishii Ryōsuke, "Chiso" 86, 755. See also Ishii Shirō, *Nihon Kokuseishi kenkyū* 1 (Tokyo, 1966), 202-203, and Wakita Osamu, *Kinsei hōkensei seiritsushi ron* 2 (Tokyo: Tōkyō Daigaku Shuppan Kai, 1977), 22.

[33] Araki, *Bakuhan taisei shakai*, pp. 228-35.

of definition of terms) hinges upon the precise nature of the persons whose names were recorded in the cadastral registers as "owners" of cultivated land. Specific points of disagreement turn on whether these individuals were in all cases the actual "owner cultivators" of the land, or whether there were among the registrants free or bound tenants of large landowning farmers, or whether in fact some names were those of large landowners who had their fields cultivated by household tenants. In other words, was the kenchi intended to create a single class of owner-cultivators who as "serfs" of the daimyo or the military hegemon owed allegiance (and taxes) directly to this higher authority? If this was the case, as Araki claims, it would have given rise to the classic Marxian "feudal" relationship whereby the lord exercised direct control over the serf. It is from this standpoint that Araki asserted that the kenchi brought about a "revolution *into* feudalism."[34] The work of Miyagawa Mitsuru differs from that of Araki in detail, but he too is in general agreement that the Taikō kenchi had a "progressive" influence upon Japanese rural society, since it gave new freedoms to the peasantry by moving the status of the bulk of the cultivating class from a form of household slavery into what he claims is closer to serfdom.[35]

In the years since the start of the Taikō kenchi debate it has become clear that the kenchi-chō records alone do not contain all the answers. By taking a more flexible approach, it has become possible to claim meanings quite at odds with Araki's. Recently, for instance, Wakita Osamu has proposed that the emphasis on the intent of the kenchi be placed more on the local proprietary class, the jizamurai. He contends that the main thrust of the kenchi was to deny the status of proprietor (ryōshu) to those samurai who did not move out of the village to become di-

[34] Ibid., p. 221.
[35] Miyagawa explains his idea of "relatively reformist" consequences of the Taikō kenchi (*sōtaiteki kakushin seisaku*) along with differences between himself and Araki in *Taikō kenchi ron*, 1, 24-32.

rect retainers of daimyo.[36] The fact that many types of cultivators were listed on the registers would seem to show that the leveling of village society was not a prime consideration. In fact, former samurai were permitted to survive as village leaders, holding land cultivated at least in part by dependent households, so long as they accepted the status of hyakushō.[37] As becomes evident in the evaluation of mura administration under the bakuhan system, samurai government depended considerably on the existence of a "village leader" class (*yakke* or *yakunin*) to administer the mura and to act as responsible agents in the delivery of the annual tax. But although former samurai could remain in the village as villagers, except in a very few instances they were denied the political powers that jizamurai or dogō had enjoyed. Where "village leaders" still held such power, a struggle between them and the daimyo continued into the Tokugawa period.[38]

Whatever the precise legal status given the hyakushō individually, for the village community as a whole the kenchi all but completed the movement toward autonomy in internal mura affairs begun during the Muromachi era. There were still some changes destined to take place in the relationship of samurai government to village administration under the Tokugawa regime, notably the more complete withdrawal of private samurai interference in village affairs and the general spread of a more uniform and evenhanded method of village administration by daimyo and shogun. There were also changes *within* the village in the relationships between hyakushō and other levels of the cultivator society. But although the hyakushō were made

[36] This point is also made by Ishii Ryōsuke, *Ryakusetsu Nihon kokka shi*, pp. 90-91.

[37] For a treatment of village leaders of this sort, see among others Gotō Yōichi in Shakai Keizaishi Gakkai, ed., *Hōken ryōshusei no seiritsu* (Tokyo: Yūhikaku, 1957), pp. 41-110.

[38] As a case study of this latter effort of the daimyō to reduce the powers of village leaders as recorded in Bizen, see Shibata Hajime, "Sengoku dogō," 52-63.

more secure, they were also placed under numerous con-
straints. As a result both of the kenchi and later social legislation, the hyakushō were bound to their status as cultivators. No matter how much land a hyakushō might have
listed on the village register, he had no way of gaining proprietary rights to it and thus becoming a samurai.[39] While
this condition was implied in the kenchi itself, it was more
specifically expressed in Hideyoshi's 1591 Edict on Change
of Status. This nationally promulgated edict gave orders
that no former samurai should attempt to assume the
status of either townsman or farmer, and that no farmer
should leave his village to enter another occupation.

Although there is little direct evidence of how thoroughly these social injunctions were enforced at the time,
another control measure had immediately visible results.
This was the so-called "sword hunt," by which the non-
samurai classes were disarmed. Weapon confiscations had
already been attempted sporadically by daimyō in their
own territories and by Hideyoshi against certain groups,
such as the militant religious communities, but the first
nation-wide effort at confiscation followed Hideyoshi's
edict of 1588. Farmers were singled out as objects of a
thorough prohibition against private possession of swords
and firearms. Daimyo were ordered to collect all such
weapons from the countryside. Although the official reason given for the sword hunt was to lessen the chances of
rural unrest and opposition to tax collections, its most significant result was social. It helped to underline the social
distinction between samurai, whose social mission it was to
handle weapons for protection and the maintenance of
order and security, and hyakushō, whose job it was to cultivate the soil and pay taxes. Hideyoshi's achievement in disarming the peasantry, is shown by the fact that there are no

[39] There were certain exceptions: a village headman could on occasion,
usually for services rendered, obtain the right to "surname and long
sword" (*myōji-taitō*), but usually only for one generation. With respect to
land, such a person would rarely be given the samurai's right to stipend.

recorded repetitions of the *katana-gari* edict under the Tokugawa shogunate. The hyakushō remained effectively
disarmed for the next two centuries.

ESTABLISHMENT OF THE KOKUDAKA SYSTEM

As Wakita Osamu has stated, of all aspects of Hideyoshi's
domestic policies, the perfection of the kokudaka system
was most central to the sixteenth-century revolution in
Japanese political and social institutions.[40] Essentially a
procedural method of property assessment and taxation, it
became the prime basis for defining property and income
rights for all classes under the Tokugawa bakuhan government. Asao Naohiro has suggested that the adoption of
the kokudaka system may well have been a logical necessity
to handle the situation created by the separation of the
warriors from the peasantry.[41]

The Taikō kenchi imposed several techniques that differed from existing practices. First, it enforced a fundamental shift in emphasis from tax *figure* to tax *base*. In the
preexisting system, the *taka* had referred to the actual
amount of tax expected from a given plot of land; in the
kokudaka system the taka referred to the estimated productive capacity of a given plot, and thus became the tax
base upon which the annual tax, and various other dues,
could be levied. Second, the kokudaka system, implying as
it did payment in kind, completely eliminated the kandaka
(cash payment) system, which had been giving trouble to
several of the Sengoku daimyo. What recommended this
move is not altogether clear. But, as is apparent in Nagahara Keiji's essay above, the kandaka practices were neither
universally in use nor uniform in their application across
the country. The capacity to enforce a strict accountability
of argicultural production and of payment in rice resulted

[40] Wakita, "The Kokudaka System," pp. 302-14.
[41] Asao, "Kinsei hōkensei ron," p. 3.

from the improved local administration achieved by Hideyoshi and his vassal daimyo, and in improved transportation. It also rested upon the improved capacity to enforce a standard system of measures across the land. Another fundamental feature of the Taikō kenchi was the use of a new linear measure in which the *jo* was 300 rather than 360 *shaku* (ca. one foot) and upon the *kyōmasu* (Kyoto measure) as the standard for volume measure.

All told, as adopted, the kokudaka system was more flexible in application and more effective as a technique for the standardization of land-tax procedures than earlier practices. How it worked is as follows. We have already noted that the kenchi had made an assessment of the productive capacity of each piece of cultivated land. This calculation was made in volume of rice as measured in koku. The tax base for each piece reduced to koku, or fraction thereof, was known as the *koku-mori*; and the total of all koku-mori for a given village was called the kokudaka. Taxes imposed upon the village were figured as a percentage of the kokudaka, commonly from 40 to 60 percent.

The kenchi itself provided the national hegemon, be he the Taikō or the shogun, with accurate information on the country's productive land base, thereby enabling him to peg more precisely the status of daimyo within the political hierarchy to the wealth of their domains. Once the kenchi had accounted for all productive land in the country and kokudaka figures had been calculated, the hegemon acquired a relatively exact means by which he could measure the wealth (and hence presumed power) of each daimyo. Such figures were matters of public knowledge, making known to the entire country the relative status of each daimyo. The hegemon also used the kokudaka figure as a base for calculating the amount of military and labor service required of each daimyo.

But even more significant was the fact that daimyo could be granted their domains from Hideyoshi in terms of kokudaka instead of land area or specific location. Larger daimyo tended to retain domains based on hereditary holdings that conformed to the boundaries of old provinces, so that their assigned kokudaka was often simply a confirmation of the total kokudaka figure of the province rather than an arbitrarily determined figure. The vast majority of daimyo and shōmyō, however, were assigned *ryōchi* or *chigyo-chi* at round figures of ten or twenty or fifty thousand koku. Such "domains," especially the smaller ones, had no clearly drawn geographical boundaries, although they might center on a small headquarters castle. Instead, an appropriate number of villages, or even fractions thereof, whose total koku would add up to the required figure were awarded to a daimyo. Since the allotment was made in terms of koku, not land, it became largely immaterial whether a fief was changed from one location to another. Indeed, the frequency of new assignments and reassignments of domain under Hideyoshi and Ieyasu gave rise to a popular phrase, "potted-plant lords" (*hachiue ryōshu*).[42]

A further extension of this situation, as noted above, was the increased use of the term "to entrust" (*azukeru*) in the granting of domains. By Hideyoshi's time daimyo were presumed to hold domains as "a trust from the overlord." Their rights of exploitation were carefully spelled out by the hegemon and were matched by the citation of responsibility for good administration and loyal military service. Their rights were administrative, not proprietary.

Withdrawal from land possession was even more extreme for the rest of the samurai class. Although in Hideyoshi's time a good portion of the upper-class samurai retainers of the hegemon or daimyo held chigyō (roughly, what we would call fiefs), the vast majority of the samurai

---

[42] This point should not be overstated, however. As the Tokugawa regime became stabilized, so that changes of domain became less frequent, daimyo acquired a sense of attachment and identification with a given region, especially to the headquarters town.

Hall

class had given up direct land proprietorship for stipended service in the lord's castle town. Increasingly, even the chigyō were converted into stipends.[43] Such stipends were calculated in koku or bales of rice without reference to location of fief or name of village. Having no title to land as income-producing property, samurai could not transfer land privately among their own class, nor could they acquire land by purchase from hyakushō. As Wakita Osamu has aptly stated, superior proprietary land ownership under the kokudaka system belonged not to individuals but to "the samurai class as a whole."[44] Thus a samurai's income could be increased only by the acquisition of net increases of fief or stipend in the service of daimyo or shogun. The kokudaka system stands out as one of the most remarkable land-tax systems in history. That it became fully established under Hideyoshi must surely be one of the major results of his domestic policy.

CONCLUSION

The above pages have laid out most of the factual data relating to five areas of political and social change that preceded the formation of the Tokugawa bakuhan polity; but these were not necessarily the whole of the story. If we take 1650 as the point at which the "Kinsei (Tokugawa) system" reached maturity, we can see that there were several aspects of the overall polity that have not been touched on in our review of Hideyoshi's policies. Among these are the anti-Christian and seclusion (*sakoku*) policies, the effects of urban growth as seen in the newly formed castle towns, and the spread of neo-Confucian thought.[45] Strictly speak-

[43] Kanai Madoka, "Hōroku seido," in Heibonsha, *Sekai rekishi jiten* 17 (Tokyo: Heibonsha, 1953), 249-50.

[44] Wakita, "The Kokudaka System," p. 310.

[45] Contemporary scholars have given various definitions of the "essential characteristics" of Kinsei Japan. Asao Naohiro's selection is: hei-nō bunri, the kokudaka system, and *sakoku*; "Kinsei hōkensei ron," p. 3. In

ing, the origins of these developments can be traced to Hideyoshi's Japan. But they did not become major parts of hegemonic policy until after the establishment of the Edo shogunate, and until the first three Tokugawa shoguns put their weight behind them. For this reason they have not been elaborated in this analysis. By putting Hideyoshi's policies and their implementation into five specific historical contexts, we have seen that he moved Japanese society a great step along a broad continuum of change. As we noted at the outset of the study, Hideyoshi was neither the sole instigator nor the ultimate completor of the actual changes that occurred in his time. But he was surely the prime mover in the establishment of a new national order, an order that historians call the early modern bakuhan state.

---

his contribution to this symposium, Asao stresses the importance of foreign policy to the legitimation of the Tokugawa shogunate under Hidetada, the second shogun.

Chapter 7

The Commercial and Urban Policies of Oda Nobunaga and Toyotomi Hideyoshi

WAKITA OSAMU

WITH JAMES L. McCLAIN

MANY SHARP CONTRASTS in such areas as commercial organization, urban formation, and marketing structure mark the transition from medieval (Chūsei) to early modern (Kinsei) society in sixteenth-century Japan. Among the more conspicuous changes were the replacement of the trade monopolies or guilds (za) by direct daimyo control of trade through the regulation of merchants and artisans, the emergence of a countrywide marketing system linking the central Kinai region merchants with the various domain traders, and the shift in urbanization patterns from one of self-governing communities to one dominated by the castle towns from which military lords and their retainers directed the political and economic affairs of their territories.[1]

[1] There is a great deal of research concerning these topics. Some of the major works include: Ono Hitoshi, *Kinsei jōkamachi no kenkyū* (Tokyo: Shibundō, 1928); Toyoda Takeshi, *Chūsei Nihon shōgyōshi no kenkyū* (Tokyo: Iwanami Shoten, 1952); Wakita Haruko, *Nihon Chūsei shōgyō hattatsushi no kenkyū* (Tokyo: Ochanomizu Shobō, 1969). For more recent publications, see Sasaki Gin'ya, "Rakuichi-rakuza rei to za no hoshō ando," in Nagahara Keiji, ed., *Sengoku-ki no kenryoku to shakai* (Tokyo: Tōkyō Daigaku Shuppankai, 1976), pp. 157-230; Wakita Osamu, *Kinsei hōkensei seiritsu shiron* (Tokyo: Tōkyō Daigaku Shuppankai, 1977), 2 vols.; and Wakita Osamu, "Kinsei toshi no kensetsu to gōshō," in *Iwanami kōza Nihon rekishi* 9 (*Kinsei 1*) (Tokyo: Iwanami Shoten, 1975), 155-94.

Virtually every daimyo of the late sixteenth century played some role in this process, but obviously the two most important actors were Oda Nobunaga and Toyotomi Hideyoshi. It is important to recognize that there were both continuities and clear discontinuities between the policies of these two men.[2] Perhaps the most apt characterization of the Oda administration is that it exemplified the military-based centralized power of the typical Sengoku daimyo. The Toyotomi administration, on the other hand, achieved the more complete and unified authority of an early modern, or Kinsei, daimyo. The purpose of this essay is to clarify the transformation from medieval to Kinsei society as reflected in the commercial and urban policies of these two men, and to illustrate how the similarities and dissimilarities in their approaches are related to the differences in their bases of power.

THE REORGANIZATION OF COMMERCE AND INDUSTRY

In the medieval period the guilds, under the patronage of the imperial family, court nobles, and religious institutions, had achieved a near monopoly over the conduct of trade. Sengoku daimyo trying to extend their own authority over commerce and industry, therefore, found it necessary to modify (and later abolish) the old structure of privileges. The Sengoku daimyo also strove by various means to build up the economy of their domains and unify their control over the land. Policies designed to concentrate men and resources in their castle towns under their personal control included a system of census registration to identify and lure to their service merchants and artisans important to the domain economy—especially those who specialized in castle construction and the provision of armaments—and the use of officials appointed from among the merchants and artisans themselves to extend daimyo control over all

---

[2] Wakita Osamu, *Oda seiken no kiso kōzō* (Tokyo: Tōkyō Daigaku Shuppankai, 1975); and Wakita, *Kinsei hōkensei*.

merchant and artisan groups. Many daimyo swept away the checkpoints that had obstructed the free flow of trade, leaving in existence only those barriers located on the boundaries between domains.[3]

But the appearance of domain-based economic systems should not be equated with the functional implementation of autonomous and completely self-supporting economic systems. Even in the Sengoku period, the economic power concentrated in the Kinai region in such urban centers as Kyoto and Sakai had already begun to form the nucleus of a national economy. Here, in what may be called the capital marketing area, was the heart of domestic commerce and the terminus for trade with continental East Asia. Moreover, Kyoto was the center for important handicraft industries not to be found elsewhere. Despite the warfare of the Sengoku era, daimyo continued to export to this area specialty crops and such products as raw materials for handicrafts, in return for armaments, textiles, and other necessities unobtainable in their own domains.

The conduct of trade in the capital marketing area continued to be subject to guild monopolies and barriers through most of the Sengoku period. The experience of merchants from the province of Echigo offers a convenient illustration. Ramie (*aoso*), a fiber used for textiles, was grown in the province of Echigo, and during the medieval period merchants of the ramie guild in Tennōji, under the patronage of the noble Sanjōnishi family, monopolized trade in this fiber, buying it in Echigo and selling it in Kyoto. When Echigo was brought under the military control of the Uesugi family early in the sixteenth century, local merchants using the daimyo's backing managed to wrestle away from the ramie guild their monopoly on purchase rights. But the Echigo merchants still had to pay a fee to the Sanjōnishi family for permission to sell the fiber in

[3] For more on the domain economies of the Sengoku daimyo, see Fujiki Hisashi, *Sengoku shakai shiron* (Tokyo: Tōkyō Daigaku Shuppankai, 1974), pp. 287-325.

areas such as Kyoto. This is one example of how the Sengoku daimyo could effect changes in market relations. Yet in the vicinity of the capital, medieval styles of market relations persisted, an anomaly to which the Sengoku daimyo were forced to adjust.[4]

The administrations of both Oda Nobunaga and Toyotomi Hideyoshi came into existence against this backdrop of marketing relations and marketing structure, and each administration, in its own way, undertook a set of reforms. Oda Nobunaga, who began his career as a typical Sengoku daimyo and only later became nationally influential, put into effect in his home domain policies that were essentially the same as those of other Sengoku daimyo, such as appointing a certain Itō Sōjūrō to supervise the merchants in his base provinces of Owari and Mino, ordering "free markets and free guilds" in the castle towns of Azuchi (in Ōmi) and Kanō (present-day Gifu), and, in an effort to create a larger volume of trade, abolishing checkpoints within his domains. However, Nobunaga did not implement these policies in the environs of the capital. Previous opinions have held that Nobunaga followed in Kyoto the same policies he had initiated earlier in his home domains;[5] but this is not so. Outside of the castle towns he controlled, we can find no evidence of any ordinances calling for free markets and free guilds.[6] Moreover, guild organizations remained active in Kyoto and Nara, and Nobunaga protected the established guild merchants and recognized their special rights.

A dual policy structure is also evident in the case of checkpoints. While eliminating these in Owari, Mino, Ise,

[4] Wakita Haruko, *Nihon Chūsei shōgyō*, pp. 371-85.

[5] In his *Chūsei Nihon shōgyōshi no kenkyū*, Toyoda Takeshi argues that Nobunaga abolished the special privileges of the oil guild in Ōyamazaki, but his evidence is weak and inconclusive.

[6] Nobunaga issued the ordinances proclaiming free markets and free guilds in Kanō, Azuchi, and Kanamori, which for the purposes of this essay may be treated as a castle town.

and some other places, the Oda administration recognized the imperial checkpoints at the seven entrances to Kyoto.[7] Moreover, in Ōmi province Nobunaga acknowledged the special rights of the four famous merchant groups known as the *shihon* merchants, who conducted trade with the Ise area, as well as the special rights held by the shipping guild at Tsuruga, and by the group at Katata that controlled shipping on Lake Biwa. In short, at the same time that the Oda administration was abolishing checkpoints, it permitted transportation associations (*nakama*) to retain their traditional privileges and to control trade along the major transportation routes.

Nobunaga clearly did not destroy in a single stroke the medieval style of market relations; rather, he found it expedient to allow old and new practices to coexist. This was in large part due to the fact that the Oda political and military organization never achieved as completely centralized a control as the later Toyotomi administration would; nor was the society at large characterized by as complete a separation between the *bushi* and the commercial and agricultural classes.[8] The movement of goods on the scale that later typified Japan under the Toyotomi administration was not necessary: the Oda administration could satisfy its economic requirements through existing commercial institutions. Though the Oda administration brought the capital marketing area under its control, most of the local markets outside this area remained in the hands of Sengoku daimyo antagonistic to Nobunaga. Even as late as 1582, the year of his death, Nobunaga did not

[7] In 1568 Nobunaga issued the ordinance abolishing barrier checkpoints only in Owari, Mino, and the southern part of Ōmi, although it is likely that he enforced this ordinance in other territories under his control. In the same year he authorized the imperial barriers. Previously, it was thought that the law abolishing checkpoints was enforced throughout the entire nation, and that the imperial barriers were exceptions.

[8] For example, Oda Nobunaga's retainers continued to hold personal fiefs, as did local military commanders allied with Oda.

have command of the Inland Sea, and on the Japan Sea coast he had only a very tenuous hold on the area from Noto to Hōki, near present-day Tottori. But guild organizations, under the patronage of court nobles and religious institutions, continued to engage in trade throughout Japan and, by not interfering with their operation, Nobunaga preserved both the predominant economic role of the capital area and his access to provincial goods.

It remained to the administration of Toyotomi Hideyoshi to bring into being what we know as Kinsei market relations. In the beginning, of course, the policies of Hideyoshi differed little from those of Nobunaga. His abolition of the checkpoints at the seven entrances to Kyoto in 1582, his issuance in 1583 and 1584 of guild charters to his Kyoto deputy Maeda Gen'i, and his levy of a tax on ships entering Hyōgo all evidenced a certain expediency in dealing with the old market structure. But soon Hideyoshi began implementing policies designed to break guild monopolies and to terminate the domination of trade by court nobles and religious institutions. An entry in the "Hideyoshi jiki" for the ninth month of 1585 reads: "Dues levied by nobles, religious institutions, and common merchants are to be ended; and guilds are to be abolished."[9] This order was intended to put an end to various taxes such as the *sekisen*, levied on goods at barrier checkpoints, and the *jōbunsen*, a kind of business tax that court nobles, bushi families, and certain powerful merchants had previously exacted from merchant and artisan organizations in return for protection or patronage. In late 1585, Hideyoshi sent to his daimyo followers a letter severely criticizing the noble Susuki family for levying taxes on the

[9] This entry is actually dated the tenth month in "Hideyoshi jiki." However, from evidence in the "Kanemi kyōki" and the "Kobayakawa Ke monjo" in Shiryō Hensanjō, ed., *Dai Nihon komonjo iewake* (Tokyo: Tōkyō Teikoku Daigaku, 1929) 11, p. 2, pp. 401-403, we can conclude that this occurred in the ninth month.

trading of cattle.[10] Orders were given to guilds not to exact fees from any newly arising nonguild merchants. And there remains extant today a document in which Asano Nagayoshi reprimands the innkeepers at Imazu, in Ōmi, for collecting a fee for each traveler and each piece of baggage.[11]

The policies of Hideyoshi's administration were obviously designed to assert direct lines of authority over persons engaged in commerce and industry, but did not necessarily imply totally unrestricted trading rights for merchants and artisans. Hideyoshi's economic objectives were more complex. For example, Hideyoshi abolished the guild organizations at the port of Katata which controlled shipping on Lake Biwa, only to turn around and authorize the establishment of the "100 Ship Nakama" at Ōtsu (the chief port on Lake Biwa) and the publication of official shipping codes and shipping rates, which included stipulations on rates to be charged ordinary as well as special customers (such as daimyo). There was a comparable situation on the Yodo river in the formation of the "Yodo Kashosen Nakama."[12]

The key technique in Hideyoshi's effort to destroy the autonomous character of the old guilds and to gain more direct control over commerce was the registration of merchants and artisans, such registration becoming the basis for levying corvée. The Oda administration had never brought this technique to full fruition. In Azuchi, for example, the administration offered merchants and artisans special benefits, including exemptions from corvée levies, in order to induce these persons to settle in the castle town. The Toyotomi administration was able to exert a

[10] Doc. 463 in the section "Kobayakawa Ke monjo" in *Dai Nihon komonjo iewake* 11, p. 2, pp. 401-402. The letter carries the date of the eighteenth of the ninth month, and presumably was written in 1585.

[11] "Kawarabayashi monjo" in Shiga-ken, ed., *Shiga-kenshi* (Tokyo: Sanshūsha, 1928) 5, 376.

[12] Wakita Osamu, *Kinsei hōkensei* 2, 142-46.

more complete control over artisans and merchants by abolishing corvée exemptions. This became a general trend. In castle towns throughout the country, the daimyo lords moved to do the same, although, of course, continuing to grant exemptions from land taxes as a means of encouraging merchants and artisans to come into their domains.

THE EMERGENCE OF KINSEI CITIES

The late Sengoku period was an era of tremendous urban growth in Japan, and the cities that began to flourish all across the land can be separated into a number of types: castle towns (*jōkamachi*), post towns (*shukubamachi*), commercial towns that grew up in front of temples and shrines (*monzenmachi*), and commercially oriented towns that were first established within temple compounds (*jinaimachi*). The emergence of what can be called the Kinsei-style city was greatly influenced by the Oda and Toyotomi administrations. The policy of concentrating men and resources in the castle towns was fundamental to this transformation, as were the measures taken by the daimyo to differentiate their policies toward city and village, commerce and agriculture.[13]

Urban development prior to the rise of Oda Nobunaga reached its highest level in the economically advanced capital marketing area centered in Kyoto, where such cities as Sakai, Tennōji, and Hiranogō had grown up within a short distance of each other. Most cities in this area first took form as small-scale market centers for surrounding agricultural villages, as distinguished from cities whose origin lay in some function, such as a transshipment point, within the economic systems that served the capital or the provincial nobility.[14]

[13] Ibid., pp. 168-70.
[14] Wakita Osamu, *Kinsei hōken shakai no keizai kōzō* (Tokyo: Ochanomizu Shobō, 1963), pp. 284-312.

At one point in this pre-Oda development, urban residents began to achieve a high degree of self-governance. Even in Kyoto, the seat of aristocratic power, commoners fashioned a system of district self-government; the examples of Sakai and Hiranogō are well known. The attainment of self-government meant that the community as a corporate group exercised judicial and police powers, including the right to investigate and prosecute crimes, and directed self-defense programs, such as constructing and managing moats. This kind of urban self-government was also to be found in certain jinaimachi. In a few cases, like the Ishiyama jinaimachi and Imai in the Yamato area, the temple built the commercial section and retained ultimate political authority. But in the more usual type of self-governing jinamachi—Tondabayashi, Daigazuka, and Kaizuka, for example—urban residents held collective responsibility for managing the community.

The history of Tondabayashi, located in Kawachi near present-day Osaka, typifies the creation of these communities. The first buildings of what was to become Tondabayashi were put up on the property of Kōshōji temple in 1558 by eight men from four nearby villages.[15] The men had to pay 100 *kanmon* (strings) in copper to the governing shugo in order to obtain rights to use the land, and probably also had to come to some kind of agreement with each of the villages that held various special rights in the locality.[16] The new town was situated on high ground along the Ishikawa river, and was protected by a moat and by gates at the main entrances. In 1560, Ami Naomasa, a retainer of the shugo of Kawachi, granted to Kōshōji, and thus to the

---

[15] Wakita Osamu, "Jinaimachi no kōzō to tenkai," *Shirin* 4 (January 1958), pp. 1-24.

[16] Although this was a rough and desolate area, the eight-man group probably had to indemnify the villages in the vicinity. Money had to be paid to the Amagasaki city government when constructing the jinaimachi at Honkōji in Amagasaki. Wakita Osamu, "Amagasaki to jinaimachi," *Chiikishi kenkyū* 7 (January 1977), 1-24.

town, exemptions from certain taxes and corvée and from debt moratoriums. Added to these exemptions were police powers, the right to control the judicial process, and the right to possess private property. These rights were recognized by Kōshōji temple, which held ultimate, but nominal, proprietary powers. This meant the Tondabayashi, as a corporate entity and in the manner of Ishiyama Honganji, had become a self-governing town.[17]

In the area of the capital, the attainment of a high degree of economic prosperity and the constant disputes among capital-based landed interests prevented the appearance of any single dominant military power, and thus created an environment hospitable to the growth of self-governing communities. The contesting court-centered and smaller military proprietors were in the habit of recognizing the jinaimachi of the area and granting them special rights in the hopes of receiving, in return, military and economic assistance from the sects, such as the Shin and Nichiren, to which the temples belonged. Self-governing communities now associated with temples were also recognized and granted special rights by the daimyo or kokujin of the location.

The above trends in urban development provided the context within which the Oda and Toyotomi administrations developed their urban policies. At the outset the main objective of both of these national leaders was to encourage the movement of artisans and merchants into their newly emerging castle towns. The offering of special rights and privileges to merchant and artisan families was central to their policies. Typical are the ordinances for Azuchi, the castle town headquarters of Oda Nobunaga; the codes for this castle town called for free markets and free guilds, specified exemptions from various taxes, including the tax on households, confirmed exemptions from debt mora-

---

[17] This acquisition of special rights was similar to the case at Honganji. See Imai Shūhei, "Ishiyama Honganji jinaimachi ni kansuru ichi kōsatsu," *Machikaneyama ronsō* 6 (1973), 1-18.

toriums, and authorized monopolies for groups that lodged visiting merchants or bought and sold horses throughout the domain. Although Nobunaga did not at this time permit exemptions from the city land tax, such exemptions became general under the administration of Hideyoshi. Daimyo throughout Japan were enacting similar policies in their respective castle towns. In doing so, they obviously sacrificed some revenues that they could have extracted from merchants and artisans. But in return, the daimyo hoped to entice into their service artisans and merchants necessary to the domain's economic development.

Although the special rights granted to commoners in the castle towns were similar to the prerogatives exercised by the self-governing communities, there were definite differences between the two types of urban settlement. Castle towns served as the military headquarters of territorial lords, and were spatially organized to suit requirements of military defense. Moreover, in castle towns it was the daimyo who held all proprietary rights to the land, monopolized political and administrative powers, and controlled the police and judicial machinery. In Azuchi, for example, townsmen were permitted only a very narrow range of self-government under the close supervision of samurai-class magistrates (*bugyō*).

The structural reorganization of already existing cities represents one of several ways in which Kinsei-type cities were brought into being. Immediately after his arrival in Kyoto, Oda Nobunaga began to challenge militarily the independence of existing self-governing cities such as Sakai and Hiranogō. As such communities submitted to him, this type of self-governing city became extinct. But despite the superiority of Nobunaga's military power, he was not able to achieve total jurisdictional authority by force alone. In Kinai, for example, Yoshiaki, the last Ashikaga shogun, retained considerable authority, especially in Sakai which was located on lands under the direct control of the shogunate.[18] In time, Nobunaga received one section of Sakai as a fief held in his wife's name. This gave Nobunaga the right to post a representative, or *daikan*, and thus extend the range of his influence over the area. This example also shows that, although historians use the term "Sengoku," or the era of warring states, to describe this period, actually claims to proprietary lordship and control over territory were not challenged in capricious, random fashion.

After the collapse of the Ashikaga shogunate, Oda Nobunaga still was unable to exert total control over Kyoto and the capital-area jinaimachi, where numerous religious institutions and noble families held proprietary rights. The Oda administration exercised some administrative control over Kyoto through its appointed representatives (*shoshidai*), but Nobunaga acknowledged the landownership rights of the vested order and their partial powers to investigate and prosecute criminals. After Nobunaga burned Kamigyō (the northern half of Kyoto) in 1573, he granted some exemptions from the city land tax. But the fact that the exemptions were not granted throughout all of Kamigyō attests to the limitations on his authority. Nobunaga never achieved a unified jurisdiction over Kyoto.[19]

Nobunaga also reconfirmed the vested interests of the proprietary classes in those jinaimachi that were not antagonistic toward him. Tondabayashi, a jinaimachi associated with the Shin sect, and Tonda, in Settsu, are cases in point.[20] During his battle with Ishiyama Honganji, Nobunaga received aid from the Nichiren sect and, in return, approved the construction of a jinaimachi at Chōenji in Amagasaki. Further, he granted to the town government

---

[18] Wakita Osamu, *Kinsei hōkensei* 2, 244-53.

[19] Ibid., pp. 189-92.

[20] "Shimizu monjo," in Takatsuki-shishi Hensan Iinkai, ed., *Takatsuki-shishi* (Takatsuki: Takatsuki-shi, 1973), 4, 548, 584.

special rights, such as the power to investigate and prosecute criminals.[21] In this way, the self-governing communities retained certain rights and prerogatives which prevented the Oda administration from fully extending its political authority over these communities.

Toyotomi Hideyoshi was more successful in asserting his authority over urban areas. The Toyotomi administration implemented a variety of policies whose basic purpose was to encourage the concentration of men and resources in the castle towns, an especially effective one being the skillful use of taxing powers. For example, to induce merchants and artisans to move to Osaka from places like Sakai and Hiranogō, Hideyoshi granted exemptions to the land tax in Osaka, but continued to levy that and other taxes in Sakai.

Important also was the implementation of the *kokudaka* system. As this system was instituted, the Toyotomi administration legally defined each locality as either an urban settlement or village, and fixed the amount of tax (*nengu*) due from each village. By classifying certain communities with concentrations of merchants and artisans as villages, and by holding these men responsible for the payment of nengu, the administration was able to promote the migration of talent to cities such as Osaka, where tax obligations were lighter. Thus, under the terms of the Taikō land survey, jinaimachi such as Tondabayashi, Hiranogō, and Tonda were defined as villages, and the prerogatives of the corporate city community were eliminated.

Among the large existing cities, the one most adversely affected by Hideyoshi's policies was Kyoto, home of noble court families and religious institutions. It was no easy matter for Hideyoshi to achieve complete control over the city; but in 1591, following a land survey, he was able to get the noble families and religious institutions in central Kyoto to give up their holdings and accept substitute land in the

---

[21] "Chōenji monjo," in *Amagasaki-shishi* (Amagasaki, 1973), 4, 297.

suburbs.[22] He also divided Kyoto into residential sections, constructed an earthen wall around the city, created a special quarter for temples, and began to grant exemptions from corvée and property taxes. This was a watershed in Kyoto's evolution into a Kinsei-type of city.

CHARACTERISTICS OF THE KINSEI CITY

The dominant type of Kinsei city was the castle town. These were, first of all, the headquarters of territorial military lords and the locus of political and military power. Thus they were often located at militarily strategic points, and were laid out in accordance with the security requirements of the daimyo. Likewise, samurai retainers and privileged merchants and artisans who purveyed goods and services to the daimyo were allowed to live within the castle complex, while ordinary townsmen and even lower levels of the samurai were relegated to the unprotected sections of the cities. This use of urban space illustrates the degree to which the shogun and daimyo had strengthened their claims to control over the land. The concomitant was an erosion of the townsmen's right to land; the contemporary conception was that the townsmen were merely using land over which the military class held ultimate proprietary rights.[23]

Kinsei cities also became the home of many ordinary, non-privileged artisans and merchants. Intent on keeping these useful people under personal command, the territorial lords enforced a status system that separated the peas-

---

[22] Ono Kōji, "Kyōto no Kinsei toshika," *Shakai keizai shigaku* 10 (October 1940), 1-32.

[23] Townsmen did own houses and have the right of usufruct over the land the house sat on. Dwellings were bought and sold, but the practice of buying and selling land alone did not exist in the early part of the Kinsei period. It is under these conditions that we say townsmen owned homes. For a specific example of the special arrangement of a castle town, see James L. McClain, "Castle Towns and Daimyo Authority: Kanazawa in the Years 1583-1630," *Journal of Japanese Studies* 6:2 (Summer, 1980).

antry from the merchants and artisans, and in other ways encouraged the latter to settle in castle towns. Having done so, the daimyo levied labor and service taxes as a way of benefitting from their skills and talents. One can find examples, such as in Azuchi, in which townsmen received exemptions from such levies; but in general townsmen bore the burden of a tax system in which service levies predominated.[24]

The self-governing character of late medieval urban settlements virtually disappeared during the Kinsei period. This was due to several factors, not all of them political. First, we should note that the European type of corporate community did not exist in Japan in the Kinsei era. Guilds in Japan did not acquire the right to a voice in city administration. The monopoly rights possessed by guilds did give them the right to deal with certain types of crime, but the regulations creating "free guilds" (*rakuza*) in Japan closed any possibility of an evolution parallel to that of Europe. Furthermore, the residential quarters (*machi*), which in the Sengoku period had banded together as communities for the purpose of self-defense and had practiced self-government, found themselves by the end of the sixteenth century under daimyo or shogunate political control, and with only a very limited degree of autonomy. In addition, shogun and daimyo, whose principal concerns were with the military security of the castle towns and the preservation of public peace and order, forced the townsmen to shoulder the cost for civil improvements and public works programs essential to the townsmen's own well-being. These included the construction and maintenance of roads, bridges, and sewage systems. By holding the townsmen responsible for these expenses, the military class in effect was taxing the townsmen, even though exemptions from land taxes were common. In sum, unlike the

---

[24] There were temporary levies in Azuchi. Moreover, in Edo, Osaka, and other major cities, the townsmen had tax obligations. See Wakita Osamu, "Kinsei toshi no kensetsu to gōshō."

situation that had existed in some earlier self-governing towns, it was now the lord of the castle town who decided defense policy, specified tax regulations, and controlled the judicial machinery.

Other evidence also shows that, in contrast to the situation in Europe, institutions established by samurai government did not provide a great deal of legal protection for merchant interests. For example, in general the bakufu and daimyo preferred that the townsmen make out-of-court settlements in money and debt disputes. Moreover, when the number of lawsuits submitted by townsmen to the magistrate's office grew too large, the magistrate might refuse to hear any cases at all—and, in fact, the bakufu issued orders to this effect in 1685 and 1702. Although artisans and merchants constituted a substantial proportion of the population in Kinsei cities, the military class did not give commensurate attention to their interests.

THE KINSEI ECONOMIC STRUCTURE

The policies of Oda Nobunaga and Toyotomi Hideyoshi affected both the merchant-artisan community and its urban context, giving rise to the economic structure characteristic of early modern society. The basis of the Kinsei economic structure was the kokudaka system and the method of collecting land revenues from the peasant population. Rice was the most easily marketed and commercialized product of the time, and *ryōshu* instituted policies designed to extract, to the fullest possible extent, rice and local specialty products from the countryside. The daimyo did not consume the whole of this tax income, but sent portions of it to markets to be sold as a commercial product. One consequence of this process was to limit the degree to which the peasantry could participate in the commercialized sectors of the economy. Since the shogun and daimyo drained off in the form of taxes the rural products that could be marketed—that is, rice and specialty products—the peasantry was locked into the domain-based economy while the territorial lords were able to dominate the national markets.[25]

The Kinsei nationwide marketing structure consisted of the central marketing area, which centered upon the Kinai region, and the various domain markets, which were based in the castle towns. Within the domain marketing areas, some specialization of function between rural and urban areas had evolved, but because the rural economy continued to play an important role, specialization had not advanced to the fullest possible extent. In the castle towns themselves, the commoners of most consequence were the privileged artisans and merchants who purveyed goods and services to the daimyo and samurai. The fact that most commercial transactions were conducted in marketing places distinguishes yet another characteristic of the castle town economic systems. The daimyo collected rice and specialty products in the form of taxes, and then sold a portion of these within the domain at mines or fishing villages, as well as in the castle town itself. Another portion would be sent outside the domain to be sold at central markets in places such as Kyoto, Sakai, and Osaka, and later Edo. In return, the daimyo purchased in the central markets certain luxury or specialty goods not available in their home areas.[26]

Standing above the domain markets were the central markets of the Kinai, and later the Kantō, area. The policies instituted by the Oda and Toyotomi administrations had a direct impact on the evolution and importance of these central markets. As outlined earlier, the Oda administration reconfirmed the special rights of the guilds, and thereby helped ensure that goods would be traded on a nationwide basis and that the capital area markets would play a major role in that process. The Toyotomi administration, as was befitting a regime with a more consolidated

---

[25] Wakita Osamu, *Kinsei hōkensei 2*, 8-25.

[26] Wakita Osamu, *Kinsei hōken shakai*, pp. 95-112.

basis of authority, pursued policies that did much more to enhance the importance of central markets. For example, Hideyoshi held personal fiefs in each region of the country, so that his administration was able to obtain, in the form of tax receipts, rice and specialty products from each area.[27] The administration established a set of market prices for its own rice, and the effect was to keep prices low in the producing areas and high in the consuming areas. For instance, with ten *ryō* of gold one could purchase 240 *koku*, or about 1,200 bushels, of rice in Tsugaru and Akita to the north, but just 30 *koku*, or 150 bushels, in Ōmi. This price differential would seem to indicate the existence of deliberate price manipulation, the purpose of which was to provide a margin of profit to cover transportation and other costs. This, of course, promoted the flow of commodities into the central marketing areas and stimulated the development of a nationwide marketing structure built around the core central markets.[28]

Developments during the Tokugawa period changed the nature of this marketing system. Because the Toyotomi house had held small personal fiefs within many of the daimyo domains, most daimyo were not able to exercise complete autonomy in their economic policies. This indicates that the Toyotomi administration made a strong effort to centralize authority, even to the point of interfering in the internal affairs of vassal domains. The Tokugawa administration, however, ended this policy, and by and large gave the individual domains local autonomy in their domain economies. As a result, the closed character of domain markets intensified. The trade connections between central markets and domain markets continued, but prices in domain markets now reflected prices in the central markets; in fact, in certain instances prices in consuming areas such as Osaka could actually be equal to or lower than

[27] Ibid., pp. 15-22. See also Fujiki Hisashi, "Toyotomi-ki daimyō-ron josetsu," *Rekishigaku kenkyū* 287 (April 1964), 31-41.

[28] Wakita Osamu, *Kinsei hōken shakai*, pp. 23-36.

those in domain markets. The development of this sort of nationwide price structure constitutes one of the chief characteristics of the national marketing system during the early modern period.

Another distinguishing feature of the Kinsei economy was the functional separation of rural villages and urban communities, and the rapid growth of a strictly urban-based economy. This trend was due in large part to the effect of government policies conducive to urban growth and to the growing role of cities in domain economic structures. In the early Kinsei period, as we have noted, conditions in the rural areas favored a flow of population into the emerging urban centers. Particularly conspicuous was the development of such cities as Kyoto, Osaka, Fushimi, and later Edo, all of which served at one time or other as strategic bases for the men who unified Japan. With the adoption of the alternate attendance (*sankinkōtai*) system, the daimyo from the entire country traveled from their castle towns to Edo periodically, and left hostages there on a permanent basis. The consumption demands of the samurai and service-class residents of both the existing large cities and the new castle towns stimulated the growth of urban commerce and industry. It is difficult to measure with certainty the development of this urban-based economy, but servants' wages provide a clue. Until well into the Edo period, servants in rural households did not work for wages. Rather, they served for indefinite periods, at times even their entire lives, in exchange for room and board, and perhaps a lump-sum settlement made to their parents when they became servants. In contrast, we can find examples as early as 1602 in Kanazawa, the castle town of the Maeda family, in which servants in bushi households received the exceptionally high yearly wage of 12 *hyō* (roughly 24 bushels) of rice.[29]

Large-scale construction projects, such as the building of

[29] See the doc. in vol. 1 of *Kaga-han shiryō* (Tokyo: Ishiguro Bunkichi, 1929), under the date Keichō 7 (1602)/3/26, pp. 851-52.

Osaka castle begun by Hideyoshi and the flood-control projects along the Yodo river, provided employment for tens of thousands of artisans and day laborers, drawn both from the domains and from the country's major cities. Unfortunately, historical documents that would allow us to judge accurately the total economic impact of these projects in the capital area have not yet been found, but the example of Tokugawa construction projects at Osaka during the 1620s give some idea of their magnitude. The Tokugawa administration required the various domains to contribute toward the construction expenses. Obama, which had an assessed productive capacity of 92,000 koku, contributed more than 100 kan of silver yearly. If other domains contributed on a similar basis, total project expenses may have amounted to the equivalent of 260,000 koku of rice annually.[30] If this estimate is correct, and if we assume that the project continued at the same pace for five years, the total amount of expenditures staggers the imagination, and must have delivered an enormous stimulus to the economy. And when we put together the many construction projects Hideyoshi sponsored at Osaka, Fushimi, and Yodo castles,[31] with the similar sorts of large-scale construction projects carried out in the early Tokugawa cities such as Nagoya and Edo, we can imagine that these projects alone were a major factor in creating the expanding urban-based economy.

Demographic statistics yield evidence corroborating these trends. Although many gaps exist in the population

[30] According to the "Kyōgoku Ke monjo" (in the document collection at Osaka castle) wages for day laborers and artisans came to roughly 40 percent of the total construction expenses in 1624. Total construction expenses were 114 *kan*, 697 *monme*, 8 *bu*, 7 *rin*; wages amounted to 46 *kan*, 939 *monme*.

[31] Epistles of the missionary Gnecchi-Soldi Organtino speak of levies by ryōshu, taxes in Sakai, and the development of urban commerce. See Okamoto Yoshitomo, *Toyotomi Hideyoshi* (Tokyo: Chūōkōronsha, 1963), pp. 78-79. Concerning the construction of Osaka castle, see Okamoto Ryōichi, *Ōsaka-jō* (Tokyo: Iwanami Shoten, 1970).

statistics available for the first half of the seventeenth century, some recent estimates have put the 1634 population of Kyoto and Osaka at 410,000 and 405,000, respectively.[32] These figures were previously discounted because they surpass by far the generally accepted population figures of 300,000 for the second half of the seventeenth century. However, when considered against the backdrop of the enormous stimuli given the economy of central Japan by Hideyoshi and the early Tokugawa shoguns, it may well be that the 400,000 figures approximate the actual populations.[33] We must also acknowledge the possibility of subsequent population loss. The scale of the urban-based economy and its objectives were heavily dependent on shifts in locations and needs of the ruling military class. At the opening of the Edo period, townsmen from Fushimi were compelled to migrate to Osaka, and towns on the outskirts of Kyoto, such as the post towns of Yamazaki and Rokujizō, suffered economic downturns.[34] The termination of the large-scale construction projects in Kinai brought economic recession even in Osaka and Kyoto, and the population of these two cities declined. So it is quite likely that the population of these two cities was greater in the first half of the seventeenth century than in the second half.

[32] Honjō Eijirō and Kuroha Hyōjirō, eds., *Ōsaka hennenshi* (Osaka: Ōsaka Shiritsu Chūō Toshokan, 1968), 5, 130; and the document "Rakuchū haishaku no koto," in Okada Nobuko and Iwao Seiichi, eds., *Kyōto oyakushomuke taigai oboegaki* (Osaka: Seibundō Shuppan, 1973) 1, 269-71.

[33] For example, earlier we reckoned the annual yearly expenditures for the renovation of Osaka castle in the Genna period (1615-1624) at 260,000 koku. If we assume the annual per-person rice requirement at that time was 3 koku, these expenditures would have supported a population of nearly 90,000 persons. When we take the ripple effect into consideration, we can see that the construction-related expenses alone could have supported a population base of over 100,000 persons.

[34] For information on Yamazaki, see Shimamoto Chōshi Hensan Iinkai, ed., *Shimamoto chōshi* (Tokyo: Shimamoto Chōshi Hensan Iinkai, 1975) 1, 350-51. For information on Rokujizo, see Uji Shishi Hensan Iinkai, ed., *Uji-shishi* 2 (Tokyo: Uji Shishi Hensan Iinkai, 1975), 232-37.

The economic investments in the cities by the shogun and daimyo, such as the construction projects mentioned above, came to an end during the first half of the seventeenth century. This was due not so much to any arbitrary turnabout in shogunate and domain policies as to the economic exhaustion of rural areas. That is, with the economic impoverishment of agricultural villages and the onset of the great famines of the early 1640s, the flow of investment into cities declined, and the urban-based economy entered a period of recession. The improvement of the economic conditions in cities in the latter half of the seventeenth century was directly related to the return of prosperity to rural areas.

This stagnation of the urban-based economy resulted in changes in shogunal policy, a fact noted by Sasaki Junnosuke in his essay in this volume. In 1634, Iemitsu, the third shogun, visited Kyoto and signaled an end to the policy of granting special privileges to urban areas by terminating the land-tax exemptions of Kyoto and Sakai residents and the special grants of money advanced to Kyoto merchants. In addition, the shogunate eased the policies designed to separate merchants and peasants, which had been in effect since the Toyotomi administration. It was also during this period that systems for administering the pariah class and dealing with the urban poor started to receive special attention. These examples show that the earlier conditions which had led to the implementation of policies designed to stimulate the urban economy had changed. Underlying this policy shift was the fact that the urban-based economy, which had been expanding in the earlier period, had begun a downturn.

SUMMARY

This essay has discussed the basic transformations in commercial organization, urban structure, and market relations that occurred in the late sixteenth and early seventeenth centuries. Clearly, the policies implemented by Oda Nobunaga and Toyotomi Hideyoshi were crucial to these transformations. A comparison of the two administrations uncovers both similarities and dissimilarities in their approach to problems. The Oda regime abolished barrier checkpoints and attempted to control merchants and artisans through the technique of census registration and the appointment of merchant officials. In the castle towns, Nobunaga decreed free markets and free guilds, and encouraged the flow of human and material resources into these military strongholds. On the other hand, because Nobunaga also granted charters to guild organizations, guild merchants continued to conduct business throughout the Kinai and Ōmi regions and to monopolize trade on the main roads and trunk lines. The imperial barriers at the seven entrances to Kyoto also continued to function. Thus, in the capital marketing area, the Oda administration was compelled to recognize the old guild organizations, although in some areas, especially away from Kinai, Nobunaga initiated policies that were identical to those used by other Sengoku daimyo. Given the problems that Nobunaga faced, this was perhaps his most effective option, and it fit in with his fundamental policy of reconfirming the rights of court nobles and religious institutions. Nobunaga's policies toward cities also reveal the dual nature of his approach. Where cities emerged in areas that had been under military proprietorship, he attempted to establish direct control. But in those urban areas that were the preserves of court nobles and religious institutions, he necessarily tolerated the continuation of the previous special rights and interests. Accordingly, only under Toyotomi Hideyoshi do we finally see the dissolution of guild organizations, the abolition of barrier checkpoints, and the fruition of Kinsei-style urbanization in Kyoto and the jinaimachi.

The above developments were the result of policies common to both the Oda and Toyotomi administrations.

But there were also clear discontinuities between the two regimes, such as their dissimilar policies toward the special prerogatives of court nobles and religious institutions. Although one should be cautious not to overestimate these discontinuities, in many ways they were profound. It is fair to argue that Oda Nobunaga possessed authority typical of a Sengoku type of daimyo, while Toyotomi Hideyoshi attained the more fully consolidated basis of authority typical of the Kinsei daimyo. A look at these contrasting bases of authority helps to clarify the differences between the two administrations. During the era of Oda Nobunaga, the court families and religious institutions still exercised considerable power, and Nobunaga had little choice but to recognize their special rights and interests. Toyotomi Hideyoshi, however, had built a stronger power base and achieved the status of a national hegemon, as symbolized by his appointment by the court as *kanpaku*, the traditional post of adviser to the emperor. He was thus able to go beyond what Oda had done, and finally dissolve the guilds and stop the development of the jinaimachi. Likewise, the implementation of the kokudaka system, an epochical event in the evolution of Kinsei society, redefined land rights throughout Japan and had a decisive impact on the marketing structure and on the development of the urban-based economy. In short, the urban and commercial policies of the Oda and Toyotomi administrations must not be considered as a succession of discrete, individually conceived policies, but must be placed within the context of changed power configurations and the broad structural transformations that society was undergoing. Seen in this way, the discontinuities between the two administrations take on a deeper meaning.

Chapter 8

Shogun and Tennō

ASAO NAOHIRO
WITH MARIUS B. JANSEN

IT HAS BEEN made clear in several previous chapters that under the bakuhan system the emperor held no real power, but only the symbolic authority involved in the granting of court offices and ranks and the determination of era names. Nevertheless, when we reflect on the nature of the modern emperor system, the end product of the elevation of the *tennō* that followed the collapse of the Tokugawa order, it is clear that we cannot avoid consideration of the position of the emperor within that order.

In this essay, although I begin with the Sengoku era, my main focus is on the formative stage of the shogun-tennō relationship as it was institutionalized under the bakuhan system. In Sengoku times, when the old political order centered on the Muromachi bakufu entered its final crisis, the shogun became a shadowy figure, as did the court nobility. The authority of the emperor declined to such a degree that he could barely enforce the use of his era names in preference to those in use in various other parts of the country; it seemed that the tennō was little more than one of many private sources of authority in the land. Some provinces were autonomous domains under Sengoku daimyo; others were under the control of lay *ikkō-ikki* sectarians, and the fragmentation of political power was extreme. In spite of this, powerful Sengoku daimyo such as Nagao Kagetora of Echigo, Asakura Takakage of Echizen, Ōuchi Yoshitaka of Suō, Mōri Motonari of Aki, Imagawa

Yoshimoto of Suruga, and Oda Nobuhide (Nobunaga's father) of Owari all made special trips to Kyoto or sent emissaries there to pay respects to the shogun, the tennō, and the court nobles by presenting them with money and with gifts. This so-called "Kyoto orientation" of the Sengoku daimyo was symbolized by the fact that in 1568 Oda Nobunaga himself professed to enter Kyoto in response to an imperial edict of Emperor Ōgimachi and a summons from Ashikaga Yoshiaki. One problem we have to deal with is why these daimyo should have troubled themselves with acts of homage to Kyoto at such a time. Then, keeping this in mind, we shall go on to see what forms the relationship between shogun[1] and emperor took after Nobunaga, through the Hideyoshi years, and in the formative years of Tokugawa rule. In doing so it is my goal to give order to recent research and to present a new approach.

LORD-VASSAL AND OFFICIAL SYSTEMS

The relationship between shogun and tennō has frequently been argued from the perspective of comparative history, with the focus on which—tennō or shogun—should be regarded as having had the powers of a feudal monarch.[2] It has also been suggested that the tennō should

[1] It should be made clear that the term "shogun," as it is used here, is not limited to the office of the *sei i taishōgun*. It refers in a broader sense to shogunal power and, at times, applies to such hegemonic figures as Oda Nobunaga and Toyotomi Hideyoshi. See Asao Naohiro, " 'Shōgun kenryoku' no soshutsu," *Rekishi hyōron*, nos. 241, 266, 293 (1970-1974).

[2] For discussions of the emperor's "power of the king," see Kuroda Toshio, "Chūsei no kokka to tennō," *Iwanami kōza Nihon rekishi (Chūsei 2)* (Tokyo: Iwanami Shoten, 1963), pp. 26-30, also in *Nihon chūsei no kokka to shūkyō* (Tokyo: Iwanami Shoten, 1975). On an opposing view that regards the shogun as having the characteristics of "kingship," see Nagahara Keiji, in "Chūsei kokka-shi no ichi-mondai," *Shisō*, no. 475 (1964), pp. 42-51, and in *Nihon chūsei shakai kōzō no kenkyū* (Tokyo: Iwanami Shoten, 1973). Kuroda does agree, however, that it was the shogun who had the "power of the king" in Tokugawa times.

be seen as having had a spiritual authority comparable to that of a pope rather than the power of a monarch.[3] It is my own preference, however, to seek the roots of that relationship in the social system of medieval Japan and in the historical evolution that led to the Tokugawa order of early modern times.

In earlier discussions of the formative stages of the bakuhan structure, I have suggested that Tokugawa political authority struggled to overcome a dualism that was inherent in military rule—the relationship between (feudal) lord-vassal and (imperial) bureaucratic-official systems.[4] Since some misunderstanding seems to remain on this point, let me briefly clarify it.[5]

The samurai, precursors of the Tokugawa bushi, emerged after the Heian period with a distinct social status, institutionalized in the thirteenth century by Kamakura law: samurai had a special standing before the law. In criminal investigations they were not to be examined by torture. If found guilty, they could be subject to confiscation of property or monetary fine, but never to physical punishment. Besides their privileges of having surnames and carrying swords, they wore a special style of headgear, loose-fitting *hitatare*, and hunting outfits that distinguished them clearly from ordinary people. Since the bakufu forbade commoners to become retainers (*gokenin*), this discrimina-

[3] Inoue Kiyoshi, "Tennōsei no rekishi," in *Rekishika wa tennōsei o dō miru ka*, edited by Rekishigaku kenkyūkai (Tokyo: Shinseisha, 1946; 3rd. ed. Tokyo: San'ichi Shobō, 1948), pp. 1-113.

[4] Asao Naohiro, "Shōgun seiji no kenryoku kōzō," *Iwanami kōza Nihon rekishi, Kinsei* 2 (Tokyo: Iwanami Shoten, 1975), pp. 1-56, and *Sakoku*, vol. 17 of *Nihon no rekishi* (Tokyo: Shōgakkan, 1975).

[5] On this problem Miki considers the development as the process of diffusion of both lord-vassal authority and sovereign authority as they are discussed in Satō Shin'ichi, "Muromachi bakufu kaisōki no kansei taikei," in *Chūsei no hō to kokka*, edited by Ishimoda Shō and Satō Shin'ichi (Tokyo: Tōkyō Daigaku Shuppankai, 1960), pp. 449-511. See Miki Seiichirō, "Sengoku Kinsei shoki ni okeru kokka to tennō," *Rekishi hyōron*, no. 320 (1976). My sense of problem, though inadequately developed, is made clear in "Zenkindai Ajiya ni okeru kokka," *Rekishi hyōron*, no. 207 (1967), pp. 12-22.

tion came to set the pattern of the Kamakura lord-vassal system. However, many of the emoluments of samurai status were very similar to the privileges enjoyed by those with imperial rank and office, as prescribed in the imperial legal codes.[6] Moreover, in the provinces, governors extended samurai status to rustic warriors whose names appeared on the local office register, appointing local notables to various police and semimilitary offices with titles such as *tsuibushi, ōryōshi*, and *kebishii*. Such men were gradually assimilated into the local imperial officialdom, while at the same time they organized themselves into regional warrior groups.[7] The feudal lord-retainer system of Europe was based on a private relationship between the lord and his vassals, with ties expressed through personal oaths of homage and fealty in performance of reciprocal obligations and services. In Japan this was the case for the most part, but it also is clear that in medieval times the system of local political-military organization remained strongly rooted in the earlier official appointment system. Any attempt to understand the positions of tennō, court nobility (*kuge*), and shrines and temples within the evolving shogunal hegemony must start with a recognition of the persistent duality in authority structure at the local level.

Even during the disorder that followed the fourteenth-century struggle between the northern and southern courts, this symbiotic relationship between lord-vassal and official systems did not fundamentally change. The lord-vassal tie was probably weakened by the frequent insubordination called to mind by the term *gekokujō*, in that the element of contractual relationship geared to mutual self-interest became more important in the relations between a lord and his vassals. In terms of comparative history, it may have been during the fourteenth century that conditions in Japan came to resemble the *lehn* system of Europe most closely. But there was also another side to gekokujō. The

[6] Tanaka Minoru, "Samurai-bonge kō," *Shirin* 59:4 (1976), pp. 1-31.

[7] Ishii Susumu, "Chūsei seiritsu-ki gunsei kenkyū no ichishiten," *Shigaku zasshi* 78:12 (1969), pp. 1-32.

violence of the peasant uprisings of the time shook the very foundations of the lord-retainer system, and prevented its severance from the court-centered system of official appointment. Despite sayings like "power produces a master, and dependence produces a follower,"[8] when both master and follower are threatened by peasant uprisings, the need to meet that threat had to come first. Genealogies could be fabricated so that higher status could be claimed, but a fake remained a fake. Unless local military lords could retain control of their peasants, and on that basis develop a regional military organization with some claim to legitimate authority, the very survival of the retainer system would be in question. Numerous statements could be cited that show how sharp their realization was of the danger they faced from insubordination on the part of peasants as well as retainers.[9]

For the provincial lords, the shogun was the ultimate authority for the validation of their status as samurai rulers. In the gekokujō era, however, the shogun might be killed or put to flight. The military lords, therefore, had to join together to maintain their own precarious position by force, and thus to demonstrate their samurai standing. Minor lords staked their lives in battle to uphold their honor and status as swordsmen. Regional and domainal lords issued statements that, "reluctant as we are," the times made it necessary to "maintain order on our own," and issued law codes for their provinces.[10]

It has been pointed out by Katsumata Shizuo above that the house laws of the Sengoku daimyo were modeled on those of the Kamakura *Go-seibai shikimoku*.[11] Since the au-

---

[8] Tsuji Zennosuke, *Yoshino-Muromachi jidai-Azuchi-Momoyama jidai, Nihon bunkashi* 4 (reprint, Tokyo: Shunjūsha, 1970), 39.

[9] Asao Naohiro, " 'Shōgun kenryoku' no soshutsu."

[10] "Imagawa kana mokuroku tsuika," 20, *Chūsei hōsei shiryōshū* 3 *Bukekahō* 1 (Tokyo: Iwanami Shoten, 1965), 130.

[11] Ishimoda Shō, "Kaisetsu," in *Chūsei seiji shakai shisō* 1, vol. 21 of *Nihon shisō taikei* (Tokyo: Iwanami Shoten, 1972), pp. 565-646 says the same.

thority of the Muromachi bakufu was not well established, lords had to invoke the authority of the Kamakura bakufu to buttress their own. This was particularly evident in the eastern provinces. But in the west, as the *Honpukuji atogaki* shows, the peasants who challenged samurai government did so under the shadow of an ideology that had imperial and religious overtones, and claimed for themselves the standing of "imperial servitors" (*ōson*). It was a powerful device for the bushi to be able to portray their control over the peasants in terms of rank and title deriving from the imperial court, although it was also essential to be able to invoke the authority of the shogun as commander of all warrior groups.

Mōri Motonari provides a good example. The Mōri came to power in 1550, and during the next twenty years their power expanded steadily.[12] When Emperor Ōgimachi succeeded to the throne in 1560, Mōri Motonari showed his respect by offerings of rice for the enthronement banquet. He was rewarded with the title *Mutsu-no-kami*, and the office of *Daizen-taifu* was bestowed on his eldest son Takamoto. But what is not always pointed out is that the son was at the same time given the post of Aki *shugo* by Ashikaga Yoshiteru, and that both father and son were also named to the shogun's private guard (*shōban-shū*).[13] Promotion to high court office greatly increased Motonari's authority, and it was clearly important to the expansion of his power. A chain reaction was set up; Motonari's ties to the shogunate were strengthened, and his authority was strengthened by his seizure of new police and military powers.[14] One can say that at this time the Muromachi bakufu was built into both the imperial-official and the lord-vassal systems.

[12] Asao, " 'Shōgun kenryoku.' "

[13] *Dai Nihon komonjo—Mōri-ke monjo* (reprint, Tokyo: Tōkyō Daigaku Shuppankai, 1970), pp. 200-333.

[14] Subsequently Ashikaga Yoshiteru also appointed Takamoto to the offices of shugo of Bitchū, Bingo, Nagato, and Suō, and it goes without

Asao, Jansen

The Sengoku daimyo's "Kyoto orientation" thus included attention to both the shogun and the emperor. The priority a daimyo gave to each was determined by the particularities of his geographical and historical setting.

NOBUNAGA, HIDEYOSHI, AND SHOGUN AND TENNŌ

Oda Nobunaga's entry into Kyoto in 1568/9/26 was ostensibly in response to the wishes of Emperor Ōgimachi and Shogun Ashikaga Yoshiaki, and seemed well within the pattern of behavior we have just noted among Sengoku daimyo. A few months later, however, Nobunaga's tactics showed that a new era and purpose, which prefigured the Tokugawa relationship of early modern times, were at hand. I have treated these matters at length elsewhere,[15] and since the main events of that period are taken up by other contributors to this volume, I will limit this account to those details that bear most directly on the changing relationship between the imperial bureaucratic and lord-vassal system that is our focus.

Three and a half months after his entry into Kyoto, Nobunaga presented the shogun with regulations (*denchū on'okite*) that can be compared with the seventeen articles of the *kinchū narabini kuge shohatto* that Tokugawa Ieyasu served on the court and nobility in 1615. Nobunaga's regulations stripped the shogun of virtually all his authority. He was limited to contacts with his personal entourage, denied contact with warriors of consequence and even with his own guard, and ordered not to intervene in administrative decisions and quarrels. Additional restrictions were issued in 1570, and seventeen more in 1572. Nobunaga was clearly determined to depersonalize the shogunate and re-

saying that this played a great role in enabling Mōri to dominate the central provinces. See ibid., pp. 334-35.

[15] See Asao, " 'Shogun kenryoku,' " and "Bakuhansei to tennō," in *Taikei Nihon kokka-shi* (*Kinsei* 3) (Tokyo: Tōkyō Daigaku Shuppankai, 1975), pp. 189-224.

duce the shogun to a symbol of authority within the court structure.[16]

Oda Nobunaga was thus unwilling to continue recognition of the shogun as head of the military houses and arbiter of police and military power. He saw the shogunate as having declined, together with the imperial court with which it had become entwined. It was no longer able to function as center of the lord-vassal system or as the legitimizer of samurai status. By his actions Nobunaga tried to institutionalize this perception and to reduce the shogunate to nothing but an office of the imperial court. Inevitably, the powers it had surrendered would end in his hands. Ashikaga Yoshiaki was unwilling to accept the limitations of the new power structure that Nobunaga contemplated, but the struggle between them was unequal, and Yoshiaki was driven into exile.

Nobunaga now had to make explicit what might otherwise have seemed to have shogunal sanction: he alone would stand as arbiter of samurai status. As such he demanded single-minded devotion to himself. In 1575 he declared to a retainer that "you must resolve to do everything as I say . . . you shall revere me and shall bear me no evil thought behind my back. Your feelings toward me must be such that you do not even point your feet in the direction where I am. If you act that way, you will be blessed with good fortune forever, as befits proper samurai."[17] In other words, if a warrior subordinated himself to Nobunaga, his samurai status would be confirmed. Nobunaga's red-seal certificate (*shuin-jō*) was designed for this purpose. Since recognition depended on victories achieved on the battlefield, the source of power (and hence of status) had become purely military. Recent studies show that Sengoku daimyo, on a smaller scale, had used military service as their criter-

[16] Okuno Takahiro, *Oda Nobunaga monjo no kenkyū* 1 (Tokyo: Yoshikawa Kōbunkan, 1969), 239, 343, 565, for the text of the regulations.

[17] For the *Okite* to Echizen province, see Okuno, *Oda Nobunaga* 2, 88-89. George Elison's translation.

ion for differentiating samurai from peasants.[18] Nobunaga's action was similar in concept, though different in scale.
    There was another, major difference between Nobunaga
and those daimyo: it was substantially within his power to
manipulate the tennō. Azuchi castle, which he began in
1576, contained in its plans a hall designated as the "Hall of
the Imperial Progress" (*Gyokō-no ma*), thus giving evidence
of Nobunaga's intent to receive an imperial visit.[19] He had
been named a high court noble (*kugyō*) in 1574, and from
then until 1578 he climbed steadily through the court
ranks until he was named to the second rank and was made
Minister of the Right (*udaijin-utaishō*). This achieved,
Nobunaga resigned these ranks and held no court posts
thereafter. It was his plan to institutionalize the powers he
had seized over status, police, and military functions by
means of the abdication of the tennō[20] and a visit to Azuchi
on the part of the new tennō. The four years during which
he held court rank were his years of confrontation with the
court, which opposed these plans; by resigning his rank,
Nobunaga moved a step closer to their implementation.
Upon completion of the Azuchi castle in 1579, he turned
over communications with the court to his agent, the
Shoshidai, secured the move of the heir apparent to the
Nijō palace, and extracted an imperial edict as a device for
making peace with the Ishiyama sectarians. From then on
until his death at the Honnōji in 1582, Nobunaga pursued
an unbroken advance toward absolute power, an advance
of which his military procession (*umazoroe*) in Kyoto and

[18] Katsumata Shizuo, "Sengoku daimyo kenchi ni kansuru ichi-
kōsatsu," in *Sengokuki no kenryoku to shakai*, edited by Nagahara Keiji (Tokyo: Tōkyō Daigaku Shuppankai, 1976), pp. 3-34, and "Sengoku hō," in
Iwanami kōza Nihon rekishi (Chūsei 4) (Tokyo: Iwanami Shoten, 1976).

[19] Hashimoto Masanobu, " 'Azuchi gyōkō' o shimesu 'Tokitsunekyō-ki'
shihai monjo no ittsū ni tsuite," in *Shojō kenkyū* 4 (Tokyo; Tōkyō Tegami
no Kai, 1976), pp. 175-201.

[20] On Nobunaga's request for Emperor Ōgimachi's abdication, see
Okuno Takahiro, "Oda seiken no kihon rosen," *Kokushigaku*, no. 100
(1976), pp. 29-58. It is Okuno's view that Nobunaga had requested appointment as shogun.

his continued determination to replace the reigning tennō by the heir apparent were symbols. What must be particularly stressed, however, is that throughout all this Nobunaga was especially intent on emphasizing the way proper to the warrior—and particularly insistent on his own prerogatives as arbiter of samurai-status determination.

When Hideyoshi came to control Kyoto after Nobunaga's death, the situation did not change fundamentally; his first need was to show his qualifications as undisputed leader of the samurai class. As a result of his military setbacks at Komaki and Nagakute, however, Hideyoshi found himself making greater use of the court appointment system than Nobunaga had. Hideyoshi outranked Tokugawa Ieyasu in standing at court, and he used this to extend his control over the military houses. In 1588, on the occasion of the visit of Emperor Go-Yōzei to his Jurakutei residence in Kyoto, Hideyoshi had thirty-one daimyo pledge to guarantee the lands of the court and nobility, and in that way bound these daimyo followers into an organization based on common interest (the *kōgi*)[21] that now also included tennō and *kuge*. Since Go-Yōzei had been helped to

[21] Kōgi is addressed at some length by other contributors to this volume. I view it as a polity that reflected the confusion and strife of the Sengoku period, when the establishment and maintenance of class (samurai) dominance was of primary concern. Common interest among regional leaders required a leader against both external (samurai) and internal (peasant) threats. Thus Ieyasu, on the death of Hideyoshi in 1598, pledged his fellow bugyō "not to harbor private grudges against the retainer corps" (*sho hōbai ni taishi watakushi no ikon o kuwadatte oyobu bekarazu*) "for the sake of the kōgi." Once such leadership was established and found competent, however, the leader's view of kōgi would differ from that of his fellows; kōgi came increasingly to mean the locus of superior force. In Tokugawa times the bakufu polity (*ōkōgi*) was distinguished from the kōgi of the domains. I have discussed this at some length in my "Bakuhan sei to tennō," *Taikei Nihon kokka-shi*, pp. 202-204, "Toyotomi seikenron," *Iwanami kōza Nihon rekishi (Kinsei* 1) (Tokyo: Iwanami Shoten, 1963), and "Shogun seiji to kenryoku," *Iwanami kōza Nihon rekishi (Kinsei* 2), 14ff. The Ieyasu statement is from Nakamura Kōya, ed., *Tokugawa Ieyasu no kenkyū* 2 (Tokyo: Nihon Gakujutsu Shinkōkai, 1959), 306.

the throne by Hideyoshi, the new hegemon was in a position to secure the daimyo's pledges in full confidence that he alone had final say in the assignment of court ranks and appointments. Even Ashikaga Yoshiaki, who had fled to Bingo, now joined this structure and was assigned lands producing ten thousand koku. In time, also, the "long sleeves" (nobles) and priestly hierarchy were incorporated. With the formation of this kōgi power structure, it was possible to exercise command over the warrior class and protect the lord-vassal system. Farmers could be ordered to tend their rice paddies, be deprived of their weapons, and be separated from the samurai.

Nevertheless, as can be seen from his relations with Tokugawa Ieyasu, Hideyoshi never succeeded in completing a pyramidal hierarchy among the military houses. And so he strove to supplement his prestige through the acquisition of court titles and official appointments. This is the reason why, with the inauguration of his rule as *kanpaku*, he issued the call to military action on the continent. When we read the twisted and scolding tone of his statement that "I have been able to subjugate even Japan, with all its armed strength, with my five hundred or one thousand warriors" (*Kobayakawa monjo*, no. 507), it is not difficult to see what was at stake. Similarly, once the invasion failed, it was inevitable that the Toyotomi power structure would disintegrate.

Hideyoshi's power structure also served to implant in emperor and court nobles the idea of reestablishing their former positions, for it drew no very sharp division between kuge and warrior houses at the outset. This can be seen in the case of Konoe Nobusuke, who dreamed of having power revert to the court by taking part in the military invasion of Korea. But this was by no means Hideyoshi's intent. After he ordered the suicide of his heir Hidetsugu (1598/8), his plans for complete domination of the land were clear. Together with the *okite* he issued to the military houses forbidding insurrections and lateral alliances, his *okite-tsuika* (supplement) directed court nobles and court

related temples to make sure their codes conformed to the
kōgi structure. Temples and shrines were ordered to concentrate on scholarship and religious services.[22] In this
manner his control over the warrior houses was strengthened, and a clear line was drawn to set them off from the
court nobility. These measures were taken to ensure that
the aristocracy would not be able to influence the lord-
vassal system. They were also taken to ensure that the court
nobles and court-related temples would orient themselves
politically toward the kōgi structure and not toward the
emperor personally.

TOKUGAWA AUTHORITY: SHOGUN AND EMPEROR

Tokugawa Ieyasu's victory in the battle of Sekigahara, in
which almost all the daimyo in Japan were involved, gave
him an unchallengeable position as leader of the military
houses and holder of supreme military command. Ieyasu's
power could have been institutionalized right then, except
that the remnants of the Taikō network of alliances remained to be dealt with. Young Toyotomi Hideyori was
only eight years old, but his rank and office at court put
him on a level with Tokugawa Ieyasu, who, though he held
real power, had not yet received authority to determine
court office and rank. Until the fall of Osaka, the power to
guarantee samurai status was divided between him and
Hideyori. In his two years and five months as shogun,
Ieyasu felt obliged to spend one year and nine months at
Fushimi keeping his eyes on both Kyoto and Osaka. It can
be imagined how galling he found it to hold his position as
shogun by court appointment. During that period, the influence of court and aristocracy seem to have been on the
rise, because Ieyasu and Hideyori vied with each other in
their offers of respect for the court.

In 1605 Ieyasu followed the examples of Nobunaga and

---

[22] *Dai Nihon komonjo–Asano ke monjo* (Tokyo: Tōkyō Teikoku Daigaku,
1906), 265-66.

Hideyoshi by turning his office over to his son Hidetada and taking the status of *ōgosho* (retired shogun) without court office. He now gave up the role of top soldier to take up that of top political power holder. The daimyo were ordered to turn in registers of their villages and maps of their territories, thereby demonstrating Ieyasu's authority in governance while defining their own regional authority. The kokudaka figures were based on Hideyoshi's surveys, and thus provided for continuity, but although Hideyoshi had ordered his kenchi on imperial authority while serving as kanpaku, this time the call for registers served as one more step in the direction of separation of warriors from court authority. In 1606, the court was notified that in the future recommendations of court ranks and offices for military houses were to come from Ieyasu. Ieyasu removed himself to Sumpu, which became the center of political authority, and the ōgosho era began. In 1608 the construction and expansion of the palaces for the current and the retired emperor were completed, and the residences of the court nobles and abbots of court-related temples were renovated. This done, the hegemon showed his readiness to intervene in a change of emperors.

In 1609, Ieyasu seized the opportunity provided by a scandal among certain court ladies to intrude into court affairs by placing the investigation in the hands of his agent in Kyoto, the *shoshidai*. Through this and other confrontations with the court on matters such as the forms of abdication and coming-of-age rites, the emperor and court nobles were made to realize that their activities were under his control. All this was capped by the promulgation of the *Kuge-hatto* and the *Chokukyoshie-hatto* in 1613, which institutionalized control over the nobility. Meanwhile, Ieyasu had arranged for the accession of Emperor Go-Mizuno-o (1611/3/27), and had secured control of court appointment powers. In 1611 Ieyasu received Toyotomi Hideyori at the Nijō castle as a public display that the Tokugawa political structure was now all-embracing. But the fulfillment of this claim did not come until the house of Toyotomi had been destroyed in 1615. The first campaign against Osaka was explained in part by Hideyori's failure to clear with Ieyasu the appointment of some of his retainers to court offices,[23] and the second winter campaign followed Ieyasu's refusal to allow the court to intercede.[24] At this juncture, Ieyasu was determined to deny the throne any interference with his authority over the military houses, and to make it quite clear that power was his alone.

Even before Ieyasu was named shogun, he had ordered the daimyo of the whole country to provide labor and materials for the construction of the city of Edo. Once in office, he required of them additional service for the construction of the castles at Fushimi and Hikone, as well as his own in Edo. In addition, he strengthened the ties of vassalage with the powerful daimyo of Japan, and also began to require them to leave hostages in Edo.[25] In other words, even while Ieyasu played out his role as court official at Fushimi, professedly faithful to Hideyoshi's kōgi, he was demanding that the daimyo provide service for the Tokugawa private castle, and thus showed he was planning a substantive change in the pattern of vassalage. This was the background condition that motivated the daimyo from Kai and Shinano and provinces to the east, *tozama* and *fudai* alike, to accompany Hidetada to Kyoto when he succeeded his father as shogun in 1605. The shogun was now, in fact, military leader of the warrior bands of eastern Japan, but still on the strength of the Ōgosho Ieyasu at Sumpu.

In 1611, immediately after Go-Mizuno-o had been in-

---

[23] On this entire section, see Asao, "Bakuhansei to tennō."

[24] *Honkō kokushi nikki* 3 (Tokyo: Zoku Gunsho Ruijū Kanseikai, 1968), p. 88. On this point Kurita believes that it was due to Ieyasu's "distaste for court interference in military affairs." Kurita Motosugu, *Edo jidai shi* 1, vol. 9 of *Sōgō Nihonshi taikei* (1927; reprinted Tokyo: Naigai Shoseki, 1939).

[25] Takagi Shōsaku, "Edo bakufu no seiritsu," in *Iwanami kōza Nihon rekishi* (*Kinsei* 1), pp. 117-153.

stalled as tennō, Ieyasu presented the daimyo with a three-part pledge of loyalty to the shogunal house, to which they had to swear. The first article stated that "orders from Edo must be obeyed as has been true of all regulations issued by shoguns since the time of the Minister of the Right," thereby taking as his model the first shogun, Minamoto Yoritomo.[26] Ieyasu thus made clear that, unlike Nobunaga and Hideyoshi, he was going to institutionalize the position that his victory at Sekigahara had given him by holding up the example of the Kamakura bakufu. Another article of the pledge specified that no daimyo was to give shelter to anyone who had opposed shogunal regulations and laws, nor was anyone to take rebels and murderers as retainers or enlist such persons into his service. These articles provided new meaning for Tokugawa authority. (The third, which specified arrangements for guard service, was soon superseded.)[27] Under these provisions, the daimyo were granted judicial powers within their own fiefs, and at the same time they were jointly charged with maintenance of the lord-vassal relationship. In these respects the new shogun departed from the example of his Kamakura predecessors, to base himself on the existence of regional authority while he himself stood out as national hegemon and head of the warrior houses. The strength of this structure was demonstrated in the two campaigns against Osaka by the fact that daimyo from all parts of Japan fought under Ieyasu's command.

The first article of the *Bukeshohatto* of 1615 revealed the expectations that were held of the warrior class: "Literary as well as military arts are to be cultivated side by side."[28] But it is to be noted that this statement does not have an independent, individual samurai in mind; the third to

[26] *Dai Nihon shiryō* 12:8, p. 152; 12:9, p. 293.
[27] *Ōban* military service modeled upon that of the Muromachi bakufu had already been abolished. At a time when daimyo had structured their retainer force and were themselves in *sankin* attendance at Edo and Sumpu, the clause about guard service was superfluous.
[28] *Dai Nihon shiryō* 12:22, pp. 18-22.

seventh articles, and the ninth, twelfth, and thirteenth, all address the chief of the lord-retainer units of each province or district—in other words, the daimyo.[29] And it was the shogun who confirmed the daimyo in their status. By extension, within the local area the daimyo, basing themselves on the prestige and power of the shogun, were to define and assign samurai status for their retainers. This practice was quite different from that which obtained under Nobunaga, who kept in his own hands the confirmation of status for samurai in all regions (even including rear-vassals) and tried to control them as his direct retainers. The new system was brought into being along with the establishment of the kokudaka system by Hideyoshi, and one can think of it as having been fully institutionalized by the time of Ietsuna, the fourth Tokugawa shogun.[30]

Ieyasu's regulations for the court and nobles (*Kinchū narabini kugeshohatto*) were issued at virtually the same time (1615/7/17) as those for the military houses (*Bukeshohatto*) (1615/7/7), and it is obvious that consolidation of power over the bushi would have been impossible without the simultaneous achievement of control over the court. The first article of the regulations directed toward the court stated that "scholarship is to receive priority among the accomplishments of the emperor (*tenshi*)," thus limiting the emperor's range of activities. Additional articles specified the protocol and seating order for all nobles below the ministers of state, left, and right, and laid out the qualifica-

[29] In the documents of this period, the terms in use are *daimyō*, *shōmyō*, and *shokyunin*; the status definition for daimyo would come only in 1635. Basically, however, it is probably permissible to take these terms to mean daimyo.

[30] Hideyoshi crossed borders to claim men as direct retainers, but not in the same way; he had additional criteria for this, while Nobunuga's demands were total. Nobunaga's ideas of territorial unification were also clearly formulated. In Ietsuna's time, one can cite the abolition of the hostage system (under which daimyo kept their principal retainers' families in the Edo *yashiki*) in 1665 as a sign of the maturity of the system. See Asao Naohiro, "Shōgun seiji no kenryoku kōzō," in *Iwanami kōza Nihon rekishi* (*Kinsei* 2), 42ff.

tions for those offices and that of regent. Still others governed the dismissal, promotion, punishment, and attire of court nobles and priests, and set rules for the determination of era names. The seventh article, which warned that "official appointments for members of the military houses are beyond the concern of court officials," fenced off the bushi class from court intervention and finally put an end to the duality of vassalage and court status that had characterized the samurai since medieval times. The samurai would no longer be charged with concomitant service to the court,[31] although they could be given court titles and ranks at the pleasure of the shogun. The opportunity for the tennō to manipulate the warrior elite through appointment to court office was forever destroyed. The emperor was fixed in a purely symbolic position of authority. At the same time, the shogun ceased to function as a court official. Instead, as Tokugawa Ieyasu had desired, the shogun emerged as the absolute head of the warrior aristocracy and the authority in actual control of the affairs of government.

Once the shogun's position was institutionalized in this manner, the Ōgosho was no longer necessary for the Tokugawa. At the time of the Osaka campaigns, Hidetada summoned and led the daimyo of eastern Japan, but those from western Japan, whose earlier loyalties had been to Hideyoshi, came in response to Ieyasu's command. By the time of Shimabara, however, there were no problems of divided loyalty. A shogunal vassal daimyo, Matsudaira Nobutsuna, could be delegated to command an army of fudai and tozama daimyo.

STATUS AND HOUSE

After the death of Ieyasu in 1616, Shogun Hidetada was left with a number of unsettled problems. First, it was

---

[31] Kurita, *Edo jidai shi* 1, 241.

necessary to make sure that the new codes would mean something in practice as well as on paper. Second, there was still a residue of traditional duality in the relationship between shogun and tennō that the new codes were supposed to resolve. Finally, and prerequisite to all this, Hidetada had to establish himself as the first among samurai, the national hegemon.

At this time, the power of the house of Tokugawa had not yet been fully extended to the western provinces. With the exception of a few fudai daimyo assignments in western Japan, Tokugawa authority essentially stopped at a line east of Harima. Since it was especially the daimyo in the western provinces who had had close connections with the Hideyoshi polity and had known the prestige that accompanied the holding of court appointments, this had dangerous implications for the first and second problems mentioned above. Hidetada tried to solve these deficiencies in his power structure by combining a prohibition on Christianity with tight controls on trade as national policies.[32] This was done by orders issued in 1616/8. The prohibition of Christianity was issued as the posthumous instruction of Ieyasu; the daimyo incorporated in the Tokugawa kōgi could hardly oppose it because of their moral duty (*meibun*) to the departed leader. The Hidetada bakufu itself ordered that in all territories Christianity was to be ruled out for all social classes, however low, and the daimyo had no choice but to look to the control of their retainers and their commoners. In consequence, Hidetada's grip on the entire country was greatly strengthened. That grip was further increased as this prohibition was combined with new controls on trade. With the exception of Chinese ships, foreign traders were limited to Nagasaki and Hirado. In time the bakufu had its opportunity to restrict all foreign trade to Nagasaki alone, and thus was able to move smoothly toward a full monopoly over foreign trade.

[32] These matters are treated at greater length in Asao, *Sakoku*, vol. 17 of *Nihon no rekishi* (Tokyo: Shōgakkan, 1975).

The example of Shimazu shows that the operation of this policy had a profound effect on even that daimyo, whose house had profited from foreign trade since the end of the Heian period.[33] With these restrictions on trade, the daimyo in the western provinces, who had constituted the most urgent threat to the Tokugawa supremacy, lost their chance to maneuver either politically or by economic means. Thereafter, Tokugawa Hidetada (1617/5/26) issued uniform red-seal certificates of investiture to all daimyo, something that not even Ieyasu had ever done all at once, and, basing himself on the *Bukeshohatto*, asserted his authority over all daimyo without distinction between fudai and tozama.

Hidetada's problem can also be expressed as one of continuing the kōgi, which had been established by his predecessor by use of force, in an era of peace. Since the Sengoku period, kōgi had been maintained by the military hegemon, whether Tenkabito, Taikō, or Ōgosho. Without warfare, how was Hidetada to prove that his power was legitimate and he himself the country's military leader? It is here that the problem of Christianity came opportunely to hand. The Christians could be credited with the potential for combining internal insurrection with external subversion, and they could be imagined as enemies who sought to disturb the peace. Because they were competing for trade, Spain and Portugal and Holland were each prepared to denounce each other, and so confirm Japanese suspicions. The road led straight toward the seclusion edicts of the 1630s.

Meanwhile the bakufu, using the provisions of the

[33] The Shimazu had authority to manage the cargoes from China before the time of the Kamakura bakufu, and Dazaifu had never tried to interfere with this. See Ōyama Kyōhei, *Kamakura bakufu*, vol. 9 of *Nihon no rekishi* (Tokyo: Shōgakkan, 1974). In 1588 Toyotomi Hideyoshi sent Ishida Mitsunari and others to the Shimazu territories in an attempt to control the flow of trade with "black ships." *Dai Nihon komonjo; Shimazu ke monjo* 384. The 1616 edict still did not apply to ships from China. But in 1635 they were confined to the single port of Nagasaki.

Bukeshohatto to order the transfer and reduction of daimyo holdings, consolidated the military and labor services daimyo were required to provide. In case after case— Hidetada's ouster of Fukushima Masanori from Hiroshima in 1619 for repairing his castle, Iemitsu's removal of Katō Tadahiro from Kumamoto in 1632 for improper transfer of a minor holding, and Ietsuna's move against Kyōgoku Takakuni, to name only three particularly striking occasions—powerful tozama daimyo were disciplined for infractions of "the ancestor's regulations." With the passing of time these practices gradually became ritualized, and took the form of a fictive battle in which the shogun, as military commander, rewarded and penalized his subordinates.

These measures did not suffice to legitimate the process of hereditary succession. Hidetada tried to solve this problem by becoming a maternal relative of the tennō. This possibility had already attracted the consideration of Ieyasu, who had decided on the betrothal of his granddaughter in 1614, when she was only seven. Hidetada carried out that plan over the objections of a reluctant court, and his daughter Kazuko was married to Go-Mizuno-o in 1620. Hidetada thereby became father-in-law of the tennō and eventually grandfather of the express Meishō (born 1623, succeeded 1629). But although Hidetada added substantially to his prestige through these connections, the marriage of his daughter to the tennō also confused things by making the relationship between the shogunal and imperial houses more ambiguous. The emperor, who had been excluded from the circles holding military power, which had unified the country, now became a family member of the most powerful house of all. The relationship between the two houses was thereafter characterized by pendulum swings between leniency and severity on the part of the shogun throughout the Edo period.

Nevertheless, there was no question of where the power lay. Initially Hidetada found it useful to employ the Kyoto setting to exert his control of the tozama of the west, and even after Iemitsu succeeded him as shogun he appeared in Kyoto once every four years. Hidetada used his first visit to Kyoto after Ieyasu's death (1617) to issue certificates of investiture to the daimyo of the west. Two years later he was in Kyoto again at the time of Fukushima Masanori's ouster from Hiroshima. By the time of Iemitsu's visit to Kyoto in 1626, however, the Tokugawa presence there was more a demonstration of unification than a device to bring it about. The contrast between Hideyoshi's reception of Go-Yōzei tennō at his Jurakutei mansion and Iemitsu's reception of Go-Mizuno-o at Nijō castle illustrates this. Hideyoshi, as imperial kanpaku, went to the emperor's palace (*gosho*) to attend the tennō on his journey. Iemitsu, too, went to welcome Go-Mizuno-o, who was his senior, but not as a court official, and Ōgosho Hidetada awaited the tennō's coming at Nijō castle. He saw no need to use the occasion for new pledges from or grants to the daimyo.

At the time of his daughter Kazuko's marriage, Hidetada had taken steps to end the listing of shogunal titles (and also, of course, those of the daimyo) in the *Kugyō-bunin*, the list of court appointments. This was one step in the implementation of the *Kinchū-narabini-kuge shohatto*. In 1627 a further opportunity presented itself in connection with the so-called *shie-jiken*, an incident in which the bakufu set aside the court's approval of titles requested by two great Kyoto temples on grounds that they had not obtained prior approval from Edo. Edo's generosity was amply shown at the time of Meishō tennō's enthronement. For that occasion the bakufu sent two senior councillors (*rōjū*) from Edo, restored ceremonies long discontinued, and paid all expenses. But when Go-Mizuno-o, as retired sovereign, showed an inclination to reestablish the office of Cloistered Emperor (*In*), the bakufu reminded him through the shoshidai that the In's discretion was limited by shogunal regulation to matters of costume, and that matters of expense and entourage were to be maintained on the level of a simple retirement as maintained by Go-Yōzei before him.

All this went hand in hand with further controls over the daimyo. The 1629 version of the *Bukeshohatto* institutionalized the *sankin kōtai* system for alternate daimyo attendance at Edo,[34] specified the military services required of the daimyo, and regularized the *kōgi* by placing administrative and judicial duties in the hands of the shogun's immediate retainers. The bakufu seized the opportunities offered by the suppression of the Shimabara revolt to install fudai daimyo as far away as western Kyushu, with the result that shogunal power now extended to all parts of the country both formally and effectively. This was symbolized by the 1644 order to the daimyo to prepare domain maps and submit village registers giving details on land size and productivity. As a further effort at stabilizing society, Iemitsu accentuated the current distinctions of social status by ordering harsh punishment for samurai who engaged in commercial activities.[35] Finally, a new movement was launched to deify Ieyasu as the *Tōshō daigongen* (Great Shining Deity of the East). The cult was based on the legacy of Tokugawa Ieyasu, "the *chinju* of Yashima," who was to stand at the center of Japan (Yashima) as the guardian deity for the whole world. An imperial proclamation directed worship of the Tōshōgū at Nikko in 1645, thus elevating the shrine to the same status as the imperial shrine at Ise. From then on, imperial emissaries were sent on special occasions from the court to both Tōshōgū and Ise.[36] This was the climax of the Tokugawa effort to fix the relationship between the shogun and daimyo within the context of a national *kōgi* system that included the imperial symbol of unity. There were a few further developments. Under Ietsuna, the fourth shogun, a uniform system of granting fief investitures to daimyo was adopted. As a

[34] For discussion as to whether earlier *sankin* requirements applied to Kyoto, see Asao, "Shōgun seiji to kenryoku kōzō," pp. 20-21. Now, at any rate, the *hatto* specify "Edo" for the first time.

[35] Miura Hiroyuki, *Hōseishi no kenkyū* (Tokyo: Iwanami Shoten, 1919), p. 273.

[36] Asao, *Sakoku*, pp. 271-78.

measure of peasant control, the bakufu ordered the preparation of annual temple registers as part of the effort to stamp out Christianity. For its time, the Tokugawa system of governance by shogun and daimyo was securely founded.

But there were weaknesses. The Tokugawa house was able to establish its direct control over the peasantry only through measures taken to counter the imaginary danger of Christianity. By the end of the Tokugawa period, the inadequacy of bushi rule began to be apparent throughout the country. In face of those challenges, the shogun and daimyo sought to open up their retainer bands by employing "men of talent" and relaxing the emphasis on status by inheritance. This led, in turn, to the political developments of the Meiji period, when the leaders once again moved to centralize control over the peasant population by using the emperor as nucleus for unification.[37]

[37] Shibahara Takuji, *Meiji Ishin no kenryoku kiban* (Tokyo: Ochanomizu Shobō, 1965), introduction and chapter one.

Chapter 9

The Changing Rationale of Daimyo Control in the Emergence of the Bakuhan State

SASAKI JUNNOSUKE
WITH RONALD P. TOBY

THE ESTABLISHMENT of the Tokugawa shogunate did not lead immediately to the creation of what historians now call the Kinsei *bakuhan* state. Just as the shogunate required time to establish its ideological basis of legitimacy—the creation of a new and more comprehensive *kōgi* structure—so also the daimyo needed time to create the mature Kinsei daimyo domain or *han*. The seventeenth century, in most parts of Japan, constituted a period of domain building, and the mature han did not come into being until a variety of institutional changes had been successfully carried out.

These changes resulted in the creation of a political structure or polity in which the daimyo was able to exert direct control both over his own retainers and over the peasantry and other residents of his domain. So long as a daimyo had to recognize the continued existence within his domain of independent fiefs held under the proprietorship of his vassals, what we have termed "Sengoku practices" remained. Daimyo relied substantially on the use of force to secure full control over their domains, but they also had to legitimate their control ideologically. It was at this juncture that the concept of kōgi (or *taito*), in the sense of "public authority," came into play.

In this essay I propose to outline the changing contexts

or structures of legitimacy served by the concept of kōgi in the evolution from the Sengoku daimyo through the establishment of the mature Kinsei type of han.[1] For my argument I will use two primary examples: the Go-Hōjō of Odawara,[2] as exemplary of the Sengoku daimyo model, and the Ikeda of Okayama,[3] as illustrative of the Kinsei daimyo model.

The basic structure of Go-Hōjō social and political control clearly fits the Sengoku model of kōgi (daimyo) over *ryōshu* (vassal) over *hyakushō* (cultivator),[4] but there are only

[1] I shall use the term "Sengoku period" for the period from the Ōnin War to the death of Oda Nobunaga (1582), "early Kinsei" for the period from the rise of Toyotomi Hideyoshi to the middle of the Shogunacy of Tokugawa Iemitsu (1582-ca. 1636), and "Kinsei" for the Tokugawa period after about 1636.

[2] The Hōjō family, lords of the Kantō headquartered in Odawara until their destruction by Hideyoshi in 1590, are commonly referred to as the "Go-Hōjō," or "Later Hōjō," to distinguish them from the earlier Hōjō family that dominated the Kamakura bakufu as regents in the thirteenth and early fourteenth centuries. For clarity, I shall refer to the them throughout this essay as the Go-Hōjō family.

[3] The Ikeda family enfeoffed at Okayama has been the object of study in English by John W. Hall, *Government and Local Power in Japan, 500 to 1700, A Study Based on Bizen Province* (Princeton: Princeton University Press, 1966).

[4] In contemporary documents, the terms kōgi, taito, and kubō, are used interchangeably in the sense of "public authority," as distinct from "private authority," but with the strong suggestion that this public authority was independently legitimated, or that it derived its legitimacy from the emperor, and not from any supervening levels of authority within the military class. These terms were also used to denote the person of the daimyo or the shogun, in a sense roughly equivalent to the Machiavellian "Prince," and by extension the government of the daimyo or the shogun. Ryōshu, proprietors of fiefs and lesser domains within the Go-Hōjō domain, formed the Go-Hōjō vassal band. It is important to the argument that follows to note that the degree of ryōshu independence as proprietors, and of ryōshu subordination to the Go-Hōjō authority as vassals, was in flux at this time, and varied from ryōshu to ryōshu within the Go-Hōjō domains. The tension between their status as private proprietors and their status as vassals, and the implications of that tension, for the relationship among kōgi, ryōshu and hyakushō, was one of the key issues of the period. Hyakushō, a general term for peasant, included most of the non-warrior population of the Go-Hōjō domains.

a very few extant documents that help us to understand the interrelationships among the components of this model. One such document is an edict of 1580, "orders to all ryōshu in regard to the villages in Tagata [district], Izu province."[5] The Go-Hōjō issued this decree in an attempt to revitalize agrarian villages devastated by warfare, and to discourage peasant flight and vagrancy. The daimyo could maintain his economic and strategic base only by keeping the peasants on the land and the villages functioning smoothly. Of particular interest to us is the final paragraph: "Although the above regulations should not [in principle] apply to private domains, still we have issued these orders, since they concern all the peasantry. If the above regulations are not carefully carried out, and [fields] allowed to lie fallow, the ryōshu shall be punished for it."[6]

In this document those referred to as possessing "private domains" (*shiryō*) are clearly the vassals or fief holders (ryōshu) of the Go-Hōjō. With this in mind, if we examine the document in terms of the relationship of kōgi, ryōshu, and hyakushō, we find evidence of two mutually contradictory objectives and principles. The first of these, evident in

[5] "Hōjō-ke shuinjō Zushū gōson no gi ni tsuite sōryōshu e mōshideru sujime no koto," in *Shizuoka ken shiryō* 1 (Shizuoka, Shizuoka-ken, 1932), 258ff.

[6] The interpretation of this document is in dispute. See Katsumata above who asserts that the "private domains" do not include "all the peasantry," that is, that the peasants indicated are only those outside the "private domains." However, my construction of the document is that "all the peasantry" is subsumed within the "private domains," that the edict recognizes the principle of nonintervention as a fundamental policy, and that the "entire peasantry" is taken up here *despite* that principle, as a temporary expedient. I have discussed this point at length in "Sengoku daimyō no kenryoku kōzō ni tsuite," in *Rekishi kōron*, no. 3-4 (1977), pp. 41ff., and "Bakuhansei kokka ron," in Sasaki Junnosuke, et al., eds., *Taikei Nihon kokka shi* (5 vols., Tōkyō Daigaku Shuppankai, 1975-1976), vol. 3 (*Kinsei*), p 21. See also Nagahara Keiji's use of this same document in his "Daimyō ryōkokuseika no nōmin shihai," in Nagahara, ed., *Sengoku ki no kenryoku to shakai* (Tokyo: Tōkyō Daigaku Shuppankai, 1976), p. 127f. My critique of Nagahara's evaluation of the document is in my "Sengoku daimyō no kenryoku kōzō ni tsuite."

the phrases "private domains" and "should not apply" (*iroi ni oyobazu*), is that the Sengoku daimyo regarded his vassals' governance of the peasantry within their own fiefs as a private form of control. In addition, the daimyo ought not to interfere in that relationship, or in the internal affairs of vassals' fiefs. This is set forth in the edict as a fundamental principle of Sengoku daimyo policy.

The second principle, the Sengoku daimyo's interference in the governance of private domains, implies a direct relationship between the daimyo as kōgi, and the peasantry, without reference to vassals' prerogatives. Here it is presented as an expedient, a temporary policy resorted to only because of the exigencies of war. Warfare, however, was a constant element of the Sengoku daimyo's existence, and thus the contradictions inherent in the two principles—the principle of the private nature of the ryōshu's governance of his fief and the principle of a direct relationship between the daimyo-as-kōgi and the peasantry—persisted throughout the years during which the Sengoku daimyo developed.

The meaning of the phrase "all the peasantry" (*shohyakushō*) in the 1580 edict also demands attention. It may be taken to refer to the general agrarian population of the Go-Hōjō domain, but it is important to note that this may not be congruent with the more idealized concept of "peasantry" meant in the kōgi-ryōshu-hyakushō model set up above. The agrarian village in actuality consisted of several discrete levels, which together constituted the "peasantry" as a generalized entity. We must therefore turn to an analysis of what is meant by "all the peasantry" in terms of the general context of how control was exercised over the agrarian populace.

Warrants for the return of absconded peasants are a particularly useful source for clarifying Go-Hōjō policy toward the agrarian class. Absconded peasants were a problem of particular concern to the Go-Hōjō, for depopulation of the countryside would undermine their ability to collect the dues that provided the economic basis for their rule. Indeed, if the Hōjō can be said to have had an overall agrarian policy for their domain, control over the movement of peasants may fairly be called the fundamental concern of that policy, so great was the stress laid on it.[7] In the light of the two conflicting principles outlined above, it is significant that there were numerous instances in which peasants fled from the control of particular ryōshu-vassals and escaped to areas under the direct control of the daimyo. This inevitably created tensions between those ryōshu who had previously governed peasants under the principle of private control and those persons who would thenceforth administer peasants by acting as agents for the daimyo. Any attempt by the daimyo to cope with this problem directly brought into play his superior function as kōgi. Absconding peasants became the problem that brought the two conflicting principles into confrontation.

Other evidence of Go-Hōjō policy toward the movement of peasants yields additional clues to the internal structure of "all the peasants." In 1586 Hōjō Ujikuni addressed an order to the peasant (hyakushō) Yojirō of Akuma, Chichibu-gun, Musashi province, concerning the cases of three peasants who had absconded from their village.[8] Investigation of the cases showed that the peasants were not of fully hereditary servant (*ichien fudai*) status, and therefore could not be forcibly returned to their former domiciles. That is, this particular category of peasant was not subject to the daimyo's ban on peasant movement.

Since there are many warrants for the return of peasants, and since the ichien type of hereditary menials was not an object of daimyo concern, it can be assumed that the ban on peasant movement and absconsion was directed toward a particular subgroup of the lesser hyakushō. This subgroup consisted of unfree peasants who lived in

[7] For a fuller discussion see Araki Moriaki, "Taikō kenchi no rekishiteki zentei," in *Rekishigaku kenkyū*, nos. 163, 164 (1953), the most important article on the subject.

[8] Sugiyama Hiroshi and Hagiwara Tatsuo, comp., *Shinpen Bushū komonjo* 1 (Tokyo: Kadokawa Shoten, 1975), 687f.

monogamous nuclear families, called by such names as
hyakushō no mono or *fudai no mono*, and who were subordinated or subservient to the hyakushō, or full-fledged peasants. What this evidence does is to identify for us a category
of lesser peasants (*kobyakushō*) who were for the most part
unfree agricultural servants (*fudai-genin*). The evidence
also tells us that a basic conflict existed between this level
and those above. The kogi-ryōshu-hyakushō hierarchy in the
Go-Hōjō domain may be schematized as in the diagram.

A	kōgi ryōshu hyakushō

B	kobyakushō (including hereditary agricultural servants)

The effect of the growing confrontation between groups
A and B was to intensify the contradictions between the
two principles of governance that colored relationships
among the levels of group A. This is because the absconsion of subordinated peasants, as an expression of class
confrontation between the hyakushō and the kobyakushō,
threatened collapse of the productive capacities of the
hyakushō, which were based on exploitation of the unfree
peasantry. This is also the reason why both the daimyo and
his vassals, who functioned as private proprietors, sought
to return the kobyakushō to an unfree status.

The Sengoku Daimyo and the Status of Kōgi

Although the Sengoku daimyo constantly strove to establish his position as kōgi, his efforts were hampered by the
contradictions originating in the tensions between groups
A and B within domain society. These contradictions arose

because the daimyo was obliged to acknowledge the existence of private control over hyakushō by his vassal ryōshu
at the same time that he was trying to assert his own direct
control over those hyakushō. As I have discussed in detail
elsewhere,[9] it was impossible even for Oda Nobunaga, who
became in essence the most powerful Sengoku daimyo,
fully to establish his identity as kōgi. Nevertheless, many
Sengoku daimyo, including the Go-Hōjō, struggled to attain the status of kōgi within their own domains, and frequently applied the term to themselves. Specifically, they
tried to advance the principle of the kōgi's superior right to
deal with absconded peasants, and to adjudicate confrontations among ryōshu or between ryōshu and peasants.

There were three separate elements in the Go-Hōjō's effort to achieve local recognition as kōgi. The first touched
on the question of daimyo military power and availability
of force for the maintenance of local rule. The second involved the fundamental problem of legitimizing daimyo
rule, especially in terms of the daimyo's relationship to traditional authority as symbolized by the office of emperor.
The third involved the daimyo's ability to acquire power by
gaining access to sources of wealth within the domain.

The compilation by the Go-Hōjō of the *Odawara-shū
shoryō yaku chō (Register of Fiefs and Military Obligations of the
Odawara Vassal Band)*[10] during the Eiroku period (1558-
1570) defined both the military organization of the domain
and the service obligations of its residents. It clearly
marked the maturation of the Go-Hōjō as a Sengoku
daimyo in military terms. However, this was not sufficient

[9] Sasaki Junnosuke, "Nobunaga ni okeru 'gaibun' to 'tenka' ni tsuite," in
Niigata shigaku 8 (1975). For my overall evaluation of Nobunaga's regime,
"Tōitsu seiken ron no rekishiteki zentei," in *Rekishi hyōron* 253 (1971), pp.
86-97; "Bakuhan taisei," in Yamaguchi Keiji and Sasaki Junnosuke, eds.,
Taikei Nihon rekishi 4 (Tokyo: Nihon Hyoronsha, 1971).

[10] Sugiyama Hiroshi, ed., *Odawara shu shōryo yaku chō* (Tokyo: Kondō
Shuppansha, 1969), is a carefully annotated printed edition. For an
analysis see Ikegami Hiroko, "Sengoku daimyō ryōgoku ni okeru shoryō
oyobi kashindan hensei no tenkai—Go-Hōjō ryōguku no baai," in Nagahara, *Sengoku ki no kenryoku to shakai*, pp. 35-103.

in itself to demonstrate that the Go-Hōjō had obtained kōgi status in military terms, for they still had to compete with their own vassals for control over certain segments of the domain's population. This is evident in documented instances in which the Go-Hōjō attempted to enlist as direct retainers (*taito no hikan*) some of the peasantry who lived under vassal rule. In addition, there were numerous instances in which peasants took advantage of this daimyo-vassal competition to transform themselves into direct low-ranking retainers of the daimyo, which was tantamount to using the power of kōgi as a means of escaping from the private control of the ryōshu.

For the Go-Hōjō, however, the most serious obstacle to the establishment of their identity as absolute hegemons within their domain was the weakness of their basis of legitimacy. The problem of legitimacy must be examined both in terms of the manner in which Go-Hōjō claims to public authority were recognized by the historic centers of authority in Kyoto, and in terms of the recognition afforded those claims by persons living under Go-Hōjō rule. The former was a question of traditional legitimacy, the latter, of consent.

The relationship of the Go-Hōjō to traditional authority is well illustrated by their numerous confrontations with Toyotomi Hideyoshi, which culminated in their destruction in 1590. In 1588, for example, Hideyoshi, who by then had attained the rank of *kanpaku* and hence could claim imperial backing for his hegemonic status, ordered the Go-Hōjō to send a hostage to Kyoto in order to demonstrate submission to his authority. This demand was accompanied by the charge that Hōjō Ujimasa and his son had "usurped authority in the Kanto, scorned [Hideyoshi's] royal authority (*ō'i*) . . . and utterly despised kōgi."[11] Unable to secure an equally valid claim to traditional legitimacy for himself, Ujimasa was forced to choose between submitting to the supreme "royal authority" of

[11] Sasaki Junnosuke, "Futatsu no monjo kara," in *U.P.* 42 (1976); "Bakuhan sei kokka ron."

Hideyoshi's kōgi or resisting Hideyoshi through military means. Using Tokugawa Ieyasu as an intermediary, the Go-Hōjō attempted to bargain for a compromise. Eventually, Ujimasa's brother, Hōjō Ujinori, was dispatched to Kyoto in response to Hideyoshi's demands, but this was not sufficient to stave off Hideyoshi's attack on Odawara in 1590, which resulted in the total elimination of the Go-Hōjō as a force in national politics.

The inadequacy of the Go-Hōjō legitimacy was also evident within their domains, where it expressed itself in the form of a lack of public consent. The 1566 decree banning the proselytizing activities of the Ikkō sect is a well-known case that can serve as a useful illustration.[12] The Go-Hōjō claimed that the cessation of sectarian debate and proselytization was necessary in order to maintain public order and to limit the number of lawsuits, which had been increasing dramatically. Unable to suppress the sect by sheer force, the Go-Hōjō were likewise unable to ban it outright, since even though they saw it as a serious threat, the flawed nature of their legitimacy made it impossible to achieve a consensus that would support such a ban.

The incompleteness of Go-Hōjō legitimation, and the effect this had in weakening their foundation of support, was evident also in the economic dimensions of local governance in Odawara. In order to establish himself as kōgi within his domain, a Sengoku daimyo had to attain a status distinct from and superior to that of his vassal ryōshu, a status distinction based on a superior capacity to grasp control of the modes of production. This was particularly evident in problems related to the distributive process, especially in domains like that of the Go-Hōjō, where the cash payment (*kandaka*) system of tax collection was in use.[13] As long as the Go-Hōjō were able to assert control over the distributive process through the use of the kandaka system,

[12] From the Azabu Zenpukuji collection, in Bushū Shiryō Kankōkai, comp., *Bushū monjo* 6, private mimeographed publication (Tokyo, 1960), 544.

[13] On the kandaka system see Nagahara's essay in this volume.

they could maintain the power necessary to rule their vassals, even while recognizing the principle of private control within their vassals' fiefs. In other words, the locally enfeoffed ryōshu were forced to recognize a level of control over the distributive process that was categorically different from the private control they exercised over their fiefs.

Clearly some form of domainwide control of the distributive system was essential to the local ryōshu for their maintenance of private control. This is because the market is, at least in theory, an arena for the competition of spheres of private control and thus, in the Sengoku period, should not be under the private control of any single locally based fief holder. This does not mean that competition within the domain was limited to the exchange of goods produced within the individual vassal holdings. The domain was also an arena for competition between fief holders and daimyo. Many of the warrants issued by the Go-Hōjō ordering absconded peasants returned to their original places of residence specified the places to which they had fled, and in most cases these were post towns or market towns. Market towns therefore became the scene for particularly acute conflicts between the two different principles of control that characterized the evolving Sengoku daimyo domain. Control of market institutions became a necessary foundation for any claim by the daimyo to the status of kōgi in economic terms.

Most of the attempts of the Go-Hōjō to remove peasants from the private control of their vassals and convert them into low-ranking officials of the daimyo occurred in the area of marketing and post towns. Furthermore, to the extent that peasants perceived marketing and post towns as places of refuge from private control, these became the places where the principle of direct rule between kōgi and hyakushō was realized. Indeed, the flight of peasants from private control—in most cases these were unfree peasants (kobyakushō)—was nothing less than a flight to this principle.

There is a final ironic twist to the evolving relationship between daimyo and vassal fief holder within the Sengoku domain. Absolute private control within the local fief was, of course, impossible, since the ryōshu's position was always to some degree dependent upon his relationship with the daimyo. In the first place, the daimyo's effort to secure recognition as kōgi involved him in the attempt to elevate his own position above that of the vassal ryōshu. This accorded with the ryōshu's expectations of the daimyo. In other words, the vassal subordinated himself to the daimyo in expectation of receiving protection through the daimyo's assumption of kōgi. Thus, up to a point, the effort of the Sengoku daimyo to gain recognition as kōgi, and the vassals' effort to safeguard their private control within their fiefs were two aspects of the same process. It is this condition that distinguishes the Sengoku daimyo type of lord-vassal relationship: two contradictory principles of control were obliged to coexist.

The Go-Hōjō frequently referred to themselves as kōgi or taito when dealing with the peasantry, distinguishing themselves from their vassals and asserting their authority to govern the hyakushō directly. This was necessary not only because of the personal ambition of the Go-Hōjō daimyo, but also because the concept of kōgi as legitimate authority in this period was deeply rooted in the peasants' consciousness of themselves as something more than private serfs. I have noted elsewhere, for instance, that the peasants' use of terms such as "imperial descendants" (*ōson*) and "honorable peasants" (*ohyakushō*) symbolized a growing revolutionary consciousness in the late medieval period.[14] To the extent that the kōgi-hyakushō principle was founded upon peasant consciousness of a domainwide identity which, in turn, was acknowledged by the daimyo, the Sengoku daimyo was historically progressive. But that progressiveness was clearly limited by the Sengoku dai-

[14] Sasaki, "Tōitsu seiken ron no rekishiteki zentei."

myo's simultaneous acknowledgment of the contradictory principle of private control. This limitation was evident in the failure of the Sengoku daimyo's attempts to exercise his asserted kōgi status in his relationship to the peasantry.

One set of documents clearly summarizes the problems inherent in the Go-Hōjō attempt to gain full recognition of kōgi status. These were general mobilization orders issued from Odawara during a domainwide census in 1582, which subjected the entire population of the domain to military conscription. One such order, dated in the spring of 1582, closes by stating: "In times of war such as the present, all the people of the domain must participate in the war effort. Anyone who fails to follow orders [to report for duty] will be summarily punished. Such [punishment] is not an injustice [committed by] the lord (taito)."[15] The assertion that the daimyo may not be held accountable for the harm that befalls those who flout his orders is an appeal to an external rationale, a rationale that was necessary if domainwide universal conscription was to be enforced. Had the Go-Hōjō allowed the statement, "anyone who fails to follow orders will be summarily punished," to stand alone, it would have appeared to emanate from the daimyo's intrinsic authority. The addition of the following sentence is a denial of that authority, an assertion that the right of mobilization is a priori and does not derive from the logic of the daimyo's authority as kōgi. More than that, the disclaimer undermines the asserted unimpeachability of taito. That the daimyo had to add this passage is clear indication that he was as yet unable to force recognition of kōgi status from the hyakushō.

THE SEPARATION OF THE MILITARY AND THE AGRARIAN CLASSES

The general recognition of the daimyo's kōgi status was finally achieved during the early Kinsei period. In terms of

[15] Nuki Tatsuto, comp., *Kaitei shinpen Sōshū komonjo* 1 (Tokyo: Kadokawa Shoten, 1965), 233, doc. 127.

the three elements of daimyo power postulated above—
legitimation, economic power, and military dominance—
the early Kinsei polity realized the first when it incorporated the traditional authority structure headed by the
emperor into its own logic of governance.[16] It also created
a domestic military system of unprecedented strength
through a mode of mobilization that has been called "unlimited military obligation."[17] In both these areas, it is fair
to say that the early Kinsei hegemons went far beyond the
limitations that had inhibited the Sengoku daimyo. National unification was, of course, an important element in
lending legitimacy to the new polity, and massive military
power was an essential tool for the realization of unification.

With respect to the second element, we have noted that
transformation of the material foundations of daimyo control could only be achieved by denying the principle of private control, including both the ryōshu's authority over the
general peasantry and the hyakushō's control of unfree
peasants. The early Kinsei state was also successful in ac-
complishing this. The instrument through which this was
accomplished was the series of land surveys carried out
under Toyotomi Hideyoshi.[18]

[16] See the historiographically important work of Ono Shinji on the relationship between the bakufu and imperial institution, "Bakufu to tennō,"
in *Iwanami kōza Nihon rekishi* 10 (1963), which summarizes the current
scholarship on this point.
[17] On "unlimited military obligation," see Yamaguchi Keiji, *Bakuhan sei
seiritsu shi no kenkyū* (Tokyo: Azekura Shobō, 1974). On the major issues in
regard to military obligations (gun'yaku) in the bakuhan state, see Sasaki,
"Gun'yaku ron no mondai ten," in *Rekishi hyōron*, nos. 146, 147 (1962).
[18] These land surveys had been the subject of much heated historical
debate, especially since the publication of Araki Moriaki's "Taikō kenchi
no rekishi teki zentei," in *Rekishigaku kenkyū*, nos. 163, 164 (1953). There
followed a special meeting of the Shakai Keizai Shi Gakkai devoted to the
Taikō kenchi, the papers from which were published as *Hōken ryōshu sei no
kakuritsu* (Tokyo: Yūhikaku, 1957). See also Miyagawa Mitsuru, *Taikō kenchi ron* (Tokyo: Ochanomizu Shobō, 1957); Araki, *Bakuhan sei shakai no
seiritsu to kōzō* (Tokyo: Ochanomizu Shobō, 1959); Araki, *Taikō kenchi to
kokudaka sei* (Tokyo: Nihon Hōsō Shuppan Kyōkai, 1965).

The chief purpose of these surveys was to restructure certain confrontations—especially the fundamental class confrontations—that had characterized the Sengoku daimyo domains. Therefore it is fair to say that these surveys were an historic attempt to reorganize the peasantry, and that the goal of this reorganization was the emancipation of the formerly unfree segment of the peasantry (kobyakushō) from their subordination to the free peasants (hyakushō), subjecting them instead to direct tax exploitation by the daimyo. The effect was a total denial of private control.

The reorganization of the free and unfree peasantry into a new class of general peasantry (also called hyakushō) was achieved by liberating the unfree peasant from the domination of the already free peasant. The land surveys did not immediately establish the former kobyakushō as independent agriculturalists and important members of the agrarian village.[19] Rather, the land surveys themselves and the reorganization of the peasantry gave rise to a new set of relationships, particularly that between village landlord and tenant cultivator, which became the source of the contradictions that characterized the early Kinsei state.[20]

The Taikō kenchi had been instrumental in bringing about the separation of the military and agrarian classes. This, in turn, made possible the daimyo's elimination of private vassal control within the domain. But this was achieved only by the adoption of a new concept that transformed the nature of the control which the early Kinsei daimyo was able to assert over his domain. The new rationale that supported the daimyo's governance of his domain relied on the concept that the domain was but a single element in the unified national polity which the shogun

[19] For examples see Sasaki, "Jūroku-jūshichi seiki ni okeru 'shōnō'-jiritsu katei ni tsuite," in Ōsaka Rekishi Gakkai, ed., *Bakuhan taisei kakuritsuki no shomondai* (Tokyo: Yoshikawa Kōbunkan, 1963), pp. 1-42.

[20] For details on the landlord-tenant cultivator relationship, see Sasaki, "Bakuhan taisei-ka no nōgyō kōzō to murakata jinushi," in Furushima Toshio, ed., *Nihon jinushi sei shi kenkyū* (Tokyo: Iwanami Shoten, 1958), pp. 51-139, and my "Bakuhan sei kokka ron."

had organized. In this structure, individual daimyo kōgi
units became fully subordinated to the general, nationwide
kōgi embodied in the shogun.

How this new conceptualization transformed the relationship at the local level between daimyo, vassal, and
peasant will be clearer if we look at the way in which one
early Kinsei daimyo explained his legitimacy. The instructions of Ikeda Mitsumasa to his district magistrates in 1657
provides an excellent example:

> His Majesty [the shogun] desires nothing but that
> there be no one in the entire country who is starving or
> cold, and that the entire country prosper. However,
> since he cannot accomplish this alone, he has en-
> trusted whole provinces [to major vassals] and has
> even dealt similarly with lesser vassals. . . . Likewise, I
> cannot compass all the affairs of the domain alone,
> and so I have entrusted [parts of it] to all of you in fief
> (*chigyōsho*), and have commanded you to govern them
> in accordance with my original intentions. And yet you
> all act as if [these fiefs] were your own private prop-
> erty, so that things have now come to the point that
> you exploit the lower orders (*kamin o musabori*), and
> you do not even realize that there are people starving.
> There are no words to describe your lack of devotion.
> It would be bad enough if you were thereby being dis-
> loyal only to me, but, since ultimately you owe all to
> His Majesty [I cannot allow your transgressions to go
> unnoticed]. . . . If we rule carelessly, and govern so
> that there are people who are starving and cold or so
> that parts of the province are depopulated, then we
> shall not escape confiscation of the domain by His
> Majesty.[21]

[21] Ishii Ryōsuke et al., comps. *Hanpō shū*, 1 (*Okayama han* 1) (Tokyo:
Sōbunsha, 1959), 265, Meireki 3/3/2. For another pronouncement by
Mitsumasa in the same spirit, see ibid., p. 335, tr. in Hall, *Government and
Local Power in Japan, 500-1700*, p. 403: "The shogun receives his authority
from heaven. The daimyo receives authority over the people as a trust
from the shogun. The daimyo's councillors and retainers should aid the

This injunction is an excellent expression of the basic philosophy of the Kinsei daimyo as he stood on the threshold
of a new mode of government. In Mitsumasa's case the sole
rationale for his authority lay in his relationship to "His
Majesty," the shogun as kōgi; he legitimated himself solely
as a representative of that superior kōgi.

The early Kinsei daimyo, however, had not yet worked
out a stable relationship between himself, his vassals, and
the peasants in his domain. Since the fundamental relationship between daimyo and shogun was defined by the
daimyo's military service obligations, it was inevitable that
the daimyo's control of his domain would be defined by his
military service expectations toward his vassals. In the case
of the daimyo's control of the peasantry, too, the system of
corvée for military purposes inevitably became as important as, and sometimes even more important than, the system of exploitation through the land tax. The continuance
of local subinfeudation (*jikata chigyō*) and corvée (*yakuya*),
the increasingly prevalent landlord vs. tenant cultivator relationship, and the intense peasant resistance to the corvée
led to a general condition of peasant restlessness that characterized the early Kinsei period. The early Kinsei state
had a strong military character, and this became the basis
of its ever deepening contradictions.[22]

The Formation of the Mature Daimyo Domain —the Han

Ikeda Mitsumasa's injunctions to his officials reveal another
problem that beset the early Kinsei daimyo.[23] The daimyo,

daimyo in bringing peace and harmony to the people." Hall's comparison
between Mitsumasa and Ukita Naoie is strikingly relevant to the present
discussion.

[22] See Sasaki, "Tōitsu seiken ron no nōto," in *Rekishi hyōron*, no. 253
(1971), pp. 86-97.

[23] Examples from other daimyo domains appear in Sasaki, "*Daimyō to
hyakushō*" (Tokyo: Chuō Kōronsha, 1966).

he maintained, had "entrusted" to his vassals portions of the domain, which had itself been "entrusted" to the daimyo by the shogun. Yet his vassals had "acted as if [the subfiefs] were their private property," and had reduced the peasantry to starvation.[24] That is to say, the vassals had reestablished de facto private control within their fiefs, a fact that Mitsumasa saw as a threat to his very survival as a daimyo, because of its potentially adverse impact on his relationship to kōgi (the shogun).

The reappearance of private control by the daimyo's vassals in the early Kinsei period raised the specter of peasant impoverishment. This was the result of the contradiction between the denial of private control, which had been the purpose of the Taikō kenchi, and vassal control of subfiefs as the foundation of the daimyo's military service relationship to the shogun. Repudiation of private control in the village resulted in the liberation of the kobyakushō from subservience to the free peasants. However, daimyo governance was also based on the military service system in which vassal ryōshu were in charge of conscripting peasant corvée labor for military purposes. For this, the vassals needed some form of private control over the peasantry. This gave rise to a contradiction that manifested itself in the increasing poverty among the agrarian class, especially the kobyakushō.

This was the situation in the Ikeda domain of Okayama in 1657, and it was common on both bakufu and daimyo lands at about the same time. Faced with the prospect of the impoverishment of the peasant village, the bakufu began to change its policies.[25] The Osaka campaigns of 1614-1615 had put an end to domestic warfare, and the

---

[24] For a different view of the background to this injunction see John W. Hall, "Ikeda Mitsumasa and the Bizen Flood of 1654," in Albert Craig and Donald H. Shively, eds., *Personality in Japanese History* (Berkeley and Los Angeles: University of California Press, 1970), pp. 57-84.

[25] For a discussion of these changes see Sasaki, *Bakuhan kenryoku no kiso kōzō* (Tokyo: Ochanomizu Shobō, 1964).

policy of national seclusion adopted in 1639 had eliminated fears about international warfare. Thus there was
less need for a governmental system predicated on the an-
ticipation of war. It was against this background that the
bakufu initiated the policy changes that ultimately produced the Keian military reform and the Keian Edicts of
1649.[26] It is typical of the conditions of the mid-seventeenth century that these reforms, military on the one
hand and agrarian on the other, were promulgated almost
simultaneously.

Of particular interest is the statement in the Keian Edict
that expressed the bakufu's sentiments about the fundamental importance of the cultivator "the jitō (daimyo) may
change, but the hyakushō remains on his fields forever."
This reaffirmation of the hyakushō-first policy by the
bakufu had a great impact on the way daimyo interpreted
another basic principle that "all edicts of kōgi (the bakufu)
must be obeyed."[27] The desolation of agrarian villages was
a problem common to both bakufu and daimyo. Although
in principle the daimyo were obligated to follow bakufu
policy, it was now recognized that in fact they might have to
deviate from it in order to accommodate the special conditions of their own domains. Accordingly, in what is now
considered to be the first major period of domain reforms
in the 1650s, the emphasis on strict adherence to the laws
of kōgi had been transformed so that the Ikeda daimyo

[26] For a discussion of the significance of the Keian military service reforms, and the points at issue, ibid., pp. 355-389, and Sasaki, "Gun'yaku
ron no mondai ten." On the Keian Edicts, see Sasaki, "Bakuhan sei kokka
ron." The texts of the "Gun'yaku ninzu wari" and the *Keian no ofuregaki*
appear in many collections of Tokugawa period legal documents, including *Tokugawa kinrei kō zenshū* (Tokyo: Sōbunsha, 1959), 5, 158-164; 6, 90ff.
John Hall has discussed these measures in English in *Government and Local
Power in Japan*, pp. 371, 373ff.

[27] *Hanpō shū*, 1 (*Okayama han* 2), 939. There are many passages in the
documents of the Keichō to Kan'ei periods (1596-1644) expressing the
same sentiments, e.g., ibid., pp. 952, 958.

could inform his officials: "Whatever His Majesty (the shogun) commands, whatever the *rōjū* (the shogun's senior councilors) order, you are to put forward [for my consideration] whatever you think best for all classes of people [even if it is at variance with bakufu precedents]."[28] This is a clear expression of the growing particularism of daimyo governance.

Although the results of these early han reforms varied in detail from domain to domain, the overall effort was a common response to the general problem of the decline of the agricultural village. The reform measures therefore tended to assume a common pattern, and they led eventually to the creation of the mature han.[29] In the process— and this was not the result of bakufu orders—the daimyo almost universally proceeded to abolish vassal-held fiefs (*chigyō*) within their domains or to reduce them to a fictional status. These acts constituted the final repudiation of private vassal control over village life. And with the abolition of private control, the true han was brought into being.

Under the bakuhan system, the samurai class brought the agrarian and urban classes, which it exploited for taxes and labor services, under unitary control on a domainwide basis. From their newly occupied quarters in the daimyo's castle-town headquarters, the samurai set to work to construct institutions necessary to perpetuate their rule. The establishment of general peace led to a reduction of military obligations. Meanwhile, the concentration of vassal bands in castle towns, and the concomitant employment of large numbers of domestic servants in samurai households, reduced the need to conscript corvée services from the peasantry. These developments, along with the adoption by the bakufu of national institutions for their secure main-

[28] *Hanpō shū*, 1 (*Okayama han* 1), 264.
[29] Many specific han are discussed in this connection in Sasaki, *Daimyō to hyakushō* and *Bakuhan kenryoku no kiso kōzō*.

tenance, resulted in the ultimate negation of private control as a general condition throughout Japanese society.

To recapitulate, in the early Kinsei state, vassal subfiefs were administered privately and separately from the fisc lands. The transformation of subfiefs into stipends, or into merely fictive holdings, involved more than the simple incorporation of subfiefs into the daimyo's fisc. This transformation constituted, rather, a unification and reorganization of subfief and fisc in such a way as to create a new entity, the integrated mature han. This is the critical point: the han was no longer an entity for private governance by the daimyo. His domain was, on the one hand, a military organ, a part of the military organization centralized under the authority of the shogun as kōgi. At the same time, the han was also the organ to which the shogun had "entrusted" local government, "because he cannot accomplish this alone." Thus the han, as part of this broader state structure, also became a mechanism for the repudiation of private control, which was antagonistic to the principle of kōgi.[30]

A fundamental characteristic of the bakuhan state was its attempt to bring the petty peasantry, the now independent kobyakushō, under its direct governance. This is, of course, just the other side of the denial of private control, and it served for the moment to overcome the contradictions inherent in the early bakuhan state's control of the peasantry. The transition in agrarian policy within both bakufu and daimyo domains from the 1640s therefore stressed the maintenance and development of the kobyakushō. At the same time, however, it greatly accelerated the growth of tenant cultivation and landlord-tenant relationships based on the exploitation of land rents in kind.

[30] For a discussion of these developments see Sasaki, "Tōitsu seiken ron," "Bakuhan taisei no kansei," in Kitajima Masamoto, ed., *Taikei Nihon shi sōsho* 2 (*Seiji shi* 2) (Tokyo: Yamakawa Shuppansha, 1965), pp. 21-156; and *Bakuhan kenryoku no kiso kōzō*.

These relationships formed the economic foundations of the Kinsei state.

Kōgi and Hyakushō in the Kinsei (Bakuhan) State

In light of the above discussion, what institutional developments were needed for the "maintenance of the kobyakushō"? The shogun (kōgi), as we have noted, had decreed that "the lord is a transient" entity. Moreover, as was evident from Ikeda Mitsumasa's injunctions, the daimyo clearly recognized that stable governance was an important element in their proof of loyalty to the shogun. The bakufu frequently referred to the domains of both the daimyo and the Tokugawa enfeoffed retainers (*hatamoto*) as "private domains" (shiryō) but, as should now be clear, what was meant was quite different from the "private domains" of the Sengoku period. The critical factor here was the form taken by the "mutual consent" existing between ruler and ruled within the newly structured han.

Mutual consent between the daimyo of this new form of shiryō and the people of his domain had to be based on the historically developed consciousness of the people of the domain. What was called for was a new principle that would justify the authority of the daimyo to govern the hyakushō (including kobyakushō) of his domain. The new *shiryōshu* (daimyo) sought to establish this authority as an extension of his own relationship to ultimate kōgi.[31] This attempt was manifested, for example, in the practice of Kinsei daimyo in many han of referring to themselves as kōgi while calling the shogun "greater kōgi" (*dai kōgi*). Note that the statement here that the daimyo was kōgi was not an assertion that he himself was the ultimate authority; rather, it was an acknowledgment that this authority was based upon his relationship to the shogun, the "greater

---

[31] Discussed in Sasaki, *Daimyō to hyakusho*, and "Bakuhan sei kokka ron."

kōgi." Moreover, a new and more universal conception of kōgi linked these two levels together. For the people of Kinsei Japan, kōgi came to mean the entire Tokugawa polity, which comprised the shogun at its apex, the daimyo (or shiryōshu), and their vassals. To this entity I propose to give the name "kōgi system."[32]

Under the "kōgi system" the shogun recognized the rights of the daimyo to those fiscal and judicial powers necessary to the governance of the domain. But this recognition was not total. The shogun (kōgi) reserved ultimate judgment over both the collection of the land tax and the administration of justice. Similarly, the domain's military forces were, in principle, completely integrated into the "kōgi system," in that they were conceived of as units of the shogun's military organization.

Within the "kōgi system" we can identify a further development in the relationship between kōgi authority and the hyakushō. As a general principle, the hyakushō viewed the higher authority (kōgi), not as an individual shogun or daimyo but as an impersonal representative of authority within the "kōgi system" that embraced them all. I suggest that this new development be thought of as a "kōgi system"—hyakushō relationship. The general consensus referred to above was achieved through the acknowledgment by those who were governed of the acceptability of this new relationship. This acceptability was based on recognition by the governed of the necessity and inevitability of being governed. For the agrarian class, the necessary secure conditions of production—particularly irrigation and forage land, on the one hand, and goods that they could not produce themselves, on the other—were under the control of higher authority. For this reason, the peasantry realized that some form of outside control was inevitable.

Other classes were also incorporated into the "kōgi system," but somewhat differently. As a general rule, one of

[32] This is further elaborated in my "Bakuhan sei kokka ron."

the most important functions of state power is to oversee the organization of production, that is, the ordering of the division of labor, which in the premodern state results from the imposition of political organization on the people. In the bakuhan state this was accomplished through the adoption of a fixed status system (*mibunsei*), which was founded on the class-specific role consciousness of the various strata of the governed, including, in addition to the peasantry, artisans, merchants, and outcastes.

The status system matured over the course of the seventeenth century.[33] By the end of the century the peasants were claiming that they were distinct from the townsmen and, as a rule, ought to live and think differently.[34] Popular among the merchants and artisans of the towns were tales of former peasants who had migrated to the town and made great successes of themselves. This reflects the predominant interest of the urban classes: how townsmen could become wealthy by pursuing their own way of life. By the end of the seventeenth century, then,

[33] Recent research on the former outcaste class has shed light on the development of the *mibunsei* in the early Kinsei and Kinsei periods, suggesting three stages of growth. The first stage, starting with the policies of Hideyoshi, was characterized by legislation establishing status group distinctions by occupation—agriculture, commerce, crafts—and place of residence—rural or urban—and, ultimately, status-group specific principles of ownership. In the second stage, from about 1640, terminology denoting outcaste groups changed from occupational terms like "leather-worker" to pariah terms like *eta* (polluted), tending to fix these groups as objects of discrimination. The mature stage, from the late seventeenth century, is discussed below. Minegishi Kentarō's paper "Bakuhansei kokka no kakuritsu to mibunsei," presented at the 1977 meeting of the Rekishigaku Kenkyūkai, is especially stimulating in this connection. See the review of the proceedings of the panel on status, the village, and ideology, "Mibun, mura, ideorogii-bakuhan sei no kokka kōken to jinmin shihai," in *Rekishigaku kenkyū*, no. 444 (1977), pp. 44-47. Also see Seiban Chiiki Hananomura Monjo Kenkyūkai, ed., *Kinsei burakushi no kenkyū* (Tokyo: Yūzankaku, 1976).

[34] Sasaki, "Yoshimasa to Saikaku ni tsuite," in *Chihōshi kenkyū* 124 (1973), vol. 23, no. 4.

each status group had come to advocate a way of life appropriate to its own status. The stabilization of status-group consciousness represents the successful establishment of the Kinsei status system as a whole.

This stabilization of status-group consciousness made more rigid the discriminatory attitudes against outcaste groups. It also started the process of reshaping inter-stratum relationships in terms of fictive relationships among juridically defined status groups, namely, the peasants, artisans, merchants, and outcastes. Thus, in conceiving of the totality of the Kinsei polity, we must recognize that we are dealing with more than simply a "kōgi system"—hyakushō relationship. We are in fact dealing with a "kōgi system"—peasant/artisan/merchant/outcaste structure. It is this juridically defined status system headed by kōgi (as principle) that characterized the mature Tokugawa polity.

From the era of the Sengoku daimyo to the establishment of the mature bakuhan state, the rationale used to justify political authority evolved from the kōgi-ryōshu-hyakushō model to the kōgi-mibunsei model. This model sustained the Tokugawa polity for a time. But by the mid-eighteenth century, that model began to disintegrate. As the number of peasant uprisings increased in the latter half of the eighteenth century, there developed among the peasantry a consciousness of a "peasants' world" (*hyakushō teki sekai*), which in turn gave birth to the idea of "rectification of the world" (*yonaoshi*) prevalent in the later years of the Tokugawa period.[35] I believe that this idea of yonaoshi constituted a denial of the kōgi-mibunsei consciousness, which had evolved from kōgi-hyakushō consciousness.

[35] Sasaki, "Bakumatsu ki no shakai jōsei to yonaoshi," in *Iwanami kōza Nihon rekishi* 13 (Tokyo: Iwanami Shoten, 1976), pp. 247-308, reviews the yonaoshi phenomenon.

Chapter 10

Dimensions of Development: Cities in Fifteenth- and Sixteenth- Century Japan

WAKITA HARUKO

WITH SUSAN B. HANLEY

THE SENGOKU PERIOD marked a turning point in the development of Japanese cities and in the growth of urban population. To understand this development, we need to have a clear conception of what differentiated the city or town from the village and of the key factors involved in urban growth. In much of the research to date on the subject, Japanese historians have taken European urbanization as a model in their attempts to define the medieval city and to understand the urbanization process. Typically, the emphasis has been placed on the degree to which the communities, as corporate entities, possessed rights of self-governance, directed the defense of the settlement, and controlled the judicial machinery.[1] On this basis, scholars sought to identify the existence of cities with similar characteristics in Japan. Some have stressed the limited degree of self-government in Japanese medieval cities, and others have drawn attention to similarities in patterns of urban government between Japan and Europe.[2]

[1] See, among others, Toyoda Takeshi, *Nihon no hōken toshi* (Tokyo: Iwanami Shoten, 1952) and *Chūsei Nihon shōgyōshi no kenkyū* (Tokyo: Iwanami Shoten, 1944); and Harada Tomohiko, *Chūsei ni okeru toshi no kenkyū* (Tokyo: Kōdansha, 1942).

[2] There is a good summary of the various viewpoints in Sasaki Gin'ya, "Nihon chūsei toshi no jiyū-jichi kenkyū o megutte," *Shakai keizai shigaku* 38 (October 1972), 96-111.

This approach to the study of cities has limitations, however. Even in the study of European medieval cities, we are beginning to discover that there were different types and degrees of self-government, varying according to nation and even among cities within the same country. The time has passed when we can analyze the development of cities merely by measuring the degree of self-government.[3] Furthermore, we now know that there also existed in villages during the medieval period the kind of communities (*kyōdōtai*)[4] from which self-government emerged both in Japan and Europe. During the fourteenth and fifteenth centuries in Japan, many of the villages in the Kinai area adopted a system of paying taxes to the proprietor on a collective basis (*jigeuke*) and gained the rights to administer justice in their own communities (*jikendan*). These developments indicate that, in terms of self-governance, villages differed little from cities. Although I do not deny the usefulness of analyzing the various rights to self-government, these rights do not in themselves indicate that a city existed.[5]

[3] Takahashi Kiyonori, "Komyūn-ron no ichi keikō," in Harafuji Hiroshi and Koyama Sadao, eds., *Hō to kenryoku no shiteki kōsatsu* (Tokyo: Sōbunsha, 1977), pp. 291-327.

[4] The term *kyōdōtai*, though originally a Western concept, has no equivalent in English today. When the author uses the term, she is referring to what Pirenne called "a corps, a *universitas*, a *communitas*, a *communio*, all the members of which, conjointly answerable to one another, constituted the inseparable parts. Whatever might be the origin of its enfranchisement, the city of the Middle Ages did not consist in a simple collection of individuals; it was itself an individual, but a collective individual, a legal person." Henri Pirenne, *Medieval Cities: Their Origins and the Revival of Trade*, translated by Frank D. Halsey (Princeton: Princeton University Press, 1925), p. 187. In this essay, the term kyōdōtai has wherever possible been translated into English as community, community association, or community interests, but where none of these terms seemed appropriate, kyōdōtai was left in the original Japanese. (Translator's note)

Translation of the term *ryōshu* also presents problems. In this essay, it refers to any person or institution—temple, shrine, court noble, samurai, or daimyo—that held ultimate proprietary rights to a parcel of land. It has been translated as proprietor or proprietary lord, depending on context.

[5] Amino Yoshihiko discusses the differences between cities and villages

In this essay I will attempt to define the basic characteristics of a city and to distinguish city, or town, from the
village in medieval Japan. I will first examine the economic
base of the city, focusing upon methods of urban tax collection.[6] Next I will deal with the unique characteristics of the
machi-kyōdōtai, or urban communities, and illustrate how
they differed from rural communities.[7] Further, I will attempt to pinpoint the elements of urbanism that are not
found in villages. In particular, I will be concerned with the
establishment of private property rights; that is, the rights
to adjudicate cases concerning property rights and land
ownership. These rights emerged principally as a result of
the growth of urban communities. I believe that the clearest contrast between cities and villages in the evolution of
these legal rights is that villagers, working actively through
organized movements, demanded *tokusei-rei* (decrees cancelling sales or debts), while urban residents struggled to
obtain the right to be exempted from the application of
these decrees.

Finally, I will examine the conflicting relationships that
existed between proprietary lord and the urban kyōdōtai
in the matters of tax collection and rights to adjudication.
Merchants and artisans in urban areas often prospered because of benefits and rights obtained for them by the lord,
but their relationship with the lord was always potentially

in "Chūsei toshi ron," in *Iwanami kōza Nihon rekishi*, 8 (*Chūsei* 3) (Tokyo:
Iwanami Shoten, 1975), pp. 253-303. In contrast to the relations (*en*)
within villages, Amino regards cities as *muen*, places without strong inter-
personal relations. However, *en* and *muen* are terms whose meanings are
only relative, and to be useful they must be more precisely defined. Katsumata introduces the concept of *ko*, individual entities, as contrasted with
a group (*shūdan*). In this essay, I use private ownership (*shiyū*) in place of
ko, as used by Katsumata.

[6] In his "Chūsei toshi ron," Amino discusses urban forms of tax collection, but his examples often seem to illustrate the similarities between
cities and villages.

[7] Both Toyoda Takeshi and Harada Tomohiko speak of the "village-
like" characteristics of medieval Japanese cities, but neither specifically
defines what constitutes a city or village.

hostile because their basic aims were often in opposition to
the interests of the overlords. The following study should
shed light on the structural differences and similarities between the castle towns controlled by proprietary lords
(*ryōshu*), who obtained this control through their domination of the economy, and the self-governing cities, which
constantly fought to keep as free as possible from overlord
control.

TYPES AND GENERAL CHARACTERISTICS
OF SENGOKU CITIES

Cities in the Sengoku period can be classified into the following four types:

1. Metropolises: Kyoto and Nara, which first emerged as
large urban settlements as early as the ninth century.

2. Entrepôt cities: cities that developed during the thirteenth and fourteenth centuries as a base for long-distance
trade, such as the port and post cities of Sakai, Hakata, and
Kuwana, and *monzenmachi*, such as Yawata, which developed from the communities and markets that grew up near
powerful temples.

3. Country towns (*zaimachi*): towns such as Hiranogō and
Izumisano that evolved from rural markets as the result of
agricultural growth, and *jinaimachi*[8] (towns formed within
the compounds and under the auspices of temples) in the
Kinai, such as Tondabayashi and Amagasaki.

4. Castle towns (*jōkamachi*): towns built through the
initiative of proprietory lords; these will be referred to

[8] In jinaimachi most people were members of the Jōdo-Shinshū sect, although there were also some followers of the Nichiren sect. There were
three types of Shinshū jinaimachi: 1. towns established by the temples
(Ishiyama, Yamashina, and others), 2. towns created when a powerful
dogō commended to the sect a region in which the people subsequently
became sect adherents (Kyūhōji and others), and 3. towns created when a
group of believers purchased or occupied a designated area (Kaizuka,
Tondabayashi, and others). What concerns us here is the third type.

as early castle towns, in contrast to the Tokugawa castle towns.

The listing of these types of cities follows the general order in which they developed. The characteristics of these towns often overlapped, however. Naturally, a port town could grow in accordance with the demand for its goods and services from neighboring villages, but it could also become a castle town if incorporated into territory controlled by a proprietory lord. Cities of the first three types tended to become self-governing.

The size, administrative organization, and political control of each of these types of cities were somewhat different.

1. Metropolises. Kyoto grew from the city of Heian-kyō, whose physical shape followed the ancient Chinese-style "city plan." Its growth took place through the separate expansion of the upper (northern) sector, known as Kamigyō, and Shimogyō, lower (southern) Kyoto. These were the two largest sectors of the city, each about one kilometer square in area. Urban communities also grew up around the core in sectors known as Kiyomizu, Gion, and Kitano, and these monzenmachi were also incorporated into the composite city of Kyoto. The basic units of both Kamigyō and Shimogyō were the *oyamachi*, or "parent" wards, which were grouped together into larger units (known as *machigumi*) of as many as fifteen wards each. Kamigyō and Shimogyō each contained five machigumi and about sixty oyamachi. The total population of Kyoto at the end of the fifteenth century, after the Ōnin War, was in the range of 150,000 to 180,000, which included an estimated 100,000 merchants and artisans.[9]

2. Entrepôt cities. The population of Sakai, Hakata, Tennōji, and Echigo Kashiwazaki was about 30,000-35,000 each. The city of Sakai began as a series of houses built along the thoroughfare named Kumano Ōji, but by the six-

---

[9] Kyoto Shi, ed., *Kyōto no rekishi* 3 (Tokyo: Gakugei Shorin, 1968), 38.

teenth century it had developed into a city with an estimated twenty oyamachi and 6,000 houses. Ōtsu, Sakamoto
and Kuwana, each with a population of about 15,000, and
Yawata, Tennōji, and Nishinomiya all had characteristics
common to monzenmachi.[10] These towns are well known
as commercial centers whose marketing networks were
closely tied to and focused on Kyoto. There were other entrepôt cities such as Kusado Sengen (in present Hiroshima
Prefecture),[11] but there are no extant records concerning
these cities.

3. Country towns (zaimachi). During the first half of the
fifteenth century, village markets began to appear in the
Kinai region and also in the areas located between Kinai
and the less developed peripheral areas of the country.
Markets serving a zone of two to three kilometers in radius
developed in areas where peasants had started paying
taxes in cash. As commerce grew, these grew into market
towns (*ichimachi*). In Owari province, for example, these
market towns began to merge with the castles of the
upper-strata domainal lords, and by the sixteenth century
there were approximately nineteen castles with ichimachi,
each about four to six kilometers apart.[12] A similar development occurred in Ōmi province, indicating that this
pattern was repeated throughout central Japan.

Another type of small city also developed in the Kinai.
These were the zaimachi, such as Hiranogō and Izumisano, in which the village landowning class rather than
the proprietary lords exercised political leadership. For
example, Tondabayashi was a jinaimachi in form, in that it
was located within the compounds of a temple. But in fact

[10] Harada, *Chūsei ni okeru toshi no kenkyū*, gives details on the population
and number of houses in cities.

[11] Hiroshima-ken Kyōiku Iinkai, ed., *Kusado Sengenmachi iseki*
(Fukuyama: Kusado Sengenmachi Iseki Chōsa Kenkyūjo, 1973-1977).

[12] Kobayashi Kentarō, "Daimyō ryōgoku seiritsu-ki ni okeru chūshin
shūraku no keisei—Owari heiya no jirei kenkyū ni yoru kentō," *Shirin* 48
(January 1965); 87-125.

eight upper-class peasants (*hyakushō*) provided the community's political leadership, so it can also be termed a
zaimachi. Tondabayashi comprised seven major streets
and eight wards (called simply *machi*), covering an area of
100-200 meters north to south and 200-300 east to west.
During the early seventeenth century, Tondabayashi
had a total of 285 households, of which 79 housed merchants, 33 artisans, and the remainder day laborers.[13] The
city sat on a knoll and was surrounded by a dirt wall containing four gates. (Many other zaimachi also built walls or
moats around the city; both Hiranogō and Sakai were surrounded by moats, of which Sakai's was the better known.)

4. Castle towns (jōkamachi). As outlined above, when a
market town (ichimachi) developed under the aegis of a
daimyo, a combined market town-castle town resulted. But
there were also cases in which ports, post towns, or monzenmachi were absorbed into castle towns. If we trace the
historical development of castle towns, we see that beginning in the eighth century, local administrative towns were
founded in the provinces, and in later centuries the shugo
daimyo tended to convert these into their headquarters
(called *fuchū*).[14] Still later, many Sengoku daimyo settled in
the fuchū, continuing the long history of these towns as
centers of local political power. For example, during the
Tokugawa period, the central portion of the castle town of
Kasugayama occupied the site of the medieval provincial
capital. Kasugayama also contained within its boundaries
the former castle towns of Yamashiro and Funai, and outlying areas that surrounded the port of Naoetsu. The castle
town of Funai alone contained 6,000 houses, and the fact
that this became only one section of Kasugayama indicates
how large the total population of the city must have been.
As a result of this pattern of growth, Kasugayama eventu-

[13] Wakita Osamu, "Jinaimachi no kōzō to tenkai," *Shirin* 41 (January
1958), 11.
[14] Matsuyama Hiroshi, *Nihon chūsei toshi no kenkyū* (Tokyo: Daigakudō
Shoten, 1973).

ally contained elements within it of castle town, post town, port town, and monzenmachi.[15]

The castle towns of the daimyo competed with those of their leading vassals for control over markets. Over time, the daimyo's castle towns were more successful in extending their control over the commerce and industry within their domains. This was reflected in the structure of the castle towns. According to the research of Matsumoto Toyohisa, the center of these cities was often the castle town at its earliest stage. As the castle towns grew, they gradually absorbed the local zaimachi surrounding them, creating districts within each castle town that continued to use the names of the original zaimachi.

Later, in the beginning of the sixteenth century, towns began to be separated into sections, each section occupied by persons engaged in the same type of business. The main growth during this stage took place in handicraft industries that produced goods to meet the military needs of the daimyo.[16] The newer castle towns were more apt to be subdivided according to occupational groupings than the older ones, indicating that they had developed after daimyo had begun to congregate their vassals in the castle towns following the separation of samurai and peasants. This new pattern of growth also implied the separation of merchants and artisans from peasants, and signified the maturation of this type of urban settlement.

THE CHARACTERISTICS OF CITIES AS REFLECTED IN THEIR METHODS OF TAX COLLECTION

At the beginning of the fourteenth century, the basis of rent assessments in Kyoto changed from acreage to frontage (*maguchi shakubetsu*). This change reflected the growing

---

[15] Harada, *Chūsei ni okeru toshi no kenkyū*, pp. 91-93.

[16] Matsumoto Toyohisa, *Jōkamachi no rekishi chirigaku-teki kenkyū* (Tokyo: Yoshikawa Kōbunkan, 1967), p. 186.

importance of frontage as commerce developed, and it signified a distinct difference in the method of assessing rents between city and village.[17] Three points in regard to this method of rent collection merit discussion.

First, before this new practice was adopted, dues in both cities and villages were collected by lords who claimed proprietary rights over land on the twin bases of rent and *zatsukuji* (often corvée or miscellaneous dues on various products, as opposed to *nengu*, annual land tax, levied per unit of paddy only).[18] But at the beginning of the fourteenth century, cities began to use the method of collection called *yajishi*, which was a fixed rent paid in cash. No longer were there any personal obligations owed to the proprietor; it was strictly a cash relationship.

Second, the yajishi system evolved in response to the increased buying and selling of land by those who claimed property rights as owners of the land in question.[19] In a sense, this method of rent collection can be said to have resulted from a weakening of the proprietor's control. Certainly its use by the court nobles reflected the fact that they no longer possessed strong enough political power to do otherwise.[20]

Third, yajishi rates were quite high, ranging in Kyoto

[17] Wakita Haruko, "Chūsei kōki Kyōto no tochi shoyū ni tsuite," in Nagahara Keiji, ed., *Sengoku-ki no kenryoku to shakai* (Tokyo: Tōkyō Daigaku Shuppankai, 1976).

[18] Amino Yoshihiko, "Chūsei toshi-ron," p. 270. He considers this to be an urban tax, but I am unable to agree with his view.

[19] The difference between ryōshu-type landholding and that by landlords (*jinushi*) was the absence or presence of the proprietary judicial rights and control over the day-to-day activities of the residents. See the Wakita essay cited above. Seta Katsuya, on the other hand, makes no distinction between the kind of landholding found in Kyoto and that by landlords throughout the medieval period. Seta Katsuya, "Kinsei toshi seiritsu-shi josetsu" in *Nihon shakai keizaishi kenkyū* (Tokyo: Yoshikawa Kōbunkan, 1967).

[20] For a discussion of the differences in the rights of residents living on land held by ryōshu and those residing on land held by landlords, see Wakita Haruko, "Chūsei kōki Kyōto."

from 30 to 50 *mon* (cash) per *shaku* (.994 feet) per year, about three to four times the amount of nengu collected in the villages in the same period. But although yajishi rates were high, by paying them city residents were able to extricate themselves from all other relationships and ties to the proprietors.

The situation in some other cities was similar to that in Kyoto. In Minami-no-shō in Sakai, where "yajishi was collected in lieu of dues on land," the urban residents in 1431 agreed to pay, collectively, a tax bill totaling 730 *kanmon* of cash.[21] It is likely that this tax assessment was based on units of frontage. At a somewhat later date, a letter of agreement signed in 1525 for renting a house listed only the amount of frontage,[22] indicating that yajishi was levied on frontage and not on total area.

Unfortunately, there are very few other records indicating how urban rent was paid in medieval Japan. One of the few other towns for which records are available is the village market for Niimi-no-shō in Bitchū province,[23] and these exist only for the fourteenth century. In 1334, rent for fourteen of the merchants and artisans in this market was collected on the assumption that each building lot occupied an area of 10 *shiro* (60 *tsubo* or 198 sq. meters), each having an equal frontage. Rent on the vacant land behind the houses was collected at a rate one-tenth that charged on the land containing houses. The rent on the houses in this market town was five times that levied during the same period on land cultivated by the peasants of Takase village in the same estate. However, the village rents were aug-

[21] "Gozen rakkyo hōsho." Eikyō 3 (1431)/11/8 (unpublished materials in the collection at Naikaku Bunko).

[22] See the document entitled "Furoyashiki sadame kinsei jōjō anmon," dated Daiei 5 (1525) in the section "Sugawara Jinja monjo" in Sakai Shiyakusho, ed., *Sakai-shishi* 4 (Sakai: Sakai Shiyakusho, 1930; reprint Osaka: Maeda Seibundō, 1976), 229.

[23] "Tōji hyakugō monjo," *ku* 1-4, *Kemmu* 1 (1334), Bitchū-no-kuni Niimi-no-shō tōhōjitō-gata sommō kemi narabi ni nōchō, *Bitchū-no-kuni Niimi-no-shō shiryō* (Okayama: Setonaikai Sōgō Kenkyūkai, 1952).

mented by various labor taxes (zatsukuji), so the effective
rate in the market town can actually be considered to have
been three to four times that on cultivated land.

It cannot be assumed from the preceding examples that
the method of collecting rent according to frontage was
necessarily used in market towns in other provinces. From
extant cadastral survey records of Erinji in Kai Province
for 1563,[24] for example, we learn that taxes on land built
on by merchants in the market communities consisted of
nengu (equal to rent) and corvée. But treatment was not
identical, and it is apparent that rent was levied on the basis
of area rather than frontage. Some city plots were exempt
from both nengu and corvée, since the holders discharged
"public" (*kuji*) duties, such as supplying horses, providing
lumber for construction, or serving as night watchmen.
Other households paid their dues by providing barrels or
by serving as sawyers, and for these households all nengu,
corvée, and kuji were waived. This form of dues collection
replicates in essence that used during the early medieval
period, when merchants and artisans supplied goods and
services in exchange for stipendiary land, and it was a
completely different system from rent assessment based on
frontage.

One of the problems in analyzing the systems of taxation
is in categorizing the taxpayers. Those listed as *naukenin*
(taxpayers) in the cadastral surveys were not necessarily
merchants and artisans located in the market. Many of
them lived in nearby areas, and some of them were even
kyūnin (stipended retainers of proprietors) and peasants. A
few of the names listed on tax rolls had the entry *jinushi*
(landlord) beside their names, and thus they must have
been landholders who were receiving rents, most likely
from merchants and artisans. All of this suggests that soci-

[24] See the "Erinji monjo" documents contained in Miyagawa Mitsuru,
Taikō kenchi-ron 3 (Tokyo: Ochanomizu Shobō, 1963), pp. 55-91. See also
the discussion of these sources in Katsumata Shizuo, "Sengoku daimyō
kenchi ni kansuru ichi kōsatsu," in Nagahara, *Sengoku-ki*, pp. 3-34.

ety was becoming stratified, with the powerful proprietors at the top, under them the landholders, and finally the merchants and artisans. When a powerful daimyo established a castle town, he attempted to exert direct control over the merchants and artisans by eliminating the intermediary collectors of dues, the landlords. Toward the latter part of the Sengoku period, merchants and artisans in the commercial districts of the castle towns were listed directly as taxpayers.[25]

We may mention here that since attempts at urban planning in the castle towns were undertaken from the outset, there was a fixed distance between streets, thus enabling taxes to be assessed easily by measuring frontage. But one should not conclude that taxation based on frontage in the castle towns was necessarily the same as the yajishi levied in Kyoto. Rather, the uniform distance between streets meant that the depth of the property was fixed, and so only the width of each lot had to be measured in order to assess taxes on acreage.

During the medieval period, proprietary lords maintained their hold over land and people through the collection of nengu and zatsukuji. The new system of imposing rent based on the amount of frontage meant that proprietors could no longer directly impose their control over human labor, that is, corvée. The imposition of fixed rent (yajishi) thus represented an attempt by the proprietors to retain some degree of authority over individual merchants and artisans.

During the early Kamakura period, merchants and artisans depended on nobles and on shrines and temples for their livelihood, and they acquired the privilege of tax exemption or were given stipendiary fields. Gradually they began to organize *za*. Consequently, the basic system of tax collection on merchants and artisans differed little from

[25] Matsumoto Toyohisa has analyzed urban growth in the province of Tosa in his *Jōkamachi no rekishi chirigaku-teki kenkyū*.

that in the villages during the same period. During the middle to late Kamakura period, however, the imperial court and its offices began to levy business taxes, first in Kyoto and then elsewhere, for the purpose of obtaining revenue from the growing commercial activity in the city. This meant that the urban-based merchants and artisans lost the tax exemptions accorded them in exchange for the dependent status they had held, and a new system uniformly taxing merchants and artisans was born.[26]

Two developments are implicit in the above changes. First, one precondition for the adoption of this new tax policy administered by the imperial court was an increase in the number of merchants and artisans who had become independent of the leading noble houses. These merchants and artisans coalesced into regional groups based on various za or guild-like organizations. A second development was the appearance of new types of za structured around specific occupational functions. That is, za that had been fashioned by merchants and artisans to provide services to the imperial household, nobles, and temples (*hōshi no za*), broke away from those patrons and were transformed into za that took the conduct of business (*eigyō no za*) as their primary purpose, and that paid business taxes in order to obtain this right.

A strong cohesion among members characterized these new za. They were soon able to negotiate reductions in taxes and achieved a degree of control over their craft or trade, especially the right to determine who was to be a za member. Through these means, they gradually began to acquire monopoly rights. These rights were in conflict with the right of the imperial bureaucracy and nobles to levy taxes, however. These authorities tended to assess a fixed tax on each merchant and artisan; their revenues increased as the number of merchants and artisans increased. When

---

[26] Wakita Haruko, *Nihon chūsei shōgyō hattatsushi no kenkyū* (Tokyo: Ochanomizu Shobō, 1969), pp. 235-261.

merchants and artisans formed za with monopoly rights, and the za limited the number of members in order to maximize the profits of each, they placed obvious limits on the revenues obtainable from this source.

It must be noted, however, that both the imperial bureaucracy and the Muromachi bakufu (which continued the practices of the former) did exercise the right to levy business taxes. The Muromachi bakufu taxed sake merchants and pawnbrokers, and used za-like organizations to facilitate the collection of these taxes.[27] Furthermore, the Muromachi bakufu did not permit these two za to limit their membership or to exercise monopoly rights, with the exception of the sake brewers in Kyoto, who were permitted monopsonistic rights in importing sake from the countryside.[28] In other words, while the bakufu would not tolerate the growth of za power within Kyoto, it did allow the za to exert monopsonistic power in the countryside, since this would establish distribution channels that would serve the interests of the bakufu-controlled markets in Kyoto. However, as the power of the Muromachi bakufu waned in later years, the za united, and their power increased. Faced with these circumstances, the bakufu fell back on levying a fixed amount of business tax from the za, a situation that paralleled the earlier policies of the imperial court.

In contrast, the commercial policy adopted by the Sengoku daimyo[29] eliminated the monopolies exercised by the merchant za of Kyoto, and placed increased reliance on the

[27] See Wakita Haruko, "Towards a Wider Perspective on Medieval Commerce," *The Journal of Japanese Studies*, 1:2 (Spring 1975), 335; and Kuwayama Kōnen, "Muromachi bakufu keizai kikō no ichi kōsatsu," *Shigaku zasshi*, 73 (September 1964), 12-14.

[28] Ono Kōji, *Nihon sangyō hattatsushi no kenkyū* (Tokyo: Shibundō, 1941), p. 264.

[29] Toyoda, *Chūsei Nihon shōgyōshi*, pp. 301-475; Sasaki Gin'ya, *Chūsei shōhin ryūtsūshi no kenkyū* (Tokyo: Hōsei Daigaku Shuppankyoku, 1972), pp. 42-58; Fujiki Hisashi, "Daimyō ryōgoku no keizai kōzō," in Nagahara Keiji, ed., *Nihon keizaishi taikei* 2 (*Chūsei*) (Tokyo: Tōkyō Daigaku Shuppankai, 1965), part 3; and Wakita Haruko, *Nihon chūsei shōgyō*, pp. 371-85.

privileged merchants (*goyōshōnin*) and artisans within the daimyo's own domains. However, Sengoku daimyo frequently followed policies reminiscent of the Muromachi bakufu. That is, they used the organizations of the guilds formed by their own privileged merchants and artisans to levy taxes, and also prohibited za monopsonies over major commodities that were produced within the domain but marketed outside. At the same time, in order to establish a domainwide market through which the Sengoku daimyo could exert their authority over commercial activity, privileged merchants and artisans were permitted monopolies *within* the domain. Both the za and the daimyo thus coexisted until the inherent conflicts between the two eventually made such coexistence impossible.

THE ESTABLISHMENT OF
URBAN COMMUNAL ASSOCIATIONS (*Kyōdōtai*)

Urban trade guilds originated in the formation of cooperative associations among merchants and artisans who earned their livelihood exclusively from commerce and the production of goods for the market. In this sense, we can say that the development of trade guilds corresponded to the establishment of guilds in Europe. There were certain features of the giant za in Kyoto and Nara that indicate their character. For example, all members exercised equal rights in the election of za officials, received an equal distribution of profits on shared capital ventures, and were equally subject to the rules adopted by the za.[30] The interests of these new za, which possessed monopoly rights, clearly conflicted with those of the newly emerging merchants in the surrounding villages, as well as with the interests of the proprietary lords.

[30] See the document "Gion shaki goshinryōbu 11" in Yasaka Jinja Shamusho, ed., *Yasaka jinja kiroku ge* (Kyoto: Yasaka Jinja Shamusho, 1961). On the subject of *dosō*, see Okuno Takahiro, "Muromachi jidai ni okeru dosō no kenkyū," *Shigaku zasshi* 44:8 (1934), pp. 974-1025.

These new guilds were established according to three principles: the equality of all members who collectively possessed monopolistic rights; the non-recognition of the rights of any individuals who were not za members; and a specific ranking system among the various za.[31] However, during the Sengoku period, class distinctions among za members and a breakdown of the cohesion of these guilds began to appear. Rights to za membership began to be traded, and za came under the domination of a few members whose positions of leadership were secure. Although some za tried to resist this trend and actually strengthened the principle of equality among members, the growth of output and commerce during this period meant that merchants who were not za members were able to find opportunities to engage in commerce, especially if they were protected by a military lord. Confronted by these challenges, the influence of the za waned. Eventually, they were replaced by wholesalers (*ton'ya*) who came to control commerce, gradually absorbing the rights once enjoyed by the za.

If we examine the eventual demise of the za within the context of urban development, the question arises as to why the trade guilds did not provide the structural basis of urban government.[32] In the medieval cities in the West,

[31] Wakita Haruko, "Muromachi-ki no keizai hatten," in *Iwanami Kōza Nihon Rekishi* 7 (*Chūsei* 3), 75-77.

[32] In research on medieval cities in Europe, Hans Planitz argues that the self-motivated actions of international traders provided the basic stimulus for the development of urban communities. In contrast, Edith Ennen believes that the expansion of guilds explains neither the creation of communities in which citizens pledged themselves to the formation of a community, nor the evolution of urban communities in general. Rather, the principal prerequisite for the establishment of these urban communities was the existence of regional self-governing communities that had their own systems of justice and interacted with communities based on religious parishes and guild-type economic communities. The original works of both Planitz and Ennen are in German, but a brief description of their theories can be found in Sehara Yoshio, "Yoroppa-chūsei toshi no kigen" *Ritsumeikan bungaku* 315 (1971), 4-5.

representatives of the guilds governed market towns, but in medieval Japan, guilds did not become the governing bodies of cities, even after federations of za had emerged. Rather, a geographical unit, the ward (machi), became the basis of town government. Part of the explanation for this difference may lie in the historical development of guilds in Japan and in Europe. In early medieval Japan, the za, which served the proprietary lord, were organized on a village basis by persons who specialized in a specific occupation. Although a few of this type of za continued to exist, during the late medieval period trade guilds more commonly took the form of organizations of members of the same occupation who lived in many scattered wards.[33] Furthermore, federations of guilds were never formed, and thus the machi kyōdotai, or urban communities consisting of members of various za organized on a geographic basis, emerged as the basis of city government.

By the late Sengoku and Tokugawa periods, persons engaged in the same craft did tend to live in the same ward of a castle town. But these wards resulted from the separation of handicrafts and processing from agriculture and from the formation and growth of the ward structure itself.[34] And this did not lead to occupational self-government because most of these developments were initiated by the daimyo.

In both the castle towns and self-governed cities, the basic unit of urban government was the machi, or ward, which had a defined geographic area. The development of the machi kyōdōtai, or communal associations within the ward, had its origin in the *ryōgawamachi*, which were communities of merchants who conducted business in shops lo-

[33] From their addresses, it is clear that sake brewers, cotton merchants, and merchants belonging to the lumber za lived in scattered locations throughout Kyoto. Also, residences belonging to the noble and samurai classes were intermingled with those of merchants.

[34] Matsumoto, *Jōkamachi*, believes that the system of assigning a section of a town to a specific craft group provides an index of the development of the ward.

cated along both sides of roadways. We should note that the development of these communities, in which roads provided the focal point for community development, differed distinctly from that of communities formed within the administrative divisions of the city, in which roads were used as dividing lines between administrative units or blocks. Furthermore, ryōgawamachi were formed as privately organized entities by groups of artisans and merchants.[35]

Both types of ward organization existed during the Muromachi and Sengoku periods. For example, ryōgawamachi communal associations in Shimogyō sponsored floats in the Gion Festival in Kyoto during the late fourteenth century,[36] and this suggests that these associations were created by merchants during this strife-ridden period in order to promote business and perform police functions.[37] The conversion in many cities to rent based on frontage occurred about this same time. Also, it was precisely at this time that those merchants who maintained a regular residence in the ward, as well as those persons who acted as administrators pro tem for the machi kyōdōtai, came to be called *chōnin*, or townsmen.[38]

Eventually, a pyramid-like pattern developed in Kyoto whereby fourteen or fifteen wards were combined to create a larger unit, the *machigumi*, and together these served as the basis for city government. Both Kamigyō and Shimogyō eventually contained five machi-gumi each, though these were not all created at the same time. Each ward (the smallest of the units under discussion) selected a

[35] Akiyama Kunizō, "Jōbō-sei no 'machi' no hen'yo katei—Heian-kyō kara Kyōto e," in Akiyama Kunizō and Nakamura Ken, eds., *Kyōto 'machi' no kenkyū* (Tokyo: Hōsei Daigaku Shuppankyoku, 1975).

[36] Ibid., p. 165; Wakita Haruko, "Chūsei no Gion-e—sono seiritsu to henshitsu," *Geinō-shi kenkyū* 4 (1964), pp. 88-169.

[37] Akiyama argues that the formation of the ryōgawa-machi occurred during the Sengoku period.

[38] Wakita Haruko, "Nihon chūsei toshi no kōzō," *Nihonshi kenkyū* 139-40 (1974), pp. 24-27.

representative (*toshiyori gyōji*)[39] from among the house-
holder merchants according to their seniority. These representatives took turns monthly in acting as *gatsugyōji*, or
administrator for the month. The gatsugyōji of the larger
ward groups meeting together governed Shimogyō (or
Kamigyō).

This form of ward administration would seem to indicate that merchants were on an equal footing with each
other; but, in reality, small groups of leading merchants
controlled the administrative apparatus in Shimogyō and
Kamigyō. And the same was true for other self-governed
cities. There are several reasons that government by powerful merchants emerged from a form of government that
suggested equality among participants. First, there were
differences in the political power of the various machigumi, such as between those containing the most prosperous merchants and those containing the least prosperous.
Among the machigumi of Kamigyō, the *Tachiuri oyamachi-
gumi* was the first to come into existence, and its monthly
representatives were able to dominate the government of
Kamigyō. Second, the residents of *edamachi*, the less prosperous wards fronted on back roads, contributed only a
small portion of city expenses[40] and were not permitted to
have their own representative. Thus they did not have an
equal voice in the government of the city, but merely followed the dictates of the stronger members. Third, those
people who lived in rented houses did not qualify as bona
fide members of a ward. Fourth, outcastes (*semmin*) and
outcaste communities could not become members of either
a ward or a ward group. As communal bonds grew
stronger, so did discrimination against the outcaste. However, outcastes were involved in government in that they

[39] Akiyama Kunizō, *Kōdō enkakushi* (Kyoto: Moto Kyōto-shi Kōdō
Kumiai, 1944).
[40] Kinoshita Masao, "Kyōto ni okeru machigumi no chiiki-teki hatten—Kamigyō Tachiuri-gumi o chūshin to shite," *Nihonshi kenkyū* 92
(1967); and Imaizumi, *Kyōto no rekishi*, 4, 121.

were used to carry out some police functions, such as the execution of criminals and the razing of vacant buildings.[41]

What was the situation in other cities? In Sakai, where merchants had arranged to pay rents collectively as early as the opening decades of the fifteenth century, the first records of the formation of ryōgawamachi are for 1535,[42] although some type of ward system may have existed as early as 1400.[43] Also, we know that Sakai was composed of two sections, *Kita-no-shō* and *Minami-no-shō*,[44] and that edamachi also existed. Because there was even a *kaisho* (municipal office), it is likely that the governing structure was similar to that of Kamigyō and Shimogyō. Also, the city of Yawata consisted of four sections whose elders formed a governing body that exercised police and administrative functions.

The most extensive documentation exists for Ōyamazaki, which was separated into two sections, Kami (composed of six divisions, or *ho*), and Shimo (composed of five *ho*). Their residents governed the city through a body of elders who were probably selected on the basis of age from among the *samurai-shū* (peasant-samurai consisting of upper-class peasants), most of whom engaged in the lamp oil business under the protection of temples.[45] However, it is unlikely that the units in Ōyamazaki were the equivalent of the wards that developed out of ryōgawamachi, since they retained many rural characteristics.

In contrast, Tondabayashi and Imai-chō, which emerged as jinaimachi, both originated as ryōgawamachi. Both de-

[41] Harada Tomohiko, *Nihon hōken toshi kenkyū* (Tokyo: Tōkyō Daigaku Shuppankai, 1957), p. 57.

[42] See the document "Nenbutsu sashichō nikki" in Aguchi Jinja, ed., *Aguchi jinja shiryō* (Aguchi: Aguchi Jinja, 1975), pp. 103-106.

[43] "Ashikaga Yoshimochi Kishinjō," in *Aguchi Jinja shiryō*, p. 98.

[44] Miura Keiichi, "Sakai wa jiyū toshi de atta ka," *Nihon rekishi no shiten* 2 (Tokyo: Nihon Shoseki, 1973), 335; and Toyoda Takeshi, *Sakai* (Osaka Shibundō, 1966), p. 69.

[45] See the document dated Eiroku 11 (1568)/12 in the section "Rikyū Hachimangū monjo" in *Shimamoto Chōshi, shiryō hen* (1976).

veloped self-governing bodies (*sōchū*). Tondabayashi was governed by eight elders, two from each of the four nearby villages that had put up the necessary cash to purchase proprietary rights from a local lord and had placed the community under the nominal proprietorship of Kōshōji temple. The exact relationship between the elders and the residents of the urban wards is unclear. Since the eight elders seem to have had proprietary interests in land in Tondabayashi,[46] that is, some kind of rights over the merchants who lived in the town, we can assume that the elders had some type of authority over the governed.

Finally there was the jōka-ichimachi. In Yamaguchi, an early castle town in the Ōuchi domain, we can assume from the existence of wards that used *kōji* (street) in their names, such as *Katakōji-machi* and *Kubokōji-machi*, that these were originally ryōgawamachi. An analysis of the cadastral survey records of the Chōsōkabe of Shikoku shows that combination castle towns-market towns in their domain were in the form of ryōgawamachi, that is, they were originally built along a highway and were organized differently from farming villages. However, because these towns were established upon the initiative of lords—and therefore were not self-governing—further study is needed before we can tell whether they were established at the same time that self-governed ryōgawamachi were formed by merchants and artisans.

In the castle town of the Yūki domain, the daimyo actually decreed that each ward organize an association, and further ordered that the members take turns serving as gatekeepers and night watchmen. A decree issued by the Yūki stated that "even those who possess no dwellings shall be members if they are heads of families."[47] Thus, even

[46] Wakita Osamu, "Jinai-machi no kōzō to tenkai," p. 7, and his essay in this volume.

[47] See article 82 in the "Yūki-shi shinhatto," in Satō Shin'ichi and Ikeuchi Yoshisuke, eds., *Chūsei hōsei shiryōshū* 3 (Tokyo: Iwanami Shoten, 1965), 248-49.

renters were included in the associations organized by the lord for the purpose of better policing the city. This case indicates that in order to flesh out the lower levels of their administrations, daimyo sometimes had to create community organizations, which were otherwise formed by the people out of communal interest.

Castle towns increased in size as they attracted artisans from local towns throughout the domain. As the cities grew, new wards were created. The new wards often included those inhabited by people in the same trade, in addition to those organized in a specific locale and which still retained the name of the town they had once been.[48] An example is the Honai-machi in the castle town of Ōmi Ishidera. In this case, equality of membership, which had existed within the za communities of the medieval period, disappeared as a result of the emergence of a status structure within the za and the lord's appointment of leaders (*zatō*) who became the basis of a new structure of government.[49] Commerce was now controlled by these urban leaders who became *goyōshōnin* and *goyōshokunin* (merchants and artisans by appointment to the lord). We can assume that once this occurred, equality among members (house owners in the ward) and the selection of ward representatives on the basis of age were no longer practiced.

Daimyo interference affected other aspects of urban self-government. In the self-governed cities in the Kinai, the city as a whole won the right to be exempted from debt moratoriums (*tokusei-rei*)—a crucial victory in establishing the right to adjudicate civil matters.[50] However, in the castle towns of the Sengoku daimyo the authorization to buy and sell land and the right to be exempted from the moratoriums were granted individually to specific mer-

[48] Matsumoto, *Jōkamachi*, p. 189.
[49] Wakita Haruko, *Nihon chūsei shōgyō*, pp. 503-504.
[50] Wakita Haruko, "Tokusei-rei to tokusei menjo—shoyū no ronri o megutte—," *Tachibana Joshi Daigaku kenkyū kiyō* 4 (1976).

chant houses.[51] Castle towns, as corporate entities, did not win the right to be exempt from the moratoriums until the issuance of the free market decree (*rakuichi-rei*) by Nobunaga.[52]

Castle towns in the Kinai achieved a greater degree of self-government than did castle towns in any other part of the country. Evidence from 1556 for the castle town of Amagasaki in Settsu indicates that the Amagasaki *sōchū* (governing body) could borrow money. It also sold land that it owned collectively to Honkōji temple of the Nichiren sect for the construction of a jinaimachi.[53] Although we are uncertain of the details concerning the internal structure of this governing body, we can assume that it held considerable powers of self-government. But this example is limited to the Kinai area.

THE ADMINISTRATION OF JUSTICE

In medieval Japan land was held by nobles, temples, or by members of the samurai class as their proprietary holdings. Within their respective holdings, each proprietor in principle possessed the right to prevent intrusion of any kind into his property (*fu'nyū-ken*) and the rights of adjudication. By the fourteenth or fifteenth century, however, the rights of adjudication came to be exercised either by a public authority (imperial court, bakufu, or shugo) or by the inhabitants themselves.

In Kyoto, proprietary rights to land within shrine and temple precincts, such as Kitano and Tōji, were recognized

[51] In addition, guarantees called *baitoku ando* were given by Sengoku daimyo such as Date, Ashina, and others. See Shimomura Ko, "Sengoku-Shokuhō-ki tokusei no ichi keitai—Tosa Chōsokabe-shi no baichi ando-jōhyō-tokusei o megutte—," *Kokugakuin zasshi* 77 (August 1978), 1-15.

[52] Sasaki Gin'ya, "Rakuichi rakuza-rei to za no hoshō ando," in Nagahara, *Sengoku-ki*, p. 206.

[53] Wakita Osamu, "Amagasaki to jinai-machi," *Amagasaki chiiki-shi kenkyū* 18 (1977).

by the bakufu as belonging to the temples or shrines themselves. In contrast, in most of the city proper, including the
wards both in Kamigyō and in Shimogyō, the proprietor's
rights of adjudication were superseded by the rights of the
bakufu.[54] Thus proprietors were reduced to mere landholders who collected rent. The machi-kyōdōtai had their
own administrative structures to deal with festivals, public
works, and other functions necessary in ordering the day-
to-day affairs of the community, but for police and criminal matters they were dependent on the bakufu. However,
due to the virtual disappearance of bakufu power by the
middle of the sixteenth century,[55] the machi-kyōdōtai
exercised self-adjudication and sometimes took collective
action to refuse to pay rents. Thereafter, how much self-
government the association was able to exercise waxed or
waned depending on how much power the proprietors
were able to exert at any one time.

In Yawata, which developed as a monzenmachi of the
Iwashimizu Hachiman shrine and became an important
regional entrepôt, the shrine itself served as proprietary
lord and exercised the rights of adjudication in the four
administrative jurisdictions located within the temple holdings. During the Muromachi and Sengoku periods, however, the elders began to exercise adjudicative powers. In
port towns such as Sakai, Hakata, and Kuwana, where the
municipal administration was in the hands of a council of
merchant elders (*egōshū*), which operated by consultation
among representatives of the townspeople, the council
exercised the rights of adjudication. It was no easy task for
these towns to retain the right to self-government, however. Their success depended on the regional power balance among contesting lords, and at times on their ability
to supply rations and cash to warring military factions. The
people of Ōyamazaki, for example, made a practice of con-

[54] Wakita Haruko, "Chūsei kōki Kyōto."
[55] Hayashiya Tatsusaburō, "Machishū no seiritsu," in *Chūsei bunka no kichō* (Tokyo: Tōkyō Daigaku Shuppankai, 1953), pp. 210-211.

tributing cash (*mainai-sen*, literally money for rations, but in fact a bribe) to the leaders of competing camps on the eve of major battles, receiving in return a promise from the warring groups not to quarter military forces in the town and a guarantee of the continued right of urban government.

Generally speaking, in areas where civil proprietors, temples, shrines, and nobles were weak, urban residents were able to acquire the rights to self-government under the pretext of protecting the rights of their proprietors from incursion by daimyo and other military powers. This ruse was carried out in many jinaimachi associated with the Jōdo and Nichiren sects in the Kinai. The temples became only nominal proprietors, while merchants and artisans in fact governed the cities themselves, and even held rights of adjudication.

Disputes among za members were usually arbitrated within the za itself, following its own individual rules. But when a dispute involved persons outside the za, it was not uncommon for the disputants to resort to force in settling the issue. When a dispute involved more than one za or persons not belonging to a za, the matter had to be adjudicated by the proprietor, provided that all parties involved resided within his territory. If a dispute involved the proprietor himself or residents from various territories, then the shugo, or later, a daimyo had to be enlisted to adjudicate the matter. Similarly, if a dispute was interprovincial, then the bakufu adjudicated the matter.[56]

In areas that had gained rights to self-adjudication, the elder in charge of municipal administration served as judge in civil matters. To cite some examples, in Kuwana, four of the elders issued judgments concerning a dispute that involved a za of Ōmi merchants.[57] In Sakai during the Sengoku period, the governing council, consisting of

[56] Wakita Haruko, *Chūsei shōgyō hattatsushi*, pp. 573-578.
[57] "Imabori Hie-jinja monjo" (undated but known to be 1558), "Kuwana-shū yonin rensho origami."

thirty-six merchants, administered the city, while ten *nagayashi* (merchants in the warehousing business) heard cases concerning disputes.[58] It is most likely, however, that the leading members of the governing council were in charge of making the final decision in any dispute. Sometimes bakufu aid was also solicited, as in the 1430 case involving the inheritance of the wealthy merchant, Notoya.[59]

In Kyoto, prior to the Muromachi period, civil disputes were handled by the imperial capital police, the *kebiishichō*.[60] As this body's authority declined, the larger za began to take over its functions. For example, by the middle of the fourteenth century sake producers and the moneylenders in Kyoto who enjoyed the patronage of Enryaku-ji were able to enforce their own decisions concerning debt payment.[61] But even then, there existed no formal judicial structure maintained by groups of za. The Muromachi bakufu from the beginning prohibited za from carrying out private judicial decisions (*shikkōken*), and limited the judicial authority of individual proprietors. Eventually the bakufu absorbed the powers of the capital police to claim jurisdiction over all civil matters in Kyoto.[62] Despite its loss of political power, bakufu control of the judicial process was generally maintained until the end of the Sengoku period. In the castle towns, naturally, civil matters were under the jurisdiction of the townspeople (chōnin). In other words, the chōnin held certain rights to administer justice within the framework of their institutions of self-government, but any civil and criminal matters of consequence were dealt with by the daimyo, who retained higher rights over judicial matters.[63]

[58] Toyoda, *Sakai.*

[59] "Gozen rakkyo hōsho."

[60] Gomi Fumihiko, "Shichō no kōsei to kinō," *Rekishigaku kenkyū* 392 (January 1973), 11-12.

[61] Wakita Haruko, "Nihon chūsei toshi no kōzō," p. 26.

[62] Satō Shin'ichi, "Muromachi bakufu ron," in *Iwanami kōza Nihon rekishi* (*Chūsei* 3) (Tokyo: Iwanami Shoten, 1963), p. 37.

[63] For example, Article 140 of the "Ōuchi-shi okitegaki," in Satō and

In medieval Japan, decrees abrogating creditor and debtor relationships (*tokusei-rei*) were frequently issued in response to demands by various groups to abrogate their debts. Thus one can scarcely say that rights to private property acquired through transaction were fully respected. The most important kind of private property was, of course, land. Because private property rights to land could be obtained only through the grant of fief (*chigyō*) by a lord, private transactions in land were theoretically illegal. Thus the rights to transfer land lay solely with the imperial court, the bakufu, and the daimyo. Even if a peasant purchased land, he had to receive permission from his lord to claim ownership. Likewise, in Kyoto, over which the bakufu held judicial responsibility, merchants and moneylenders who could claim no special relationship with anyone in power found it difficult to buy land or retain land ownership because of the constant threat of abrogation decrees. Most of the townspeople were not landholders, therefore, but houseowners who paid rent on their land to landlords, who were mostly of the proprietary class and therefore legally able to hold land.[64]

In Sakai and many other self-governing cities, merchants bought and sold land, and the establishment of private property rights in matters concerning land must have been considered indispensable. For the surrounding farm villages, moreover, where moneylenders from the city did a brisk business, the issuance of debt moratoriums was a matter of grave concern. The first evidence of any group acquiring the right to be exempt from a moratorium pertains to the merchants of Ōyamazaki in 1520. After this date, Sakai, Hirano, Katada, Hakata, Yawata, Tondabayashi, and most of the other self-governed cities received this same right from the bakufu or from various daimyo. Con-

---

Ikeuchi, *Chūsei hōsei* 3, 90-91, makes clear that Ōuchi adjudicated a civil dispute between Somedonoya (a dyer) and Ashidaya (a *geta* maker).

[64] Wakita Haruko, "Chūsei kōki Kyōto," pp. 311-325.

comitantly, these cities made preparations to defend themselves against attacks from mass movements advocating the abrogation of debts (*tokusei ikki*), and in some instances townspeople became involved in actual combat.[65] We can conclude, then, that in self-governed cities, where property was more important to the inhabitants than debt cancellations, the principle of rights to private property acquired through transactions became secure. This distinguished the city from the village, and clearly characterized the self-governed cities whose economic base was commerce and moneylending.

In Kyoto, the machi-gumi were able on occasion to win injunctions against specific moratoriums, but they were not able to acquire general exemptions from all moratoriums. However, appeals to the bakufu for *bun'ichi tokusei-rei* (decrees permitting debtors to pay a certain percentage of their debts in order to be exempt from liability for the rest) were made far less frequently by urban debtors than by rural debtors.[66] Debtors in the towns not only were subject to strong pressure from the leading merchants who were the creditors, but also had to abide by the system if they were to continue to be urban dwellers.

Conditions were different in the castle towns governed by the Sengoku daimyo. There, privileged merchants and artisans were given assurance of the inviolability of transactions they made and were exempt from all debt moratoriums. When military hegemons established castle towns in the Kinai and surrounding regions during the late sixteenth century, they could attract merchants and artisans only by according them the same privileges they had received earlier under various military leaders in the region. Consequently, some of the commercial guarantees first ex-

[65] Wakita Haruko, "Tokusei-rei to tokusei menjo," p. 93.
[66] Wakita Haruko, "Tokusei ikki no haikei," in Kobata Atsushi Kyōju Taikan Kinen Jigyōkai, ed., *Kokushi ronshū* (Tokyo: Kobata Atsushi Kyōju Taikan Kinen Jigyōkai, 1970), p. 515.

tended to privileged merchants were extended to the entire merchant community.

CONCLUSION

Let me now summarize the major points I have made, and add some perspective to the preceding discussion.

During the early medieval period, tax levies on agriculturalists consisted of nengu and zatsukuji. However, merchants and artisans were exempted from all or part of these dues, and in exchange for this exemption paid taxes in the form of their products and services. As the cities grew, a new tax collection system evolved based on yajishi, which was levied according to the frontage of a lot, and various forms of business taxes. The yajishi was generally three to four times higher than the taxes levied on the villages, but in exchange, the city residents were able to extricate themselves from the judicial authority of the proprietary overlords. By contrast, in the combined castle town –market town (jōka-ichimachi) outside the Kinai and its environs, it is most likely that the tax collection system remained similar to that found in the villages. Proprietary lords remained strong in Kyoto and accumulated a great deal of land. In the self-governed cities, on the other hand, proprietors had only limited power, and the townspeople won the right to pay taxes on a collective basis and to administer justice in their own communities.

Community associations within the cities consisted of za, which united persons of the same trade, and wards (machi), which were organized on a geographic basis. These two types of communities were distinct but coexisted in the same city. It was the latter type, however, that grew into the basis of city government. Machi kyōdōtai, or urban communal groups, originally developed from the ryōgawamachi, which were built along roads during the Namboku-chō period. The members of a machi kyōdōtai were townspeople who owned and occupied houses facing the main street, who also conducted business there as members of a za, and who were on an equal footing with each other. However, among the machi there were relative rankings, and, in time, the leading merchants emerged as the principal decision makers. In castle towns there were similar forms of government, the major difference being that leading merchants were appointed by the daimyo to serve in the lower echelons of the urban administrative structure.

The structure of urban government was based on the federation of the various machi kyōdōtai or communities of the townspeople. The most fundamental right characterizing this kind of city government was jurisdiction over all civil cases. The self-governing organizations (*sō*) of farm villages also possessed civil authority, but what clearly distinguished the cities from the villages was that the townspeople obtained both secure rights to private property acquired by transaction and the right to be exempted from debt moratoriums. This was the sine qua non of the city's existence. Although village sō dealt with matters pertaining to moratoriums, their interests were directly opposite to those of the cities.

The Muromachi bakufu, which worked to suppress the power of the za, nevertheless used the za structure to collect taxes and to encourage commerce oriented toward Kyoto. The policy vis-à-vis cities adopted by the Sengoku daimyo was basically an extension of that pursued by the Muromachi bakufu. The Sengoku daimyo were nevertheless able to exert their authority over cities, because they possessed sufficient power to dominate commerce in the countryside and to build castle towns that incorporated outlying towns.

Oda Nobunaga's policy toward castle towns was influenced by the fact that it was formulated after the self-governing cities in the Kinai had come into being. To attract merchants to the castle towns he had no choice but to recognize their exemptions from debt moratoriums. Since he was compelled to treat all merchants and artisans in a city equally, his policy had the effect of making all of the people in the castle towns into *goyōshōnin* and *goyōshokunin*; that is, all merchants were given special privileges in exchange for special services.

The Toyotomi administration exempted merchants and artisans from land rent in order to facilitate its control of the cities. In Kyoto, the rights of the proprietors to receive land rents were still recognized in principle, and exemptions from rent were given to merchants and artisans only after the proprietors, chiefly nobles and temples, were given land elsewhere to substitute for the rents they would lose in Kyoto. These policies were similar to those adopted in the early castle towns to extend direct daimyo authority over merchants and artisans by eliminating parties who had rights to rents and who stood between the merchants and artisans and the ultimate authority of the daimyo. In contrast, the tax system employed in medium to small self-governed cities, such as Hiranogō and Tondabayashi, was the same as that used in the villages. Although residents of these towns paid a much lower rent than the yajishi levied in the medieval period, they continued to maintain the right to govern themselves.

This essay has analyzed many of the characteristics of cities during the medieval period. The major characteristics are the system of taxation, the unique function of the urban communal associations, and the acquisition of the right to administer justice. It is important to note that the castle towns that formed the urban base of Kinsei society did not simply evolve from medieval cities in a single, unbroken line of historical progression. The castle towns of the Sengoku daimyo were substantively different from medieval cities. When creating the castle towns of the late sixteenth century, the daimyo abolished the rights of self-government that had typified cities of the Kinai. However, in order to attract merchants and artisans to the castle towns, the daimyo had to grant some degree of self-government and extend other privileges, such as free markets and exemptions from debt moratoriums and land rent.

Chapter 11

Returns on Unification: Economic Growth in Japan, 1550-1650

Kozo Yamamura

THE ECONOMY of Japan underwent a significant transformation during the century of political unification from 1550 to 1650. Agriculture was so fundamentally changed that, using the standards employed by most economic historians, we can only characterize these changes as constituting an "agricultural revolution." The colorful century of the Sengoku daimyo and their unifiers Nobunaga, Hideyoshi, and Ieyasu also witnessed an acceleration in the growth of commerce. During the lifetime of Ieyasu (1542-1616), an economy basically composed of local and regional markets was replaced by a highly integrated national market. As the total output of agricultural products rose rapidly, the total volume of trade across local and regional boundaries also increased visibly. The economy in the 1660s, when the eastern and western shipping circuits around the islands of Japan came into service, differed significantly from that in 1549, when the Sengoku daimyo Rokkaku created a "city of unfettered commerce"—rakuichi—the first of many cities for which we have reliable evidence.

The magnitude and rate of increase in both agricultural output and productivity in this period was markedly greater than those attained during any of the preceding centuries. The closely interrelated factors accounting for

the pace of increase in output included an unprece-
dentedly large number of large-scale irrigation and reclamation works, a discernibly more rapid rate of increase in
population, a fundamental transformation in the landholding system characterized by the rise of small peasants who
came to enjoy more secure rights to land, improvements in
farming technology and management, and the rapid
growth of commerce that stimulated, as well as resulted
from, the growth of agriculture.

The rapid growth of commerce was a product of the
agricultural revolution and the quickening pace of the ongoing process of political unification. As the result of the
revolution, the total agricultural output continued to rise.
This provided the margins necessary for increased commercial activity, while the accelerating process of political
change provided the crucial incentive to the Sengoku
daimyo and later to the Tokugawa bakufu and its daimyo
to adopt a wide range of policies designed to encourage
commerce.

The first section of this essay describes the major factors
that contributed to the agricultural revolution. The second
section advances the hypothesis that the peasants' incentive
to increase agricultural productivity played a dominant
role in the agricultural revolution. I shall argue that agricultural productivity increased principally because an increasing number of peasants, whose rights in land closely
approximated that of exclusive private ownership, were
able to benefit from their own efforts. Such a view, I am
fully aware, contrasts sharply with the view, shared by most
Japanese scholars, that the lot of the peasant remained basically unchanged at best, and possibly declined, as the
process of political unification continued and was completed. My intent in advancing an alternative view, therefore, is to encourage a fresh reexamination of the economic history of this period. The third section of the essay
describes the major changes in transportation and other

factors that contributed to the accelerated growth of commerce and premodern manufacturing activities.

An Outline of the Agricultural Revolution

The most visible evidence of the agricultural revolution was a sustained and rapid rise in major water-control, irrigation, and reclamation works that sharply increased the acreage in paddy and contributed to a rise in agricultural productivity. Two factors bear special mention in any discussion of this phenomenon. First is that during the intense warfare of the sixteenth century, the Sengoku daimyo acquired a profound interest in developing the agricultural bases of their domains and began to pour considerable effort into the water-control and irrigation projects, which were crucial to any major increase in agricultural production. With the end of interdaimyo warfare at the beginning of the Tokugawa period, it became possible to devote still more resources to projects of this sort, and large-scale reclamation projects were undertaken more vigorously than ever.[1]

The second factor bearing mention here is that the period from 1550 to 1650 was one of rapid technological development in Japan. The tendency to treat the history of this period primarily in terms of the military upheavals that characterized its early decades has naturally had the effect of focusing attention upon the striking advances that were made in the fields of castle building and of mining and excavation. It was, however, the equally significant advances in the fields of irrigation and water control that had the greater long-term impact on Japanese society.[2]

One indication of this lies in the very number of major

[1] See Hōgetsu Keigo, *Chūsei kangaishi no kenkyū* (Tokyo: Meguro Shoten, 1950), especially p. 350.

[2] Ōishi Shinzaburō, "Kinsei" in Kitajima Masamoto, ed., *Tochi seidoshi* 2 (Tokyo: Yamakawa Shuppansha, 1975), 24. For a good description of the

reclamation projects that were undertaken. In a massive study produced some fifty years ago, the Japanese Academy of Sciences (*Nihon Gakushiin*) found that of the 118 major projects known to have been undertaken between 781 and 1867, 49 (or 39.9 percent) of the total were completed during the 1467-1651 period, with 33 of the 49 being completed between 1596 and 1651. Since it can be shown that most of the 16 projects that were undertaken between 1467 and 1596 were carried out during the second half of the sixteenth century, it is apparent that more than 40 of these major reclamation projects were completed during the century from 1550 to 1650. That is, of a total of 118 major projects initiated during the millennium studied by the Academy scholars, about 34 percent were undertaken within this single century.[3]

Nor can there be any doubt that these projects marked a major change in the patterns that had characterized land reclamation throughout most of the middle ages. Hitherto, most reclamation projects had been attempted in small valleys through which minor tributaries flowed, and each project had yielded but a few acres of additional paddy. The great projects of the sixteenth and seventeenth centuries, on the other hand, were designed to reclaim the sedimentary basins of Japan's largest rivers, and each of them resulted in the creation of several hundred acres of additional land.[4]

Under the impact of these projects—a representative sample of which is presented in Table 11.1—the total area of rice paddy in Japan increased dramatically. Although precise quantitative data are impossible to obtain, there are

---

rapid increase of irrigation and water-control projects see also Hayama Teisaku, "Kinsei zenki no nōgyō seisan to nōmin seikatsu" in *Iwanami kōza Nihon rekishi* 10 (*Kinsei* 2) (Tokyo: Iwanami Shoten, 1975), 184-86.

[3] Nihon Gakushiin, ed., *Meiji izen Nihon dobokushi* (Tokyo: Doboku Gakkai, 1936). Also see Ōishi, "Kinsei," pp. 25-26.

[4] Ōishi, "Kinsei," pp. 27-28. See Hōgetsu, *Chūsei kangaishi*, for a discussion of medieval irrigation and reclamation.

TABLE 11.1
SELECTED MAJOR RECLAMATION PROJECTS, 1550–1650

River	Location	Year	Political Leadership	Notes
Kitakami	Sendai	1623–1626	Date	The largest river in the Tōhoku region was diverted to flow southward to merge with two other rivers, creating paddies "along the banks of these three rivers."
Ara	Odawara	1574, 1629	Go-Hōjō Bakufu official	Today's Arakawa was created. Newly excavated channels between Arakawa and Irumagawa created a large amount of superior quality paddy fields.
Kiso	Mino-Ise-Owari	1586, 1609	Ieyasu	A major rechanneling of the region's largest river was carried out to create new paddies and to control floods.

TABLE 11.1
SELECTED MAJOR RECLAMATION PROJECTS, 1550-1650

River	Location	Year	Political Leadership	Notes
Fuji	Kōfu	1560s, 1621-1645	Takeda Bakufu official	An immense dike was built to control the Fuji river and its major tributaries; taking more than a decade to complete on its first stage, the project resulted in a phenomenal gain in productivity in the region.
Ashida	Fukuyama	1619-?	Mizuno	A new dike extending over 1,500 *ken* (nearly 3,000 yards) was built to control floods. The result was one of the best rice paddy belts in this region.
Otake	Aki-Suō	1603	Fukushima	A large river in this region, which demarked Aki and Suō, was controlled to assure stable yields.

River	Domain	Date	Builder	Description
Jōgani	Toyama	1580	Sasa	The major river in this region was controlled by building a new bank. This contributed to creating today's major rice-producing region in Toyama.
Chikugo	Saga	1550s, 1620s	Ryūzōji (?) Saga official	The banks of the largest river in Kyushu were strengthened to control flooding and to create new paddy fields along the river.
Shiro & Midori	Kumamoto	1603	Katō	This major river in the Chikugo Plain was controlled by means of creating a new tributary, resulting in the largest concentration of rich paddy fields in the center of the plain.
Onga	Fukuoka	1600? 1620?	Kuroda	This large river was controlled by erecting a major new dike, and the yields of the paddy fields in this region were thereby increased.

SOURCE: Ōishi Shinzaburō, "Kinsei shakai no seiritsu," in Kitajima Masamoto, ed., *Tochiseido-shi* 2 (Tokyo: Yamakawa Shuppan-sha, 1975), 25–27. See footnote 3 for the source used by Ōishi.

a number of sources that provide estimates for the extent
of rice paddy at various points in Japan's history, and these
estimates are presented in Table 11.2. Assuming that these
estimates are reasonably accurate, it would appear that
paddy acreage increased by more than 70 percent between
1450 and 1600, and by another 140 percent by 1720. Since
it can be shown that the majority of large-scale reclamation
projects undertaken between 1450 and 1600 took place
after 1550, and that most of the new paddies created during the Tokugawa period were created by 1650,[5] it is probably safe to conclude that the amount of rice paddy in
Japan more than doubled in the period from 1550 to 1650.

TABLE 11.2
TOTAL PADDY FIELDS

Year	Paddy Fields [a]	Original Source
Around 930	862 (91.1)	*Wamyōshō*
Around 1450	946 (100.0)	*Shūgaisho*
Around 1600	1,635 (172.8)	*Keichō 3-nen daimyo-chō*
Around 1720	2,970 (313.9)	*Chōbu shita kumi-chō*
In 1874	3,050 (322.4)	*Dai ikkai tōkeihyō*

[a] In 1,000 chō; the numbers in parentheses are the index, using the total
paddy fields in 1450 as 100.
SOURCE: Same as for Table 11.2.

It is quite clear, then, that large-scale reclamation projects constituted a major factor in producing the environment in which the agricultural revolution of the late sixteenth and early seventeenth centuries took place. It is all
the more important to note, therefore, that an important
contributory factor was that the daimyo of this period en-

[5] For a detailed description and discussion of the increase of paddy
fields in the 1550-1867 period, see Kimura Motoi, *Kinsei no shindenmura*
(Tokyo: Yoshikawa Kōbunkan, 1964), pp. 1-12; and Susan B. Hanley and
Kozo Yamamura, *Economic and Demographic Change in Pre-industrial Japan*
(Princeton: Princeton University Press, 1977), p. 74.

joyed enough control over the territories they ruled to give them considerable incentive to undertake the projects we have just described. The tax dues and rents of the *shugo daimyo* and the local military lords (*kokujin*), it should be remembered, had been defined within the economic framework left over from the earlier estate (*shōen*) system. In contrast, the Sengoku daimyo of the second half of the sixteenth century, and the Tokugawa shogunate and its daimyo of the first half of the seventeenth, enjoyed domains that were increasingly secure, in nearly all cases contiguous, and much larger in size than the areas over which effective political control had been exerted by any local powers of the preceding centuries. All of this meant that, in comparison to the shugo daimyo and kokujin, the Sengoku and Tokugawa daimyo had an increasingly strong political capacity to mobilize manpower as well as the resources needed to undertake large public works and capture all the direct and indirect gains that resulted. That is, the domains that they ruled were large enough so that even if the returns on an investment made upstream in a river accrued to areas downstream, the daimyo were in a position to benefit from the returns; the increased security of their domain justified commitment of large amounts of resources from which returns could be captured only over many years; and they had the political, economic, and administrative abilities to maintain the completed public works, to settle intradomain disputes resulting from the diversion of water from one area to another, and to take the necessary measures for moving cultivators to work new paddies.[6]

Another major factor contributing to the agricultural revolution was a substantial increase in population, with the consequent growth in the size of the agrarian labor force. Though no reliable population data exist, both demographers and historians specializing on this period

[6] See Hōgetsu, *Chūsei kangaishi*, pp. 262-324.

agree that the population increased more rapidly during the 1500-1700 period than in either the preceding several centuries or in the second half of the Tokugawa period. Hayami has argued in a recent study, for instance, that the annual growth of population during the first 150 years of the Tokugawa era must have been in the range of 0.96 to 1.34 percent per year;[7] and another study has concluded that the rate of population growth began to accelerate rapidly around 1500 and remained at a level of 0.78 percent per year throughout the period from 1600 to 1750.[8] Although these figures are necessarily crude, and Hayami's estimate has been criticized for being inflated,[9] they do suggest that the rate of population growth accelerated during the period, and that the rate of growth in population may have been roughly similar to the rate of increase in the total acreage planted to rice.

Two major factors that produced the agricultural revolution, then, were a dramatic increase in the amount of arable land and a roughly proportional increase in the supply of labor to cultivate it. There were, however, a number of other factors that merit discussion, such as the more effective use of water resources, the creation and dissemination of higher-yielding varieties of rice, the availability of low-cost hoes suitable for small-scale farming, the increased application of fertilizers, and a more efficient allocation of labor due to the greater contiguity of landholdings and the emergence of more efficient labor units.

The effective use of water resources has always been a crucial problem for Japanese agriculture, and we have already seen that the period under consideration was one of widespread reclamation of arable land from the sedimentary basins of Japan's major rivers. But the water-control

[7] Hayami Akira, *Kinsei nōson no rekishi jinkōgaku-teki kenkyū* (Tokyo: Tōyō Keizai Shinpōsha, 1973), p. 23.

[8] Shakai Kōgaku Kenkyūjo, ed., *Nihon rettō ni okeru jinkō bunpu no chōki jikeiretsu bunseki* (Tokyo: Shakai Kōgaku Kenkyūjo, 1974), pp. 42-57.

[9] Hanley and Yamamura, *Economic Change*, pp. 38-68.

projects of the late sixteenth and early seventeenth centuries achieved more than the creation of new fields. As Minegishi has noted, 20 to 30 percent of the land tilled in western Japan during the thirteenth and fourteenth centuries could have been subjected to double- or triple-cropping had more water been available.[10] Once the great water-control projects of the Sengoku and Tokugawa periods got under way, therefore, it was a simple matter to increase production dramatically in these hitherto underutilized fields.

In this regard, it is worth noting that the political and economic importance of the careful management of water resources was not lost on the daimyo of these periods. The law codes of several Sengoku daimyo contain provisions regarding the allocation of water among landholdings, and it is quite apparent that the daimyo were determined to control access to water in order that they might both increase agricultural production and control the peasantry.[11] A similar determination had been held by the landed proprietors of the earlier middle ages as well, of course,[12] but the far greater political power vested in the Sengoku daimyo and their successors was what finally made such control possible.

The dissemination of more productive varieties of rice was also an important phenomenon of this period. Southeast Asian varieties such as Champa rice, which were resistant to drought and insect infestation, had been imported

[10] Minegishi Sumio, "Sonraku to dogō" in Rekishigaku Kenkyūkai and Nihonshi Kenkyūkai, eds., *Kōza Nihonshi* 3 (Tokyo: Tōkyō Daigaku Shuppankai, 1970), 141.

[11] Readers interested in this question are referred to Nakamura Kichiji *Kinsei shoki nōseishi kenkyū* (Tokyo: Iwanami Shoten, 1970; originally published 1938), pp. 418-61; and Hōgetsu, *Chūsei kangaishi*, pp. 348-66.

[12] For a discussion of irrigation and water management during the Muromachi period see Nagahara Keiji with Kozo Yamamura, "Village Communities and Daimyo Power," in John W. Hall and Toyoda Takeshi, eds., *Japan in the Muromachi Age* (Berkeley and Los Angeles: University of California Press, 1977), pp. 113-115.

via China sometime during the earlier middle ages and were planted widely in Kyushu, Chugoku, and Shikoku by the early Sengoku period.[13] Soon many more new varieties were added to these strains, which were continually improved, and by the end of the seventeenth century the number of varieties of rice approached one hundred. Peasants were thereby able to select the seed best suited to local agricultural conditions and to make most efficient use of their labor by planting rice of differing (early and late) planting and harvesting times. Also, as the hazards of nature affected each variety of rice differently, planting a wider variety of rice strains enabled the peasant to distribute his risk.[14]

During the second half of the sixteenth century, moreover, new small hoes became available at low cost. These hoes were ideally suited for small peasant families, who often did not own draft animals and who could now hoe deeply and increase the soil's productivity through better aeration and a deeper and more effective mixing of composts. Because of an increase in the supply of iron and a growth of markets, hoe prices declined to a level well within the reach of all cultivators; in 1586, for instance, one hoe sold at 20 cash (*mon*), a price equivalent to only 4 *shō* of soybeans.[15] Furthermore, it appears that the daimyo may have recognized the hoe's value in increasing production and therefore taken direct action to encourage the distribution of hoes among the peasants of their territories.[16]

Fully as important as the daimyo's contributions to technological change in his territories were his contributions to a fundamental reworking in the patterns by which

---

[13] Sasaki Gin'ya, "Kaigai bōeki to kokunai keizai," in *Kōza Nihonshi*, p. 184.

[14] See Hanley and Yamamura, *Economic Change*, pp. 99-103.

[15] Araki Moriaki, *Bakuhan taisei shakai no seiritsu to kōzō* (Tokyo: Ochanomizu Shobō, 1964), pp. 211-14; and Hayama, "Nōmin seikatsu," pp. 190-91. A shō is equivalent to 1.8 litres.

[16] Hayama, *Kinsei nōson no rekishi*, p. 180.

agricultural labor was organized. Because the evidence regarding this transformation is subject to a variety of interpretations, however, it is an issue that must be approached with some care. Before going on to discuss how productivity was further increased through the more intensive use of fertilizers and through greater efficiency in the use of labor, we must first discuss a factor which may have been the most important one involved in raising agricultural productivity during this century: the peasants' motivation.

INCENTIVES FOR PRODUCTIVITY INCREASES

More and more small peasants, during the period 1550-1650, acquired a strong incentive to increase their agricultural productivity as a result of their being made "independent"—that is, given explicitly sanctioned, more secure rights to the land they worked—and of their being freed of complex obligations to pay rents and other dues in kind and in corvée. These obligations, which used to be paid to various persons claiming proprietary rights in the land cultivated by the peasants, were replaced by direct annual payments (*nengu*) to Sengoku and Tokugawa daimyo. To be sure, the process by which small peasants became "independent" differed according to the political and economic conditions of the particular time and region. The changes in the methods of tax payment, in some instances, occurred in stages, as is discussed in Nagahara's essay in this volume.

My purpose here is to offer a description of the changes in contractural arrangements and landholding systems that occurred during the century from 1550 to 1650 and to advance the hypothesis that the newly acquired "independence" of the small peasants provided them with a strong incentive to increase agricultural productivity.

Let us begin with a brief outline of the contractual arrangements that prevailed before the emergence of the independent peasants. Although we know that there were wide regional variations in patterns and timing, it is possible to say that the agriculture of the late fourteenth century to the mid-sixteenth century had two general characteristics. First, it was characterized by the legacies of the shōen system—a complex system of contractual arrangments between cultivators and various levels of claimants to the cultivators' agricultural output and labor. Second, we find a clearly discernible trend of change in the contractual relationship to one increasingly dominated by the *kajishi myōshu*—that is, by well-off peasants, some of whom were *jizamurai* (peasant-samurai, literally "samurai of the soil"), who purchased the rights to kajishi, a de facto rent that was usually paid in kind.[17]

Underlying this second characteristic was a gradual increase in the man-land ratio. In other words, while population continued to increase slowly but steadily during the Muromachi period, new paddy fields could be created only with increasing difficulty due to the existing technology and the limited abilities of the shōen holders, kokujin, and other local powers to provide the necessary resources. This, in turn, meant that an increase in output could only be realized through more intensive cultivation accomplished through such labor-intensive means as double-cropping, well-maintained irrigation works, and the use of more fertilizers (ashes and composts that were then in use were themselves labor-intensive to produce).

However, the prevailing tenurial arrangement was a legacy of the shōen system—large units of paddies were man-

[17] This is a highly abbreviated description of complex changes in the land-holding system and "contractual" terms which occurred during this period. For a fuller discussion, see the following contributions in Takeuchi Rizō, ed., *Tochi seidoshi* 1 (Tokyo: Yamakawa Shuppansha, 1973): Nagahara Keiji, "Muromachi bakufu; shugo ryōgoku seika no tochi seido," pp. 339-94; Minegishi Sumio, "Jūgoseiki kōhan no tochi seido," pp. 395-446; and Fujiki Hisashi, "Sengoku-ki no tochi seido," pp. 447-505.

aged by village landowners (*myōshu*) and cultivated by many dependent peasants who, having little or no rights in land, worked basically under the supervision, managerial control, and protection of the myōshu. This arrangement proved to be ill-adapted to increasing productivity, since intensive agriculture could be efficient only with well-motivated cultivators working under little or no supervision. The most effective way to provide such motivation was to evolve a new contractual arrangment that gave strong rights in land, incentives to share in increased output, and a larger scope of individual freedom in managing labor and land. This is, in fact, what came about.[18] The myōshu became a class of rentiers who gave up their management of cultivation and contented themselves with the receipt of kajishi. The cultivators themselves now managed their land and labor, and were accorded what were called *sakushiki*, "rights to cultivate." Though not exclusive private property rights, these sakushiki were quite effective in providing the incentives and freedom necessary for intensive agriculture.[19]

Of course, this newly evolving contractural arrangement was also affected by the steadily shifting balance of political power against the economic background of the changing man-land ratio noted above. As the central political structure of the Ashikaga bakufu continued to grow weaker, the shugo daimyo, kokujin, and jizamurai struggled to gain a secure political foothold in the provinces. The kokujin and the jizamurai, with better-established economic bases than the shugo daimyo, gradually came to exercise more and more local power, providing the peasantry with protection, law and order, and leadership in maintaining and improving irrigation and water-control works.

Then, with the outbreak of the Ōnin War, the already weakened political order was subjected to the severe shock

[18] This highly abbreviated discussion will be fully elaborated in my book-length work currently in progress.
[19] See the sources cited in note 17.

of intermittent, but large-scale civil wars among the shugo daimyo and certain kokujin who were beginning to emerge as Sengoku daimyo, and who relied on the jizamurai and other kokujin for military force. Undoubtedly prompted by the necessity of specializing in military confrontations, many kokujin, and an increasing number of jizamurai, became tax collectors, relinquishing their role in farm management. That is, so long as they received their dues, they were willing to let the contractual arrangements change, and those "upper-class" peasants, temples, or merchants who were able to buy kajishi rights increasingly did so. The result was a contractual arrangment in which land rights were fundamentally divided into two categories—rights to receive rent from land and rights to cultivate it. The concept that land rights were related to the functions one purportedly performed within an outmoded shōen structure was completely abandoned, and individuals frequently held *myōshu-shiki* (that is, rental rights) to some lands and sakushiki (cultivation rights) to others. In the long run, moreover, rights of cultivation even came to be preferred over the old-fashioned myōshu-shiki as being the more secure.[20]

It is against this background that the cadastral surveys of the Sengoku daimyo, Nobunaga and Hideyoshi, and the early Tokugawa bakufu must be understood. As early as the first half of the sixteenth century, the Imagawa family had begun a pattern of cadastral survey and land registry that offered no recognition of the right to collect kajishi.[21] This sort of policy, which would ultimately produce a contractual arrangement in which the only land rights recognized were the overall lordship of the warrior class and the cultivating rights of individual peasants, was not consis-

[20] See Miyagawa Mitsuru, *Taikō kenchi-ron* 2 (Tokyo: Ochanomizu Shobō, 1957), 47-48.

[21] Nagahara Keiji, *Sengoku no doran*, vol. 14 of the Shogakkan *Nihon no rekishi* series (Tokyo: Shōgakkan, 1975), p. 217.

tently pursued until the great cadastral surveys of the 1580s and 1590s.[22]

By the early seventeenth century, in fact, a contractual order had emerged in which the peasants had for all intents and purposes become the owners of the land they tilled. Wakita Osamu's description of this situation is particularly apt:

We can say that the peasants' rights of ownership were in fact property rights in land—strong rights. Rights belonged to an individual but could be divided among members of a family. Though the property rights tended to be held by the household head, in principle they could be held by any individual but not by a village or a household. This meant that property rights in land were clearly established among the individual peasants, such that even between parents and children the rights were specifically assigned [for example] to a retired father [*inkyo*] or to a widow.

Inheritance, acquisition, and alienation of land by sale were all determined by the peasants' own volition. The political authority of the early period [from the early sixteenth century to the mid-seventeenth century] did not impose any restrictions concerning these matters. We know that decrees were issued prohibiting the alienation and division of land and restricting the types of crops to be planted, but such limitations on the peasants' rights were exercised only after the mid-seventeenth century, when famines became a problem and measures were needed to aid the sound management of peasants' land. [The fact the decrees were issued] indicates to us that the peasants' property rights

[22] See Sakudō Yōtarō and Takenaka Yasukazu, eds., *Nihon keizaishi* (Tokyo: Gakubunsha, 1973); Takenaka Yasukazu and Kawakami Tadashi, *Nihon shōgyōshi* (Kyoto: Mineruva Shobō, 1965), pp. 73-74; and Wakita Osamu, "The Kokudaka System: A Device for Unification," *The Journal of Japanese Studies* 1 (Spring 1975), 297-320.

were feudal and differed from modern property rights. However, it is evident that these decrees had little effect even during the half-century following their promulgation.[23]

Nor is it difficult to understand why the samurai rulers of this period should ultimately have settled upon a policy of creating "independent" small peasants. On the contrary, they had every incentive to accelerate the already visible trend toward the increase of independent peasants, because by doing so they would eliminate all "middlemen" and obtain an enlarged and directly controlled tax base. Moreover, there were strong political and military reasons for disallowing the rights of middlemen to share in the output of the cultivators. These arose from the fact that military rulers who hoped to maintain a strong foundation of power were compelled to achieve two urgent and closely related goals.

The first goal was to eliminate the economic, and thus the political and military, base of competing powers. Such powers were both real and potential, ranging from recalcitrant jizamurai and local kokujin leaders to the stubbornly independent major kokujin. The other goal for the Sengoku daimyo and the Tokugawa bakufu was to create fiefs that could be granted to local and regional military leaders—jizamurai, kokujin, and daimyo—who were either forced to become the vassals of the rulers or chose to do so of their own accord. These fiefs—regardless of whether they were actually donated by one's lord or were in fact current holdings over which the lord was willing to reconfirm one's rights—were the most effective way to insure a vassal's continued loyalty, manifested in his performance of military service.[24]

[23] Wakita Osamu, *Kinsei hōkensei seiritsushi-ron* 2 (Tokyo: Tōkyō Daigaku Shuppankai, 1977), 82.

[24] For a further discussion of this process, see Wakita Osamu, "The Kokudaka System: A Device for Unification," and the Nagahara essay in this volume.

If we agree that the rulers had an incentive to create small indpendent peasants, we then may ask how the fact of becoming independent affected the small peasants. Similar developments in the economic history of Europe tell us that such a change in the contractual arranagement can be presumed to have been a powerful factor in raising the peasants' incentive to increase their productivity.[25] Was this also the case, however, in Japan between 1550 and 1650?

We must approach this question with care, since the works of many Japanese specialists either totally neglect to discuss, or at most only cautiously hint at, any possible relationship between changed contractual arrangements and increased peasant incentives. Some Japanese historians, in fact, go so far as to argue, either explicitly or implicitly, that the nengu burden might have increased after the peasants were made independent. They believe that nengu absorbed all of the increase in output resulting from the increase in productivity, and may even have exceeded it.[26] The historians who hold such a view can scarcely be expected to concern themselves with peasant incentives. Productivity, these historians imply, increased because of more intensive cultivation, more widespread use of fertilizers, and other factors that resulted because the peasants were attempting to maintain, or to prevent a decline in, their living standard. Since this view is shared by many Japanese scholars, those who do discuss increases in productivity generally choose their words carefully. A typical example is: "Though there was some variation in the specific condi-

[25] See Douglas C. North and Robert P. Thomas, *The Rise of the Western World* (Cambridge: Cambridge University Press, 1973), pp. 12, 39-40, 59-60, 92.

[26] See the examples included in the Nagahara essay in this volume. Some college textbooks used in the United States clearly reflect the views of Japanese scholars. See, for instance, Mikiso Hane, *Japan: A Historical Survey* (New York: Charles Scribner's Sons, 1972), pp. 138-39. Sir George Sansom, however, presents a more balanced assessment in his *A History of Japan, 1334-1615* (Stanford: Stanford University Press, 1961), p. 317.

tions according to region, despite the heavy tax burden of the nengu, small peasants became the core of agricultural production and gave new direction to the growth of agricultural productivity."[27]

There are, however, a few Japanese historians who fully recognize the increased efficiency of agriculture that resulted from an increase in the number of the small independent peasants. These writers thus come close to recognizing the increase in peasant incentive as a factor that contributed toward a rise in their productive capabilities. One such scholar is Hayama, who wrote,

> Three fundamental elements to be found in the farming of small peasants (*shōnō*) were: (i) family cooperation, basically within nuclear family units, (ii) use of simple implements such as hoes, and (iii) cultivation of intricately arranged small strips. Combining these three elements, it was possible to realize the productive capabilities unique to small-scale farming. Basic to the small peasants' capabilities to increase productivity was their ability to increase the yield per unit of paddy. Family cooperation enabled them to use their labor most efficiently, i.e., large quantities of labor and fertilizer were applied to each parcel of paddy and small implements were used. In effect, closely managed and intensive farming was made possible. All these factors contributed to the development of small farm management.[28]

What is implicit in Hayama's observation is the strong peasant incentive to produce more through improved "small farm management." Our hypothesis is that these changes summarized by Hayama occurred because, in Miyagawa's words, "the cadastral surveys officially recognized that a new class of peasants had the rights to cultivate" and this gave them "a sense of satisfaction,"[29] and a

[27] Takenaka and Kawakami, *Nihon shōgyōshi*, p. 74.
[28] Hayama, "Kinsei zenki," pp. 189-90.
[29] Miyagawa, *Taikō kenchi-ron*, p. 42.

motivation to work harder and more efficiently. In other words, peasants now had the motivation to hoe deeply, to seed carefully, to minimize loss of time, to maintain irrigation systems carefully, and to apply more fertilizer. The fact that the new contract was a de facto share-cropping arrangement, enforced much less arbitrarily and more predictably than the rent arrangements of the middle ages had been, gave them still more incentive to increase production.[30] Unlike the "dependent" peasants who labored for myōshu, the new class of peasants had every reason not to shirk because they could now share in the gains.

Here we should state explicitly the difference between our view and that held by most Japanese scholars. The latter would readily agree that one of the reasons agricultural productivity rose was improved agricultural management, and they would probably also concede that peasants worked harder and more efficiently. The crucial difference between this view and ours is in answer to the question: who gained from the increased productivity? Most Japanese historians maintain or imply that the gain accrued only to the samurai rulers. In contrast, we argue that the peasants increased productivity and shared in the fruits of their labor with the rulers. While most Japanese scholars believe, in effect, that the increasingly powerful Sengoku daimyo and the unifiers of Japan had sufficient power to coerce the peasants into producing more, we suggest that the self-interest of the peasants was the dominant factor in raising the yield per acre. Our disagreement, in short, concerns whether the peasant was motivated to increase productivity by "the carrot or the stick."

The disagreement is a fundamental one. For the many Japanese scholars who hold that the conflict of interest between tax collectors and cultivators served as an agent of

[30] Though many qualifications must be added, and some pertinent facts cannot be clearly established, it is generally accurate to say that the medieval nengu burden tended to be fixed, while the 1550-1650 period saw the establishment of de facto share-cropping. See Wakita, "The Kokudaka System."

historical change, the dominant role was played by the stick. The strength of this theoretical orientation in Japan explains why Hayama and other scholars chose to describe the changes they observed in productivity and farm management in such a way as not to offend their colleagues. Are most Japanese scholars right in suggesting that the Sengoku daimyo and the unifiers of Japan possessed sufficient political power to coerce the peasants to change the daily management of their paddy fields, to work more efficiently and to produce more, only to see the fruits of their labor taxed away? Can they be right in suggesting that there were no "carrots" at all because Hideyoshi's "cadastral surveys, whatever the ideal behind them, brought suffering to the peasants"?[31] Is it in fact reasonable to believe that because "the shōen became fiefs, each fief was thoroughly assessed for tax purposes, and all fiefs came under the control of Oda," the peasants faced a situation in which "a giant political power extending over an entire province had emerged, and their struggle against a shōen ryōshu could no longer obtain for them tax deductions for poor harvests, however critical this might be in sustaining their lives"?[32]

Though we are reminded of the still tentative nature of our hypothesis, we submit that to overemphasize the power of the Sengoku daimyo and the unifiers of Japan during the 1550-1650 period is to neglect the basic economic realities of the century. We believe that the demand for labor to work the rapidly increasing amount of paddy was such that it gave the peasants sufficient "bargaining power" to deter the rulers from increasing the effective tax burden. We should recall that the rates of increase in both population and paddy—both new fields and those made usable again because of the improved supply of water—were roughly of

[31] Hayashiya Tatsusaburō, *Tenka ittō*, vol. 12 of Chūō kōron *Nihon rekishi* series (Tokyo: Chūō Kōronsha, 1975), p. 436.
[32] Fujiki Hisashi, *Oda-Toyotomi seiken*, vol. 15 of Shōgakkan *Nihon no rekishi* series (Tokyo: Shōgakkan, 1975), p. 147.

similar magnitude. Given the growth of towns, the political desires of the rulers of this period, and the demonstrated efficiency of intensive agriculture, the rulers were well advised to remain cognizant of the peasants' "bargaining power." Moreover, we maintain that the rulers were aware that the increase in productivity benefited both the peasants and themselves under the new form of contractual agreement that was slowly evolving through the cadastral surveys and the creation of independent peasants.

To demonstrate that the views held by Japanese scholars need to be examined, we will here enlist evidence provided by them in support of their view, and point out why it is inadequate or at best inconclusive. At the same time, in order to prove that our view is analytically consistent, we will demonstrate the existence of sufficient evidence in the findings and observation made in the Japanese literature to support our own arguments. Let us begin with an examination of the "bargaining power" of the peasants, which is crucial in assessing the rulers' ability to coerce them. We will then proceed to show that both the evidence on changes in the effective rate of the tax burden and on the living standard of the peasants is far from sufficient to prove the view held by the Japanese scholars. Indeed, if the evidence used to support the contention that the burden of taxation on the peasant did increase is at best inconclusive or limited, then this lack will provide a good reason for further testing our hypothesis.

Despite the frequently cited words of Hideyoshi to the effect that the cadastral surveys were to be carried out "even if all the peasants in one or more villages had to be killed,"[33] Japan's rulers, especially the Sengoku daimyo, were hardly in a position to take peasant labor for granted. Though we can present only a few examples, there is abundant evidence indicating that the actions taken by the rulers were frequently moderated and motivated by their

[33] Ōishi, "Kinsei," p. 52.

desire to retain labor to work the paddies. The bargaining
power of the peasants appeared in the form of absconding
or in threats to do so, in the concern shown by rulers in
preventing their vassals from arbitrarily imposing corvée
on the peasants, and in various concessions given to the
peasants in setting the effective tax rates levied on them.[34]

The following quotations, drawn from the works of Japanese scholars themselves, will serve to illustrate this bargaining power more concretely.

A decree was issued in 1551 by the Go-Hōjō for the
purpose of obtaining labor to reclaim new paddies.
The three measures stressed in this decree were: issuance of notices of invitation to peasants, exemptions
of various dues and corvée, and grants of seed rice and
other agricultural necessities.[35]

After defeating Akechi in 1582, Hideyoshi forcefully
carried out a cadastral survey in Yamashiro, which was
under his control. But he met here with strong opposition from the peasants, who resorted to absconding or
refusing to plant. When he received a report that
"more than one half of the peasants have absconded,"
he reacted at first by saying that he would be satisfied if
the arrears in the nengu of the past year were made up
and that, if this were difficult, he was prepared to have
the arrears paid after the harvest of that year. In any
event, he was anxious to have the peasants get back to
work on the neglected paddies.[36]

A decree issued in 1603 by Ikeda Terumasa stated that
"should there be peasants who abscond, take measures
to effect their return as soon as possible. . . ." And a
decree issued in 1610 in the domain of Okazaki read:

[34] Nakamura, *Kinsei shoki*, pp. 81-101.

[35] Fujiki Hisashi, "Daimyo ryogōku no keizai kōzō" in Nagahara Keiji,
ed., *Nihon keizaishi taikei* 2, *Chūsei* (Tokyo: Tōkyō Daigaku Shuppankai,
1965), p. 271.

[36] Fujiki, *Oda-Toyotomi seiken*, p. 272.

"If houses become vacant because of absconding, do not destroy them. They should be kept for peasants who may return or who may newly arrive in the village."[37]

Absconding peasants were frequently captured and returned [during the late Sengoku period]. But more frequently, the peasants' return was encouraged by offering them immunity from prosecution. Rather than enforcing the domain laws [prohibiting absconding], an offer of real inducements was made more effective.[38]

It is clear, moreover, that in many cases the absconding peasants fled to cities and towns, which were frequently delighted to receive them. As Nakamura has observed,

Active measures were taken to induce people to come to towns, and, with promises of special considerations to be granted, many came to the towns. . . . It was natural for many peasants to be attracted there. . . . It is known [for instance] that, after Mitsui Motonobu's adoption of an unwise cadastral policy, the peasants of Suō and Nagato absconded in large numbers to create new wards called Suō and Nagato within the city of Kokura, which was then adopting an active policy of enticing people to settle there. . . . [According to an investigation made by the magistrates of the town of Kiyosu in Owari province in 1594], there were at this time 2,729 houses. The long-time residents of the town occupied 1,553 houses and the remaining 1,176 houses were occupied by new arrivals of recent years. . . . We must note that most of the new arrivals were peasants.[39]

[37] Nakamura, *Kinsei shoki*, p. 166.
[38] Ibid., pp. 122, 141, 389, 416; and Fujiki, "Daimyō ryōgoku," pp. 265-72.
[39] Nakamura, *Kinsei shoki*, pp. 214-15, 217-18.

These samples clearly suggest that the peasants of this period—who could abscond to other villages, to newly reclaimed paddy fields, or to the growing towns—may have possessed considerable bargaining power. Many Japanese historians, however, interpret such evidence as a reflection of the desperate reactions of an overburdened peasantry. Undoubtedly there were many who absconded to escape the harsh demands made on them. But for one to surmise, often on the basis of only a few examples, that absconding and migration per se reflected the oppressive impositions of the ruling class is clearly unwarranted. Though the final verdict must await more study, we believe that future research should carefully consider the hypothesis that most of the absconding and migration occurred because this period was one in which migrating peasants were welcomed to work the land and to people the cities.

We should add that our hypothesis in recognizing the bargaining power of the peasants also receives support from the actions taken, and decrees issued, by the rulers concerned with securing peasant labor. From Go-Hōjō Sōun to Tokugawa Ieyasu, for instance, rulers took pains to see that no arbitrary imposition of corvée was placed on the peasants, lest they flee to an area where such burdens were lighter.[40]

Just as the facts relating to absconding and migration leave ample latitude for an interpretation in support of our hypothesis, so also do the facts relating to the effective rate of the tax burden and the changes in the living standard of the peasants. The tax rate and the peasants' living standard provide our most crucial and direct evidence of the peasants' ability to share in the fruits of the productivity increase. Leaving aside the more categorical statements that some Japanese scholars are prone to make on this issue, let us note only a small fraction of the many other statements that tend to demonstrate that the effective increase of the tax burden is not as great as claimed:

[40] Ibid., pp. 81-101.

[According to article 24 of the house laws of the Rok-kaku], peasants who do not honor "the established precedents" and pay nengu accordingly were to be punished by the ryōshu, who were entitled to exercise such power. However, the ryōshu were strictly prohib-ited from instituting "new precedents" in order to levy nengu in excess of that set by the established prece-dents. This was a restriction imposed on the zaichi ryōshu who, as a class, possessed a strong impulse to establish "new precedents." Such an article, codified within the house laws of the Sengoku daimyo, symbol-ized the hard-worn legal rights of the medieval peas-ants.[41]

It is reported that, in the Go-Hōjō domain, Sōun posted decrees that read: "the prevailing rate of nengu shall be changed from 50 percent to 40 percent, and no other dues, not even one mon, shall be levied."[42]

The peasants of the Kuta-no-shō contracted in 1566 to pay dues following "precedents." . . . Their basic rice nengu had remained fixed for half a century at 21 koku 2 shō 2 gō after having been changed at the be-ginning of the sixteenth century. When the 1566 con-tract went into effect, no changes were made to ac-count either for paddies once lost to natural disasters but since reclaimed or for newly created paddy fields. . . . The *todai* [the nengu burden per tan] seems to have remained unchanged from the Kamakura period to the Sengoku period. The total nengu was 24.8 koku in 1233, 28 koku shortly before 1324 because of 2 chō of new paddy, 26.7 in 1356 when a tax deduction was given for flooding, 23 koku during the late fifteenth century, and 21 koku throughout the sixteenth cen-tury. In short, the total basic nengu peaked, due to newly added land, at the beginning of the fourteenth

[41] Fujiki Hisashi, "Sengoku-ki no tochi seido," p. 469.
[42] Nakamura, *Kinsei shoki*, p. 8.

century and continued to decline till the beginning of
the sixteenth century because of several floods. It then
became fixed throughout the Sengoku period at a
level 13 percent below its peak.[43]

[In a decree that Hideyoshi issued in 1586], he stated
that the amount of nengu was to be decided on the
basis of a negotiation between the fief holders and the
peasants. If decisions could not be reached, the year's
yield was to be assessed and two-thirds of the assessed
yield was to be paid as nengu. Hideyoshi's policy was
thus based on a division of two-to-one for the ruling
class and the cultivators, respectively. . . . However, because of the importance of the tax rate, it is unlikely
that [this policy] was followed to the point of ignoring
local customs and conditions.[44]

In addition to these observations and similar ones scattered
throughout Japanese secondary sources, we must keep in
mind the fact that many Japanese authors have a tendency
to present evidence of "peasant victories" in their "struggle" against tax collectors. In addition, most Japanese specialists of the Sengoku period do not make an effort to use
sufficiently specific evidence to demonstrate an increase in
the effective tax burden. For example, in his recent two-
volume study of the Oda-Toyotomi period, Wakita does
not present direct evidence showing that the effective tax
burden on the small peasants rose, and recognizes that a
"lenient policy" was adopted by Oda toward the upper class
of peasants.[45] We must note also that Japanese specialists
of the Tokugawa period are by and large willing to acknowledge that the seventeenth century was characterized
by a rapid increase in population, steady growth of commerce, and visible advances in agricultural technology. To
my knowledge, no quantitative evidence has been compiled

[43] Fujiki, "Sengoku-ki no tochi seido," p. 467.
[44] Nakamura, *Kinsei shoki*, pp. 11-12.
[45] Wakita, *Kinsei hōkensei*, pp. 80 ff.

to demonstrate that the effective tax burden actually rose during the 1550-1650 period.

The central point here is that a relatively thorough examination of recent works of Japanese scholars clearly reveals that much further research is required to determine the direction and magnitude of changes in the effective tax burden levied on peasants during the 1550-1650 period. The current state of our knowledge, especially if we demand objective and quantitative evidence consisting of more than a few case studies, is far from sufficient to allow us either to accept the Japanese scholars' view or to refute our own hypothesis. To be sure, further research will be demanding, as the following will be necessary: 1. the careful examination of the total burden imposed on the peasants during the period of shōen dissolution in order to establish the initial conditions of the changes; 2. an extensive and, as far as possible, quantitative study of the tax burden imposed by the rulers of this period, paying special attention to the net effects of a changing mix of tax payments in kind and in cash under both the *kandaka* (cash payment) and the *kokudaka* (rice payment) systems; and 3. a thorough analysis of the effects on the effective and real (as against nominal) burden of the changing terms, conditions, and enforcement of the *erizeni* (coinage evaluation) policies adopted by the Sengoku daimyo and by Nobunaga and Hideyoshi.

Given the complexity of the methods of assessment, enforcement, and payment, along with the local variations and the host of other factors complicating research, such an investigation will require a concerted effort by specialists. Perhaps the most immediate tasks to be performed in beginning such an undertaking are: 1. a systematic compilation of the case studies for which sufficient information exists over a long period of time, and 2. an analysis of the relative values of rice (and other commodities used in tax payment) and cash against the background of both the secular deflation that can be shown to have continued from the mid-fifteenth century to the end of the seventeenth century and the inflation that characterized the seventeenth century.[46]

To elaborate briefly, what is clearly called for is the compilation and analysis of case studies such as the Kuta-no-shō example cited above, and a thorough examination, using economic analysis, of the effects of the kandaka system and the erizeni decrees on the real tax burden of the peasants. As Fujiki has recognized, serious analysis of the kandaka system has only just begun, and "no persuasive answers" have as yet been provided to numerous questions raised by the system.[47] Questions relating to the effects of the erizeni policies, which overlap with questions relating to the effects of the kandaka system, are also numerous. The Japanese specialists who have conducted case studies and have often given ad hoc explanations are now being urged by Fujiki to undertake a more integrated general analysis.[48]

In conducting research on the changes in the effective burden of the taxes, in other words, we must go beyond the narrowly defined analyses of most Japanese scholars. Though they have, to date, given us an excellent foundation for our future study through their institutional and political analyses of the kandaka system and the erizeni policies, we must now begin to analyze the macroeconomic impact of changing relative prices, deflationary and inflationary trends, altered distribution of risks, enforcement

[46] For a discussion of price level changes and the monetary condition in general, see Kamiki Tetsuo and Kozo Yamamura, "Silver Mines and Sung Coins—A Monetary History of Medieval and Early Modern Japan in International Perspective," a conference paper for the Pre-Modern Monetary History Workshop, University of Wisconsin, August 28-September 1, 1977. For the data and a good discussion of these changes in prices, see Kamiki Tetsuo, "Chūsei kōki ni okeru bukka hendō," *Shakai keizai shigaku*, 34 (January 1968), 21-38.

[47] Fujiki, *Oda-Toyotomi seiken*, p. 184.

[48] Fujiki Hisashi, *Sengoku shakaishi-ron* (Tokyo: Tōkyō Daigaku Shuppankai, 1974), p. 282.

and transaction costs involved, and other economic, analytically significant factors within a clearly formulated framework of analysis.[49]

Just as the evidence on changes in the effective tax burden is inconclusive and awaits further reexamination, evidence on changes in the living standard of the peasants during the 1550-1650 period is also inconclusive and conflicting. Most scholars either simply assert or implicitly assume that the living standard failed to improve or, in fact, deteriorated for the small peasants. They assume that the evidence of absconding, the changes in the tax burden due to the adoption of the kandaka system and the erizeni policies, and the increase in sales of paddy fields all support their view.

It is difficult to accept the assertions of an unchanging or deteriorating standard of living, not only because of the problems involved in interpreting the evidence usually cited by the Japanese scholars, but also because of other evidence which suggests that the living standard of the small peasants may have risen. Nakamura and others present a long list of sumptuary decrees, from those issued by the Sengoku daimyo Uesugi to those issued by the Tokugawa bakufu, prohibiting the peasants from wearing certain kinds of footgear as well as "superior clothing," and from consuming food or drink "unbecoming to peasants."[50] Were these decrees issued repeatedly to make certain that the impoverished peasants stayed "in their place" and "minded only their work?" Or did the frequent issue of these decrees indicate the difficulties the rulers were having in controlling peasants whose purchasing power had begun to increase?

[49] Kyōguchi Motoyoshi, "Erizeni to erizenirei," *Nihon rekishi* 73 (1954), 2-11. Kyōguchi's discussion is confusing and, at times, seems inconsistent. He calls for a further examination of erizeni policies in relationship to changes in price levels, and this sort of analysis is long overdue.

[50] Nakamura, *Kinsei shoki*, pp. 259-69. For a detailed discussion and further examples of these decrees, see Hanley and Yamamura, *Economic Change*, pp. 84-85.

ACCELERATION OF THE GROWTH OF COMMERCE

Having detailed the way in which the growth of daimyo
power and the ultimate achievement of national unification
contributed to technological and social changes that sustained an agricultural revolution in sixteenth- and seventeenth-century Japan, I shall devote the remainder of this
essay to an explication of how unification and the growth
of daimyo power contributed to a spectacular growth in
commerce, as well. Here too we will find evidence that
throws into question the view that the sixteenth-century
peasant lived in poverty. For if, as one scholar writes, a
"cotton revolution" occurred "explosively" during the sixteenth century, could this have failed to benefit the small
peasants?[51] We have evidence that, from the Sengoku to
the Tokugawa period, "an increase in city population
created markets for vegetables, raw materials for clothing,
items for petty luxuries, [and] lamp oils."[52] Did not the
peasants gain as the suppliers of goods needed in the growing markets? Was the growth of commerce possible without increasing effective demand from by far the largest
segment of the economy? We find it difficult to imagine
that none of the rapidly increasing gains realized through
trade accrued to the peasants.[53]

It is now generally accepted that the tempo of the growth
of commerce accelerated during the 1550-1650 period as
the process of political unification was completed, and that
this created an expanding and then an unified market.
Underlying this phenomenon was an agricultural revolution that continued to increase the economic margin, providing a larger surplus necessary for this steady increase in
commercial activities. Despite the obvious economic burden and disruptions caused by the intermittent civil wars,
the relative peace maintained by stalemates and alliances

[51] Nagahara, *Sengoku no dōran*, p. 99.
[52] Sakudō and Takenaka, *Nihon keizaishi*, p. 59.
[53] A macroeconomic analysis of the Tokugawa economy is presented in
Hanley and Yamamura, *Economic Change*, pp. 19-37; 69-90.

among the Sengoku daimyo and the lasting peace that was finally won by Ieyasu had profound effects in stimulating the rapid growth of commerce. These effects consisted of heightened motivation to encourage commerce on the part of the rulers whose domains grew larger and more secure. And this motivation in turn led to provisions for increased safety, better-developed transportation facilities, and improved or new institutional arrangements that both increased market activities and enlarged their range.

Given this well-substantiated growth of commerce during the 1550-1650 period, the main objective of the analysis that follows is to offer a general perspective from which to evaluate the interaction of political change and the social and economic aspects of the growth in commerce.[54] Here again I will project my analysis against the background of evidence accumulated by Japanese scholars.

Of the many factors contributing to the growth of commerce, the most crucial were several policies adopted by the Sengoku daimyo and the three unifiers of Japan, which sought to encourage and protect commerce first within increasingly secure domains and then on a national basis. Most important were efforts made to assure the freedom and security of the market by promoting the *rokusai ichi* (local markets held six times monthly), the abolition of toll gates, and the *rakuichi* and *rakuza* decrees establishing "free markets." These subjects are touched upon in previous essays in this volume by Sasaki Gin'ya and Wakita Osamu, so I will not go into descriptive detail except for aspects of institutional and economic change not covered by them.

The growth of rokusai ichi during the sixteenth century reflected "the increased productivity of the tax-paying peasants"[55] and the Sengoku daimyos' desire to encourage the growth of commerce. That is, the growth of rokusai

[54] The basic analytical framework for these observations is the theory of institutional change as developed in North and Thomas, *The Rise of the Western World.*

[55] Sasaki Gin'ya, *Chūsei shōhin ryūtsūshi no kenkyū* (Tokyo: Hōsei Daigaku Shuppankyoku, 1972), p. 24.

ichi was on the one hand "an inevitable development" that "came about because it facilitated the necessary exchange functions for the people [*minshū*]."[56] And, on the other hand, it was facilitated by the Sengoku daimyo's adoption of various growth-promoting measures, which included "taking an active part in deciding the dates and locations of rokusai ichi."[57] Let us present a few observations which illustrate the characteristics of the developing local markets and the roles played by the daimyo in their development:

> In the domain of Uesugi . . . the markets within various regions were approximately 3 *ri* [or 7.32 miles] from each other. Under Go-Hōjō, the markets in the Chichibu basin were held on dates ending with 1 and 6 in Chichibu-Ōmiya, 2 and 7 in Niegawa, 3 and 8 in Yoshida, 4 and 9 in Ōnohara, and 5 and 10 in Kamiogano. This organization clearly indicated that this region constituted a unified market zone and that several of these zones made up the domainwide market.[58]

> During this period, the distance between markets was usually 2 to 3 ri. This enabled peasants in the proximity of these markets to leave in the morning with their carts loaded with vegetables and to return by evening. . . . The frequency of market days differed. Some markets were held only three times per month, as in Ejiri in Suruga. But markets that were held on six regularly scheduled market days [per month] were the most numerous, providing frequent market opportunities for the peasants. . . . Usually each market coordinated the date it was held with the other markets in

[56] Nagahara, *Sengoku no dōran*, pp. 233-34.
[57] Toyoda Takeshi, "Shōhin ryūtsū no yakushin," in Toyoda Takeshi and Kodama Kōta, eds., *Ryūtsūshi* 1 (Tokyo: Yamakawa Shuppansha, 1969), 95.
[58] Ibid., p. 97.

the neighborhood. Daimyo often issued decrees concerning these dates.[59]

In addition to these involvements in the markets, the daimyo adopted various policies and issued decrees to protect merchants and to encourage the smooth functioning of the markets. That is, these rulers not only "provided general police functions to protect the rokusai ichi" but also "took active measures to aid the economic functions of the markets."[60]

In 1553, Date Harumune waived all the taxes on merchants coming into the domain. These merchants were also exempted from tolls. . . . Concerned with the protection of the merchants, the villagers in [areas surrounding the markets] were collectively held responsible should a merchant from another domain be murdered. Uesugi is also known to have prohibited in 1564 a town elder of Kashiwazaki from levying any taxes on horses, oxen, or goods brought into the town for commercial purposes.[61]

The decrees that the Go-Hōjō issued during the 1560s and 1570s to encourage commerce in the rapidly growing market towns within the domain also reveal a Sengoku daimyo's policies toward the markets within his domain. A sample of these decrees reads: "none of our military personnel is allowed to enter the marketplaces of Matsuyama"; "no one shall be obliged to sell rice or horses to the quartermasters coming from the encampment in Moro"; and "however large a debt a merchant owes, he is not to be asked to make a payment while he is in the market of Matsuyama on market days."[62]

[59] Toyoda Takeshi, *Chūsei Nihon shōgyōshi no kenkyū* (Tokyo: Iwanami Shoten, 1952), p. 318.

[60] Toyoda, "Shōhin ryūtsū," p. 97.

[61] Ibid.

[62] Nagahara, *Sengoku no dōran*, p. 229. For a good discussion of the *rokusai-ichi* see Fujiki, "Daimyo ryōgoku," pp. 258-64. It should be made

Along with these measures promoting commerce, or as natural extensions of them, Sengoku daimyo began to abolish tolls and then to adopt a policy of rakuichi and rakuza in an increasing number of markets.[63] The number of toll gates abolished and "free towns" decreed correlated with the growing power of each Sengoku daimyo and the degree of military control exerted over the nation by Nobunaga and Hideyoshi. The abolition of toll gates began with individual daimyo's efforts to "eliminate impediments standing in the way of the free flow of commerce within a domain."[64] Abolition of tolls continued with Nobunaga and Hideyoshi's efforts to eliminate the toll gates in all provinces over which they held political and military dominance. There is clear evidence that Nobunaga's efforts to abolish toll gates were successful in the Kinai and the many central and western provinces that he subdued, but his success was limited when compared to what Hideyoshi was able to accomplish through his virtually uncontested military and political power.

Immediately following the battle of Yamasaki [in 1582], Hideyoshi began the cadastral survey of Yamashiro and abolished the *sotsubun* toll gates in Kyoto and other provinces. The incomes from these tolls belonged to nobles, and Nobunaga had attempted to abolish these gates but had been prevented from doing so. Around 1585 Hideyoshi also abolished all seven toll gates to Kyoto as a part of his newly adopted policy of "prohibiting the toll collections across the nation." When he embarked on a campaign to subdue Kyushu [in 1587], he ordered the abolition of all toll

clear that these authors' interpretations of the rakuichi and rakuza differ from those being offered in this essay. For a fuller discussion of these developments by the present author, see Kozo Yamamura, "The Development of *Za* in Medieval Japan," *Business History Review* 47 (Winter 1973), 438-65.

[63] Ibid.

[64] Sakudō and Takenaka, *Nihon keizaishi*, p. 42.

gates in the domain of Mōri. As the result of these actions, goods from many regions began to flow more freely into markets, and prices began to decline.[65]

The emergence of the "free towns," as described by Wakita Haruko above, parallelled the course followed in the abolition of toll gates. From the mid-sixteenth century on, the number of free towns rapidly increased, culminating in Hideyoshi's policy to establish "free towns" across the entire nation. To quote Toyoda again:

> In 1585, when Hideyoshi's political power became even better established, Ōmura Yūko wrote in *Tenshōki*: "Levies were waived for all nobles, warriors, and merchants, and the guilds were abolished. This caused joy to many and sorrow to few." In the *Tamon'in nikki*'s entry for December 1591, we read that "levies and guilds are now completely prohibited" and we know that the guilds disappeared around this period.[66]

Thus Takenaka and Kawakami conclude: "By the time of Ieyasu, the principle of free trade was so widely adopted nationally that even the expressions rakuichi and rakuza ceased to be used."[67]

Two important aspects of the growth in commerce that accompanied the growing political power of the Sengoku- and Tokugawa-period daimyo were the development of transportation networks and facilities and the initiation of such commerce-promoting measures as the unification of units of measurement and the issuance and enforcement of erizeni decrees. Since these subjects have not been fully explored in the previous essays in this volume, I will be excused for treating them in some detail.

There is little doubt that the transportation networks and facilities both on land and sea underwent substantial

---

[65] Toyoda, "Shōhin ryūtsū," p. 118.
[66] Ibid.
[67] Takenaka and Kawakami, *Nihon shōgyōshi*, p. 64.

development during this century, reflecting the initiatives taken by the daimyo as well as the efforts made by the merchants themselves. Except for periods of intermittent warfare, merchants could now travel with their wares in increasing ease. The Sengoku daimyo, while working to remove impediments in commerce, were also eager to improve transportation facilities:

> Post stations were established on all roads linking the central and smaller castles of the domain. All the Sengoku daimyo, without exception, improved the roads and facilities necessary for commerce. . . . Those eastern daimyo who gained dominant military positions in their respective areas at earlier dates—Go-Hōjō, Imagawa, Takeda, Uesugi, and Tokugawa—led the way in making effective use of the established post stations and also in promoting post stations in all nodes of their transportation network.[68]

> In the domain of Go-Hōjō . . . wholesaling establishments were placed at all of the more important post towns. These establishments also served as inns for traveling merchants, and the merchant in charge of such establishments was given the specific authority to govern post towns and to set prices for the use of post horses. . . . The appointment of the merchants in charge of wholesaling was confirmed by a red-sealed letter issued by Go-Hōjō, and in exchange for the privileges that the letter accorded them, they owed the responsibility of maintaining the post horses.[69]

Under Nobunaga and Hideyoshi transportation networks and facilities continued to be expanded and improved. Wakita Haruko provides some revealing insights into these developments. "To promote commerce in castle towns and also to increase control over commercial ac-

[68] Toyoda, *Chūsei Nihon*, p. 335.
[69] Nagahara, *Sengoku no dōran*, p. 237.

tivities, the specific trade routes were often designated [by the ruling class]. Such classification, however, was accompanied by efforts [by the ruling class] to improve the facilities and services provided on the routes."[70] As a good example of this point, Wakita presents the changes observed on the stretch of Shiozu road connecting Tsuruga and Shiozu. First a magistrate, appointed in 1580 by Nobunaga, came to supervise the development of post stations and a town on the road. Then, in 1590, another magistrate, this time appointed by Hideyoshi, came to improve the road, "using local labor."[71]

With political unification complete, the Tokugawa bakufu immediately took action to accelerate the trend of improvement in transportation networks. The first effort was to place "horses and men at post stations along all the major roads," starting with the Tōkaidō linking Edo and Osaka. Tokugawa Ieyasu then "continued to pursue a policy of establishing a nationwide transportation system."[72]

The development of a transportation network and facilities for sea transport, which were crucial for moving such important products as rice, lumber, and marine products over a long distance, was no less rapid during this period. Faced with the increasing necessity to trade in order "to acquire military material and other needs" and "to promote the economic activities of their domains," the Sengoku daimyo "paid close attention to protecting and administering the harbors and ports, the windows of trade with other domains."[73] This was typified by the increased use of Lake Biwa, the Seto Inland Sea, and many major rivers under the control and protection of the Sengoku daimyo of the western region, and by the Go-Hōjō's efforts to promote

[70] Wakita Haruko, *Nihon chūsei shōgyō hattatsushi no kenkyū* (Tokyo: Ochanomizu Shobō, 1969), p. 582.

[71] Ibid.

[72] Watanabe Nobuo, "Kaidō to suiun," in *Iwanami kōza Nihon rekishi* 10 (*Kinsei* 2) (Tokyo: Iwanami Shoten, 1975), 301.

[73] Toyoda, "Shōhin ryūtsū," p. 99.

the development of coastal shipping between Ise-Owari and the ports of the southern Kantō region.[74]

For the Sengoku daimyo, effective control and development of transportation capabilities over the water routes was both a military and an economic necessity. But their political and military capabilities were limited both by their military fortune and by the size of their domains. Thus the establishment of a truly nationwide network of sea and river transportation awaited the achievement of unification under Hideyoshi.

The new opportunities for transportation developed under Hideyoshi were more fully exploited at the beginning of the Tokugawa period, so that the growth of shipping capabilities was even more rapid than the growth of land transport. Osaka soon became the central entrepôt of Tokugawa commerce, but more remote domains also began to enjoy greatly improved access to the central markets.

> It is said that the sea transport between Osaka and Edo began in 1619 when a shipping agent in Sakai rented a 250-koku ship and sent cotton batting, oil, cotton, sake, wine vinegar, and soy sauce to Edo.[75]

> Goods from all of western Japan came to Osaka, the terminal of the Seto Inland Sea traffic. The Higaki shipping service began its operation in 1624 to ship goods to Edo. Then, as the increase in population continued to boost the demand in Edo, the *kobaya* [later called *taru*] shipping services were added to the Higaki service and provided speedier shipping by the mid-seventeenth century. The volume of trade between Osaka and Edo rose rapidly. . . . Because water transport was suited for shipping large quantities of goods,

[74] Ibid., pp. 106-107.
[75] Yasuoka Shigeaki, "Bakuhansei no shijō kōzō" in *Iwanami kōza Nihon rekishi* 10 (*Kinsei* 2), 253.

shipping services on rivers also developed rapidly in inland regions for transporting goods from one region to another, thus aiding the growth of commerce.[76]

The Nambu han, located in the northernmost part of Honshu and having virtually no sea transport service to Edo, began to send rice to Edo in 1614 or 1615. . . . Ships were built under domain auspices by shipwrights brought from Edo, and these were manned by captains and crews who were under the jurisdiction of the domain's magistrate in charge of ships. Captains who were skilled in shipping were made officials of the domain and crews were recruited from fishing villages. Both were provided [by the domain] with stipends in rice.[77]

In short, as works by Watanabe and other specialists make evident, even before the well-known Eastern and Western Circuit Shipping Services were fully established in the early 1670s, the shipping services in all parts of Japan were developed to a significant extent. New market opportunities increased rapidly in the newly pacified nation, both for merchants and for daimyo who had tax-rice and domain products to sell, and these opportunities provided a strong stimulus to the creation of shipping capabilities.

The growth of commerce during the 1550-1650 period was also aided by the efforts of rulers both local and national to standardize the units of measurement and to reduce the high costs of trading that resulted from the several types of Chinese and domestic coins of differing values then in use. As soon as they were politically able, Sengoku daimyo enforced the use of the *masu* (square wooden containers) that were customarily used in the major trading center of each domain, because "a vigorously enforced use

[76] Sakudō and Takenaka, *Nihon keizaishi*, pp. 60-61.
[77] Watanabe, "Kaidō to suiun," p. 317.

of a strictly specified measurement unit was essential in maintaining the smooth functioning of the market exchange."[78]

As is to be expected, both Nobunaga and Hideyoshi were active in their efforts to standardize measurements. "Nobunaga officially designated the *jūgō-masu* which had already been established as the masu to be used in the market of Kyoto," and promoted its use within the regions under his control.[79] Hideyoshi "promoted the wider acceptance of the masu and had it used in the cadastral surveys, in paying nengu, and in commercial transactions in general."[80] The Tokugawa bakufu also adopted a policy promoting the use of the Kyoto masu, and in 1669 was finally able to prohibit the use of the Edo masu, the last major competing masu then in commercial use. Though much of the earlier history of scales is unknown, they too were finally unified in 1665 by the bakufu.[81]

Though the story of the erizeni decrees and the minting of coins is a long and complex one, we can nevertheless state with confidence that the direction of the change promoted and enforced by the Sengoku daimyo and the three unifiers was toward "the setting of relative values of coins and assuring the stability of the values of the coins."[82] For instance, among Sengoku daimyo, the Takeda specified the coins that could be used in their domain, and the Ōuchi, Asai, Go-Hōjō, Yūki, and others issued numerous decrees that set the relative exchange rates of various coins "indicating how strongly these rulers were concerned in maintaining smooth trade and the stability of prices in the markets."[83] Nobunaga and Hideyoshi each took an interest in the problem of unifying the currency. But it was To-

[78] Toyoda, *Chūsei Nihon*, p. 327.
[79] Toyoda, "Shōhin ryūtsū," p. 116.
[80] Ibid., p. 119.
[81] Yasuoka, "Bakuhansei," p. 262.
[82] Sakudō and Takenaka, *Nihon keizaishi*, p. 42.
[83] Toyoda, *Chūsei Nihon*, p. 328.

kugawa Ieyasu who in 1595 took the lead by minting *koban* (one-*ryō* gold coins) as the medium of transaction within his great domain. Hideyoshi had minted *ōban* (ten-*ryō* gold coins) in 1583, but these were used only as gifts or as rewards for military performance, and not as a medium of transaction. Thus the minting of koban in 1595 was the first minting of a medium of exchange (except for illegal, privately minted coins) since the so-called *kōchō 12-sen* (twelve types of imperial coins) that were produced by the Ritsuryō government in the eighth century.[84] After the establishment of the Tokugawa bakufu, silver coins as well as gold were minted. Also, from 1636, a large number of copper coins were minted and circulated widely, ending the centuries of reliance on Chinese copper coins as a daily medium of exchange. And so "the period of the erizeni came to an end."[85]

These facilitating factors were part of the overall growth of commerce in the century of the agricultural revolution: growth in terms of volume, not just variety. Several Japanese scholars have demonstrated that the total quantities of rice and numerous other products traded across the nation rose steadily. "A nationwide market was created with Kinai as its center. By the Keichō-Genna period [1596-1624] nearly a million koku of rice were brought from Tōhoku, Hokuriku, and other regions facing the Sea of Japan, and from all parts of western Japan."[86] Also, "because large quantities of goods from many provinces began to be brought in on horseback and by ships . . . various economic regions were integrated through trade across regional boundaries."[87]

This gradual unification of markets reduced the wide regional price variations that characterized the medieval

[84] Toyoda, "Shōhin ryūtsū," p. 120.

[85] Sakudō and Takenaka, *Nihon keizaishi*, p. 59.

[86] Wakita Osamu, *Kinsei hōken shakai no keizai kōzō* (Tokyo: Ochanomizu Shobō, 1963), p. 75.

[87] Toyoda, "Shōhin ryūtsū," p. 109.

economy. Regional differentials in the price of rice, which ranged from up to 240 koku per 10 *ryō* in Tsuruga and Akita in the north to as low as 30-40 koku in the Kinai region in the 1580s, declined steadily. By the mid-seventeenth century, price differentials in rice had virtually disappeared, and those of many other commodities also continued to decline, as studies by Yasuoka, Wakita, and others have shown.[88] Increased volume of trade and reduced price differentials are the expected results of an economy that had succeeded in reducing the costs of transportation, and that had begun to operate on the basis of increased knowledge of prices due to an established network of transportation and the existence of a large number of towns and of merchants specializing in specific products.

Evidence of commercial growth of the kind just discussed again brings us to the question of "who profited?" Obviously the acceleration of commerce during this period yielded large gains realized from specialization, economies of scale, and reduced costs of transactions. The gain was captured by the rulers and the merchants and, we argue, by the peasant class, as well.

CONCLUSION

It is now fully accepted that during the century of political unification, the Japanese economy underwent a fundamental transformation and rapid growth that was, in its rapidity and scope, matched only by the transformation witnessed during the century following the Meiji Restoration. It is also apparent that two closely interacting forces were the principal causes of this transformation and rapid growth.

One was political unification, first pursued and later

[88] Wakita Osamu, "Tsugaru no kaisengyō ni tsuite," in Fukui Kenritsu Toshokan, ed., *Nihon kaiunshi no kenkyū* (Fukui: Fukui Kenritsu Toshokan, 1967), p. 189; and, for the Tokugawa prices, Yasuoka, "Bakuhansei," pp. 283-284.

achieved. Larger and increasingly secure territories came
to be ruled by the Sengoku daimyo, and this fact, along
with the final unification and peace achieved by Ieyasu,
provided the ruling class with the strongest of incentives to
take measures promoting economic growth. Unlike the
claimants of shōen dues or the shugo daimyo, the rulers of
this period succeeded in obtaining the political power
necessary to make and capture the returns from major investments of resources. They committed their resources
and administrative capabilities to undertake large irrigation and water-control projects, to carry out cadastral surveys, and to improve transportation facilities precisely because they were able to benefit from the returns that these
projects yielded. Their intense interest in and adoption of
a series of policies promoting commerce were also justified
by their ability to capture the returns.

The second cause of rapid growth was the sharply increased number of "independent" peasants, that is, the
creation of a "new class of peasants" by the rulers of the
century of unification. Daimyo encouraged the establishment of such peasants to deprive potential or real com-
petitors from weakening the domain economy, to broaden
their tax base, and to cement ties with their vassals. The effects of this newly accorded "independence" were fundamental and far reaching, both for agriculture and for the
peasants themselves. As Japanese scholars have shown, the
increase in "independent" cultivators went hand in hand
with the intensification of agriculture, resulting in increased productivity. And the agricultural revolution, a
product of increased agricultural productivity, provided
the fundamental basis for the accelerating growth of commerce.

The main interpretive point I have tried to make in-
volves the problem of the effect of the creation of the "new
class of peasants" on the economic changes of the period.
Most Japanese scholars, while acknowledging that productivity increased as a result of intensive farming by "independent" small peasants, argue or imply that the fruits of

increased productivity were taxed away by the more politically secure and strong ruling class. The peasants, they claim, were taxed often to the point of desperate revolt, and intensive agriculture that contributed to increased productivity was only the result of peasant efforts to maintain their meager existence under an increasing burden of taxation. The rulers, ever oppressive, were prone to "exploit" the peasants, and the peasants countered the demands on them by pleading, absconding, or revolting. The interests of the rulers and the ruled were mutually exclusive, and the conflicts continued as time passed.

While fully recognizing and respecting this established interpretation, the economic historian trained in neoclassical economic analysis cannot but find himself asking many questions. Perhaps the most important is the question: did these "independent" peasants work to increase productivity only to see the fruits of their labor taxed away? And did the benefits of increased agricultural output and commercial activities elude these small peasants?

To answer these questions, I have advanced a hypothesis that the increase in productivity resulted because the small "independent" peasants were able to share in the fruits of their labor; that is, they worked more intensely and effectively because they were motivated by the desire to improve their lot. This motivation, I have argued, provided the missing link between the creation of the small "independent" peasants and the recognized increase in agricultural productivity. I shall be the first to acknowledge that my hypothesis has only been sketched out, and I realize that if it is to be supported, much further study is needed. But whatever future research reveals, it seems certain that the century of unification opened a new era of both increasing agricultural productivity and rapid growth of commerce. These provided, after a period of gestation and maturation during the Tokugawa period, the economic foundations necessary for another century of rapid economic growth following the Meiji Restoration.

bakufu 幕府 The name given to the military governments headed by the Minamoto, Ashikaga, and Tokugawa families; the shogun's government; shogunate.

bakuhan 幕藩 A term coined by historians to refer to the Tokugawa system of government in which the shogunate (bakufu) constituted national authority while the daimyo exercised authority over their domains (han).

bugyō 奉行 Administrator or magistrate.

bugyōnin 奉行人 See bugyō.

buichi tokusei 分一徳政 A special debt cancellation under which a debtor might obtain forgiveness of a privately incurred debt by paying a given portion to the bakufu, or by which a creditor might prevent such a cancellation by paying a portion of the debt to the bakufu.

buke 武家 Bushi houses; the warrior estate.

bunkokuhō 分国法 Daimyo domain laws.

bushi 武士 An armed fighter, warrior; also called samurai.

chigyō 知行 Rights to the administrative control of land; by late Sengoku times the term came to be used in the meaning of fief.

chō 町 A unit of land measure; 2.94 acres until 1594, when Hideyoshi reduced it to 2.45 acres, also read machi.

daikan 代官 Deputy or manager.

daimyo 大名 Regional military lord. During the Sengoku period, this name was often applied to shugo, and then to the families (also known as Sengoku daimyo) who supplanted them. After the establishment of the Tokugawa shogunate, the term was applied to those lords whose domains were assessed at 10,000 koku or more.

dogō 土豪 Usually referred to village leaders who possessed landed wealth and, thereby, local political and even (before the disarming of the peasantry) military influence.

Similar to jizamurai and kokujin.

dosō 土倉 Pawnbrokers, whose usury formed the basis of far-flung commercial enterprises in later medieval Japan.

erizeni-rei 撰銭令 Orders prohibiting the collection of commercial or tax obligations solely in sound currency. Creditors were forced to accept a fixed proportion of base currency in payment.

fudai 譜代 A "hereditary" retainer, one whose ties to his lord were deemed to be so intimate and of such duration as to have created a particularly binding obligation to serve and a unique competence to serve in the lord's household administration.

gekokujō 下剋上 The overthrow of a superior by an inferior; a term frequently used in characterizing the political upheaval of the Muromachi and Sengoku periods.

gesakushiki 下作職 The right to cultivate the land; originally this right was referred to as the sakushiki, but with the rise of kajishi relationships the sakushiki tended to become a right to kajishi entailing no obligation to work the land itself—that right and obligation being referred to as the gesakushiki.

gō 郷 In medieval Japan, an administrative division of a shōen or kokugaryō; the medieval gō developed in some cases from the ancient administrative villages, or go, of the ritsuryō codes.

gokenin 御家人 Originally, vassals of the shogun; later many daimyo began to refer to their major vassals as gokenin, as well.

goryō 御領 The private holdings of the shogunal or of a daimyo house.

gōson 郷村 Village; in particular the self-governing village organization, also known as sō or sōson, which began to emerge during the Muromachi period and which formed the basis of the administrative village system of the Tokugawa period.

goyōshokunin 御用職人 Artisans or performers accorded special privileges in return for their services on behalf of the daimyo.

goyōshōnin 御用商人 Merchants accorded special privileges in return for their services on behalf of the daimyo.

gun 郡 "County"; or administrative division of a province; the term is also read kōri.

gundai 郡代 A gun-level administrator or magistrate, also referred to as gunji.

gunji 郡司 See gundai.

gun'yaku 軍役 A military service levy.

han 藩 A daimyo domain. The contemporary term was ryōgoku. Han came into official use only after the Restoration of 1868. It has subsequently been adopted by modern historians as the generic term for the Tokugawa-period domain.

hei-nō-bunri 兵農分離 The strict definition and separation of the warrior and peasant classes, with the former being settled in castle towns and the latter being bound to the soil.

hikan 被官 A vassal, subordinate.

hon nengu 本年貢 The "original nengu"; a term that, with the emergence of kajishi, was used to distinguish nengu from the new impost of kajishi.

hyakushō 百姓 Peasant, farmer, cultivator.

hyōjō 評定 A council of senior vassals; alternatively, the decisions or orders of such a council.

ichimachi 市町 Market towns that developed with the expansion of a local market.

ichimon 一門 A term that, within a vassal organization, refers to those vassals deemed to be kinsmen.

ichizoku 一族 A lineage (including cadet branches) tracing descent from a common ancestor.

ie 家 Household, family.

ikki 一揆 A league or alliance.

in 院 Cloistered emperor.

jitō 地頭 Gokenin appointed by the Kamakura bakufu to act as land stewards of shōen and kokugaryō holdings.

jizamurai 地侍 Literally, "samurai of the soil," or "base

samurai," this term referred to rural samurai of a sort not far removed from the peasantry; corresponds roughly to the dogō class.

jinaimachi 寺内町 Towns that grew within a temple compound rather than before its gates; see monzenmachi.

jōkamachi 城下町 Castle towns.

kahō 家法 Daimyo house laws.

kajishi 加地子 "Supplementary land tax" that members of the myōshu or dogō class began to collect from the cultivators of the land as they themselves took less part in its actual management.

kajishi myōshu 加地子名主 A myōshu or dogō of the late medieval period, who no longer took an active part in the management of the land, but rather acted as a landlord whose return from the land was the kajishi.

kakun 家訓 Daimyo house precepts.

kan 貫 In the kanmon monetary system this was a unit of cash designating 1,000 copper coins, each of which was called a mon.

kandaka 貫高 The assessed value of a land holding in terms of cash.

kanmon 貫文 See kan.

kaō 花押 A cipher or stylized signature.

kashindan 家臣団 A band of retainers.

katanagari 刀狩 The confiscation of arms from all but the warrior class.

kenchi 検地 A cadastral survey.

kendanken 検断権 The right to administer criminal justice.

kobyakushō 小百姓 Lesser peasantry.

kōden 公田 (1) That land within a holding from which its lord could extract the full range of nengu and kuji; (2) that land, whether within shoen or kokugaryō, which was listed within provincial registers as being subject to tansen.

kōgi 公儀 A term meaning both "the public" and "public authority" or "government," kōgi was used by Sengoku daimyo to refer to themselves as paramount public authority within their territories.

kokka 国家 The "state" or "polity," used to refer to the consolidated sphere of daimyo political control. For daimyo, the concept of kokka was equivalent to Oda Nobunaga's use of tenka.

koku 石 A unit of volume equivalent to 5.1 bushels.

kokudaka 石高 The assessed value of a land holding in terms of koku of rice.

kokugaryō 国衙領 "Provincial domain"; that land which, not having been absorbed into shōen, remained subject to the adminstration of the provincial office.

kokujin 国人 "Men of the province"; although the term was used by a wide spectrum of warriors to distinguish themselves from the shugo, who frequently came from outside the province, historians generally use it to refer to scions of the old jitō-gokenin families of the Kamakura period.

kokujin ikki 国人一揆 A kokujin league formed for mutual assistance in governing a province in the absence of a strong daimyo, or for the purpose of resisting such a daimyo.

kuge 公家 Court nobility.

kuni 国 Province, country.

komedome 米留 See nidome.

kuji 公事 Corvée, or dues in kind levied against men in lieu of corvée; contrasted with nengu, which were dues levied against land.

kunigae 国替 The transfer of a daimyo from one domain to another.

machi 町 Originally, divisions of a city encompassing each of the squares formed by the intersections of its streets, the term eventually came to refer to townlike communities both within cities and in the countryside.

machigumi 町組 In Kyoto, associations of members of 14 or 15 machi communities joined together for purposes of limited self-government.

mon 文 See kan.

monzenmachi 門前町 Towns that grew up before the gates of

major temples and shrines.

mura 村 Village.

munebechisen 棟別銭 A cash tax levied against peasant households in proportion to the number of buildings in their possession during the medieval period.

myō 名 A holding registered in the name of the head of a patriarchally organized group of cultivators.

myōden 名田 The rice fields contained in a given myō.

myōshu 名主 In the early medieval period this referred to the patriarchal head of a group of cultivators farming a myō; the man responsible for managing the holding and forwarding all imposts due on it. By the Sengoku period, however, there was little difference between myōshu and dogō or jizamurai.

naukenin 名請人 The peasant listed in a cadastral register as the possessor of a given piece of land; the fact of his being so listed made him responsible for rendering the nengu from that land and meant that, as far as the lord was concerned, he had both the right and the duty to cultivate it.

nengu 年貢 An annual tax or rent due from the land, as contrasted to kuji, which were service dues construed to be incumbent upon men.

nidome 荷留 A policy frequently adopted by Sengoku daimyo of refusing to allow certain goods to cross their borders; the prohibition of the export of rice, for instance, was called komedome.

oyamachi 親町 Literally "parent towns," the term refers to the old machi divisions created by the partition of a city by its grid of intersecting streets into a large number of squares or rectangles called machi.

rakuichi-rakuza 楽市楽座 Literally "free markets and free guilds," the term refers to a commercial policy whereby Sengoku daimyo abolished both monopolistic guilds (za) and the obligation to trade at certain privately controlled markets (ichi), and there to render certain special dues.

ritsuryō 律令 A term referring to the T'ang-inspired legal

codes adopted by Japan during the seventh and eighth centuries, and, by extension, to the bureaucratic imperial state established by those codes.

rokusai-ichi 六斎市 Markets that were open six days a month, that is, every fifth day; Sengoku daimyo frequently established these so as to foster trade of certain sorts within their territories.

rōjū 老中 Elders; members of the Tokugawa senior council.

ryō 両 A unit of gold currency; officially one ryō was equal to 60 monme of silver.

ryōgawamachi 両側町 Townships that grew up from associations among the merchants inhabiting the two sides of a street or road.

ryōke 領家 The central proprietor of a shōen.

ryōgoku 領国 "Domainal province," the territory under a daimyo's rule.

ryōshu 領主 Proprietary lord.

sakaya 酒屋 Sake brewers; together with the dosō, the sakaya were heavily involved in usury and long-distance trade.

sakoku 鎖国 The closed country; the policy of seclusion imposed by Tokugawa Iemitsu.

sakushiki 作職 The right to cultivate the land; see, however, gesakushiki.

sashidashi 指出 A report of the area, holder and/or cultivator, and dues incumbent upon a given parcel of land, the report being submitted by peasants or village officials at the order of the daimyo; these formed the basis of most surveys undertaken before the very end of the sixteenth century.

sekisho 関所 Toll barriers.

Sengoku daimyo 戦国大名 The type of daimyo characteristic of the Sengoku period.

shiki 職 An office and the income pertaining to it; in land tenure relationships, the nominal offices allowing various people to draw income from a given piece of land.

shirowari 城割 The destruction of surplus castles.

shiryō 私領 Private land holdings; fiefs held of a daimyo.

379

shōnin 商人 Merchants.

shōnin kashira (tsukasa) 商人頭 Merchant leaders or elders.

shōmyō 小名 A military lord of less than daimyo status.

shōryōshu 小領主 Literally "small lords," this term is used by some historians to refer to those dogō whose acquisition of a species of lordship within the village was advanced enough to distinguish them clearly from the rest of the peasantry.

shuinjō 朱印状 A document issued over a vermilion seal (shuin); during the course of the sixteenth century, the use of seals rather than kaō in issuing documents became common among many daimyo.

shōen 荘園 Private landed estate.

shōgun 将軍 The chief of the military hierarchy in medieval and early modern Japan; from the mid-fourteenth century on, the de facto ruler of the country.

shugo 守護 Province-level officials of the Kamakura and Muromachi bakufu; they became great territorial lords during the late fourteenth and early fifteenth centuries; in the latter sense they are referred to as shugo daimyo.

shugodai 守護代 Deputy shugo.

shugo daimyo 守護大名 See shugo.

sō 惣 Self-governing village organizations of the Muromachi period.

sōryō 惣領 Lineage chief; heir to the main line of a warrior family; under the sōryō system the members even of branch lineages of a warrior family remained subject to the sōryō's orders.

Taikō kenchi 太閤検地 A term referring to the cadastral surveys carried out under Hideyoshi's orders during the last two decades of the sixteenth century.

tan 段 A unit of land area equal to one-tenth chō.

tansen 段銭 A tax in cash based upon the assessed area of a holding; originally an extraordinary levy to offset certain expenses of the court, tansen became routine imposts imposed by the shugo and Sengoku daimyo.

tenka 天下 A term that in Chinese political theory referred to the empire, or "all under heaven." The term came to be used by Oda Nobunaga to refer to the "realm" whose welfare and proper rule he deemed to be his particular responsibility.

tennō 天皇 The Japanese sovereign; emperor.

toiya 問屋 Also read ton'ya; the term refers to merchants who originally specialized in transporting and disposing of goods for others, but eventually came to engage in all forms of trade on a large scale; wholesaler.

tokusei 徳政 Literally "virtuous governance," the term referred to a policy of cancelling debts so as to "ease the misery" of the debtors.

toshiyori 年寄 Elders; chief representatives of merchant communities.

tozama 外様 A retainer who was regarded as in some sense "outside" the lord's household; in contrast to the fudai, whose obligations to the lord were regarded as more or less absolute, the tozama were treated more nearly as allies.

yajishi 屋地子 Rents levied against lots within a town or city.

za 座 Usually translated as guild, the term refers to monopolistic trade organizations that manifested a considerable variety of characteristics over time—from being service organizations fairly strongly subordinated to members of the ruling class, to being free associations of merchants or artisans.

zaimachi 在町 Towns that grew up in the countryside as a result of the growth of local trade; equivalent to ichimachi.

Notes on Contributors

PETER J. ARNESEN, Assistant Professor of History, University of Michigan, received his Ph.D. from Yale University in 1977. A specialist in the history of the Muromachi period, his study, *The Medieval Japanese Daimyo: The Ouchi Family's Rule of Suo and Nagato*, was published by the Yale University Press (1979).

ASAO NAOHIRO, Associate Professor, Kyoto University, was graduated in 1954 from the Department of History of the same university, from which he also received his doctorate. He has written extensively on the Shokuhō and early Kinsei periods. His major works include "Toyotomi seiken ron" in *Iwanami kōza Nihon rekishi*, Series II (1963); "Shōgun seiji no kenryoku kōzō," in *Iwanami kōza Nihon rekishi*, Series III (1975); *Sakoku*, Shōgakkan Nihon no rekishi series, 17 (1975); and *Kinsei hōkenshakai no kiso kōzō* (1967).

MARTIN COLLCUTT, Assistant Professor of East Asian Studies, Princeton University, received his Ph.D. from Harvard University in 1975. His book, *Five Mountains: The Zen Monastic Institution in Medieval Japan*, is being prepared for publication by Harvard University Press.

GEORGE ELISON, Associate Professor of East Asian Languages and Cultures and of History, Indiana University, received his Ph.D. from Harvard University in 1969. His publications include *Deus Destroyed: The Image of Christianity in Early Modern Japan* (1973) and *Warlords, Artists, and Commoners: Japan in the Sixteenth Century* (with Bardwell L. Smith, 1980). He is currently at work on a study of Nobunaga.

FUJIKI HISASHI, Professor in the Faculty of Letters, Rikkyō University, completed his graduate work at Tōhoku University in 1963. His major study *Sengoku shakai shi ron*, published in 1974 by the University of Tokyo Press, is a careful study of the dissolution of medieval society and the rise of the daimyo in sixteenth century Japan. His *Oda-Toyotomi Seiken* (1975) is volume 15 in the Shōgakkan Nihon no rekishi series.

Notes on Contributors

JOHN WHITNEY HALL, A. Whitney Griswold Professor of History, Yale University, received his Ph.D. from Harvard University in 1950. He taught at the University of Michigan from 1948 until moving to Yale University in 1961. Among his publications, the ones most relevant to this study are *Government and Local Power in Japan, 500 to 1700* (1966); *Japan in the Muromachi Age* (with Toyoda Takeshi, 1977); *Studies in the Institutional History of Early Modern Japan* (with Marius B. Jansen, 1968).

SUSAN B. HANLEY, Associate Professor of Japanese Studies and History, University of Washington, received her Ph.D. from Yale University in 1971. Included in her publications are articles on the demographic history of premodern Japan, notably "Fertility, Mortality, and Life Expectancy in Premodern Japan," *Population Studies*, 28.1 (1974), and *Economic and Demographic Change in Preindustrial Japan, 1600-1868* (with Kozo Yamamura, 1977). A specialist on the Tokugawa period, she is currently working on the material culture and standard of living in Japan from 1600 to 1900.

WILLIAM B. HAUSER, Associate Professor of History at the University of Rochester, received his Ph.D. from Yale University in 1969. He is the author of *Economic Institutional Change in Tokugawa Japan: Osaka and the Kinai Cotton Trade* (1974). A specialist on the economic and social history of the Tokugawa period, he is at work on a history of the city of Osaka, tentatively titled "Osaka: A City in Transition, 1600-1900."

MARIUS B. JANSEN, Professor of History, Princeton University, received his Ph.D. from Harvard University in 1950. He is the author of *The Japanese and Sun Yat-sen* (1954), *Sakamoto Ryōma and the Meiji Restoration* (1961) and numerous other works dealing with late Edo and Meiji Japan. In 1968 he coedited with John Hall *Studies in the Institutional History of Early Modern Japan*.

KATSUMATA SHIZUO, Associate Professor, Faculty of Education, University of Tokyo, is a specialist on medieval law codes. His publications include "Sengoku hō" in *Iwanami kōza Nihon rekishi*, Series III (1976) and *Sengoku hō seiritsu shiron* (1979).

MATSUOKA HISATO, Professor, Faculty of Letters, Hiroshima University, graduated in 1942 from the same university. His prime area of research has been local administration in Aki province during the middle ages. Most recently he has edited *Naikai chiiki shakai no shiteki kenkyū* (1978), a collection of studies on the special historical features of the Inland Sea region of Japan.

JAMES L. MCCLAIN, Assistant Professor of History, Brown University, received his Ph.D. in 1979 from Yale University. For his dissertation he wrote on "Kanazawa in the Seventeenth Century: Castle Towns and Japan's Early Modern Urbanization." His article "Local Politics and National Integration: The Fukui Prefectural Assembly in the 1880s," appeared in *Monumenta Nipponica* (1976).

NAGAHARA KEIJI, Professor, Faculty of Economics, Hitotsubashi University, graduated from the University of Tokyo in 1944. He received his doctorate from Hitotsubashi University in 1965. His early interest was directed toward the Muromachi period, but subsequently he has ranged widely in his scholarship. His publications include: *Nihon hōken shakai ron* (1955); *Nihon hōkensei seiritsu katei no kenkyū* (1961); *Daimyō ryōgokusei* (1967); *Nihon Chūsei shakai kōzō no kenkyū* (1973); *Sengoku no dōran* (1975) in the Shōgakkan series, and many articles.

SASAKI GIN'YA, Professor, Faculty of Letters, Chūō University, graduated from the University of Tokyo in 1950, having specialized in Japanese history. His major work, *Chusei shōhin ryūtsūshi no kenkyū* (1972), published by Hōsei University Press, is a detailed study of trade and transportation in medieval Japan.

SASAKI JUNNOSUKE, Associate Professor, Faculty of Sociology, Hitotsubashi University, graduated from the University of Tokyo in 1953, and received his doctorate in 1960. His major work, *Bakuhan kenryoku no kiso kōzō* (1964), is a study of the peasant base of the *bakuhan* system. He is author of *Daimyō to hyakushō* (1966) in the Chūō Kōron series, *Bakumatsu shakai ron* (1964), and numerous articles.

RONALD P. TOBY, Assistant Professor of History, University of Illinois, received his Ph.D. from Columbia University in 1977. He wrote his dissertation on "The Early Tokugawa Bakufu and seventeenth-century Japanese relations with East Asia." His article "Reopening the Question of *Sakoku*: Diplomacy in the Legitimation of the Tokugawa Bakufu" appeared in *The Journal of Japanese Studies* (1977).

Notes on Contributors

WAKITA HARUKO, Professor at Tachibana Women's University in Kyoto, received her doctorate from Kyoto University. A specialist on medieval economic and urban history, she is author of *Chūsei Nihon shōgyō hattatsu shi no kenkyū* (1969). The article "Muromachi-ki no keizai hatten" appears in *Iwanami kōza Nihon rekishi*, Series III (1976). Her essay "Towards a Wider Perspective on Medieval Commerce" was published in *The Journal of Japanese Studies* (1975).

WAKITA OSAMU, Associate Professor at the University of Osaka, received his doctorate from Kyoto University in 1962. His major publication is a two-volume study of the Shokuhō polity, *Shokuhō seiken no bunseki*: Vol. I, *Oda seiken no kiso kōzō* (1975); Vol. II, *Kinsei hōkensei seiritsushi ron* (1977). In English, the essay "The *kokudaka* system: A Device for Unification" appeared in *The Journal of Japanese Studies* (1975).

KOZO YAMAMURA, Professor of Asian Studies and Economics, University of Washington, received his Ph.D. in 1963 from Northwestern University. He has written extensively on the economic history of Japan, and among his many publications are *Economic Policy in Postwar Japan* (1967); *A Study of Samurai Income and Entrepreneurship, Quantitative Analyses of Economic and Social Aspects of the Samurai in Tokugawa and Meiji Japan* (1974); and *Economic and Demographic Change in Preindustrial Japan, 1600-1868* (with Susan Hanley, 1977).

Index

Aizu Wakamatsu, 129-30
Akechi Mitsuhide, 158, 160, 183,
    189, 190, 192, 350
Aki, 18, 65, 88, 102, 248, 332
Akita, 241, 370
Amagasaki, 235, 298
Araki Moriaki, 14, 209, 215-16
Asai Nagamasa, 162, 169, 368
Asakura Eirin, 111
Asakura family, 57, 114, 188
Asakura Takakage, 248
Asakura Yoshikage, 152, 162, 169
Asano Nagayoshi, 230
Ashikaga family, 112-13, 120, 196,
    199-201
Ashikaga Yoshiaki (Kakukei), 121,
    149, 150-73, 176, 184, 185, 196,
    234, 248, 254-55, 258
Ashikaga Yoshihide, 149
Ashikaga Yoshimasa, 175
Ashikaga Yoshimitsu, 180-81, 197
Ashikaga Yoshinori, 166
Ashikaga Yoshiteru, 120, 149,
    150-51, 168, 253
Ashina family, 129-30
Awa, 102
Azuchi, 180-82, 227, 230, 233-34,
    238, 256
Azuchi Disputation, 178

Bingo, 258
Bizen, 10, 195
Buke-shohatto, 262-63, 266-67,
    269
Buzen, 65-66, 70, 72, 75

cadastral surveys, see kenchi
castle towns, 142, 224, 316-17;
    growth of, 231-39, 289-90, 298-

99, 301-302; marketing struc-
    ture, 134; taxes, 137, 305-306,
    325-26
Chikuzen, 65, 71, 84
China, 126, 146
Chōsokabe family, 29, 200, 315;
    house laws, 102
Chōsokabe Motochika, 102
Christianity, 9, 22, 199-200, 265,
    266
Chūgoku, 29, 183, 338
class separation, 63, 194, 207-10,
    218, 293-94, 346, 375
Cloistered Emperor, see In
coin selection edicts, see erizeni-rei
court nobles, 18, 21, 123, 196, 201,
    225, 229, 246, 251, 254, 260,
    263-64, 306, 317; shoen rights,
    31-34, 36-37

Daigazuka, 232
Daimyo house laws, 43, 72, 101-24
Date family, 57-58, 102, 200, 331;
    commercial policies, 130, 135,
    141; house laws (jinkaishū), 102,
    108, 117, 130, 135
Date Harumune, 361
Date Tanemune, 102
Dazaifu Tenmangū, 71
debt cancellation edicts, see
    Tokusei-rei
dogō, 24-25, 66, 69, 70, 76, 93,
    142-43, 208, 211-12, 217, 374
dorei, 24-25

Echigo, 10, 128, 130, 163, 226, 248
Echigo Kashiwazaki, see
    Kashiwazaki

Index

Echizen, 152, 162, 186-88, 227, 248
Echizen Fuchū, 187-88
Edo, 242, 243, 261-62, 366, 367
emperor, 7, 20-21, 123-24, 168, 173-84, 197-98, 248-70, 381
Enryakuji, 21, 144-45
erizen-rei, 113, 140, 146, 356-57, 374
Etchū, 188-89
export prohibitions, see nidome

Free markets and free guilds, see rakuichi-rakuza
fudai ("hereditary") retainers, 105, 261, 264, 266, 374
Fujiwara family, 197
Fukuoka, 333
Fukushima Masanori, 267, 268
Fukuyama, 331
Funai, 142
Fushimi, 242, 243, 261
Fuwa Mitsuharu, 187

gekokujō, 9, 251-52, 374
Gifu, 151, 156, 164
Go-Hōjō, see Hōjō
gokenin, 90-92, 374
Go-Mizunoo, 260-62, 267, 268
Goseibai shikimoku, 103-104, 252-53
Gōshi, 24, 208
goyō merchants and artisans, 131-32, 237, 309, 325, 375
Go-Yōzei, 197, 257-58, 268
guilds, see za

Hakata, 298, 299, 318, 321
hanzai, 71
Harima, 183, 265
Heian-kyo, 299
Higo, 102
hikan, 24-25
Hikone, 261
Hirado, 265

Hiranogō, 231-32, 236, 298, 301, 325
Hiroshima, 267-68
Hitachi, 177
Hōjō family, 64, 65, 272-82, 331, 350; commercial policies, 54-58, 127, 128, 143, 145, 360, 364-66, 368; kokudaka system, 134; kandaka system, 18, 28, 30, 35-43, 63, 76, 80, 87, 134; legitimacy, 114, 200; military levies, 49-51; tansen, 87
Hōjō Sōun, 9, 352-53
Hōjō Ujimasa, 278-79
Hōjō Ujinori, 279
Hōki, 229
Hokke sect, 178, 233, 317, 319
Honkokuji, 155
Honnōji, 183, 256
Hosokawa Fujitaka, 189, 190
Hyōgo, 229

Ikeda family, 272, 285-91
Ikeda Mitsumasa, 285-87
Ikeda Terumasa, 350-51
ikki, 73-75, 109, 162, 205, 211, 248, 279, 376
Imagawa family, 28, 30, 39, 43, 46-48, 57, 64, 65, 76; commercial policies, 130-32, 135-37, 140, 143; house laws, 102, 108, 127, 128, 136, 364
Imagawa Ujichika, 102
Imagawa Ujizane, 46
Imagawa Yoshimoto, 102, 135, 138, 248-49
Imai, 232, 314-15
Imazu, 230
In, 268, 376
Ise, 128, 129, 152, 227, 331, 366
Ise shrine, 269
Ishii Ryōsuke, 206, 214
Ishimoda Shō, 13
Isshiki Fujinaga, 160
Itō family, 141, 142

Iwami, 65, 86
Iwasawa Yoshihiko, 183, 188
Izu, 42
Izumisano, 298

jinaimachi (jinaichō), 231-36, 298,
    300-301, 314-15, 317-19, 376
jinkaishū, see Date; house laws
jitō, 23, 31, 71, 376
jizamurai, 24-25, 66, 142, 143, 208,
    211-12, 217, 340, 375

Kadoya family, 128, 135-36
Kai, 9, 102, 128, 129, 180, 190, 261
Kaizuka, 232
kajishi, 34, 37, 41, 60, 142, 341, 376
kajishi-myōshu, 24, 36, 340, 376
Kakitsu Disturbance, 166
Kamakura *bakufu*, 31-32, 102,
    250-51, 253, 262
Kanazawa, 242
kandaka system, 18, 27-63, 76,
    80-90, 121, 134, 146, 279, 355-
    56, 376
Kannonji, 145
Kanō, 227
kanpaku, 121, 123, 174, 179, 180-
    81, 197, 247, 258, 260
Kanshuji Harutoyo, 181
Kantō, 9, 28, 30, 35, 38, 64, 127,
    129, 130, 139, 178, 181, 240
kashindan, 90, 102, 104-12, 127,
    143, 196
Kashiwazaki, 131, 299, 361
Kasugayama, 142, 301-302
Katata, 228, 230
Katō Tadahiro, 267
Kawachi, 162, 191, 232-33
kenchi, 8, 10, 36-41, 100, 125, 194,
    305, 376; effect on peasantry,
    14, 15, 56-57, 142, 211-19, 346;
    implementation, 41-44, 75-80,
    189-93; and *kokudaka* system, 21,
    59, 61
Kennyo Kōsa, 163, 178

Kikkawa family, 86-87, 96
Kikkawa Hiroie, 102
Kikkawa Motoharu, 97
Kikkawa Tsunenori, 80
Kinai, 28, 126, 132, 179, 226, 240,
    246, 296
Kobayakawa, 96
Kōfu, 332
Kōfu Yōkaichi, 129, 191
Kōfukuji, 177, 191
kōgi, 19, 20, 22, 120-24, 166, 170,
    198, 204, 207, 257-61, 265-69,
    271-94, 377
kokka, 19, 111-24, 198, 204, 377
kokudaka system, 18, 35-37, 63,
    84-85, 134, 194, 210, 219-22,
    239, 263, 355
kokujin, 20, 24-25, 31-33, 36, 37,
    59, 90, 93, 125, 143-48, 205, 208,
    233, 335, 341-44, 377
Kokura, 351
Konoe Nobusuke, 258
Konoe Sakihisa, 179
Korea, 146, 199, 258
Kōzuke, 180, 183
Kumamoto, 267, 333
Kurata family, 130, 131, 141-43
Kusunoki Chōan, 182
Kuwana, 298, 300, 318
Kyōgoku Tadakuni, 267
Kyoto, 7, 65, 121, 126, 129-31,
    136, 149-52, 154-56, 158, 164,
    166, 169, 171-73, 180, 183, 189,
    196-98, 226-27, 229, 231-37,
    240, 242, 244-46, 249, 254, 257,
    259, 261, 268, 278-79, 298-300,
    307, 308, 309

Lake Biwa, 144, 170, 228, 230, 365

Mabuchi, 144
Maeda Gen'i, 229
Maeda Toshiie, 187-88
Maruyama Masao, 105

Index

Matsudaira Nobutsuna, 264
Matsuki family, 128, 143
Matsumoto Toyohisa, 302
Matsunaga Hisahide, 120, 162
Mikatagahara, 171
Mikawa, 10, 40, 152, 171
Minamoto Yoritomo, 262
Mino, 40, 41, 141, 150-52, 227, 331
Mito, 129
Mitsui Motonobu, 351
Mizubuchi Fujihide, 172
Mōri family, 18-19, 29, 88-89, 95-
    100, 114, 200
Mōri Motoharu, 96
Mōri Motonari, 96-97, 248, 253
Mōri Takakaga, 96
Mōri Takamoto, 253
Mount Hiei, 21, 144
Murai Sadakatsu, 172
Muromachi bakufu, 65, 102, 118,
    201, 248, 253, 308, 324
Musashi, 42, 50
Mutsu, 102, 130
myōshu, 18, 24-25, 33-34, 46, 66,
    74, 160, 208, 341-43, 378

Nagao Kagetora, 248
Nagasaki, 265
Nagato, 18, 64, 82, 92, 351
Nago, 24-25
Nagoya, 243
naitoku, 37, 60, 61
Nakamura Kichiji, 11
Nakayama Takachika, 173-74
Nanbu, 367
nengu, 35-37, 41, 43-49, 52, 56, 59,
    63, 71, 73, 77-79, 85, 236, 303,
    323, 339, 345-46, 353-54, 368,
    375, 378
Naoetsu, 301
Nara, 126, 175, 177, 191, 227, 298,
    309
national closure policy, see sakoku
Nichijo Shōmin, 158
Nichiren sect, see Hokke sect

nidome, 138-40, 378
Nijō castle, 156, 166, 169, 171-72,
    256, 260, 268
Nijō Haruyoshi, 174
Nikkō, 198, 269
Nishinomiya, 300
Noda, 171
nōdo, 24-25
Norisaka, 145
Noto, 187-88

Obama, 243
Oda Nobuhide, 248
Oda Nobukatsu, 185
Oda Nobunaga, 8, 10, 20, 135,
    147, 149-94, 224-47, 327; com-
    mercial policies, 138, 141, 317,
    324-25, 362, 368; kandaka sys-
    tem, 30; legitimacy, 119-23, 125,
    249, 254-63, 277; religion, 198-
    205
Oda Nobutada, 185, 190
Odawara, 64, 279, 280, 287, 331
Ōgimachi, 150, 153, 173-77, 182,
    248, 253, 254
Oiwake, 145
Okayama, 272
Okehazame, Battle of, 135
Okuno Takahiro, 163
Ōmi, 29-30, 102, 144-46, 153, 162,
    164, 213, 227-28, 230, 240, 246,
    300
Ōminato, 128
Ōnin War, 9, 65, 104, 147, 299,
    341
Organtino, Father Gnecchi, 178
Osaka, 191, 232, 236, 240, 241-44,
    287-88, 366
Osaka castle, 8, 201, 242-43, 259
Ōsugi, 145
Ōtomo, 29, 72
Ōuchi family, 18-19, 64-100;
    commercial policies, 136; house
    laws, 102
Ōuchi Masahiro, 65, 72, 76, 84

Index

Ōuchi Norihiro, 72, 81, 84
Ōuchi Yoshiaki, 76, 85
Ōuchi Yoshitaka, 10, 65, 76, 90, 248
outcasts, 313-14
Owari, 10, 40, 141, 150, 152, 188, 227, 249, 300, 331, 351, 366
Ōyamazaki, 314, 318, 321

pawnbrokers, 126, 135, 136, 374
provincial land tax, *see tansen*

rakuichi-rakuza, 142, 145, 327, 359-60, 364, 379
reinō, 24-25
Rokkaku family, 102, 153, 162-63; commercial policies, 144-46, 327; house laws, 102, 109, 117-18
Rokkaku Yoshiharu, 102
Rokkaku Yoshikata, 102
Rokujizō, 244

Saga, 333
Sagami, 42, 44-45, 50
Saitō Tatsuoki, 151
Sakai, 126, 128, 226, 231-36, 240, 245, 298-99, 301, 314, 318-19, 321
Sakata family, 137
sakoku, 9, 22, 199-200, 379
sakuin, 24
Sakuma Nobumori, 184-85, 190
Sanehito, 176, 179-80
Sanjōnishi, 226-27
Sansom, George B., 10
Sassa Narimasa, 187-89
Satake family, 57, 129, 136, 201
Satō Shin'ichi, 112, 115-16, 120
Sekigahara, Battle of, 8, 201, 259, 262
sekisho, 135, 145, 225-29, 246, 362-63, 379; tariffs, 129, 130, 134, 229
Settsu, 162, 191, 235

Shibata Katsuie, 186-87
Shimabara revolt, 264, 269
Shimagō, 144
Shimazu family, 114, 200, 268
Shimazu Takahisa, 10
Shimofusa, 139
Shimomura Fujio, 138
Shimōsa, 102
Shimotsuke, 131
Shinano, 9, 180, 189, 261
shōen system, 18, 25, 28-35, 37, 41, 53, 61, 74, 125-27, 144, 193, 340-41, 348, 380
Shōsōin, 175
shugo, 64, 72, 82, 85, 102, 114, 144, 186-87, 191, 253, 317, 380
shugodai, 75, 86, 93
Sue family, 77-79
Sue Hiroakira, 92
Sue Nagafusa, 73
Sue Okifusa, 74, 92
Sue Takafusa, 76
Sugara family, 102
Sugiyama Hiroshi, 105
Sunpu, 260, 261
Suō, 10, 18, 64, 73, 74, 82, 92, 102, 248, 351
Suruga, 64, 131, 135, 145, 180, 249
Suruga Imajuku, 128, 137
sword hunts, 10, 194, 376

taikō, 197
Taikō land survey, 193, 213-16, 219-21, 236, 260, 283-85, 287, 347-49, 380
Taira Kiyomori, 180-81, 196
Takeda family, 28, 30, 43, 46-48, 50, 53, 57, 65, 76, 364; commercial policies, 128-30, 136-37; house laws, 108
Takeda Harunobu, 102
Takeda Katsuyori, 180, 189
Takeda Shingen, 9, 162-64, 169-71
Takikawa Ichimasu, 191-92
Tanba, 189
Tango, 189

tansen, 33, 37, 51, 72, 73, 87, 116,
    133-34, 381
Tendai sect, 177
tenka, 20, 119-24, 161, 166-67, 170,
    186, 198, 207
Tennōji, 231, 299, 300
Tōdaiji, 74, 175
Tōhoku, 128, 370
Tokugawa Hidetada, 24, 264-68
Tokugawa Iemitsu, 267-69
Tokugawa Ietsuna, 263, 267, 269
Tokugawa Ieyasu, 8, 10, 22, 152,
    183-84, 194, 198-202, 254, 257-
    64, 267, 269, 279, 327, 331, 352,
    359, 365, 368-69, 371
Tokusei-rei, 60, 74, 118-19, 146,
    297, 321-22, 381; exemptions
    from, 233-34, 316
toll barriers, *see sekisho*
Tomono family, 128, 130, 131,
    137, 141-43
Tonda, 235
Tondabayashi, 232-36, 298, 300-
    301, 314-15, 321, 325
Tosa, 102
Tōtōmi, 60, 145, 171
Tottori, 229
Toyama, 333
Toyotomi Hidetsugu, 258
Toyotomi Hideyori, 259-61
Toyotomi Hideyoshi, 8-11, 17,
    20-22, 61, 100, 119, 123-25, 147,
    196-223, 224-48, 257-63, 265,
    268, 278-79, 325-27, 350, 354,
    362-69
tozama ("outside") retainers, 105,
    261, 264, 266-68, 381

True Pure Land sect, 162-63
Tsugaru, 128, 241
Tsuruga, 228, 365, 370
Tsutsui Junkei, 191

Ueno Hidemasa, 160
Ukita Naoie, 10
Uesugi family, 142, 200, 360, 364;
    commercial policies, 130-31,
    136, 226-27
Uesugi Kagekatsu, 131
Uesugi Kenshin, 10, 57, 131, 136,
    226-27
Utsunomiya, 129

Valignano, Alexandro, 179

Wakasa, 146

Yabe Zenshichirō, 191
Yamashiro, 159
Yamato, 162, 191-93, 232
Yamazaki, 244
Yanada family, 141-42
Yawata, 298, 300, 314, 318, 321
Yōkaichi, 144
Yūki family, 368; commercial
    policies, 139-40, 144; house laws,
    108, 140
Yūki Masakatsu, 102

za, 130-31, 137, 141-42, 224, 226-
    30, 238, 246, 306-11, 316,
    319-24

LIBRARY OF CONGRESS CATALOGING IN PUBLICATION DATA

Sengoku Conference, Lahaina, Hawaii, 1977.
  Japan before Tokugawa.

  Translation of Sengoku jidai.
  Includes index.
    1. Japan—History—Period of civil wars, 1480-1603—
Congresses.   2. Japan—History—Azuchi-Momoyama period,
1568-1603—Congresses.   3. Daimyo—Congresses.
4. Japan—Economic conditions—To 1868—Congresses.
I. Hall, John Whitney, 1916-   II. Nagahara, Keiji,
1922-   III. Yamamura, Kōzō.   IV. Title.
DS868.S37 1977a   952'.023   80-7524
ISBN 0-691-05308-1

DATE DUE

	NOV 1 5 2013		
	DEC 1 8 2013		